TOLSTOY
AND
EDUCATION

DANIEL MURPHY

IRISH ACADEMIC PRESS

This book was typeset by
Gilbert Gough Typesetting, Dublin for
Irish Academic Press,
Kill Lane, Blackrock, Co. Dublin.

A catalogue record for this book
is available from the British Library.

ISBN 0-7165-2484-8

Printed in Ireland by Colour Books Ltd., Dublin

To Fidelma, Deirdre and Nuala

I believe that the meaning of every man's life lies only in increasing the store of love within him; and that this increase of love leads a man to greater and greater blessings in this life, and to blessings after his death that are in proportion to the amount of love within him.

Tolstoy: *A Reply to the Synod's Edict of Excommunication*

. . . the success of the school depends on love. But love is not accidental. Love can exist only with freedom.

Tolstoy: *Progress and Education*

I assume that the necessity of enjoying art and serving art are inherent in each human personality, no matter to what race or milieu he may belong, and that this necessity has its rights and ought to be satisfied.

Tolstoy: *The School at Yasnaya Polyana*

The celebrated Cyprian said: 'The world is going mad in mutual bloodshed. And murder, which is considered a crime when people commit it singly, is transformed into a virtue when they do it en masse.'

Tolstoy: *The Law of Violence and the Law of Love*

Tolstoy is unique among the world's writers in two respects. Firstly, he commands our respect to a degree that no other writer does by virtue of his love of truth. . . . for Tolstoy in all things truth matters more than anything else; for this one value he will not count the cost in personal suffering, isolation or risk of ridicule. It is this which gives him his unique moral authority.

But there is another respect in which Tolstoy is unique amongst writers—that is in the degree to which he moves our inmost and deepest feelings. The reason for this lies in Tolstoy's goodness and his love of goodness which shine steadily and unwaveringly through everything which he wrote.

R.V. Sampson, *Tolstoy: The Discovery of Peace*

Contents

Preface

The motivation to undertake the present study arose in the first instance from a number of visits to the USSR which were organised as part of a Comparative Education course I have been teaching for some years to M.Ed degree students at Trinity College, Dublin. My initial debt is to the student travel authorities of the Soviet Ministry of Education for the hospitality they have extended to my students and myself during six educational tours of their country. I am particulartly grateful to them for inviting me personally to be their guest on a tour of the monastic cities of the Golden Ring—Zagorsk, Pereslavl-Zalesky, Rostov-Veliki, Yaroslavl, Vladimir and Suzdal—as part of the celebrations commemorating the millennium of Russian Christianity in 1988. My appreciation of the religious ethos of Russian culture was profoundy enriched by the whole experience and the present study has benefitted immeasurably from this. My thanks are due particularly to my hosts, Igor Chernyak, Alexander Bochkarev and Tatiana Kopteva, of the Sputnik Travel Authority, for the hospitality extended to me throughout the tour.

At the Fourth World Congress for Soviet and East European Studies at Harrogate in 1990 I had the opportunity to meet some of the world's foremost Slavic scholars and my understanding of Tolstoy's work was further enriched by this. I was particularly fortunate to be able to participate in a seminar on Tolstoy conducted by four of these scholars—R.F. Christian, R.V. Sampson, Andrei Roginsky and William Edgerton. I am especially grateful to the latter for a copy of an unpublished paper on which I have drawn extensively in the seventh chapter of this book.

I want to acknowledge the support and practical assistance I have received from Professor Valentine Rice, Director of the School of Education, Trinity College, and from my colleagues, Raymond Houghton, Patrick Wall and Michael Curran. A special word of thanks is due to my first instructor in Russian, Ian Vincent Czak.

It would be impossible to undertake a work such as this without extensive access to library resources. Because of the nature of the work, I was particularly dependent on inter-library loan services to gain access to documents not generally available in Irish and British university libraries. I am very grateful to the library staff of Trinity College and to the staffs of the Institute of Education and Senate House libraries of the University of London, and of the Bodleian Library, University of Oxford, for the courteous and generous assistance they have given me on numerous occasions.

Thanks are due finally to Dr Michael Adams and the efficient and helpful staff of Irish Academic Press for guiding the work through its final stages of production.

I

Introduction: Reappraising Tolstoy

This book attempts to meet a long-standing need in Tolstoyan scholarship: the need for a comprehensive assessment of Tolstoy's life and work as an educator. From the time he founded his first school—sometime around 1849–50 when he was twenty-one years old—right up to the end of his life, Tolstoy was consistently involved in education, and was deeply committed to bringing about fundamental reforms in the practices he had observed in contemporary schools and other educational institutions. He was involved in education in a number of capacities: as school-master, pedagogic theorist, religious and social reformer and adult educator—and he left a substantial body of writings on all these activities. But, aside from two small booklets published at the turn of the century, and some brief journal articles that have appeared periodically since then, there has not yet been a serious attempt at a full-scale analysis of his educational ideals and achievements. The present work aims to provide such an analysis; it attempts both to evaluate the worth and significance of these ideals and to determine their relevance for the needs and concerns of the present age.

It has a further objective, however, which arises from certain developments in recent Tolstoyan scholarship. While there have been few attempts to examine Tolstoy's pedagogic writings in themselves, two anthologies of these writings were published recently, each of which was accompanied by an introductory essay in which some perspectives were offered on his educational beliefs and activities. It is this writer's contention that each of these essays has seriously misinterpreted Tolstoy's aims and ideals as an educator, and that the viewpoints they offer are based on a flawed and defective understanding of what he was attempting to achieve in his various educational activities, particularly the experiments in schooling that he conducted at Yasnaya Polyana in the period from 1860 to 1862.

The first of these works is essentially a reprinted version of the translations of Tolstoy's pedagogic writings that were published in 1904 as Volume 4 of *The Complete Works of Count Tolstoy*, under the editorship of Leo Wiener, a Slavic scholar from Harvard University. Wiener's translations are the most authentic that have yet appeared, and these are the versions that are used for the quotations cited in the present study. (Where there are occasional obscurities or ambiguities in Wiener's English, interpretations have been checked against the original Russian text.) Wiener's translations, however, were reproduced in a volume called *Tolstoy on Education*, which was published by the University of Chicago Press in 1967, with an introduction by Reginald D. Archambault. In this introduction Tolstoy is depicted as a precursor of the modern progressive movement, supposedly having strong affinities both with John Dewey and A.S. Neill.

'His solutions were strikingly similar to Dewey's in their insistence on a new pedagogy based on a sensible psychology,' Archambault writes. His 'conception of educational aims and the values that underlie them', he says, 'is a radical one that antedates the American pragmatists' views by several decades, but is clearly consistent with the spirit of Emerson and the transcendentalists, as well as the German romantics.' Tolstoy, he further suggests, 'saw education as having no ultimate aim'; like Dewey, he saw its purpose as 'being generated from the educational process itself'. But he went much further than Dewey, Archambault adds, 'by creating a pedagogy of extreme permissiveness, not only regarding teaching techniques but curricular organisation and principles of discipline as well'. And he concludes: 'He was less a pre-Deweyan theorist and more a precursor of A.S. Neill who came to strikingly similar conclusions to Tolstoy's in his experiments at Summerhill'.[1] All this, it will be argued in the course of the present study, not only misrepresents the ideals put forward by Tolstoy in his educational writings, but grossly distorts the values and beliefs on which all of his work was founded.

In a much lengthier commentary introducing another anthology which appeared in 1982,[2] Michael Armstrong makes a detailed analysis of Tolstoy's pedagogy, giving particular attention to the whole relationship he envisaged between teacher and learner, to his curricular policies, his attitudes to matters such as motivation and discipline, and the manner in which he organised his school. The essay provides some valuable insights on each of these issues, and offers some particularly worthwhile comments on Tolstoy's methods of fostering creativity. But in this instance also one sees a total failure to define the basic convictions on which Tolstoy's educational thinking was founded, and once again he is categorised as an educator in the progressive movement, on the basis of superficial affinities with some of its more widely publicised features. In a section, for example, where he discusses Tostoy's methods of teaching writing, we find this comment: 'The emphasis on the purposefulness of his pupils' writing is one of the many characteristics which makes Tolstoy so unusual amongst progressive theorists of education.'[3] It is highly significant that Armstrong neglects to deal with the ethico-religious aspects of Tolstoy's philosophy or to indicate the central importance of his Christian values and beliefs in all his writings. Nor indeed does he acknowledge the highly traditionalist character of *all* his beliefs and the extent to which this determined his attitudes to matters such as the teaching of history, literature, art, music and the scriptures. Had he done so, it is unlikely he would so readily have classified him as a 'progressive theorist' in the company of educators whose basic values and ideals Tolstoy would have vehemently and uncompromisingly rejected.

The essential weakness in both these commentaries—and this is apparent in some of the journal essays also—is their failure to appreciate the integrity of all of Tolstoy's interests—artistic, pedagogic, philosophic, religious and socio-political. That integrity has been repeatedly recognised in *literary* studies of Tolstoy, most notably in recent years by writers such as Isaiah Berlin and Renato Poggioli. In an essay called 'Tolstoy and Enlightenment', for example, Berlin has shown how all his central beliefs—in divine providence, in the harmony of the natural order, in the intuitive faith of the masses—run through all his writings, fictional and non-fictional, and how each of these writings can be fully understood only in terms of the unifying vision informing all his work.[4] A similar integrity is emphasised by Renato Poggioli in an essay, 'Tolstoy As Man and Artist', where he points to a tensed but fundamental compatibility between Tolstoy's roles as artist and prophet, preacher and fiction-writer, free-thinker and moralist:

> For the last thirty years of his long existence a steady conflict, apparently without truce or issue, seemed to arm against each other Tolstoy the preacher and Tolstoy the writer, Tolstoy the moralist and Tolstoy the artist. We think that too much has been made of this conflict. Tolstoy had always been, even before his conversion, a writer with a message; and even after his conversion he magnificently performed his artist's task, as he had himself defined it at the time when he was writing his two greatest novels. 'A writer's aim is not to settle a question once and for all, but to compel the reader to see life in all its forms, which are endless.'
>
> Yet it remains true that this great and splendid writer despised literature as a profession; and that even when he took his calling seriously, he never thought that art has no end but itself. For this reason he appears to be the only exception, among the main literary creators of the modern age, to a rule once laid down by Rainer Maria Rilke, that 'the writer is the poet of a world which differs from the one of which he is the prophet.' The world of Tolstoy the creator and of Tolstoy the prophet may not fully coincide, but they are closely related to each other. . . .
>
> The unity of Tolstoy is thus to be seen in a consistent interplay of all the contrasting factors of his extraordinary personality. There took place a constant dialogue and exchange, as well as a continuous controversy and

debate, among the many souls dwelling within his breast. At times he was keenly aware of the problematic, as well as the dialectical, character of his own nature: on such occasions Tolstoy the *heautontimoroumenos* would unexpectedly reveal the serenity of an almost god-like being.[5]

To grasp the full import of Tolstoy's educational writings, it is essential, therefore, that they be located within the framework of his work as a whole, and that the precise nature of their relationship to all his other writings be fully and carefully defined. Within that integrated framework, however, yet another balance has to be maintained. More than one hundred years ago, the Russian literary scholar, Nikolai Mikhaylovsky, challenged the then pre-vailing assumption that 'Tolstoy was an outstandingly good writer of fiction but a bad thinker', and went on to demonstrate the intellectual rigour and depth of his non-fictional writings.[6] That same assumption has continued to dominate much Tolstoyan scholarship in the present century, though the position defended by Mikhaylovsky has been repeatedly reaffirmed also. Isaiah Berlin, for example, has written: 'Tolstoy was no less acute, clear-eyed and convincing in his analysis of ideas than of motive, character and action.'[7] While conceding that a high degree of subjectivity is present in his non-fictional writings, Berlin sees considerable philosophic merit in this, regarding it as the basis of a Beckett-like process of 'aporetic' questioning that was an essential feature of Tolstoy's lifelong quest for truth:

> Tolstoy's opinions are always subjective and can be (as for example in his writings on Shakespeare or Dante or Wagner) wildly perverse. But the questions which in his more didactic essays he tries to answer nearly always turn on cardinal questions of principle, and his analysis is always first hand, and cuts far deeper, in the deliberately simplified and naked form in which he usually presents it, than those of more balanced, concrete and 'objective' thinkers. Direct vision often tends to be disturbing: Tolstoy used this gift to the full to destroy both his own peace and that of his readers. It was this habit of asking exaggeratedly simple but fundamental questions, to which he did not himself—at any rate in the sixties and seventies—claim to possess the answers, that gave Tolstoy the reputation of being a 'nihilist'. Yet he certainly had no wish to destroy for the sake of destruction. He only wanted, more than anything else in the world, to know the truth. How annihilating this passion can be, is shown by others who have chosen to probe below the limits set by the wisdom of their generation: the author of the *Book of Job*, Machiavelli, Pascal, Rousseau. Like them, Tolstoy cannot be fitted into any of the public movements of his own, or indeed, any other age. The only company to which he belongs is the subversive one of questioners to whom no answer has been, or seems likely to be, given—at least no answer which they or those who understand them will begin to accept.[8]

The method of the present study is determined by all the foregoing considerations. Its primary purpose is to define and elucidate the ruling principles of Tolstoy's educational philosophy (the term 'philosophy' is used merely to signify his basic ideas and beliefs and does not have rationalist connotations of any kind), and to examine the available evidence on their practical application. It is focussed, in the first place, therefore, on the primary sources—the Pedagogic Journal, the Diary, the Letters, the autobiographical and confessional writings, the social, religious and philosophic essays, the reminiscences of Tolstoy's children, Ilya and Sasha, and of close associates, such as Pavel Biryukov and Aylmer Maude[9]—but it seeks also to identify thematic links between his educational and fictional writings, where these can illuminate his purposes more clearly. Secondly, Tolstoy is seen as an educator, not only in the direct sense in which he fulfilled that role as school-master or social and religious propagandist, but also in the indirect sense in which he conceived the role of the artist as having an oblique, but nonetheless distinct, educational purpose. As Poggioli[10] and others have shown, Tolstoy rejected the idea of art as an end in itself, and consistently maintained that its purpose is the revelation of truth— especially religious and moral truth—and to that degree he saw it as serving a purpose analogous to that which he sought to fulfil through his formal educational activities.

Tolstoy, however, was pre-eminently a *Russian* educator and his writings were deeply imbued with the traditions of Slavic culture, including those of its educational and scholastic inheritance, some aspects of which he endorsed, others of which he vehemently rejected. The next chapter is devoted, therefore, to locating his educational ideas in the context of Tsarist education in the nineteenth and early twentieth centuries. Some of the most significant developments in Russian education occurred in these years and Tolstoy, together with other liberal educators such as Pirogov and Ushinsky, was to the forefront of the reforming movements which eventually bore fruit in the creation of a modern democratic system. This whole process is being examined, however, not only to provide the necessary historical background for the analysis of the specific issues in Tolstoy's purely educational writings, but to indicate the ways in which theory and practice are inter-related in Russian education throughout the nineteenth century—a matter of considerable relevance to the evolution and character of his pedagogic ideas. The chapter devoted to 'Education in Tsarist Russia' attempts to realise both of these objectives.

A central theme of the work is Tolstoy' personal exemplification of the ideals that he advocated in his educational writings. Accordingly, a further chapter describes all his educational activities from the time he founded his first school at Yasnaya Polyana in 1849–50 until his final ventures in adult education shortly before his death, more than sixty years later, in 1910. In those years he founded a number of schools—the most successful being the experiment for peasant children conducted at Yasnaya Polyana between 1860 and 1862—he involved himself in educational controversies, wrote extensively on the subject of educational reform, struggled with government officials for improved conditions in all Russian schools, produced some of the finest school textbooks in the Russian language, and organised a hugely successful adult education movement to propagate his religious, social and political ideals amongst the masses of the people. In all these activities he manifested an extraordinary commitment and dedication to his educational ideals and beliefs, and sought relentlessly to implement them through the methods he considered most effective and most appropriate to his purposes.

The main body of the work is devoted to four main aspects of Tolstoy's work on education: the basic principles of his pedagogic philosophy; his policies on aesthetic education—and specifically on the teaching of reading and writing, art and music; his policies on moral and religious education; and finally, his views on social, community and adult education. A chapter is devoted to each. Tolstoy challenged conventional assumptions on all these issues, starting with the fundamental question of the aims and goals of the entire educational process. On this he challenged the objectives both of the prevailing traditionalist orthodoxies and of the progressive movement that had recently emerged under the influence of Rousseau. Seeing the inadequacies of both, but recognising the validity of some of their ideals nonetheless, he pointed to a third way forward that would embrace the values of tradition and individual freedom, without sacrificing the one to the fulfilment of the other. Thus, he put forward a vision of education that gave full recognition to the individuality of the learner, while simultaneously reasserting the importance of cultural rootedness and emphasising the need to promote learning not only in a spirit of individual freedom, but also in a spirit of continuity with the heritage of knowledge and truth. In all this he successfully matched the directional role of the teacher with the individual freedom of the learner—a crucial conjuncture, and one that is full of significance for modern educators struggling with the polarised claims of two conflicting pedagogic traditions.

A vital principle in his philosophy was the centrality of imagination in all learning, and a particularly valuable feature of his educational writings is their demonstration of the ways in which imaginative potentialities are nourished through the arts. It is not surprising, perhaps, that Tolstoy— himself one of the greatest artists of his age—should have demonstrated so keen an understanding of the role of the arts in education, but his contribution goes much further than this. He devised a pedagogy for reading and writing, and to a lesser degree for art and music, that surpasses anything currently available in its resourcefulness, its practicality, and its unique marriage of formative direction by the teacher with the highest possible degree of creative freedom in the learner. Additionally, he insisted on the right of everybody, regardless of cultural background or ability, to have the fullest possible access to the heritage of art, literature and music, and devised methods appropriate to achieving this in the challenging conditions of the schools for peasant children he had founded at Yasnaya Polyana.

Developing aesthetic potential, however, was an activity which Tolstoy saw as being subordinate to a higher objective: the fostering of the spirit of faith, which he considered the ultimate and all-encompassing goal of education. While regarding much of the inheritance of historical, and particularly institutional, Christianity, as a corruption of the original teaching of Christ, he relentlessly reinvoked the basic principles of that teaching through his fictional and non-fictional writings. He reinvoked it, in the first instance, through all the great novels, making it immediately accessible to the masses through the medium of fictional narrative. His pedagogic methods were based on the same principle of facilitating access to religious truth through the medium of imaginative and symbolic understanding. His pupils were enabled to discover the truths of the scriptures both through readings designed to exploit the imaginative excitement of the text, and by written responses through which they gave expression to their individual feeling for the narrative. The approach he adopted was simultaneously innovative and traditionalist: innovative in its appeal to the creative instincts of the learner and traditionalist in its concentration on the authentic word of the scripture text. This approach to religious education has much to commend it to modern educators seeking to awaken an interest in religion amongst pupils grown disillusioned with its traditions and conventions. Not only did Tolstoy exemplify the potential of an aesthetically based pedagogy, but his entire approach embodied a vision of Christianity that was radically non-dogmatic—an approach that has much to offer educators seeking alternatives to the exclusivist and socially divisive traditions which may well be at the root of the current disillusionment with religion in school classrooms. A further chapter attempts to explore these issues and to define their relevance to the needs and conditions of the present age.

The fourth aspect of Tolstoy's work to be considered is his treatment of the whole sphere of social and community education. He wrote extensively on social issues, especially during the last thirty years of his life, and advocated major reforms in various spheres of Russian society. Recognising that such reforms would require fundamental changes in the social and moral values of the people, he saw an important role for educators in fostering the attitudes appropriate to such a transformation and did much to promote this objective himself through his extensive activities in the whole field of adult and community education. Equally, he recognised the dangers of the emerging socialist ideology and warned his countrymen of the catastrophe that would follow from a revolution dedicated exclusively to social and materialist ideals. His analysis of this whole issue has acquired immense significance with the recent collapse of socialist systems throughout Eastern Europe and, because of its concentration on the ideological weaknesses of socialism, it can help greatly in the crucial redefinition of moral and socio-political values that must now be undertaken in the changed conditions of post-marxist and post-totalitarian societies. What Tolstoy envisaged was the renewal of society through the fostering of the community spirit—a task he saw as essentially one for educators—and through the promotion of radically democratic structures that would offset the dominance of state monoliths, whether of the totalitarian or capitalist modes.

By far the most pressing and most urgent of the issues that Tolstoy raised in his social writings was the problem of peace. He argued passionately for the absolute and uncompromising applicaton of the Christian ethic of non-violence to all spheres of human activity—the interpersonal, the social and the political—and provided substantial scriptural and historical evidence in support of his beliefs. It will be argued in the present study that Tolstoy's pacifism has been widely misinterpreted and that this is due, in large measure, to a failure to appreciate its intrinsically religious character. At a time when the survival of mankind is threatened by the everpresent prospect of nuclear annihiliation, it seems superfluous to emphasise the relevance of such an analysis and its importance for educators struggling to define their responsibilities in promoting the cause of peace.

II

Education in Tsarist Russia

1 The Russian Heritage in Education

There were three main strands in the tradition of educational policy and practice that was inherited by the Russian educators of the nineteenth century. Firstly, it included the distinctive heritage of Russo-Byzantine culture which had been conserved by monastic centres of learning through the centuries and disseminated both to student monks and priests through the monastic academies and to the ordinary people through the liturgical services and scripture lessons of the Orthodox Church. Secondly, it included a strong emphasis on the practical and vocational aspects of education that emerged in the period of Peter the Great and remained a significant feature of educational policy, especially in matters of curriculum and pedagogy, from that time onwards. Thirdly, it included an amalgam of foreign influences, such as the French enclyclopaedist traditions in liberal learning, the Prussian and Austro-German innovations in didactic pedagogy, and the educational radicalism of writers such as Montaigne and Rousseau—all of which were introduced to Russia during the reign of Catherine II and deeply penetrated the educational theories that emerged subsequently. All these elements were present in the writings of the major Russian theorists of the nineteenth century—especially those of liberal and forward-looking educators, such as Pirogov, Ushinsky and Tolstoy. They have continued to exert a significant influence on the pedagogic and curricular policies adopted in the USSR throughout the present period.

Surprisingly, one finds many historians beginning their accounts of the evolution of Russian education with the reforms of the Petrine period, and with the assimilation of western influences which particularly characterised educational, as well as socio- political and cultural, policies in that period. It is essential, however, to stress the existence of a distinctive Russian heritage in education that preceded the reforms of Peter the Great by several centuries, and that deeply influenced the shape of the formal education system that finally emerged. It is particularly important in the context of the present study that this be emphasised, since this centuries-old, distinctive tradition of Russo-Byzantine culture was a singularly potent influence in the educational theories that Leo Tolstoy developed for the schools he founded in Yasnaya Polyana in the 1860s.

Ironically, it was a Soviet work on educational theory—Goncharov's *Pedagogika*[1]—which drew attention to the neglect of these influences by historians of Russian education. The 1946 edition of Goncharov's work began with an historical chapter which traced the origins of Russian education to the golden age of Kievan Christianity between the tenth and thirteen centuries A.D. Goncharov stressed the scholastic and religious ethos in which Russian educational traditions originated in those years and the manner in which they were sustained by the Orthodox Church and its monastic communities through the centuries. These communities, with their great library collections of classical and Biblical literature, provided the cultural and intellectual foundation on which the educational traditions of Russia were based. While confining their formal educational activities to the training of monks and priests, they transmitted a distinctively Russian religious culture to the masses through the evangelical agencies of their churches. Every Russian home—from the humblest cottages of the serfs to the great mansions of the landed gentry and aristocracy—had its icons and other religious emblems; all attended the Orthodox services, with their elaborate liturgy, their lengthy readings from the scriptures, their chanted music and rituals, their Sunday lessons in the catechism, and thereby gained access to the teachings and the spirit of Russo-Byzantine Christianity.

Russo-Byzantine culture was itself a synthesis of two complementary elements: the sacred tradition of the Jewish and Christian scriptures and the secular tradition of Graeco-Latin learning. The first was given a central place in the curricula of all the monastic academies through the formal studies in Scripture and Orthodox theology which were prescribed for their students.[2] Classical learning, which was introduced to the monasteries in the first instance through their contact with the Greek versions of the scriptures, was reinforced through the gradual assimilation of Latin scholarship that occurred in later years. The process was accelerated in the seventeenth century by the greater availability of primers for the teaching of classical grammar (following the introduction of printing to Russia in 1563), and by the reform of monastic curricula, precipitated by the challenge of Jesuit influences coming from the West. By the end of the seventeenth century the typical monastic curriculum consisted of scriptural studies, Slavic and classical languages, theology and philosophy. With the schism of the 1650s, and the departure of the Old Believers from the Orthodox Church because of their dislike for its westernising tendencies, the classical influence became more prominent. The founding of new theological schools with strong classical curricula—such as the institute founded in a Moscow monastery in 1666[3]—the greater availability of Latin and Greek texts, the gradual emergence of scientific studies, were all manifestations of this assimilation of secular classical elements into a tradition that nonetheless retained its distinctively religious character.

By the time of the accession of Peter the Great in 1683, this tradition of sacred and secular learning had been at the centre of an educational process that served the cultural and spiritual needs of the Russian populace for centuries. It had been made available formally to an elite (which was mainly though not exclusively clerical) through the monastic academies, and informally to the masses through the evangelical work of the monks and priests who had been trained in those academies. The first state initiatives in education occurred during the reign of Peter. His reforms, however, were mainly pragmatic and utilitarian in character and were designed specifically to provide the professional personnel required for the new westernised institutions he had created. Initially, these reforms centred around the creation of a navigation school in 1701, which was modelled on the Royal Mathematical School of Christ's Hospital in London.[4] (Peter had seen this institution and been impressed by it during his travels in England.) Its function was to provide officers for the newly established naval forces. All but one of the instructors at the school were Englishmen. The Engineering and Artillery School which was founded some years later was also modelled on an English institution.

Both initiatives were to lead to the first measures taken by the state to provide a system of elementary education. The Education Act of 1714 aimed to provide a basic education in Russian, arithmetic and geometry to children in the 10-15 age group who intended to serve in various state professions, such as the navy, the army, government adminstration and the Church. The schools were of two main types—'ciphering' schools which were founded and staffed by state employees, and eparchal schools which were staffed by the clergy. The latter placed a much greater emphasis on religion than the state schools. By 1723 there were 43 ciphering schools, catering for about 3000 children, most of whom were the sons of government clerks, soldiers, and professional citizens. Garrison schools were founded specifically for the childen of soldiers in 1731. Church schools were founded in 1722 and catered mainly for the children of the clergy. By the late 1720s there were thirteen such schools in the Province of Novgorod, seven in the Ukraine, and one each in Moscow, Rostov Veliki and Nizhny Novgorod.[5]

Some initiatives occurred also in the field of secondary education during the reign of Peter. These consisted mainly in the founding of Church sponsored schools. One was founded in Chernigov in 1700, another in Rostov Veliki in 1702 and a third in Novgorod in 1706. All these schools offered the traditional curriculum of the medieval scholastic institutions. In 1721 the Holy Synod decreed that one secondary school should be established in each diocese, as a result of which there were 46 such schools by 1727. None of these schools, however, catered for the educational needs of the millions of peasant children scattered throughout Russia. Apart from the Church-sponsored schools, most of the institutions founded by Peter served a narrow utilitarian need by providing a basic education for children who could subsequently be given the specialised training that would equip them for service in the new state institutions. Popular education was never a priority for Peter: the system he created could be described most accurately as a system of vocational education, consisting of selective elementary schools which served as preparatory centres for pupils intended for special-ised training in the newly created technical and professional colleges. The emphasis given to practical, vocationally oriented, technical studies during his reign remained a potent factor, however, in the evolution of the Russian education system, and its impact was to be seen particularly in the composi-tion of school curricula at elementary and secondary levels in later years.

The nucleus of a national system of education emerged in Russia during the reign of Catherine II (1762-96). It was in this period also that French and Prussian influences became evident in the policies adopted by Russian educators.[6] Initially influenced by the ideas of the French Enlightenment, Catherine sought to provide a liberal education for Russians along the lines of the *colleges royaux* in France, with their strong concentration on classical studies. But being deeply influenced also by the landed gentry who had been largely responsible for ensuring her accession to the throne, she constructed a system that was highly selective and elitist, and provided almost ex-clusively for the needs of the privileged classes. With her adviser, Ivan Betskoy, she issued a Statute for the Education of the Youth of Both Sexes in March 1764. Through this measure she proposed to create a system that would provide fully for the education of all children between the ages of 5 and 18. This ambitious project resulted merely in the creation of two elitist schools in St Petersburg, the Smolny and Novodevichy Institutes, both of which were modelled on the famous school of Mme de Maintenon at Saint Cyr. Both provided a secondary education for girls, the Smolny for about 200 pupils, all of whom were of noble origin, the Novodevichy for approxi-mately 240, most of whom were drawn from the professional classes. The curriculum of the Smolny Institute had a strong liberal-classical character, consisting of religion, Russian, foreign languages, arithmetic, geography, history, drawing, music, law, dancing, knitting, etiquette and sewing. The curriculum of the Novodevichy Institute was substantially the same, apart from the substitution of domestic science for law. These schools became the models for a number of highly elitist, privately funded institutes which were established in Russia throughout the nineteenth century.

Side by side with these initiatives, Catherine sought to provide a national system of education that would cater for all sections of Russian society. The Commission of 1769 proposed a national plan for education, according to which elementary schools were to be provided in every parish and secondary schools were to be provided in every large town throughout the country. Elementary schools were to be financed from local sources while secondary schools were to be funded by the state. This, however, remained a noble aspiration which was never implemented. A similar plan put forward by the Holy Synod in 1777 was not implemented either. Meanwhile, strong Prussian influences became evident in Catherine's policies. At a meeting with the Emperor Joseph II at Mogilev in 1780 she learned of the successes of recent reforms in Austrian education and was urged by her ministers to introduce similar measures into Russian schools. The Austrian reforms were based on the didactics of the 'Sagan system', a pedagogic methodology developed by Johann von Felbiger at an Augustinian Monastery near Sagan in Prussian Silesia.[7] The system, which von Felbiger had first introduced at a realschule in Berlin, had been vigorously promoted throughout the Prussian school system by Frederick the Great and throughout the Austrian system by the Empress Maria Theresa. Elementary schools, or *trivial-schulen*, were established throughout Austria, with a curriculum based on the three Rs, religion, domestic crafts and husbandry; all of the schools adopted a pedagogic policy modelled on the methods developed by von Felbiger at the Normalschule in Vienna. The schools, which provided six years of instruction for pupils between 6 and 12 years of age, were maintained out of local funds and were regularly monitored by inspectors from the Ministry in Vienna. A system of *hauptschulen*, intended for pupils who had completed the six year elementary school course, was planned also, with a view to providing a complete education for children up to the age of eighteen. All this became the model for the reforms of the Russian education system that Catherine proposed to introduce in the 1780s.

In 1782 she set up the Commission for the Establishment of Schools, with a mandate to plan and organise a national education system. The Commission recommended the establishment of elementary, secondary and third-level institutions along the lines of the Austro-Prussian system. In 1786 its plans were given full legislative status in the Statute for Public Schools. Fedor Jankovich de Mirievo, a Serbo-Croatian educator who had been mainly responsible for the organisation of the Austrian and Hungarian school systems, was appointed special adviser to the Commission. A fluent speaker of Russian and a member of a Greek Orthodox congregation, De Mirievo gave a strong Slavic character to the reforms, though they retained the shaping influence of their Austro-Prussian origins. Under his guidance,

German textbooks were translated into Russian for use in the new schools and a pedagogical seminarium was founded in St Petersburg to train teachers in the pedagogic principles of the Sagan philosophy. Syllabi were prepared for two main types of school: minor two year schools, and major five year schools—each of which was designed in accordance with the Austro-Prussian model. (Provision was also made for middle schools but these were few in number during Catherine's reign.) The Statute declared that a minor school would be established in every district and a major school in every large town. The curriculum was to consist of religion, Russian, arithmetic, Latin, a foreign language and drawing in the minor schools, with history, geography and science as additional subjects in the major schools. All the schools were to be free, with teachers' salaries being funded by the state.

In practice, this ambitious project resulted in a highly selective and socially discriminatory education system. The overwhelming majority of minor and major schools were founded in cities and towns and virtually no provision was made for the education of the children of peasants and serfs, despite the fact that the Commission had specifically recommended that the schools be open to all classes of society. The number of schools in country districts was tiny—a mere 11 existed by the end of Catherine's reign and catered for only about 250 pupils.[8] The few schools that existed in rural areas had been funded through local initiative; most of them closed after a few years because of lack of financial support. A small number of peasants received their education in the urban schools, where they constituted about 5% of the numbers enrolled.

This disparity in school provision between town and country remained a problem throughout the nineteenth century and was a matter of grave concern to reform minded individuals such as Leo Tolstoy, and others like him, who sought to redress the problem by founding schools themselves. But even in the eighteenth century initiatives of this nature occurred occasionally. Nikolai Novikov,[9] a journalist and publisher with a deep commitment to education, opened a number of primary schools for underprivileged children in the countryside near Moscow in the 1780s. The schools, which were entirely free, were maintained through voluntary fund-raising. The scheme brought Novikov into conflict with the government, as a result of which he was sentenced to fifteen years in prison. After serving several years of his sentence, he was eventually pardoned by Catherine's successor, Paul I.

The same elitism which characterised the schooling system founded by Catherine was to be found in the policies she followed in higher education. Again, following the Austro-Prussian model, her government created a number of extended major schools, or gymnasia, which were designed to prepare pupils for university education. At the same time a plan for the expansion of the universities was prepared. This envisaged the creation of over fifty new Chairs in the Faculties of Philosophy, Law and Medicine in existing universities and in a number of new ones which the government planned to establish. The government announced that the new pre-university gymnasia would be open to all children 'irrespective of origin' so long as they had the required certification from the major schools. 'The way of enlightenment is open to everybody who is not of defective mind', the statutes solemnly declared. 'The sciences are called free in order to give freedom to everybody to acquire them and not in order to give this right only to free men.'[10] As a measure to assist poorer students aspiring to university education, free places were to be made available for those who could produce a certificate from the Board of Social Welfare confirming their inability to pay fees. A system of state scholarships was envisaged to provide for the maintenance of poorer students. All these changes were promulgated in the University Statutes of 1787. These Statutes, however, were never confirmed into law by Catherine and most of her grandiose plans for higher education remained unrealised at her death. The more egalitarian proposals would not have been realised in any event, despite the reformist rhetoric of the Statutes, because of the inequities inherent in the pre-university system.

Yet, for all the faults of the class-dominated system she created, significant advances were made in education during Catherine's reign. She provided the nucleus of a national system, which was developed steadily during the last ten years of her administration. Between 1786 and 1796 the number of schools grew from 40 to 316 and the number of teachers employed in them grew from 136 to 744. The number of pupils enrolled in the schools increased from 4398 to 17,341—of whom 16,220 were boys and 1,121 were girls.[11] The basic structures of the elementary, secondary and higher levels of Russian education were defined in these years, as were the curricula that were adopted in each. The structures created remained largely intact throughout the nineteenth century, despite various modifications by successive administrations. The special synthesis of Russo-Byzantine, liberal-classical and vocational elements which constituted the curricular philosophy of Russian education was also developed and implemented in these years. In its essentials, this was the curricular philosophy that Tolstoy adopted in the schools of Yasnaya Polyana, despite his reservations on the French and Prussian influences underlying it and the rigidly didactic pedagogy by which it was taught. Ironically, Tolstoy derived much of the theoretical justification for his rejection of some aspects of Franco-Prussian pedagogy from the writings of Rousseau and Montaigne—which had also been widely promoted by eighteenth century Russian educators, inspired by the enthusiasm of Catherine the Great for radical French philosophy.

2 Building a National Education System, 1804–55

The more expanded, but still predominantly privileged and class-bound education system that existed in Russia when Leo Tolstoy was born in 1828 was largely the creation of Tsar Alexander I, the grandson of Catherine the Great. The University of Kazan where Tolstoy had his first contact with the formal education system (he received his elementary and secondary education from tutors in his own home) was one of the new institutions established by Alexander. Alexander acceded to the throne in 1801, following the brief and uneventful reign of his father, Paul I. A radical political thinker, he saw education as the key to the liberalisation of Russian life and the foundation of the democratic society he intended to create. Though his achievements fell far short of his democratic aspirations, he did succeed in effecting a sizeable expansion of the system he inherited and a much higher proportion of Russian children gained access to education as a result of his reforms.

The first phase of expansion initiated by Alexander occurred in the sphere of higher education. His father, Tsar Paul, had established two theological academies at St Petersburg and Kazan and had founded a new university at Dorpat. To these Alexander proposed to add a new network of third-level institutions and a system of second-level schools where students would be prepared for entry to university education. Thus, the Statutes of 1804 defined six administrative regions, each of which was to have a university and a number of second-level schools, which were to be closely linked with the universities. To the existing institutions at Moscow, Vilna and Dorpat were now added the new universities of St Petersburg, Kazan and Kharkov.[12]

Further plans were made for a related expansion of the elementary and secondary systems along the lines of the Polish educational reforms of the 1780s. Alexander's adviser, Prince Czartoryski, was the son of the minister who had planned and implemented the Polish reforms. A 'ladder system' had been created in Poland, in which elementary and secondary education were both conceived as stages in a student's progress towards entry into higher education. Polish secondary schools were controlled by the universities and the four-year elementary schools were conceived as feeder institutes for second level and university education. It was envisaged that all children would have the right and opportunity to proceed upwards through the system. This model, which was recommended to Alexander by Prince Czartoryski, significantly influenced the direction and content of the Statutes of 1804.[13]

The democratic thrust of the statutes was considerably influenced also by developments in French education, following the Revolution of 1789. Alexander had been deeply impressed by the egalitarian ideals of his Swiss tutor, Frederic Cesar de la Harpe, and through him had been introduced to the Enlightenment philosophers and to the radical ideas of the revolutionary activists. He was particularly influenced by the educational writings of Condorcet: by his treatise on democratic education, *Sur L'Instruction Publique*, and by his Address of 1792 to the National Assembly,[14] urging the creation of an egalitarian system of education in France. The plans proposed for the reorganisation of the Russian system in the Statutes of 1804 broadly resembled the structures proposed by Condorcet to the French National Assembly. A four-tiered system was proposed, with primary schools offering one to two years of elementary instruction, district schools offering a further two years of instruction, and provincial gymnasia offering courses extending over five to seven years. This again was the ladder system, designed to facilitate ease of transfer on the basis of academic merit from one phase of education to the next.

The language of the statutes strongly echoed the egalitarian tone of Condorcet's writings and especially his Address to the National Assemby. Clause 123 declared: 'The parochial schools are open to children of all classes irrespective of their sex or age.' Clause 9 decreed: 'The district schools are open to all children of all classes who have completed the course of the parochial schools or who have completed education elsewhere according to the syllabus of the parochial school.' And Clause 14 decreed: 'The gymnasia are open to all pupils of all classes who have completed the course of the district school or received education elsewhere according to the desired standard.'[15] The university statutes decreed that students would be allocated places on the basis of academic merit exclusively.

The egalitarian spirit of the statutes was further manifested in the provisions made to ensure that poorer students got access to the upper levels of education. While initially it was envisaged that free access would be provided for all students at every level of the system, a fee-paying arrangement was introduced in 1819, which was accompanied by elaborate provision for exemptions and scholarships for poorer students. Orphans and the children of poorer parents were automatically exempted from all fees. Additionally, a system of state scholarships was established to provide for the maintenance of 'poor and capable children' at the gymnasia and universities. These grants were financed by the government and administered by the institutions themselves. In the St. Petersburg Gymnasium, for instance, a total of 60 grant-aided places was provided for poorer students, many of whom were either the children of the lower ranks of the First Army

Corps or inmates of the Home for Poor Children founded by the Imperial Humanitarian Society. Forty scholarship places were provided in the Kharkov Gymnasium and one each in every gymnasium in the Dorpat adminstrative region. Similar arrangements existed in the Moscow and Kazan regions. There was corresponding provision for grant-aided places in the universities. There were over 200 such places in Moscow University, 100 at St Petersburg and 50 each in the Universities of Vilna, Kharkov, Kazan and Dorpat. This represented over 500 grant-aided places out of a total of approximately 3000 places in the university system as a whole.[16]

The major flaw in these policies, however, was the government's failure to make adequate provision for elementary education. The founding of elementary schools was still left to the initiative of municipalities, local landowners and the clergy, with the result that large areas of the country remained without any provision for elementary education at all, despite the egalitarian rhetoric of the statutes. While six new universities, 57 gymnasia and over 500 district schools were founded during Alexander's reign, at most 500 new elementary schools were founded, giving a total of about 600 schools, which could cater for only about 70,000 children—from a population of over 50 million.[17] Millions of peasant children, therefore, were denied entry to the education system, despite the provision for scholarships and grant-aided places in the gymnasia and universities. The children of serfs could enter the gymnasia only with the permission of their owners; even then they were accepted only on the most stringent conditions. Only a small minority of girls gained entry to the gymnasia and none at all were admitted to the universities, despite the specific commitment to social equality decreed in the statutes. (There was a total of 12 boarding-schools for girls in the entire country in 1825, all catering for the daughters of the privileged classes, along the lines of the Smolny and Novodevichy Institutes in St. Petersburg.)[18]

Without adequate provision for elementary education, therefore, the democratic aspirations of Alexander I were inevitably frustrated, and the system he created, despite its quite extensive provision for second and third level education, remained discriminatory, class-bound and elitist. Following the Decembrist uprising, and the assumption by his successor that political radicalism amongst students and the intelligentsia was largely attributable to the democratic ideals of Alexander, educational policies assumed a strong reactionary character under the new administration. The spirit in which the new policies were to be conceived became evident in the Decree of August 19, 1827 in which the new Tsar, Nicholas I, declared:

> It has come to my notice that serfs are often educated in gymnasia and other

higher institutions. This leads to two-fold harm: firstly, these young men having received their elementary education from their owners or parents, who in the majority of cases are negligent, enter higher schools with acquired bad habits and infect their comrades; by this they prevent the more careful parents from sending their children to these institutions. Secondly, the most capable of them become accustomed to a life, to a way of thinking and to notions which are not compatible with their position. Its unavoidable burdens become unbearable, and thus very often in their despair they indulge in pernicious dreams and low passions.[19]

'It is necessary', Nicholas insisted, 'that in every school the subjects of instruction and the very methods of teaching should be as far as possible in accordance with the future destination of the pupils, that nobody should aim to rise above that position in which it is his lot to remain'.

Almost immediately these views found expression in policies designed to perpetuate existing class divisions. The Minister, Shiskov, condemned the previous government's aspirations towards universal education. 'To teach the whole nation to read and write would do more harm than good', he declared.[20] Count Lambert, a member of the Education Commission set up by Nicholas to 'reform' the system, declared that 'children belonging to different social groups must not be educated together'.[21] 'Such a mixture could not be tolerated in consideration of the moral qualities', he said. The Statutes of 1828 decreed that 'the general aim of all schools is to give a moral education and to furnish the young with the means of acquisition of the knowledge that each most needed according to his status.' The elementary schools would 'be open to all pupils', the statutes said; the district schools would 'cater especially for merchants and townspeople', and the gymnasia would aim to 'furnish a decent education for the children of the gentry and civil officials'.[22] Serfs were prohibited by law from entering gymnasia or universities. A government rescript required that 'instruction be appropriate to the likely future destination of pupils' and that they should be discouraged from 'striving too excessively to improve upon the situation in which fate had placed them'. Upward mobility was seen to be harmful for the serf and peasant population because . . .

> on the one hand, these youth often bring baneful habits along with them to the school; on the other hand, those who excel in application and are successful become accustomed to a way of life, to notions and to a style of thought not appropriate to their situation; the inevitable burdens of their life now become intolerable and they fall into despondency, succumbing to baneful dreams and base passions.[23]

A report issued in 1833 by the new Minister for Public Instruction,

Uvarov, declared that henceforth the guiding principles of Russian education would be 'Autocracy, Orthodoxy and Nationality'. Those principles had been undermined, he said 'by superficial education and visionary and abortive experiments'. He further condemned the democratic policies of Alexander I and explicitly committed the government to the maintenance of class privilege through selective educational provision. 'The noble youth, the best flower of the rising generation, which by birth is already destined to occupy the most important offices in the state, must be educated separately, if possible', he declared.[24] For this purpose special hostels were established for the children of the gentry at the gymnasia in Moscow, St Petersburg, Vilna, Kiev and other provincial centres. Fees were increased to 'embarrass access to gymnasia for the lower orders' and scholarships were now confined to 'children of noble birth'. By the mid 1830s over 80% of all pupils in gymnasia were the children of nobility or of state officials— less than 2% were drawn from the clergy and about 17% from the merchant classes and lower orders. A similar pattern emerged in the district schools. In 1852 out of a total of 3790 pupils attending the 33 district schools in the Vilna region, 3458 were the children of the gentry.[25]

As a further measure to eradicate the remaining traces of the democratic policies of the 1820s, a Decree of May, 1835 removed administrative responsibility for gymnasia and district schools from the universities and vested it once again in the Ministry. The appointment of teachers and inspectors was again controlled by the government, thus breaking the link between schools and universities—a crucial feature of the meritocratic system that had been created. Additionally, the Ministry was given powers of supervision over university professors; it held the right to make appointments to Chairs without reference to the University Councils and the further right to dismiss those considered to be 'disloyal'. On 11 October 1849 a decree was issued abolishing the elective principle in universities; thenceforward all rectors were to be appointed by the Ministry. Inspectors were appointed to supervise the work of the universities. Faculties were reorganised into three main groupings—philosophy, law and medicine—in accordance with the Prussian system, which served as a model for all these reforms.

Government policy was now explicitly designed to restrict university places to the children of the gentry. All applicants for places were obliged to undergo an interview with the Ministerial Curator who, in turn, was instructed to 'keep away from the universities young men who have received no education in the homes of poor parents of lower origin'[26](*sic*). Such applicants, one official document declared, are 'vain as to their capacities and attainments, generally become restless citizens, discontented with the established order of things, especially when they cannot find vent for their overexcited ambition'.[27] These measures greatly changed the social composition of university students, many of whom had been the children of clergy and of the lower classes under the previous administration. Nicholas Hans cites figures for entry patterns at St Petersburg University to illustrate the extent of the change that occurred. In 1828 only 26 of its 84 students were the sons of the gentry; 28 were state students and the rest were self-maintaining. In 1838, out of a total of 241 students at the university, 193 were the sons of gentry or civil officials, only 7 were the children of the clergy and only 6 belonged to the lower orders.[28] The universities had again become centres for the education of the privileged classes.

Paradoxically, a certain degree of progress was made in elementary education in these years. Generally, the founding of elementary schools was left to the initiative of the clergy, local municipalities and individual landowners. Progress, however, remained slow in this area; records for 1855 indicate a total of 1106 parochial schools, an increase of about 500 since the end of Alexander's reign.[29] More substantial progress was made in the schools founded by the Ministry for State Domains. Since the state itself held responsibility for approximately 17 million peasants and serfs, it was obliged under the Statutes of 1828 to make provision for their education. Before 1830 no provision whatever was made for this sector of the population. Under a decree issued by Nicholas, the government undertook to found schools specifically for the children of state peasants. These schools, the decree said, would aim to 'spread elementary useful knowledge among state peasants and prepare out of their number capable secretaries for the cantonal and village officials'.[30] The schools were open to the children of state peasants only; while no fees were charged for places in the schools, they were maintained through taxes levied on the peasants of each district. By 1853 there was a total of 2795 schools in this category, catering for approximately 153,000 pupils. The number of Church-sponsored schools also increased quite rapidly during these years. Numbering about 1500 in 1838, they had grown to 9283 by 1861 and to over 21,000 by 1865.[31] Reports suggest, however, that these schools were generally unpopular with parents. Standards were lower than they were in other primary schools and children were frequently expected to do menial tasks such as chopping wood, carrying water, feeding livestock etc. N.V. Chekhov, writing in 1912, gives this description of the Church schools of the 1850s:

> At first glance one is struck by the surprisingly rapid increase in the number of such schools. The local priests, the psalmist, the deacon—all opened schools, whether at home or using church facilities, and they opened these

schools when it was least convenient for peasant children, namely, in May or June. If one looks closer, yet another peculiarity becomes evident: sometimes in the small hamlet two or three schools were opened simultaneously, or in short order one after another, and in one school the priest would teach five, the deacon three, and the psalmist one pupil. Generally, the average number of pupils in such schools was fewer than ten, and sometimes dozens of schools in populous villages had from three to five pupils each. . . . Among the surviving population from that era, the memory lingers of these schools run by priests; if you ask an elderly literate how he learned how to read, he'll answer you: 'Ah, that was when the priests were still the teachers.'[32]

There were other state agencies willing to sponsor schools, such as the Mining Department of the Ministry of the Interior which had founded 4000 schools by 1855. Additionally, there was a good deal of informal education provided by Church sextons, retired soldiers and, in some instances, by itinerant teachers, such as those described in this account given by M.I. Demkov at the turn of the century:

> The wandering teacher who arrived in the village always stayed in the school, which at that time served also as an overnight lodging for travellers. The school was also the permanent residence of the deacon. Sometimes the wandering teacher entered into an agreement, that is, hired himself out to the local *pomeshchik* to teach his children, and on occasion, when there was no school in the village, went from house to house teaching the children. There can be little doubt that such wandering teachers made a major contribution to basic schooling and that some of them helped promote a love of learning.[33]

While statistics indicate significant progress in the provision of elementary education by the 1850s, the proportion of schools measured against the population as a whole remained small. Thomas Darlington, an English observer who wrote a lengthy report on Russian education at the turn of the century, estimated that the ratio of schoolgoing children to the total population was 1:170 in 1854 and 1:117 in 1864—a far cry from the goal of universal education set by Alexander I.[34] By the 1850s there were still thousands of villages with no school at all and, even where schools existed, most children attended for no more than one year. Absenteeism was high because of fears that school enrollment would lead to conscription into the armed forces; in the case of Old Believers absenteeism was further due to the fear that their children would be indoctrinated in the heresises of reformed Orthodoxy.

Statistics on school provision furthermore conceal the reality that the quality of the education was generally poor. Reports suggest that pedagogic practice in the elementary schools was crude, that physical conditions were primitive, and that discipline was usually harsh and severe. This is the

picture that emerges from Miropol'skii's study, published in the 1870s, one
of the most widely cited sources on Russian education in the years before
the Great Reforms. Pedagogic theory, he says, was a mixture of Prussian
didactics, the strict injunctions of the *Domostroi* (a sixteenth century treatise
on moral conduct), and Poroshkov's *Paternal Testament*, which urged
parents and teachers to 'teach the faith diligently and keep children in
dread'.[35] While the influence of reformist educators such as Pestalozzi was
in evidence in a minority of urban schools, the old methods prevailed
overwhelmingly in rural areas, where a heavy concentration on rote
memorisation in the teaching of grammar and arithmetic, and the use of the
aphabetic method in the teaching of reading, were the standard methods of
instruction. This report on conditions in the Tula Province—the region
where Leo Tolstoy founded his schools in the early 1860s—describes the
kind of teaching methods that were employed there. (The report is being
quoted at some length because illuminating comparisons can be made
between the conditions described in it and those existing in Tolstoy's
schools, which will be discussed in a later chapter).

> The teachers had no pedagogical training: they included semi-literate
> peasants, a deacon, a psalmist, and even the wife of the local priest, who could
> scarcely make out a word. Literacy consisted of the ability to read Old Church
> Slavonic and a smattering of writing. For textbooks there were the Church
> Slavonic *azbuka* and the psalter. In our Kibensk school the teacher was a local
> peasant named Boris who was sixty years old. His literacy consisted of being
> able to read the psalter for the deceased; I think he knew virtually the entire
> book by heart. School was held in his house, a wooden building six arshins
> in length, with only one window, and of the black izba type. The teacher
> received payment individually from the pupils—50 kopecks each for the
> winter, along with an apartment. The school year lasted from the first snow
> till the snow disappeared from the ground.
> We learned by the alphabet method. The teacher would choose the lesson
> by pointing with his finger 'from here to there' and would begin, as they used
> to say, by 'leading' the pupils—he would say along with them 'Az! Az!
> Buki!' and so forth. . . . From the school issued forth an unremitting clamour
> from morning to dinner. After dinner the noise began again, for reading in
> unison was the only skill our 'pedagogue' had. He taught writing by requiring
> memorisation of the alphabet book, and sometimes the poor pupils studied
> for two winters and still didn't know how to write the letters of the alphabet.
> . . . For them to retain what they had learned by rote each morning upon
> arriving in class the pupils had to repeat what they had just learned; during
> this time one could hear a concert of voices of children aged ten to seventeen.
> . . . If, God forbid, one of the pupils had failed to memorise the homework,
> then fists, shoves and hair-pulling were brought into use, while for a weak
> performance a flogging was administered. . . .

When he was absent for several days in a row, the teacher turned over the class to his son, Daniel. Daniel was entirely illiterate; he could not even name a single letter. So in his father's absence Daniel would take a switch, or even a stick, and walk around the classroom striking each pupil in sequence saying 'Read! Read!' The pupils could not complain to their parents, because the mother or father would simply add some punishment, saying 'You idiots won't learn anything without the rod'—of course, parents had learned this cruelty in their own treatment by their masters. And all of the teachers named above—the deacon, the psalmist, and the widow of the priest—applied the same method and the same discipline as Old Boris. The only variation was in the way fees were levied. Boris took money, the deacon and psalmist were paid in kind,—someone brought flour or grain, another brought a hen or a piglet, yet another a wagonful of straw, and so forth.[36]

Reports can be cited from various other regions suggesting that the kind of pedagogic practice existing in the Tula region was typical of what existed througout the whole system. Mechanistic instruction, learning through rote memorisation, the stifling of individual creativity, strict, regimental styles of discipline were the norm in most of the primary schools. Alternatively, the reports speak of extreme negligence on the part of the teachers and widespread absences from school by the pupils. 'There are almost no books in the schools', one observer wrote, 'and the children are more likely to end up sextons than literate peasants. . . . So little attention is devoted to lessons that for half the year they never go to school . . . after attending school for more than a year the boys can barely read, and at that only slowly and hesitantly; they can't even write two words correctly, even when they are regarded as having completed the course.'[37] The historian, E.A. Zviaginstev, concluded: 'The reports all demonstrate the extremely impoverished condition of the schools, the abysmal levels of instruction, the transience of individual schools, and popular indifference—in fact, some peasants and children in state peasant villages regarded school attendance as a means of fulfilling their state imposed obligation.'[38] By the time of the Great Reforms it was estimated that more than half the rural schools were either inoperative or considered incapable of equipping pupils with the basic levels of literacy and numeracy needed for their employment. In Tula it was recorded just before the Emancipation Act of 1861 that half the local serf-owners had reported that there were no literate peasants on their lands. Gearóid T. Robinson in *Rural Russia under the Old Regime* concluded:

In the decades that intervened [between the 1804 Statute and the Emancipation Act] some progress was made in establishing official numbers of unregistered primary schools, maintained sometimes by the peasants themselves and sometimes by the landlord. A beginning had thus been made, but the great mass of the serfs on the private estates and of the peasants on the State domain had hardly been touched by the cultural changes which since Peter's time had so deeply affected the nobles and the bourgeoisie.[39]

Yet, for all the defects of the education that was offered in these schools, far greater numbers of children were given access to it than had been the case under the previous administration. The policies of Nicholas I ensured that Russian education remained severely divided along social class lines yet, paradoxically, his reign saw an improvement in the *provision* of elementary education, the area which had been most neglected during the administration of Alexander I. 'It is one of the minor ironies of history', Ben Eklof writes, 'that this paternalistic autocrat, who had little use for the Enlightenment principles toyed with by his elder brother and who worked hard to dismantle the ladder system, did far more than Alexander to promote primary education.'[40] Firmly believing in the stability of a rigidly demarcated class system, Nicholas had sought to maintain this through his educational policies. In a speech of 1842 he had condemned the evils of serfdom while complaining that certain landowners were providing their serfs with an education that was inappropriate for their lowly status. It seemed perfectly consistent to him that he should promote an elitist system of secondary and higher education to provide for the needs of the gentry and bureaucracy, while attempting to provide for the needs of the lower orders exclusively through the medium of basic education.

3   The Years of the Great Reforms, 1855–81

The years of the Great Reforms have a special significance for the present study since this was the period when Leo Tolstoy embarked on his most prolonged and most successful experiment in the education of peasant children. It was a period not only of major legislative advances in the provision of education for the masses of the Russian peasantry, but one which also saw the emergence of some of the country's most innovative and enlightened educational theory. As well as Tolstoy, three other major theorists—Pirogov, Ushinsky and Stoyunin—produced their most significant work in these years and established a tradition of pedagogic theory that continued to develop and grow throughout the Soviet period. The reforms which were introduced by Alexander II, shortly after his accession to the throne in 1855, were part of a general process of social change initiated by a government badly shaken by its defeat in the Crimean War and alienated from its intelligentsia by the reactionary policies of Nicholas I. The abolition of serfdom on 19 February 1861 was the signal for a wide-ranging liberalisation of Russian society. In accordance with the terms of the Emancipation

Act, serfs were to be allotted plots of land by the landowners for which they, in turn, were to be compensated by the government, until they could recover the costs of the transfer from the peasant freeholders. New local authorities, or zemstvos, were to be elected by all sectors of the population at provincial and district level and were to be given particular responsibility for the organisation of education in the regions they controlled. The reforms in education were greatly assisted by these measures. As the biographer of Alexander II wrote: 'The issue of spreading primary education among the people, of teaching the peasants literacy, flowed directly from the changes taking place in their daily lives with the onset of the emancipation from serfdom.'[41] Landowners, freed from the fear that an educated serf population would revolt against their conditions of bondage, were no longer opposed in principle to their education, and many were actively engaged in providing it through the local and provincial zemstvos.

The major educational reforms were spread over a period of ten years, beginning with the Statutes of 1864 and culminating in the Statutes of 1874. Various preparatory measures had been initiated, however, shortly after Alexander's accession to the throne. In November 1855 he issued a decree repealing the restrictions on university entry that had been imposed by his father. This was followed by another decree of 17 January 1857 lifting the restrictions on the founding of private schools. This led to an immediate increase in the numbers of schools established by individual landowners and various voluntary agencies. Consultative bodies, set up to advise the Minister of Public Instruction on the formulation of educational policy, immediately began to work on a major reform programme for the entire system. Condemning the utilitarian bias of existing legislation, the Minister, Norov, declared that a more liberal philosophy would inform the new policies. 'The Ministry recognises the importance of a utilitarian bias in science', he declared, 'but it regards the intense predominance of an utilitarian bias in education as a pernicious extreme. The Ministry thinks that intellectual as well as moral and aesthetic development demand the restoration of their former importance to classical languages, at the same time, not connecting with it the former privileges of classical scholars.' A particular commitment was made to the equalisation of educational opportunity for different sectors of society. 'The unification of nationalities and classes can be achieved not by administrative decrees', the Minister said, 'but only by moral measures, which would bring together different minds, nationalities and classes by a unity of aims obtained by a common system of education.' Further recognition was given to the need to provide more equitably for the female population: 'The vast system of education in Russia has up to the present only had in view one half of the population—namely, the males',

Norov said. 'It would be of the greatest benefit to our country to establish day girls' schools in provincial and district towns and even in large villages.'[42]

These policies were greatly reinforced by the pedagogic writings of Pirogov and Ushinsky. Both men strongly condemned the socially discriminatory attitudes that had characterised educational policy during the previous reign. A surgeon by profession, Pirogov had served in the armed forces during the Crimean War. In 1856 he published an essay, 'Problems of Life', in which he denounced the narrow vocationalism of existing policies and advocated a balancing of moral and utilitarian aims in educational planning for the future.[43] Impressed by his ideas, the Minister, Norov, appointed him Curator of the Odessa educational region—which he administered from 1856–58—and subsequently Curator of the Kiev region, which he administered from 1858 to 1861. In a number of pedagogic essays, which appeared in 1862, Pirogov advocated a common basic curriculum for all children, irrespective of social background, sex or nationality—a remarkably far-seeing proposal for the 1860s and one that was to serve as the foundation principle of the egalitarian manifesto proclaimed by A.V. Lunacharski in November 1917. 'Everybody without distinction of class or position should be compelled to follow the general course of a secondary school', Pirogov wrote. 'In this way, if this were to be compulsory for all citizens, education would spread equally among all groups of society.' He proposed the establishment of a fully democratic system, even to the extent of providing a third level education for everybody. 'The ideal and normal condition of education in society', he wrote, 'would be if all, without any distinction, entered life by the same way i.e. by the high way of university education.'[44] However, even an administration as liberally disposed as that of Alexander II found these views too radical and too extreme for the time, and Pirogov was eventually forced to resign from his post. Idealistic and naive though his views might have been for the 1860s, they greatly influenced government policy nonetheless and gave considerable momentum to the reforms that were then being planned.

Less influential in the short-term, but immensely supportive of the plans to universalise educational opportunity, was Pirogov's contemporary, Konstantin Ushinsky.[45] An inspector of schools, author of numerous textbooks for elementary education, and editor of a popular teachers' journal, Ushinsky argued that Russian education had been dominated by foreign influences in pedagogic philosophy and by the westernised classical model of the curriculum. Stressing the importance of basing all learning on the child's experience and immediate environment, he devised a radical pedagogy appropriate to a society proposing to offer an elementary education to millions of peasant children whose lives were far removed from the world of the classical disciplines. 'In order to lead public education on a direct and proper path', he wrote, 'one must examine not what is necessary for Germany, France, England... but what is necessary for Russia in her present condition, what is compatible with her historical traditions, with the spirit and needs of her whole people from the small to the great.'[46] A strong supporter of local control, his ideas found expression in the measures taken to entrust the administration of education to the zemstvos, an important factor in the expansion of elementary education. On the matter of promoting Russia's indigenous traditions, his ideas took longer to bear fruit, but the democratic tenour of his writings provided strong support for the liberal measures that were then being prepared.[47]

Meanwhile, elaborate consultations were taking place between government officials, pedagogic specialists, teachers, administrators and various interested parties on the nature and character of the proposed reforms. Previously, educational policy had been determined unilaterally by the government; in this instance the extent of the consultative process that occurred was itself indicative of the government's intention to democratise educational policy-making to the greatest possible degree. Kovalevsky, the Minister, and his successor, Golovnin, sent drafts of the proposed legislation to educational specialists in France, Belgium, Switzerland, Germany and Great Britain, inviting them to comment on the planned reforms. Their responses were published in seven volumes for circulation amongst government officials, and became the basis for the measures eventually passed into law in 1863–64.

A new ladder system, fully consistent with the Norov declarations of 1856, was created by the Law of 1864. Its first clause declared: 'Education is the main basis of the state and the source of its well-being. Therefore, the profits of education ought to be enjoyed by all persons, irrespective of either sex or origin.'[48] There were to be three levels in the new system: two years of elementary schooling for 7-9 year olds, four years of secondary education in the pro-gymnasium for 9-13 year olds, and four years of gymnasium education for 13-17 year olds. Pupils would automatically advance from one level to the next as they fulfilled the appropriate academic requirements. All three types of school could be established either by government or by private agencies. Government schools were to be grant-aided by the state and administered by local boards. A particularly significant development was the provision of a number of secondary schools for girls. Before 1858 there had been no secondary schools at all for girls, apart from the highly elitist Smolny and Novodevichy Institutes in St Petersburg and about a dozen boarding schools of a similar nature in the major cities. By a Decree of May 1858 new regulations were defined for the establishment of girls' gymnasia and special funding was made available for this purpose in 1864. A large number of non-educational agencies also continued to establish and maintain schools. They included the Ministries of the Interior, State Domains and Mining, as well as the Holy Synod and various voluntary bodies. Elementary schools could also be established by private individuals, with the permission of the local schools' board.

General regulations were issued for all schools on matters relating to curriculum and pedagogy. Elementary schools were expected to provide for the religious, moral and intellectual needs of their pupils. Their declared aim was to give a broad, general, non-specialised education. Echoing the democratic thrust of Pirogov's philosophy, the Reform Act required them to 'give moral and intellectual education to such a point that everybody should understand his rights and perform his duties rationally as a human being should do'.[49] The curriculum was to consist of Russian, religion, reading, writing, arithmetic, singing and drawing. Schools would be permitted to charge fees, depending on the preference of the local authority or the founding agency, but, in practice, they were usually free. (One of the attractions of Tolstoy's school at Yasnaya Polyana was that no fees were charged.) The curriculum of the pro-gymnasia was to consist of Russian, religion, history, natural science and geography, mathematics and physics, German, French and drawing. Two types of gymnasia had evolved at this stage, the classical and the modern or real, the latter term clearly indicating its Prussian origin. In the classical gymnasia Latin and Greek were added to the pro-gymnasium curriculum and only students coming from these institutes were allowed to proceed to university. Students completing the course of the real gymnasium entered other third-level institutes, such as teachers' seminaries and the army and naval training colleges.

Elaborate arragements for the administration of this new system were set out in the Statutes of 1864. Special district boards were established for the primary sector. Each board was composed of two delegates from the zemstvo assembly, together with one representative each from the Ministries of Public Instruction and the Interior, and the Holy Synod. The boards were empowered to 'supervise instruction, open and close schools, certify teaching and distribute approved textbooks'.[50] All non-official bodies had to secure the approval of the board to establish schools. With the exception of the clergy, all teachers had to be confirmed in their posts by the board, and reports on their work were submitted regularly to the Director of Schools. All of this signified a major devolution of responsibility for the organisation and control of education from the state to provincial and district authorities; the growth of the system thenceforward depended largely, therefore, on the initiatives taken by local communities and their political representatives.

Statistics for the 1860s and 70s give some indication of the progress made under these arrangements. In those years the cost of providing elementary education was shared by the zemstvos and the local communities. Initially funding was provided for the establishment of new schools from each of these sources, but the costs of maintaining the schools and the salaries of teachers were paid for mainly by the local communities, with some assistance from the zemstvos. By 1880 it was estimated that the expenditure on elementary education by the zemstvos was about 2 million rubles, while that of the local communities was over 3 million. The provision and quality of schooling, therefore, was greatly dependent on local conditions, and inevitably, there remained large areas of the country where provision was inadequate or simply did not exist at all. Between 1864 and 1873 the zemstvos established 3917 new schools and a further 4437 between 1873 and 1882, while village communities established 3217 and 1556 schools respectively in the same periods. A total of 13,127 new schools, therefore, had been provided between 1864 and 1882. Yet the percentage of school age children registered in schools remained small—a mere 13% in Moscow, 14% in St Petersburg, 11% in Kharkov, 13% in Kiev. Teacher training facilities were also inadequate; there were only 3 teacher seminaries and 12 pedagogical institutes in the whole of the country by 1870. (This was expanded to 34 seminaries and 39 pedagogical institutes by 1875 under the ministry of Count Dmitri Tolstoy.)[51]

Under the ministry of Tolstoy certain measures were taken in the 1870s to restore some of the authority to the central government administration that had been devolved to the provincial zemstvos and district school boards in the 1860s. This process began in 1869 with the appointment of primary school inspectors who were required to report directly to the Ministry of Public Instruction on the work of the schools. While responsibility for the founding and maintenance of schools remained with provincial and district authorities, considerable control was exercised over their work through the creation of this new centralised educational bureaucracy. Government inspectors had particular responsibility for the appointment and evaluation of teachers and for ensuring that the nationally prescribed curriculum was properly implemented. They were empowered to close schools on the grounds of 'disorder' or 'harmful instruction' and held the right to dismiss teachers on grounds of negligence or incompetence.[52] All these powers were given legal force in the Statutes of 1874, generally considered to have been the brainchild of the Minister for Public Instruction, Dmitri Tolstoy.

There are widely varying viewpoints on the nature of Dmitri Tolstoy's influence on Russian educational policy in the 1870s. They range from the highly favourable assessments of Nicholas Hans and Allen Sinel—both of whom saw him as the person primarily responsible for the democratic expansion of the system in those years—to the less flattering view put forward by James McClelland that he was a reactionary bureaucrat responsible for perpetuating elitist policies, especially in the sphere of secondary education.[53] Hans has argued that the increase in pupil enrollments, both at primary and secondary levels, was largely due to Tolstoy's intervention in the affairs of provincial zemstvos—where he frequently faced opposition to educational expansion from reactionary landowners—and that this ultimately resulted in much greater numbers of children from the lower orders gaining access to education. Conceding that he maintained the socially divisive system of classical and real gymnasia, he saw this as merely reflecting a view of secondary education that was typical of all European countries at the time. With regard to his proposal that elementary education be made compulsory, he saw him as an especially forward-looking minister, determined to challenge the spurious charge from some clerical and landowning classes that the state had no right to deny parents the freedom to decide whether or not their children should be educated. To this charge Tolstoy had responded that 'the government, in compelling ignorant parents to perform their duty, is defending the right of children from being abused by parents and preventing pernicious effects on social welfare'—a position that seems much closer to a twentieth century view of education than to that which prevailed throughout most of Europe in the 1870s.

It was Tolstoy's determination to diversify second level education that lay at the root of the controversy that has surrounded his policies—even amongst twentieth century scholars who might have been expected to see this as a realistic approach to meeting the educational needs of a society so complex as that of the Russian Empire in the late nineteenth century. Recognising that the alternatives to the prestigious classical gymnasia he was proposing to create would be perceived as socially and educationally inferior, Tolstoy consulted a wide range of interested groups on the shape and content of his projected legislation. Despite petitions to the government from various quarters to increase the numbers of classical gymnasia rather than extend the system of real schools, Tolstoy—presumably on the basis of his consultations—decided to embark on the latter course and to provide a completely restructured second level system. Under the new statutes six main types of real gymnasia were created—general-technical, commercial, chemical, mechanical, mining and agricultural. Within five years fifty real schools had been established to meet the needs of students taking up careers in each of those areas or intending to proceed to further studies in higher technical and professional colleges. A common basic curriculum, consisting of Russian, religion, foreign languages, mathematics, history, geography and drawing was prescribed for the first four years of the real school programme. Specialised courses were introduced in the fifth and sixth years, side by side with more limited coursework in general studies. Normally, pupils entered these schools at nine years of age, transferring at fifteen to apprenticeships or to further studies. Judged by twentieth century criteria, these policies would probably be seen as discriminatory, insofar as the pupils of the real schools were denied access to university education; from a nineteenth century perspective, they compared quite favourably with policies on secondary and higher education throughout the rest of Europe and, in the context of Russian education alone, they provided a necessary diversification in a system rigidified by the narrow classical bias of the existing secondary schools.

One of the measures taken by Tolstoy that particularly improved opportunities for the lower orders was the support he provided for Church controlled schools. A former Procurator of the Holy Synod himself, he recognised the contribution these schools had made to the education of the serf and peasant population through the years. Despite widespread dissatisfaction at the standard of education offered in the Synod schools, they were the only means by which the masses of peasant children could gain any access to education. Since 1818 Church grants had been withdrawn from these schools and they had since been maintained through the sale of candles or through private donations from Church congregations. In 1867 Tolstoy issued new statutes for these schools and restored their government funding, on condition that they accepted children from all social backgrounds. (Previously they had favoured the children of the clergy or those intending to enter seminaries to study for the priesthood.) Secondary schools administered by the Holy Synod were given full gymnasium status and many of their graduates subsequently obtained places in universities. It was estimated by 1880 that 23% of all university students had come from schools run by the Holy Synod.[54]

Tolstoy also took some steps to reform the remaining district schools with a view to enabling greater numbers of poorer students to gain access to secondary and higher education. Initially he proposed to turn them all into pro-gymnasia but this was met with stiff opposition in offical circles, so he transformed them into a new system of urban schools designed specifically to meet the needs of poorer students. Essentially, these urban schools were extended elementary schools, but the curriculum was broadened to include Latin and foreign languages in the upper grades so that their pupils could proceed eventually to the classical or real gymnasia after four years of study.

Unfortunately, few of their pupils achieved this objective, though many of them entered teachers' seminaries and returned to work as teachers in the elementary and urban schools subsequently. Tolstoy also made considerable progress in extending the provision for the education of girls. By a decree of 1870 he transformed more than 90 existing girls' schools into pro-gymnasia and a further 30 into full gymnasia.

Not all commentators on Tolstoy's policies accept the evidence of democratisation that these measures would suggest. James McClelland, in *Autocrats and Academics*, saw his policies as inhibiting progress towards democracy through a subtle process of controlled expansion, designed deliberately to slow down the democratisation of educational opportunity. It was rare, he argued, for peasant children to proceed beyond the primary schools, if only because most of the secondary schools were located in towns, and distance proved an insurmountable obstacle for most of the children from rural areas. Secondly, he suggested the classical gymnasia were largely closed institutions, requiring a knowledge of Latin from all new entrants and, since Latin was taught only in pro-gymnasia and in the new urban schools, children coming from the remaining district schools could not gain entry. Additionally, he argued that the classically dominated curriculum, by virtue of the rigours and the highly disciplined character of its intellectual content, served to prevent or stifle the growth of radical political ideas amongst the students:

> Russian political and ideological conditions were primarily responsible for convincing Tolstoy of the virtues of classicism. One of the most disturbing phenomena of the 1860s, from the autocratic viewpoint, had been the movement of intellectual nihilism that had spread so widely among Russia's urban youth. Most of the leading lights of this movement had an irregular educational background, and did not always thoroughly understand the tenets of natural science which formed the crux of their world view. Tolstoy thought that his curriculum would help to steer the elite youth of the country away from this type of orientation mainly in two ways. First, its compulsory nature and strenuous academic rigour would put an end to the hitherto predominant tendency of many youth to pick up their education here and there, in 'bits and pieces'. Second, its emphasis on classical languages and abstract mathematics would insulate immature minds from subjects such as the natural and social sciences, which Tolstoy believed led too easily to incorrect and improper social and political generalisations. . . . He was convinced that disaffected and hence dangerous students were most likely to come from the ranks of the ill-prepared and undermotivated. The gymnasium, with its strict controls and stiff classical curriculum, was the school most likely to weed out such pupils before they reached the university level. By requiring virtually all incoming university students to have coped successfully with

several long, hard years of gymnasium study, Tolstoy thought he could control the type of students who reached the pinnacle of the education system.[55]

It would not be difficult to find examples of radical political thought amongst either the major Latin authors, or amongst students who through the centuries have been educated in the Latin classics, to refute the rather unlikely thesis that liberal tendencies in the young could be stifled by the study of classical literature. In this, as in several other respects, McClelland's portrayal of Tolstoy as a reactionary administrator seems weak and untenable. The assessments which seem, in the view of the present writer, to correspond most closely to the evidence of Tolstoy's policies and actions as Minister,are those of Hans and Sinel. Describing his administration as one characterised by 'liberal reform', Hans writes: 'The number of schools of all kinds and of scholars in them increased during this period enormously. The proportion of the increase to the population was the highest in Russian educational history. The percentage of scholars of lower origin in general and of peasants in particular in secondary and higher institutions increased during this period.'[56] This view is substantially confirmed in Sinel's study.[57] While acknowledging the centralising tendencies of Tolstoy's administration, and his determination to uphold the authority of the monarchy, he concludes that his vision of education was ultimately one where democratic rights would be advanced through a full and equitable provision of educational opportunities. That vision was frustrated by various agencies, not least those of the state bureaucracy and the political establishment, and it may have been premature in the 1870s, but it was, nevertheless, the dynamic force underlying his policies, and substantial progress was made towards its fulfilment by the time he left the Ministry:

> During the seventies and eighties, except in the larger cities, less than 30 per cent of all Russians could either read or write and a much smaller proportion could do both. Under such circumstances every school had to be wholly utilised; Russia could afford no half-empty classrooms. Even before Tolstoy became minister, zemstvos had inquired about compulsory schooling, and this time they found the new ministry receptive to their ideas. Tolstoy too wanted the greatest number of people educated . . . . After the death in 1875 of A.S. Voronov,the ministry's major proponent of obligatory schooling, Tolstoy himself pushed the matter forward. Public apathy, he declared, was paralysing elementary education. Since parents either did not send their children to school or withdrew them prematurely, 'our school's fundamental and supreme task, the strengthening of the people's religious and moral feelings and the spread of useful knowledge cannot be realised'. Believing compulsory education the solution, Tolstoy conducted Russia's first

full-scale survey on the feasibility of obligatory elementary education. The replies revealed . . . that Tolstoy's proposals were premature, that Russia could not yet supply the necessary teachers and institutions. Not until 1908 would it have sufficient schools and faculty for the government to issue legislation on compulsory attendance.

Unfortunately for Russian education, many tsarist ministers did not share Tolstoy's desire to improve and extend the primary network. . . . He established a fairly rational and expanding system of rural and urban elementary schools with their own teacher training institutions and government inspectors. Unlike some conservatives, Tolstoy recognised the ugency of his country's need for a literate population and worked conscientiously to fill this demand.[58]

4 From Reform to Revolution, 1881–1917

Following the reforms of the 1860s and 70s the remaining three decades of the nineteenth century were marked by strong reactionary tendencies in Russian education. Following the assassination of his father, the new Tsar, Alexander III, attributed the growth of revolutionary movements to the emancipation of the serfs in the 1860s and to the democratising forces that had been set loose in the country as a result of this. Determined to restore the authority of the monarchy, his attention turned inevitably to the country's educational institutions, which he saw as the main breeding grounds for the revolutionary propaganda underlying the general state of political unrest in the country. The Minister for Public Instruction, Delyanov, issued a new university statute in 1882, severely restricting the freedom of students and once again abolishing the elective principle within universities. A Curator was appointed by the Ministry for each educational region, with powers of supervision over all student activities and the right to nominate rectors and professors. Fees were increased in 1887 to limit access to universities by poorer students. Universities were inspected regularly by the police and hundreds of students were arrested and given heavy prison sentences. Inevitably, in such conditions, the universities became the focus of the political struggle which culminated in the bloody upheavals of 1905 and 1917.

Various repressive measures were taken against the gymnasia on the grounds that they too were disseminating revolutionary propaganda. On 11 April 1887 all preparatory classes in the gymnasia were closed. Since most of the places in these classes were held by students from the poorer sections of society—children of the gentry usually got their pro-gymnasium tuition in their own homes—the measure had the effect of further denying the lower classes access to higher education. A decree of June 1887 specified certain occupational groups whose children would be ineligible for entry to the gymnasia: they included cab-drivers, cooks, waiters, washer-women and retail shop-keepers. 'These children', the decree said, 'should not aspire to secondary education.'[59] Special restrictions were imposed on Jewish children; the numbers accepted for entry to gymnasia and universities could not exceed 10%. (The quota was even lower than this in certain regions.) As a further measure to keep the lower classes out of higher education, a new system of vocational education was established. With the setting up of a Department of Professional Education in August 1884, and the issuing of a new Education Statute in March 1888, three new types of school came into being: lower technical schools, middle technical schools, and crafts and industry schools. The first were intended for the training of skilled foremen, the second for assistant engineers, and the third for skilled industrial work-men. The system evolved very slowly, however, despite a firm commitment by the government to its development; by 1895 there were only four middle technical schools and 48 lower vocational schools in the country.

In elementary education policy was focussed on strengthening the role of the Church, both in the administration of the schooling system and in the promotion of the principles and practices of the Orthodox faith. Under Delyanov's ministry, the Procurator of the Holy Synod, Pobedonostsev, who had direct responsibility for Church sponsored schools, acquired con-siderable influence also in the formulation of policy for schools under zemstvo control. Believing that primary education should be confined to the three Rs and religion, and that its function was simply to provide for the spiritual and practical needs of the child, he warned of the dangers of raising the expectations of peasant children by giving them an education beyond the needs of their existing status. 'Few reflect', he said, 'that by tearing the child from the domestic hearth for such a lofty destiny, they deprive his parents of a productive force which is essential to the maintenance of the home; while raising before his eyes the mirage of illusory learning they corrupt his mind, and subject it to the temptation of vanity and conceit.'[60] He urged the government to give priority to the establishment of greater numbers of Church-controlled schools, as a result of which a statute was passed in 1884 allowing priests to establish schools through a combination of state and local funding. These were mostly two-year schools, offering a curriculum con-sisting of religion, reading and writing, singing and arithmetic. (Russian history and sacred history were added in the schools that offered a four year course.) These schools were established side by side with the zemstvo schools and intense rivalry existed between them. Zemstvo schools regarded Synod schools as inferior educationally, while the Synod schools regarded the others as not giving sufficient attention to the religious and moral formation of the child. In 1891 Delyanov issued a decree requiring all who proposed to found a school to seek permission from the Holy Synod. That permission was usually refused in any area where a Synod school already existed. As a result, the numbers of Church controlled schools increased from 4348 to 31,835 between 1880 and 1894.[61] Generally, Church schools were inferior to zemstvo schools—their teachers were poorly qualified, buildings were usually in a bad condition, and resources were inadequate— and parents preferred to send their children to lay schools, whenever they could.

Generally the reign of Alexander III was marked by stagnation in educational policy-making and little progress could be recorded in any sphere by the time of his death. Nicholas II, who succeeded him in 1895, could see the signs of an impending challenge to the Tsarist autocracy from the thousands of young dissidents, disaffected by years of intellectual repression, and from the new class of industrial workers emerging in the cities who were determined to improve the inhuman conditions to which they were being subjected by the new capitalist entrepreneurs. His reign was marked by persistent unrest in the universities, where serious disturbances occurred regularly, resulting in the arrest and expulsion of thousands of students. In Moscow University alone, between 1890 and 1900, over 2000 students were either expelled by the authorities or arrested by the police and sentenced to lengthy periods in prison.[62] Repeatedly, universities were closed for long periods as students organised long-term strikes against the authorities. In some cases the entire body of students in a university was arrested *en masse*. In July 1899 the Emperor decreed that all students expelled from universities should henceforth be enlisted in the ordinary ranks of the armed forces—a measure which led to the further growth of radical student movements, as well as to strikes, demonstrations, expulsions and mass arrests. Following the assassination of the Minister, Bogolepov, in 1901, a Commission set up to inquire into the conditions in universities reported that repressive measures had led to an increase in student unrest, the growth of secret societies and widespread discontent amongst university teaching staff. Some reforms were introduced in 1901; a limited form of self-government was allowed for universities, student grants were improved, and the right to form societies was conceded. The measures came too late, however, to stem the tide of unrest; strikes and demonstrations continued, as did the waves of arrests, expulsions, prison sentences and the banishment of thousands of students to the remote reaches of Siberia.

Recognising the need to placate the masses through some measures in educational reform, Nicholas embarked on a programme of expansion that resulted in a huge growth in the number of pupils and schools in the two decades remaining before the Revolution. A Commission was set up in July 1899, involving representatives from every educational region, to review government policies on primary and secondary education. In its eight-volume report the Commission identified the lack of continuity between the different stages of the education system as the main obstacle to the imple-mentation of democratic objectives. Denouncing the privileged status of the classical gymnasia, it recommended the creation of a three-tiered system, proposing a first level school for 7-12 year olds, a lower second level school for 12-15 year olds, and an upper second level school for 15-18 year olds—all of which was based on the Norwegian school reforms that had recently come into being. A common school programme was to be taught for the first five years, consisting of Russian, religion, a foreign language, mathematics, geography, drawing and singing, with science and history as added subjects in the fourth and fifth years. The second level schools were to offer the same range of courses, with philosophy, a third language and some specialised courses as additional subjects. The proposals were signi-ficantly modified, however, in the next two years and were only partially implemented. Gymnasia and real schools continued to exist side by side with the new schools and the envisaged ladder system never came into being.

Nevertheless, the period was marked by an immense leap forward in the provision made for the years of elementary schooling. Large sums were made available for this purpose, both by the Churches and the state, and, to avoid the conflicts that occurred in earlier decades, new regulations on the founding of schools were set out in the Statute of 1902 to ensure that no duplication occurred between Church-sponsored and state-sponsored schools. Much of the cost was met by provincial and district zemstvos, thus relieving the peasant communities of the burden of directly financing the founding of schools. By the early 1900s the zemstvos were contributing 95% of the cost of founding primary schools; by comparison they con-tributed only 6% of the cost of second level schools. Within ten years the numbers in primary education almost doubled, from an enrolment figure of 2.5 million at the begininng of Nicholas's reign to 4.7 million by 1905—making this the period of greatest expansion in Russian education before the Revolution. Yet the government was still a long way from achieving the goal of universal primary education. By 1905 there were still only 3.8 children in school per 100 inhabitants (the corresponding figure for secondary education was .24 per 100).[63]

Once again statistical data on the provision of schools conceals some harsh realities regarding the quality of the schooling that was offered. There are various reports available on the conditions that existed in the schools of the 1890s, all indicating standards that were less than satisfactory in various respects. The status of teachers and perceptions of their competence by the communities amongst whom they worked provide clear indications of the conditions that existed. A Report from the Moscow Literacy Committee in the 1890s gives a vivid description of attitudes to teachers in the schools in that region and of the harsh conditions in which they worked:

> The situation of the teacher . . . is most unenviable. He is often forced to do without even the essentials; meat and even the necessary clothing often have to be foregone. There is no money left to order books which would give him the opportunity to supplement his knowledge and keep up with the latest methods and discussions; newspapers and journals are financially out of reach. . . . For a family man there can be no talk of saving any money or sending his children to a school with tuition, for he can't even afford shoes for his offspring.[64]

There was a great deal of movement from school to school as teachers constantly sought to improve their positions and to get better working conditions. Various measures were taken by the zemstvos to try to deal with the disruption that resulted from this. Salary supplements were introduced in the 1890s to top up the meagre payments made by the district boards, and pension arrangements were introduced in 1900. The 1908 School Bill fixed the minimum wage for teachers at 360 rubles per annum, described by one historian as 'the lowest possible amount on which a single rural teacher could survive'.[65] This figure has to be contrasted with average earnings for lawyers of between 2000 and 10,000 rubles per annum, for agronomists of 3000 rubles per annum and for doctors of 1200. Eklof, who provides detailed statistics on the material conditions of teachers, writes: 'Hardly recognised as professionals, rural teachers were removed entirely from the social world by their income. In fact, their salaries were close to those of facory workers; in all industries the average yearly wage was 264 rubles, ranging from 192 rubles in textiles to 396 in the metal industries. Primary school teachers were paid the same as *fel'dshers*, those medical orderlies who stood on the same low rung of the status ladder, although they too provided vital services to the population.'[66]

Given the low level of their earnings and the poor conditions in which they worked, it is not surprising to discover that teachers were generally held in low esteem both by the village communities and the officials under whom they served, and that they themselves had an extremely negative view of their work. One teacher wrote to a Zemstvo Congress in 1911: 'Only martyrs, accepting the burden of poverty and deprivation, or those unable to hold a job anywhere else would remain in the profession.'[67] Another teacher from the district of Ekaterinoslav wrote: 'The best talent leaves this profession, seeking service offering better material remuneration. . . . Many take up the career of teaching simply as a temporary expedient, pursuing one or more of the following goals: to take advantage of the military deferments or to wait for the opportunity to meet the right man and get married.'[68] In the village schools they were at the mercy of local bureaucrats, inspectors and various other functionaries, by whom they were constantly harrassed and humiliated. A report from the district of Chernigov, cited by Eklof, describes the kind of relationship that existed between the teacher in the school there and the local bureaucrats:

> The Gelendzhinski village elder and clerk have conducted themselves disrespectfully and coarsely with the local teacher. . . . These officials, taking advantage of each opportunity when the teacher had to contact them on school matters, not only rendered no assistance but also interfered peremptorily with her teaching, asked impertinent questions, and even pried into her personal life. Although the main villains were the assistant elder and clerk, who have been dismissed, still I recommend a strict reprimand for the elder as well, for allowing this to happen. . . .
>
> Having every reason to believe that insufficient respect is shown the rural teacher by local authorities elsewhere as well, I find it necessary to include in this instruction a proposal to all local authorities to persuade peasant officials under their jurisdiction to show the necessary respect to teachers of both sexes . . . and to point out that simply because a village society contributes to the upkeep of a school, this does not give rural authorities the right to interfere in school affairs.[69]

Since the local peasant communities contributed to the cost of teachers' salaries and to the upkeep of the schools, they frequently tended to interfere in the manner described in this passage. There were reports of communities withholding material support in areas where they considered the teacher was incompetent. Reports from the Tula province (the home area of Leo Tolstoy) indicate that the peasants withheld their taxes for a certain period because of their dissatisfaction with the work of local teachers. In the village of Budugovische parents refused to send their children to school because of their dissatisfaction with the teacher.[70] Parents in Aransk asked that the teacher appointed by the local school board be replaced by a retired soldier they felt 'could be much more useful teaching our children'.[71] An inspector investigating school closures in a district called Krachkovskii found widespread evidence of negligence; in one school the local priest was absent so frequently that parents had ceased to send their children to the school; in another the teacher was frequently drunk and the inspector reported that most of the children had not even learned to read.[72] Teachers also endured a great deal of unpopularity as they were often seen as outsiders in the communities amongst whom they worked. This comment occurs in a report on teachers in the Moscow province: 'In the eyes of the peasants the male teacher is a figure alien to their world, quite remote from their vital interests. ... The teacher is a newcomer, lacking a hearth in the community and having no personal interest in communal affairs other than that of the school'.[73]

Church schools received strong government support during the reign of Nicholas II. Though committed to promoting literacy through an efficient schooling system, he was also determined to combat secularism by promoting the traditions of the Orthodox faith, and saw the Church-controlled schools as having a key role to play in this. These schools increased in number from 21,400 to 34,000 during his reign and pupil enrolments increased from 626,100 to 1.9 million.[74] The regulations stipulated that they should 'strengthen the Orthodox faith and Christian morality amongst the people while imparting useful elementary knowledge'.[75] The schools were of two types: some provided two year courses, others provided four. By a revised statute of 1902 the courses were lengthened to three and five years respectively. In the first type of school the curriculum consisted of the Bible, Church choir, reading and writing in Russian and Church Slavonic, and the rudiments of arithmetic. To this was added further instruction in Russian and Church history in the four-year school. Teachers in these schools were usually priests who were assisted, in some instances, by deacons.

A significant event in the evolution of Church-controlled education was a government ruling in May 1891 which entrusted responsibility for the new literacy schools to the Holy Synod. These *shkoly grammaty*, or reading and writing schools, had been started in the 1880s by the zemstvos as a cheap expedient to reduce the very high levels of illiteracy reported by government officials.[76] Following the ruling of May 1891 thousands of them were taken over by the Church and converted into full parochial schools, thus swelling the numbers of Church-controlled schools. Yet reports continued to show that staff were poorly qualified in most of the Church schools, that their buildings were dilapidated and poorly furnished, and that parents still preferred to send their children to zemstvo-controlled schools.[77] The decline of the Church schools began in 1907 when yet another programme of expansion was undertaken in elementary education. Since the Church was excluded from the funding arrangements for the new schools, the numbers under their control were dramatically reduced as parents transferred their children in large numbers to the new, free and well-equipped schools that were being established as part of the last of the major educational initiatives to occur in Tsarist Russia.

That initiative was set in motion by the Bill on Universal Elementary Education that was passed by the Duma in February 1907. This Bill declared that elementary education would be made available to all children throughout the state and decreed that it would be the duty of every zemstvo to provide a school within three versts of each district under its control. A maximum figure of 50 pupils per teacher was set for each school. Grants were to be provided by the central government to finance the expansion programme; a sum of over 3 million rubles was eventually provided. It was also decreed that in future all schools would provide four years of primary education, as had been customary with many of them on a voluntary basis already. Minimum salaries were laid down for teachers and every school was to receive a grant for equipment and furnishings. As the plan was put into effect, a massive expansion in numbers occurred, so that by 1915 there were 116,234 elementary schools in the country, catering for over eight million pupils. The numbers of primary schools had almost quadrupled and enrollments had almost trebled during Nicholas's reign (the number of schools increased from 45,000 to over 116,000 and the number of pupils from 2.2 to 8 million).[78] A Bill proposing to make primary education compulsory for all children came before the Duma in 1915 but had not yet passed into law by 1917. The objective of universal primary education, advocated almost a century before by Tsar Alexander I, was not to become a reality until after the Revolution.

Ironically, the expansion that occurred in primary education under Nicholas II was to a great extent a response to the political agitation that had been a continuing feature of life in the country during the two decades of his reign. And that agitation intensified as greater numbers of newly educated young people, increasingly more aware of their own rights and of the scale of injustices occurring in the country, joined radical political movements in their thousands, especially in the universities. With the growth in the economy and the expansion of the country's industrial resources that occurred from 1905 onwards, a greater proportion of students from the lower orders were entering second and third level education and swelling the ranks of dissident political movements. The number of university students doubled from about 20,000 in 1904 to over 40,000 by 1909.[79] Mass meetings, arrests, the sentencing of students to imprisonment and exile, and their enforced enlistment into the armed forces, continued. While the elective principle was restored to universities by a new statute of August 1905, it was again abolished in 1907, following the political turmoil that occurred in the interim. During the Ministry of L.A. Casso particularly severe methods were used to stem the tide of student unrest; detectives disguised as students infiltrated universities, students were expelled for non-attendance at lectures, meetings were proscribed, and thousands were arrested and brought before the courts. It was students such as these who turned out in large numbers to welcome Leo Tolstoy on his last visit to Moscow in 1908, and who demonstrated in their thousands against capital punishment—a cause he deeply espoused—on the occasion of his death two years later. Despite all the political turmoil, however—or perhaps because of it—significant growth was recorded in higher education during these years. By 1917 there were more than 90 institutes of higher education in Russia, catering for a total of about 125,000 students.[80]

Much of the agitation that occurred in universities spread to the second level system after the Revolution of 1905. In October of that year all the secondary schools joined the general strike and demanded the setting up of a Constituent Assembly. The strike lasted for several months, during which the students virtually controlled the schools. Teachers sympathetic to the movement formed the All Russian Teachers Union. In 1907, the Minister, Kaufmann, sought to introduce more democracy into second level education by proposing to found a system of 'higher urban schools', but the scheme was never implemented. The next minister, Schwarz, also tried to diversify the system by increasing the number of real or modern gymnasia, from which he proposed to allow students proceed to university education, but this scheme was also postponed. A Bill on Secondary Education was put before the Duma in 1911, under the ministry of Count Ignatiev, and was passed into law in 1915. Its main effect was to reform the curriculum, the principal change being a greater emphasis on modern languages and the humanities. Some growth was recorded in the second level system in the last decade before the Revolution; the number of schools increased from 863 to 2153; the latter figure, however, was clearly inadequate to serve a population of 175 million people.[81]

Throughout the nineteenth century Russian education was subject to alternating movements towards democratisation and retrenchment. Policies designed to achieve a more equitable provision of educational opportunity were constantly being frustrated by reactionary elements manifesting an equally strong determination to undermine the fruits of those policies in every way they could. The progressive initiatives of Alexander I and II were each followed by retrogressive policies designed to stem the movement towards political democracy to which those initiatives would inevitably have led. Yet, in a curious way, the system continued to expand—elementary education in particular gained momentum even from the reactionary policies that were designed to ensure that educational expansion would proceed selectively, with secondary and higher education being restricted to the privileged classes, while a basic education designed to provide for the needs of manual workers and minor clerical functionaries was being made available to ensure they remained content in the lowly positions to which destiny had consigned them.

If statistics alone were adopted as a yardstick by which to determine the progress made throughout the nineteenth century, there was evidence of significant growth in the education system, at least in terms of the recruitment of teachers and the physical provision of schools. Though far short of the goal of universal education, the figures for the last years of Romanov rule suggest that considerable progress had been made towards making that objective a foreseeable reality. By 1911 90% of the zemstvos had concluded agreements with the government on the funding arrangements necessary to implement the terms of the Education Act of 1907, which committed them to the provision of elementary education on a compulsory basis for the entire school-going population. The greatest progress recorded was in European Russia—the proportion of the school-going population enrolled in Moscow Province was 84.2%; it was in 54% in Arkhangelsk and 58.4% in Smolensk. These figures must be contrasted, however, with enrollment rates of 2.4% in Samarkand, 1.6% in Fergana and 9.4% in Semirech'e. On a national basis the percentage of school-age children registered in schools was estimated at 44.8%. (Count Ignatiev, the Minister, claimed it was a highly inflated 91%.) Yet this figure must be qualified by evidence of high drop out rates and persistent absenteeism; it was estimated that the proportion of children completing four years of elementary education was at best 10%.[82] Additionally, the evidence on the poor quality of education, as illustrated from the reports cited earlier in this chapter, would suggest that much of what passed for educational provision could scarcely be described as such in any meaningful sense of that term. And while it might be claimed that half the child population was receiving some form of education as Russia entered the twentieth century, most of the progress made had occurred in the last two decades of Tsarist rule. Throughout the nineteenth century the majority of the peasant population were denied access to education of any type or form. Apart from those lucky enough to get access to state- or Church-sponsored schools, the remainder were dependent on the generosity of enlightened individuals, such as Leo Tolstoy, who considered they had a moral obligation to provide for the educational as well as the material needs of the masses of deprived and poverty-stricken people amongst whom they lived.

Tolstoy the Teacher: A Biographical Profile

1 *Formative Years, 1828–50*

A study of Tolstoy's life as an educator must begin with the impressions he formed of the whole educational process in the years when he experienced it from the standpoint of the young pupil and student. Like most Russian landowning families of the nineteenth century, the Tolstoys entrusted the education of their children to governesses and tutors who were charged with the responsibility of providing for their moral and academic formation in the secure and comfortable surroundings of their own home. Tolstoy has left vivid memories of those years in *Childhood, Adolescence, Youth*, his fictional autobiography, which he completed while still a young man in his twenties. While essentially a work of fiction, its descriptions of the events of Tolstoy's childhood correspond quite closely to the biographical accounts of those years provided by his children, Ilya and Sasha, and by close associates, such as Aylmer Maude and P.I. Biryukov.[1] It can therefore be considered an authentic, if somewhat embellished, version of the experiences that shaped his childhood formation and growth. It provides vivid and frequently dramatic accounts of his progress from childhood to adult life, beginning with his recollections of his parents—both of whom died tragically while he was still a child—and concluding with his ignominious departure from the University of Kazan without a degree in 1847.

Two contrasting images dominate the early chapters of this work. The first is a warm and affectionate image of his first tutor, the eccentric, slightly comic, volatile, kind and good-natured Fyodor Ivanovich Rossel, who is known in the autobiogaphy as 'Karl Ivanych'. The second image is that of the tutor who replaced Rossel, a stern, authoritarian Frenchman, Prosper de St Thomas, who is known in the autobiography as 'St. Jerome'. These two images convey a great deal both of what Tolstoy approved and what he rejected in his conception of the role of the educator. It would be wrong, however, to see them as representing rigidly demarcated pedagogic philosophies, since much of the strength of Tolstoy's educational thinking derived from its assimilation of diverse and apparently contradictory influences. Yet these two images provide valuable pointers to the elements which eventually shaped his vision of education and especially his conception of the role and mission of the teacher.

Describing the years he was taught by Rossel, Tolstoy recalls mornings spent contentedly in the classroom, while Rossel taught 'the language of Goethe', and afternoons spent in the surrounding countryside, picking mushrooms and blackberries, fishing in the Voronka, or playing with the children of the peasants from the nearby village of Yasnaya Polyana. 'What time could be better than that when the two highest virtues, innocence and joy and a limitless need to love, are the only mainsprings of life',[2] he wrote euphorically. Rossel was the key figure in this idyllic picture of early childhood. Tolstoy's description of him emphasises his simplicity, his bookish and kindly nature and, most importantly, his easy and spontaneous relationship with his pupils:

> I can still see the tall figure in the quilted dressing-gown and red cap from under which his thin grey hair protrudes. He is seated beside a small table, and the disk with the hairdresser on it casts a shadow on his face. In one hand he has a book, the other rests on the arm of his chair; beside him are a watch with a huntsman painted on the face, a checkered handkerchief, a round black snuff-box, a green spectacle case and a pair of snuffers on a little tray. All lie so decorously and neatly, each in its proper place, that this orderliness is sufficient to convince one that Karl Ivanych's conscience is clear and his soul is at peace.
>
> Many were the times when having run about to my heart's content in the salon downstairs, I would tiptoe stealthily up to the schoolroom to find Karl Ivanych all alone, sitting in his armchair, reading one of his favourite books with an expression of calm dignity. Sometimes I would come upon him at a moment when he was not reading: his spectacles would have slipped down in his large aquiline nose, his half-closed eyes would have a peculiar expression, and his lips would be turned up in a sad smile. It would be still in the room where the only sounds were his regular breathing and the ticking of the watch with the huntsman on its face.
>
> He would not notice me, but I would stand by the door thinking: 'Poor, poor old man! There are so many of us; we play and have fun, but he is all alone, with no one to comfort him. He's right when he says he's an orphan. And the story of his life is so dreadful! I remember him telling it to Nikolai. How dreadful to be in his situation!' And I would feel so sorry for him that I would go up to him, take his hand and say: '*Lieber* Karl Ivanych!' He was pleased when I addressed him thus; he would always pet me, and I could see he was touched.
>
> Maps hung on the other wall, most of them torn but pasted together skilfully by Karl Ivanych. On the third wall, in the middle of which was a door leading to the stairs, there hung on one side two rulers; one of them, all scored, was ours, and the other, a new one, was his own, which he used more for incitement than for ruling lines; on the other side was a blackboard on which our serious misdemeanours were marked by naughts and our lesser ones by

crosses. To the left of the board was the corner in which we were made to kneel when we were punished.[3]

The conditions created by Rossel seem to have been conducive to effective learning as well as to childhood freedom and happiness. Tolstoy recalled that he gained a good command of German under his tutelage, and additionally, that Rossel was responsible for releasing and nurturing his potentialities as a writer. The methods that Rossel used to stimulate the children's learning abilities were quite similar to those used by Tolstoy himself in the school he founded for the children of the peasants of Yasnaya Polyana three decades later. These were based on direct observation of children's needs, interests and learning styles. 'Fyodor Ivanovich', Alexandra Tolstoy wrote, 'did not hold any educational theory, possessed little knowledge or real discipline, simply loved his charges, understood them, always could gauge their characters with great perceptiveness.'[4] Whether Rossel became a role model for Tolstoy when he himself undertook the responsibilities of a teacher is difficult to say, but like Rossel, he also rejected the principles of theoretical pedagogics and based his teaching style on direct observation of the needs of individual children. Similarly, he believed that a trusting and authentic relationship between teacher and pupil was the essential factor in the whole process of education and the foundation principle of successful teaching and learning. Rossel embodied those qualities, as Tolstoy himself did in his various educational endeavours from the period when he was schoolmaster at Yasnaya Polyana to his work as an adult educator in later years.

Tolstoy's second tutor, Prosper de St Thomas, was Rossel's opposite in most ways. Described by Alexandra Tolstoy as 'a narrow-minded, conceited, swaggering Frenchman whose whole appearance, natural pomposity and almost theatrical affectation were repelling to any sensitive boy',[5] his arrival in the Tolstoy household proved to be traumatic for everyone subjected to his teaching. Responding angrily to the authoritarian methods of the new tutor, Tolstoy became defiant and intransigent. 'I stood there livid with anger', he recalled in a description of one particularly bitter encounter, 'and told myself I would die on the spot sooner than kneel in front of him, but he leaned on my shoulders with all his strength, bent my back and forced me to my knees.'[6] Becoming increasingly rebellious as a result of the harsh treatment and the humiliations he had to endure, he began to question not only the authority of his new tutor but the validity and truth of his teaching, especially in matters of religious faith. A good deal of his resentment of the methods used by St Thomas could be attributed, however, to his dislike for the assessments which the latter conducted regularly. There are persistent references in *Childhood* to his fear of obtaining marks of 2 or 3 (representing failure or unsatisfactory attainment on the traditional 5-point scale). Marks were awarded both for attainment and behaviour and embraced criteria such as diligence, deportment and courtesy as well as levels of achievement in the various disciplines. Threats of punishment—which were rarely carried out—added to the tensions associated with assessment.

Yet, despite all his complaints, the chapter from *Childhood* in which Tolstoy examines his feelings about St Thomas, suggests there was a good deal of ambivalence underlying the whole relationship. This excerpt indicates even a grudging respect on Tolstoy's part for the tutor's dedication and professionalism, side by side with deep personal resentment and animosity:

> Yes, this was a genuine feeling of hatred, not the hatred they write about in novels and which I do not believe, a hatred which is supposed to find satisfaction in doing someone harm, but the hatred which fills you with an overpowering aversion for a person who yet deserves your respect and causes his hair, his neck, his gait, the sound of his voice, all his limbs, all his movements to seem repulsive to you, while at the same time some incomprehensible force draws you to him and compels you to follow his every action with uneasy attention. I experienced this feeling towards St. Jerome.
>
> St Jerome had been with us for a year and a half. In judging this man cool-headedly now I find that he was a good Frenchman, but a Frenchman to the highest degree. He was quite clever, rather well-educated, and fulfilled his duties towards us conscientiously but he possessed, common to his fellow-countrymen and so contrary to the Russian character, the distinctive features of frivolous egotism, vanity, insolence, and the conceit of ignorance. I disliked all of this in the extreme. Needless to say, Grandmother had explained her views on corporal punishment to him and he did not dare to thrash us; but in spite of this he often threatened us, and especially me, with the rod and uttered the word fouetter (pronouncing it *fouatter*) as disgustingly and in such a tone of voice as though it would have given him the greatest of pleasure to whip me.[7]

With the passage of time the relationship seemed to improve, at least to the extent that Tolstoy was attributing his academic progress to the efficacy of St. Thomas's methods of teaching. Gradually one sees a distinct change in the tone of his comments on his tutor: 'I am a diligent pupil. Not only do I await my tutors without dread, I even find a certain pleasure in my lessons. . . . St Jerome is pleased with me and praises me; I no longer hate him and when he sometimes says that with my abilities and my mind it is a shame not to do such-and-such I even think that I like him.'[8] St. Thomas continued to supervise Tolstoy's academic progress until he took the entrance examinations of the University of Kazan in 1844 at the age of sixteen. He credits St Thomas with helping him to develop good study habits and to overcome his tendency to day-dreaming—'my occupations', he writes, 'consisted in solitary, incoherent day-dreaming and contemplation' —and he declared his intention to commit himself wholly to his university studies: 'I will take down the lectures, and will even prepare the subjects in advance, so that I shall be first in my year and will write a dissertation; in my second year I shall know everything in advance and may pass directly to the third year, so that at eighteen I shall graduate as First Candidate with two gold medals; then I will take my Master's and Doctor's degrees and become the leading scholar of Russia.'[9]

Initially, Tolstoy's ambitions seemed likely to be realised. He matriculated successfully, gaining full marks in oral history, French and mathematics, and obtained high grades in Russian literature and history, German, Arabic, Turko-Tatar, English, logic and binomial mathematics. Because of a low mark in Latin and a failure in the written papers for history and geography, he was obliged to repeat those subjects in a subsequent examination, and did so successfully. He generously acknowledged his tutors' part in in his success: 'Had it not been for my tutors, if not for St Jerome, who occasionally and reluctantly excited my ambition . . . the spring and my new freedom should have made me forget everything I had known and I should never have passed my examinations.'[10] At that time the University of Kazan was renowned for the brilliance of its Faculty of Oriental Languages and Tolstoy decided to enter this faculty with a view to becoming a diplomat.

At University he continued to develop his literary and musical interests. By then he had read widely in Russian, French, English and German literature, and had made a close study of the Bible, giving particular attention to the Old Testament. He continued to develop his passion for music, practising the piano, attending concerts and recitals, and even attempting piano compositions himself. (One biographer describes how he replayed one of these early compositions—a melody for a waltz—on the piano at Yasnaya Polyana in 1906 when he was 78 years old.)[11] In *Childhood* he attributed his love for music to his mother; one of the most moving sequences in the book describes her playing Field and Beethoven for her children shortly before her death.[12] In Chapter 30 of *Youth*, which is entitled 'My Occupations', Tolstoy describes his musical interests in the years at Kazan as being predominantly classical, though he regrets not aways treating them as seriously as he felt he should. 'Had any one at that time taught me to regard music as an end in itself, as a pleasure in its own right and not as a means of charming young ladies by the facility and emotion of my playing, I might perhaps, indeed, have become a decent musician', he writes.[13] Mozart, Haydn, Schubert and Chopin were his favourite composers, according to his daughter Alexandra, who adds that his classical interests in no way interfered with his fondness also for folk and gypsy music.[14] These interests proved to be deeply significant for his thinking on the fostering of imagination amongst the children attending the school at Yasnaya Polyana some years later.

Tolstoy enjoyed a lively social life at the university, as is suggested by his comments on his ability to charm young ladies by the emotional impact of his music. 'I am thankful to fate', he writes, 'that I passed my first youth in an environment where a young man could be young without touching problems beyond his grasp and that I lived a life which, though idle and luxurious, was yet not evil.'[15] Failing in Russian history and German at the end of the year—a result he blamed on the vindictive behaviour of a professor he claims held a grudge against his family—he switched to legal studies in 1845. He pursued his new studies more diligently, and passed his examinations in May 1846. Diary entries indicate the great efforts he was making to improve his study habits. On March 24, 1847 he wrote: 'I have changed a lot but I still haven't achieved the degree of perfection which I would like to achieve.' He wrote out guidelines for himself which included exhortations such as 'what you carry out carry out well', 'always read and think aloud', and 'make your mind work constantly with all possible vigour'.[16]

There are indications, at this stage, however, of a great broadening in his reading interests which was accompanied by an intense dislike for specialisation and for the restrictions of a set curriculum. That resentment was particularly manifested in his attitude to science. 'A passion for the sciences is beginning to manifest itself in me', he writes, 'but although it is the noblest of man's passions, I still never surrender myself to it in a one-sided manner i.e. completely destroy feeling, not concern myself with application, and only endeavour to educate my mind and fill my memory with facts'. 'One-sidedness is the main cause of man's unhappiness', he concludes.[17] That rejection of specialisation, side by side with an impassioned belief in the interrelatedness of all facets of human culture, became one of the mainsprings of his thought for the remainder of his life. It proved also to be a fundamental principle of his educational philosophy, one that was most fruitfully represented in his concept of a school curriculum.

In the immediate circumstances of his career as a university student it resulted, however, in an indifferent performance in his examinations. Having studied erratically and absented himself from most of the lectures while continuing to develop his wide-ranging intellectual and literary interests, he obtained poor results in most of the subjects of the law examinations and asked to be withdrawn from the university register on grounds of 'ill-health and family affairs'.[18] The division of his father's estate had recently been completed and Tolstoy now found himself the owner of the manor house at Yasnaya Polyana, the landlord of 330 peasants, and the manager of a 4000-acre estate. He set about modernising the estate and planned a number of social reforms, of which the school for the children of the peasants was to be the most notable. His Diary entries, however, indicate his determination to proceed with his studies independently and eventually to take his degree, if not at Kazan, at some other Russian university. The extent and seriousness of his commitment to independent study is demonstrated by the programme of work he set out for himself shortly after his return to the estate. The Diary entry for 17 April 1847 reads:

> Now I ask myself, what will be the purpose of my life in the country for the next two years? (1) To study the whole course of law necessary for my final examination at the university. (2) To study practical medicine, and some theoretical medicine. (3) To study languages: French, German, Russian, English, Italian and Latin. (4) To study agriculture, both theoretical and practical. (5) To study history, geography and statistics. (6) To study mathematics, the grammar school course. (7) To write a dissertation. (8) To attain an average degree of perfection in music and painting. (9) To write down rules. (10) To acquire some knowledge of the natural sciences. (11) To write essays on all the subjects I shall study.[19]

Tolstoy made one further attempt to get a degree—this time at the University of St.Petersburg, where he took the examinations in civil and criminal law in 1849, but decided not to proceed with the remaining examinations. He continued, however, to immerse himself in the vast reading programmes he had planned after he left the University of Kazan. Fostering the potential for self-education was to be one of his foremost objectives as an educator, and his commitment to developing this capacity, firstly in the young children attending his school at Yansnaya Polyana, and later in his contacts with adults through his various ventures in community education, was greatly reinforced by his personal experience of the immense benfits to be gained from it.

All these ventures were to be inspired further by a profound belief in the transforming power of religious faith, but the faith that Tolstoy preached, and the one that provides some of the most basic principles of his educational philosophy, involved a radical reappraisal of the Christian religious traditions, and especially those of Orthodox Christianity, which he had been taught as a child. That process of reappraisal can be traced also to the years when he was engaged in his university studies. Though there are passages in *Childhood* intimating a rejection of Orthodoxy at a much earlier period in his life,[20] Tolstoy tended in later years to identify it decisively with the period of his departure from the university. 'I was baptised in the Orthodox Christian faith', he wrote in *A Confession*. 'I was taught it in childhood and all through my boyhood and youth. But when I left the university in my second year at the age of eighteen I no longer believed anything I had been taught.'[21] His rejection of Orthodox, and indeed institutional, Christianity in general was based on a deep intellectual questioning of the ways in which he believed the Churches had distorted the teachings of Christ—especially on matters such as violence, property and wealth. This feeling was greatly reinforced by his discovery of two philosophers who profoundly influenced his thought on several matters, but particularly on religion and education— Rousseau and Voltaire. 'I have read the whole of Rousseau', he wrote. 'I was more than enthusiastic about him. I worshipped him.'[22] And of his interest in Voltaire he said: 'His ridicule of religion not only did not shock me but amused me very much.'[23] Yet he continued to read the scriptures— especially the Gospel of St Matthew, and several Diary entries indicate a continuing attachment to the traditions of Christianity, despite his growing hostility to the Churches. We find this entry, for example, for 13 July 1854—several years after he left the university:

> My prayer. 'I believe in one, almighty and good God, in the immortality of the soul, and in eternal retribution for our deeds; I wish to believe in the religion of my fathers and I respect it'.
> Our Father,' etc. 'For the repose and salvation of my parents'. 'I thank Thee, O Lord, for Thy mercies, for this and for that' (here recall all the happiness that has been my lot). 'I pray Thee, inspire me to good undertakings and thoughts, and grant me happiness and success in them. Help me to correct my faults, save me from sickness, suffering, quarrels, debts and humiliations'.
> 'Grant me to live and die in firm faith and hope in Thee, in love for others and from others, with a clear conscience, and with profit to my neighbour. Grant me to do good and shun evil: but whether good or evil befall me, may Thy holy will be done!'[24]

To a considerable degree, therefore, we can identify the roots of Tolstoy's educational philosophy in the experiences of his childhood and youth. Some of the influences which most significantly shaped the character of that philosophy may be traced to those years. They included the rather complex conception of the role of the educator—a concept simultaneously embracing interpersonal authenticity and pedagogic efficacy—that he formed in his recollections of the contrasting philosophies of his tutors, Rossel and St Thomas, as well as his belief in the virtues of self-education, in the importance of nurturing imaginative potential, in the benefits of a broadly based curriculum and in the need for disciplined learning. Most significantly, as we shall see from subsequent developments, they also included his belief that education should be guided by an all-embracing faith, the essential basis of which was the self-questioning freedom of individual conscience and thought he had asserted by rejecting the authority of the institutional churches.

2 Early Educational Activities, 1850–62

Returning to Yasnaya Polyana, Tolstoy assumed responsibility for the administration of his large estate. Shocked at the poverty, ignorance and backwardness he saw amongst the peasantry, he immediately embarked on various measures for social reform, including the founding of a school. Unfortunately, we know very little about this venture, apart from the fact that it lasted about two years and had to be discontinued because of financial difficulties.[25] There are no references to this first school in Tolstoy's Diary, and it gets only a brief mention in Alexandra's Memoirs and in Maude's authorised biography. It would appear that, unlike subsequent ventures in education, Tolstoy did not become directly involved in the work of the school and merely patronised its activities in his capacity as landlord of the region. The episode, however, indicates an early commitment to the cause of popular education and was to be followed by a more direct involvement a few years later. Meanwhile, he served in the army for a number of years, initially in the Caucasus and later in the Crimea. In that period he emerged as a major writer, completing, firstly, *Childhood, Adolescence, Youth* and then *The Cossacks*. More significantly, from an educational standpoint, he resolved to found a new religious movement, based on the simple Christianity of the Gospels, and especially the teachings of the Sermon on the Mount. 'Yesterday', he wrote in his Diary for 4 March 1855, 'a conversation about divinity and faith inspired me with a great idea, a stupendous idea, to the realisation of which I feel capable of devoting my life. The idea is the founding of a new religion appropriate to the stage of development of mankind—the religion of Christ, but purged of beliefs and mysticism'.[26] The realisation of that ideal was still a long way off but it gave direction and motivation to most of Tolstoy's activities from that time onward.

The events which probably gave immediate impetus to Tolstoy's decision to found a second school for the peasant children of Yasnaya Polyana were the declaration by Alexander II in March 1856 that he intended to emancipate the serfs, and the subsequent announcement by the Minister for the Interior that this would be achieved gradually through the cooperation of individual landlords. Tolstoy was one of the first to commit himself to this objective. On 22 April 1856 he noted in his Diary: 'My attitude to the serfs is beginning to trouble me greatly. I feel the need to learn, learn, learn.'[27] A few days later he drew up a plan for their emancipation and forwarded it to the Ministry of the Interior. He received little support from the Ministry, however, and convened a meeting of the serfs himself at which he proposed to transfer his lands to a village commune, allowing 12 acres to each household at a nominal rent, and freeing the serfs from all obligations to him. The serfs rejected his proposal, believing the lands would eventually be transferred to them without any rent. On this they were disappointed as the arrangements proposed by the government turned out to be less favourable than those proposed by Tolstoy, and the full liberation of the serfs was, in fact, deferred for many years. Tolstoy, nonetheless, implemented the plan as originally proposed. The provision of education for the children of the peasantry, which was part of his plan for their emancipation, was begun with the founding of the second school in 1859.

Initially, the school was located in a room of the manor-house. When work began in the autumn of 1859 Tolstoy's only assistant was the Orthodox priest who took responsibility for teaching the scriptures. The pupils (at first there were twenty-two and eventually over seventy) were taught in a converted third floor bedroom. For some time Tolstoy faced sceptical attitudes from the peasants, many of whom regarded his methods with suspicion, some even demanding that the children be flogged. Tolstoy himself taught Russian, arithmetic, religious history, Russian history and geography. The importance that he attached to the whole venture is evident from his correspondence. To his close relative, Countess Alexandrine Tolstoy, he wrote: 'You know I am sure about my occupation with a school since last year. I can quite sincerely say that it is now the one interest that attaches me to life.'[28] He wrote to his friend, Yegor Kovalevsky, to intercede with his brother, then the Minister for Education, for permission to found a Sociey for the Education of the People, through which he (Tolstoy) proposed to extend the experiment at Yasnaya Polyana into a network of popular schools.[29] He also sought subscriptions of 1000 rubles per head from nearby land proprietors to finance it. Permission was refused by the Government and the Society for the Education of the People was never founded. Tolstoy concluded that village schools founded by the local communities offered the best prospect for realising his plans for popular education.

Firstly, however, he decided to improve his own knowledge of education, particularly in the sphere of pedagogic methodology. When the first year's work was completed at the school (the children were released to help their parents in the fields throughout the summer), Tolstoy decided to undertake an extensive travel programme in Western Europe with a view to making a close study of various education systems. In July 1860 he set out with his sister, Maria, and her three children for Germany where he first visited his brother, Nikolai, who was being treated for tuberculosis in a sanitorium at Soden. In Berlin he attended evening classes for artisans at the *Handwerkersverein* where he was impressed by the lively exchanges that occurred between teachers and students. He was less impressed by what he saw in some schools in Leipzig. A Diary entry for 17 July reads: 'Visited a school. Terrible. A prayer for the king, beatings, everything by heart, frightened, morally deformed children'.[30] Compulsion he saw as the root cause of the failure of the German schools:

> Germany, the founder of the school, has not been able during a struggle of two hundred years, to overcome the counteraction of the masses to the school. In spite of the appointments of meritorious invalid soldiers as teachers made by the Fredericks; in spite of the law which has been in force for two hundred years; in spite of the preparation according to the latest fashion, which teachers receive in seminaries; in spite of the Germans' feeling of obedience to the law—compulsory education even to this moment lies as a heavy burden upon the people, and the German governments cannot bring themselves to abolish the law of compulsory education. Germany can pride itself on the education of its people only by statistical data, but the masses, as before, for the greater part, take away from the schools nothing but a contempt for them....
>
> In Germany nine-tenths of the school population take away from school a mechanical knowledge of reading and writing, and such a strong loathing for the paths of science traversed by them that they never again take a book into their hands.[31]

At Dresden he met the novelist, Berthold Auerbach who, coincidentally, had writen a story about a titled aristocrat who went to a remote village under an assumed name, following his dismissal from the army, and took up a career as a teacher of peasant children. Tolstoy identified closely with the sentiments expressed in the story. Comments such as the following find echoes in much of his own writing: 'You yourself are the best teacher. With the help of the children create your own method and all will go well. Any abstract method is an absurdity. The best that a teacher can do in a school will depend on him personally, on his own capacities.'[32] At Kissingen he met Julius Froebel, nephew of the educator, with whom he discussed his uncle's pedagogic theories. He told Froebel of his belief that the progress of the Russian people would be achieved through good popular education, based on the principles of voluntary learning which Friedrich Froebel had advocated, and contrasted this with the rigid didacticism he had witnessed in German schools.[33]

All this time Tolstoy maintained contact with his family at Yasnaya Polyana and was provided with regular accounts of the work of his school. He wrote to his aunt, Tatiana, telling her of his intention to devote himself wholly to the school on his return. 'I shall certainly return in the Autumn', he wrote, 'and intend to occupy myself more than ever with the school so I do not wish its reputation to be lost while I am away and I want as many pupils as possible from different parts.'[34] Following the death of his brother, Nikolai, which occurred at Ayeres in September 1860, he visited several schools in nearby Marseilles and again was highly critical of what he saw. The children, he complained, spent most of their time memorising the catechism, the rules of arithmetic, secular and sacred history, the rules of spelling and grammar, and methods of book-keeping—without any attempt to comprehend their meaning. He contrasted the forced feeding practised in the schools with the simple and spontaneous cultivation of intelligence occurring in the conditions of everyday life. (His comments, in this instance, refer to some *salles d'asile*, or schools for orphans, he had visited in Marseilles):

> I saw the *salles d'asile* in which four-year old children, at a given whistle, like soldiers, made evolutions round the benches, at a given command lifted and folded their hands, and with quivering and strange voices sang laudatory hymns to God and to their benefactors, and I convinced myself that the educational institutions of the city of Marseilles were exceedingly bad.
>
> If, by some miracle, a person should see all these establishments without having seen the people in the streets, in their shops, in the cafes, in their home surroundings, what opinion would he form of a nation which was educated in such a manner? He certainly would conclude that that nation was ignorant, rude, hypocritical, full of prejudices, and almost wild. But it is enough to enter into relations, and to chat with a common man in order to be convinced that the French nation is, on the contrary, almost such as it regards itself to be: intelligent, clever, affable, free from prejudices and really civilised. Look at a city workman of about thirty years of age: he will write a letter, not with such mistakes as are made at school, often without mistakes; he has an idea of politics, consequently of modern history and geography; he knows more or less history from novels; he has some knowledge of the natural sciences, he frequently draws and applies mathematical formula to his trade. Where did he acquire all that?
>
> I involuntarily found an answer to it in Marseilles, when, after the schools, I began to stroll down the streets, to frequent the dram-shops, cafes, chantants, museums, workshops, quays and book-stalls. The very boy who told me that Henry IV had been killed by Julius Caesar knew very well the history of the 'Three Musketeers' and of 'Monte Cristo'. I found twenty-eight illustrated editions of these in Marseilles, costing from five to ten centimes. To a

population of 250,000 they sell thirty thousand of them—consequently, if we suppose that ten people read or listen to one copy, we find that all have read them. In addition, there are the museum, the public libraries, the theatres. Then the cafes, two large cafes chantants, where each may enter for fifty centimes worth of food or drink, and where there are daily as many as twenty-five thousand people, not counting the smaller cafes, which hold as many more: in each of these cafes they give little comedies and scenes, and recite verses. Taking the lowest calculation we get one-fifth of the population, who get their daily oral instruction just as the Greeks and Romans were instructed in their amphitheatres.[35]

'I could write whole books', Tolstoy declared, 'about the ignorance which I have witnessed in the schools of France, Switzerland and Germany.' Despite the intensive instruction they received, the children in these schools were unable to do simple calculations in arithmetic or to answer the random questions on history that he put to them. 'More than half of the girls cannot read any other books than those they have studied', he complained. 'Six years of school had not given them the faculty of writing a word without a mistake.'[36] His complaints were the same in all the schools he visited— mechanical instruction, rote learning, compulsion, rigid didactics were the main targets of his criticism. 'School is not at school but in the newspapers and cafes', he wrote in his Diary for 13 October.[37] From all this there emerged a major essay, 'On Popular Education', in which he set out the basic principles of his philosophy, illustrating his comments extensively from his experiences in the schools he had visited.

From France Tolstoy travelled to London where he spent six weeks visiting schools and discussing education with various officials. Amongst the latter he was particularly fortunate to meet Matthew Arnold, then an inspector of schools, who gave him a letter in which he requested school principals to 'give him as far as they can all the explanations and information which he may desire'.[38] Victor Lucas in *Tolstoy in London* describes the welcome Tolstoy received in the schools as a result of Arnold's inter- vention.[39] Everywhere he went he was given opportunities to observe the activities of the schools as closely as he wished, and received mementoes from the children which he retained for the rest of his life. His impressions of these schools were a good deal more favourable than those of Germany and France, and he particularly admired the system of private schooling that existed in England. On his return to Germany he went to see the work of Minna Schelholm who ran a kindergarten at Weimar in accordance with Froebelian principles. At Jena he met a young mathematician, Gustav Keller, who returned with him to Russia and became one of the most successful teachers in the Yasnaya Polyana school. And in Berlin he met the Head of the Teachers' Seminary, Herr Diesterweg, whom he described as 'a cold, soulless pedant who thinks he can develop and guide the souls of children by rules and regulations'.[40] Apart from some notable exceptions, that description typified his impression of the educators he had met in the course of his ten months tour.

Returning to Russia, he went first to St. Petersburg to get permission to publish a new educational journal. 'In education equality and freedom is the chief thing',[41] he wrote in his Diary, pointing to the theme that was to dominate the articles he wrote in the course of the following year. Altogether, twelve issues of the journal, *Yasnaya Polyana*, appeared between 1861 and 1862. The articles written by Tolstoy explained the essential principles of his educational philosophy, and dealt with matters such as the range and content of the school curriculum, the organisation of the school, pedagogic methodology, the relative merits of day schools and boarding schools, issues relating to authority and discipline, the teaching of reading and writing, the problems of teaching religion, and various aspects of the teaching of history, geography and the arts. Inititially, at any rate, Tolstoy's writings on these matters were treated with indifference by other educators, including those of the Education Ministry. 'At that time I met with no sympathy in the educational journals nor even with any contradiction but only with the completest indifference to the question I was raising. There were, it is true, some attacks on a few insignificant details but the question itself interested no one but me', he recalled some years later.[42]

Now, however, that his ideas were reinforced by what he had read and observed during his European tour, he dedicated himself with renewed energy to the organisation of his school. In essence, its philosophy was the promotion of learning in a spirit of individual freedom. 'This work was particulartly to my taste', he wrote subsequently, 'because in it I had not to face the falsity which had become obvious to me and stared me in the face when I tried to teach people by literary means. Here also I acted in the name of progress, but I already regarded progress itself critically. I said to myself: "In some of its developments progress has proceeded wrongly, and with primitive peasant children one must deal in a spirit of perfect freedom, letting them choose what path of progress they please".'[43] Together with three assistant teachers—one of whom was the mathematician, Gustav Keller—he embarked enthusiastically on his new enterprise, determined to prove that education would flourish in the enlightened conditions he was creating. Those conditions are described vividly in this passage from his essay, 'The School at Yasnaya Polyana':

> In the village people rise with the fires. From the school the fires have long

been observed in the windows, and half an hour after the ringing of the bell there appear, in the mist or the rain, or in the oblique rays of the autumnal sun, dark figures, by twos by threes, or singly, on the mounds (the village is separated from the school by a ravine). The herding feeling has long disappeared in the pupils. A pupil no longer has the need of waiting and shouting: 'O boys, let's to school! She has begun.' He knows by this time that 'school' is neuter, and he knows a few other things, and, strange to say, for that very reason he no longer has any need of a crowd. When the time comes to go, he goes. It seems to me that the personalities are becoming more independent, their characters more sharply defined, with every day. I have never noticed the pupils playing on their way, unless it be a very young child, or a new pupil, who had begun his instruction in some other school. The childen bring nothing with them—neither books nor copybooks. No lessons are given for home.

Not only do they carry nothing in their hands, but they have nothing to carry even in their heads. They are not obliged to remember any lesson— nothing that they were doing the day before. They are not vexed by the thought of the impending lesson. They bring with them nothing but their impressionable natures and their convictions that to-day it will be as jolly in the school as it was yesterday. They do not think of their classes until they have begun.

No one is ever rebuked for tardiness, and they never are tardy, except some of the older ones whose fathers now and then keep them back to do some work. In such cases they come running to school at full speed, and all out of breath.[44]

For all the emphasis on individual freedom in this passage, we shall see when Tolstoy's pedagogic theories are examined later that, far from creating a *laissez faire* situation where every child pursued his/her interests in conditions of total disorder, the activities of the school were carefully organised, and lessons were based always on intellectually and imaginatively stimulating content, with a view to guiding the processes of individual discovery in every child towards their greatest possible degree of fulfilment.

Seeing the success of his experiment at Yasnaya Polyana, Tolstoy decided to extend it by establising a network of schools throughout the region. As Arbiter of the Peace for the First District of Krapiva in the Province of Tula, his duties consisted both of a judicial function in settling disputes and a supervisory function in ensuring that educational provision was made for the newly emancipated serfs. The number of schools he established has been estimated at about thirteen (based on calculations from official reports, diocesan records and his own journal articles), and Tolstoy took responsibility for the staffing of the schools as well as for matters relating to curriculum and pedagogy.[45] Rejecting the practice that was common in voluntary schools at the time of employing amateur teaching assistants (church deacons, sextons, retired soldiers etc.) he recruited most of his teachers from universities. In October 1861, for example, he wrote to a Professor Chicherin of Moscow University, requesting him to recruit teachers from amongst his students. 'Paragons are not to be had and I am not exacting', Tolstoy wrote. 'A semi-educated 2nd or 3rd year student who is not a scoundrel is all I want. I know there will be two capable people out of ten but you have to start with ten.'[46] Generally—apart from some exceptional cases mentioned in his Diary[47]—he seems to have been fortunate in the staff he appointed. Describing one newly arrived group in a letter to his aunt, he wrote: 'All of the twelve, except one, have turned out to be excellent people. . . . Each one arrived with a Hertzen manuscript in his trunk and revolutionary ideas in his head, and each one without exception burned his manuscripts a week later, threw the revolutionary ideas out of his head and taught the peasant children Bible history and prayers and handed round the Gospel to be read at home.'[48] Tolstoy himself provided an 'induction' course at which he initiated new teachers into the principles of his philosophy and enabled them to develop the pedagogic techniques that he favoured for work in his schools. The new teachers spent several weeks observing other teachers at work and were gradually allowed to try out their pedagogic methods under supervision from Tolstoy or from their school principals.

Tolstoy monitored all the work of his schools very closely and generally devoted Sundays and holidays to meetings with his teachers. At these meetings they reviewed their work and discussed plans for the future of their schools. The reverence with which he was regarded by the teachers is evident from various sources. In January 1862, for example, a teacher wrote to him from a distant village: 'You may rest assured that your cause has now become ours. We are all impatient for you to come back. Without you it isn't the same. It seems to me that our common task cannot go on without you to lead it, it needs the fire of your dedication.[49] Inspired by his enthusiasm and idealism, the teachers devoted themselves entirely to the needs of their pupils. 'This intense daily activity absorbs me so that I have no wish to abandon it', one of them reported to Tolstoy. 'I would spend the long winter evenings with the pupils, listening to their prayers and their thoughts. My life had mingled with theirs', another recalled.[50] Living in rough peasant huts, these men, whom Tolstoy later described as 'pure and self-sacrificing', taught the children five to seven lessons every day, six days a week, and met with Tolstoy on Sundays to prepare plans for the following week.[51] Much of their respect for Tolstoy was due to the example of dedication that he himself provided. 'The school', he wrote, 'has been my whole life, it has been my monastery, my church into which I escaped, finding refuge from all anxieties, doubts and temptations of life.'[52] Writing to Professor Chicherin, he explained why he saw teaching as a more wholesome activity than writing (a remarkable admission from someone already well established as a novelist, and shortly to gain worldwide renown as the author of *War and Peace*):

> I do not say it is necessary to work, but one must choose work the fruits of which can be seen far enough ahead to make one able to devote oneself wholly to it: ploughing land, teaching youngsters, being honest etc. The self-conceit of so-called artists . . . is, for the person who comes under its spell, most abominably low and false. To do nothing all one's life, to exploit the work and gains of others for the purpose of eventually describing them is evil, low, perhaps even perverted and vile. . . . You ask, what have I been doing? Nothing special, no trumped-up work, something which is as natural to me as breathing and at the same time from its exaltation I often like to look down, I fear with a rather sinful pride, *sur vous autres*. You would love and understand this work of mine, it cannot be described, but come when you have finished your travels, to Yasnaya Polyana, and then tell me truly if you do not envy me when you see what I have done and the calm with which I go about doing it.[53]

Reports on the work of the schools were generally favourable; many of them particularly emphasised the progress made by the children in the areas of reading and writing. Aylmer Maude, Tolstoy's close friend and biographer, cites a contemporary report which said: 'At Yasnaya Polyana school they learn everything, including all the sciences, and there are such clever masters that it is dreadful; it is said that they even imitate thunder and lightning. Anyway the lads understand well and have begun to read and write.'[54] Another report said: 'They teach the boys everything (like gentlemen's sons); much of it is no use, but still, as they quickly learn to read it, it is worth sending the children there.'[55] (Alexandra claimed in her memoirs that the children learned 'to read and write with ease inside three months';[56] similar claims are made in the memoirs of a former pupil, Vasilly Morozov.)[57] If popularity is a yardstick of educational progress, the schools were exceptionally successful. Some peasants travelled distances of twenty to thirty miles every day to bring their children to the school, and the numbers continued to grow. In the case of Yasnaya Polyana school, enrollments increased from 22 in the first year to over 70 in the second.[58] (No payment was charged for attendance.)

Largely as a result of overstretching his energies, Tolstoy became seriously ill in May 1862. Fearing he would succumb to tuberculosis like his brother, Nikolai, he set out for the Samara steppes, accompanied by two of his pupils, and sought to improve his health by taking a diet consisting mainly of fermented mare's milk (*kumys*), which was used as an energy-restoring liquid by the nomadic Bashkir tribesmen. Shortly after his departure, however, he was even more distressed to hear that police and armed soldiers, following a report from an informer that he was engaged in political subversion, had come to search the house at Yasnaya Polyana, then occupied only by his sister Maria and his aunt, Tatiana. Floor-boards were lifted, cupboards and desks were ransacked, the library books were scattered and torn, and Tolstoy's diaries, letters and manuscripts were defaced as the police examined them for incriminating evidence on his activities. The school was also searched, teachers were arrested, and the children's books and exercises were confiscated. 'All the activity in which I found solace and happiness has been spoilt', Tolstoy wrote bitterly to his aunt. 'The peasants no longer regard me as an honest man—an opinion I had earned in the course of years—but as a criminal, an incendiary, or a coiner, whose cunning alone has enabled him to escape punishment.'[59] Revolutionary ideas, especially those of Alexander Hertzen, were widely held around the region of Yasnaya Polyana at this time; it was known that Tolstoy had met Hertzen in London, and several of his teachers held copies of Hertzen's writings—all of which added to the suspicion in which he was already held by the authorities for his highly unorthodox political, religious and cultural beliefs. He complained to the Tsar about the invasion of his home and estate and received a token apology, via the Governor of Tula. Very soon, however, his troubles were compounded by a report from the Minister of the Interior that the journal he published was educationally unsound. In this report, which was addressed to the Minister of Education, his colleague wrote:

> A close perusal of the educational review, *Yasnaya Polyana*, published by Count Tolstoy, inclines me to think that by advocating new teaching methods and principles for the organisation of schools for the common people, this periodical is spreading ideas which are not only false but dangerously biased. . . . the continued publication of the periodical would seem undesirable, especially as its author, who has remarkable and persuasive literary powers, is above all suspicion of criminal intention or dishonesty. What is harmful is the inaccuracy and eccentricity of his views which, set forth with exceptional eloquence, may be convincing to inexperienced teachers and may thus orient education in the wrong direction.[60]

The Minister of Education had the journal assessed and replied that while it contained unusual views on education he found nothing harmful or objectionable in it. 'I must say', he wrote, 'that Count Tolstoy's educational activity deserves full respect and the Ministry of Education is bound to assist and cooperate with him, though it cannot share all his views, some of which, after full consideration, he will probably himself reject.'[61] As it happened, the journal had run into serious financial difficulties—a loss of 3000 rubles was recorded for 1862—and it had to be discontinued after the twelfth number. Meanwhile Tolstoy had assumed new responsibilities which, together with his difficulties with the authorities, were to bring his school experiments to an end for the time being. On 23 September 1862 he married Sofia Behrs and was shortly to become the father of a large family. (He himself told Aylmer Maude that it was these new responsibilities which finally precipitated his decision to close the school.)[62] Following the closure of the school at Yasnaya Polyana, many of the schools in outlying villages found themselves unable to continue with their work. They had, unfortunately, been over-dependent on the inspiration and organisational abilities of one man and could not continue without him. Years later, one of the teachers, Markov, recalled: 'I have never met a man capable of firing another mind to such white heat. In the course of my spiritual relationship with him I felt as though electric sparks were striking into the depths of my soul and setting in motion all kinds of thoughts and decisions.'[63] The school movement in the Yasnaya Polyana region could not continue without that leadership; most of the schools he had founded closed within a period of eighteen months, though a few survived for several years. The law of 1864 established local school councils with a view to providing popular education at community and parish level, as Tolstoy had been advocating, but it was to be a long time before that objective was realised. Meanwhile, in the changed situation in which he now found himself, Tolstoy's educational activities were about to take a new direction.

3   Further Educational Activities, 1862–76

Following his marriage to Sophia Behrs, Tolstoy soon became an educator in a more intimate sense than he had previously been as schoolmaster at Yasnaya Polyana and pedagogic mentor to the teachers of the region. Soon he had the opportunity to give further effect to his ideas on education as teacher of his own children. The evidence suggests he applied himself as vigorously to this task as he did to the two-year experiment in schooling that has just been described. Four children—Sergei, Tatiana, Ilya and Lev—were born to the Tolstoys within seven years of their marriage. A further seven— Masha, Pyotr, Andrei, Mikhail, Alexei, Sasha and Ivan—were born between 1871 and 1888. Aylmer Maude who lived with the Tolstoys for some time has described how the children were educated.[64] As was the custom with landowning families at the time, they were all taught at home by hired governesses and tutors. But Tolstoy planned and organised their education in accordance with his own principles, which by then had been thoroughly tested out in the village schools he had founded.

He himself taught arithmetic, his wife taught Russian, and the remaining subjects were taught by tutors. Amongst them was an English governess, specifically chosen by Tolstoy because of his admiration for the British traditions in schooling. This lady remained with the family for several years and became a close friend. The children were allowed a good deal of freedom; the tutors were encouraged to treat them kindly and to gain their trust. They were forbidden, however, to punish them, that function being reserved for the parents, who reprimanded them when necessary without recourse to penalties of any kind.

Significantly, Tolstoy modified his belief in the principle of self-initiated learning: a broad range of subject-matter, consisting of carefully selected literary texts, sacred and secular history and the scriptures, was laid down for the children, but they were allowed to abandon a subject if they felt they did not have the capacity to master it. Tolstoy sought particularly to acquaint them with the world of nature, fostering their love for animals, plants, insects and the whole natural environment. He also spent much of his time playing games with them, reading them stories, playing them music, walking with them in the countryside, skating on the snow, training them in gymnastics, bathing in the Voronka river—all this in the years he completed his two greatest works of fiction, *War and Peace* and *Anna Karenina*.

Tolstoy's involvement in his children's education was to lead to a further expansion of his formal educational activities. In these years he prepared a new school-primer, one of the most imaginative and far-seeing ventures in all his work for education, and secondly, he re-opened his school and undertook some further experiments in practical pedagogy. The idea of the primer originated in his feelings of dissatisfaction with existing school textbooks during the period of the Yasnaya Polyana schools, feelings that were further reinforced by the experience of teaching his own children. Alexandra describes his frustration as he tried to teach his son, Sergei, and gradually realised that Sergei's slowness as a learner was exacerbated by the inadequacies of the textbooks on which they were working: 'They were both nervous; the father was upset by the son's slowness, and the son made such an effort, strained himself to such an extent, was so afraid of not satisfying his father, that he in the end was slow-witted. Yet working with his son renewed Tolstoy's interest in teaching. He was struck by the poor quality of the textbooks, the paucity of reading-material.'[65] Following yet another trip to Samara to take the *kumys* —after the exhaustion he experienced on completing *War and Peace*—he set about producing a school primer that would provide interesting subject-matter for children learning to read, and would be sufficiently comprehensive to meet all their interests and needs. Some time before he had met Eugene Schuyler, the American Consul in Moscow, from whom he got valuable advice on the ways that different typographies could assist young children in learning to read (advice that was to be enormously helpful to Tolstoy but the cause of great distress to his printers!) In a commemorative tribute Schuyler wrote:

> One thing that constantly preoccupied him (Tolstoy) and especially drew his attention was the question of finding the best method of teaching children to read. He questioned me at length about new methods used in America, and at his request I was able to obtain for him—I believe it was done through the kindness of Mr Garrison of *The Nation*—a good selection of American methods of instruction in reading for the use of beginners and elementary schools. In one of them, I recall, the pronunciation of various vowels and consonants was depicted vividly with letters whose general appearance was that of ordinary letters but with distinctive changes which immediately were obvious. These books Tolstoy tried to adapt when he composed his primers.[66]

Tolstoy began to work seriously on the project in September 1871, though he had been planning it for some years before then. In January of the following year he wrote to his cousin, Countess Alexandrine Tolstoy: 'All goes well in the household, there are five children and so much work there is never any time. These last years I have been working on my primer and now I am printing it. It is very difficult to tell you what this work of many years, this primer, has meant to me. The coming winter I hope to send it to you, and you, out of friendship for me, may perhaps read it. My conceited ideas about this primer are these: if only two generations of all Russian children, from royal to peasant, will study this primer and receive all their first poetic impressions from it, and that, having written this primer (*sic*), I can die in peace.'[67] As the work advanced, Tolstoy indicated to Alexandrine the range of material he intended to include, and the immensity of the task that lay ahead of him: 'This primer alone may provide work for a hundred years. To write it one should know the Greek, Indian, Arabian literatures, one needs knowledge of the natural sciences, astronomy, physics, and the work on the language itself is terrific. It must be beautiful, brief, simple and, above all, clear.'[68]

Meanwhile, he decided to re-open his school and to test out the material he was preparing for the primer on his new pupils. Thirty-five children were enrolled in the third Yasnaya Polyana school, which again was accommodated in the manor house. Together with his wife, he continued to teach his own children, and occasionally some of the older ones helped him to teach the children of the peasantry. 'I recall how Papa used to teach the country children', Ilya Tolstoy wrote . . .

They were taught in the 'other house' and sometimes downstairs in our house. The country children came to us and there were a great many of them. When they came it smelled of sheepskin jackets and they all taught them together, Papa and Seryozha and Tanya and Uncle Kostya. While the lessons were going on it was very gay and lively.

The children conducted themselves quite freely, sat wherever they chose, ran around from place to place and answered questions, not one at a time but all at once, interrupting each other and pooling all their forces to remember what they had read. If one of them missed anything, immediately a second would rush in, a third, and the story or the problem was put together by common effort.

Papa was particularly appreciative of vividness and originality in his pupils. He never demanded the literal reproduction of expressions in the book and he particularly encouraged what was 'one's own'.[69]

All the children seem to have progressed satisfactorily under the methods employed by Tolstoy. This seems particularly to have been the case in the crucial domains of reading and writing: the areas in which Tolstoy's theories have been most controversial and those in which he is most widely misinterpreted. 'Tanya and Seryozha are doing fairly well', Sofia Tolstoy wrote to her sister in February, 1872. 'Within a week they knew all the letters and the syllables by ear. We teach them downstairs in the vestibule which is huge, in the small dining-room under the stairway and in the new study. The main thing is that they are taught to read and write, that there is such an urge to do it and that they study with such pleasure and enjoyment.'[70] Ever since he had opened his first school, Tolstoy had been fascinated by the whole reading process and was deeply committed to two fundamental principles of reading pedagogy: firstly, the need to foster the motivation to read, and secondly, the importance of developing the habit of voluntary or independent reading. Feeling that the available text-books discouraged children from reading and did not promote either of these two objectives, he aimed in his primer to cater for the interests of every child by providing the greatest possible variety of subject-matter. In the book, therefore, he included versions of Greek, Roman, Hebrew, Indian, Arabic, Persian and Chinese legends, stories from scripture, Russian, Ukrainian and German folk-tales, stories he himself had written specially for the anthology such as 'A Prisoner in the Caucasus' and the religious allegory, 'God Sees the Truth But Waits', stories about his dogs, Milton and Bolka, stories on horse-riding, popular historical sketches, readings from the lives of the saints and from the monastic chronicles, translations from foreign writers such as Victor Hugo and Hans Christian Anderson—all were chosen for their high literary merit, their richness of meaning, their readability and simplicity. 'If these articles have any merit', Tolstoy wrote to his friend, the literary critic, Nikolai Strakhov, 'they will owe it to the simplicity and clarity of the drawing, the line—that is, the language.'[71] In his Introduction he advised teachers that 'in order that the pupil may study well he must study gladly'. For that certain requirements would have to be met:

> In order that the pupil may study well he must study gladly; in order that he may study gladly the following is necessary: (1) that the material he is being taught be comprehensible and interesting, and 2) that the inner powers of the pupil be in the most advantageous state possible. To that end it is necessary:
>
> 1. That there should be no new, unfamilar objects about him where he is studying.
> 2. That the pupil should not be embarrassed before his teachers or comrades.
> 3. That the pupil (and this is very important) should not fear punishment because of bad work, that is to say failure to understand. The mind of man can operate only when it is not oppressed by external influences.[72]

The section of the primer which dealt with arithmetic proved particularly challenging for Tolstoy, as he was not satisfied with the conventional explanations of the rules of arithmetic and devised more elaborate explanations of his own. 'I am working myself up into a stupor finishing up arithmetic', he wrote to Strakhov. 'Multiplication and division are done and I am finishing fractions. You will laugh at me for having undertaken something out of my field but it seems to me that the arithmetic will be the best thing in the book.'[73] As well as arithmetic, the primer also included some elementary science, for which Tolstoy consulted various specialists and conducted experiments himself before describing them in the book. For the section on astronomy he made a special study of the solar system and, on occasions, stayed up throughout the night studying the stars with his telescope.

The printing of the primer, however, presented major difficulties. 'My *ABC Book* gives me no peace for any other occupation', Tolstoy wrote to A.A. Fet. 'The printing advances on the feet of a tortoise and the devil knows when it will be finished and I'm still adding and omitting and altering, what will come of it I do not know but I have put my whole soul into it.'[74] The Moscow printers he had engaged for the project were unable to provide the range of types that were necessary for the different kinds of subject-matter included in the book, and Tolstoy created further difficulties by repeatedly withdrawing the work for revision. Eventually, in desperation, Tolstoy asked Nilolai Strakhov to deal with the printers on his behalf and to take responsibility for proof-reading and for the practical aspects of the book's production. Under careful instructions from Tolstoy, Strakhov supervised

the printing and the book was published in November 1872. Initially, it sold
slowly and was criticised in several newspapers, but gradually its merits
were recognised and it became increasingly popular with teachers and
parents. Tolstoy modified its content in subsequent editions, eventually
reducing its original content of 758 pages to a more manageable 92. This
shorter edition was published in 1875 and was eventually graded into a series
of four readers which were published year after year in editions of several
thousand copies and made available to the public at a few kopecks per copy.
It was estimated that almost a million copies of the primer had been sold by
the end of the century.[75]

At the time of its publication, however, it generated bitter controversy
amongst Russian educators. 'When I brought out *War and Peace* I knew the
book was full of faults but I was sure it would be exactly as successful as it
was', Tolstoy told Strakhov. 'Publishing my *Reader* I know it has hardly
any faults and is superior to every other text-book of the same type but I am
not expecting it to have anything like the success a textbook ought to have.'[76]
Criticism was directed mainly at the 'aberrant' methods of teaching he was
advocating, especially in the sphere of reading pedagogy. On 15 January
1874 Tolstoy addressed the Moscow Society on Literacy on the best
methods of teaching children to read. He had condemned the uncritical and
excessive concentration on phonic reading methods which had then become
fashionable in Russian schools, and advocated an eclectic methodology that
would, in fact, correspond quite closely to the principles and methods of
reading pedagogy generally adopted at the present time. The German
lautiermethode, which was based on systematic instruction in phonics, had
been widely adopted by Russian teachers in a manner Tolstoy considered
too rigid and pedantic, and he condemned the arbitrary and inflexible ways
in which this method was being introduced into the schools.[77] Throughout
his writings on reading pedagogy he had particularly emphasised the
relationship between teacher and pupil; he had stressed the motivational
impact of an encouraging relationship, the importance of fostering interest,
and the ways in which the habit of voluntary reading could be promoted.
He saw the practicalities of reading instruction as being largely subordinate
to all this.

At the meeting, which took place in a large hall in Moscow, he spoke of
the dangers of imposing an alien culture on peasant children and emphasised
the need to initiate them into the universal truths of the humanities and
sciences by way of their own local culture and traditions. On the matter of
reading pedagogy, he offered to demonstrate his methods in a school
attached to a Moscow factory. The Society, however, insisted on conducting
an experiment in two Moscow schools to test the relative methods of the

Tolstoyan and *lautiermethode* approaches. In one of the schools the children were taught by a teacher using Tolstoy's methods, in the other they were taught by an expert in the *lautiermethode*. After seven weeks they were examined by a committee, the members of which disagreed on their findings and issued contradictory reports. Some of his critics claimed that the results went against Tolstoy but he disputed this, arguing that the tests had not been held under proper conditions. Classroom work, he argued, was constantly impeded by the presence of officials observing the children and, since the children mixed socially outside the schools, it was not possible, he said, to claim that their progress in reading was wholly attributable to either of the methods to which they had been exposed.

It is difficult, in the light of these facts, to comprehend the view put forward by the editor of a recently published collection of Tolstoy's educational writings that he 'made a fool of himself'[78] and was professionally discredited by these events. Firstly, the approach to reading that he advocated—with its emphasis on the stimulation of interest, the fostering of positive attitudes, and the use of a wide variety of subject-matter, side by side with his strongly attested belief in systematic instruction in letter and syllable formation—would find widespread support at the present time, whereas the rigid concentration on phonic instruction, as advocated in the *lautiermethode*, would not. Particular support would be found for his approach amongst teachers of socially or culturally disadvantaged pupils; indeed, the methods Tolstoy used with the impoverished peasant children of Yasnaya Polyana are closely paralleled in one of the classics of modern remedial education, David Holbrook's *English for the Rejected*.[79] Secondly, it seems unlikely, as Tolstoy had claimed, that definitive conclusions could be drawn from an experiment conducted in accordance with the kind of testing methods that would have been used in the late nineteenth century. Even in the 1990s great uncertainty exists regarding the reliability of testing procedures in reading; the very concept of reading attainment is held in question, because of the inseparablity of attitudinal and performance features of the reading process.

Undeterred by the outcome of this whole controversy, Tolstoy continued to press for various reforms in Russian education. Shortly afterwards he published a long article, 'On the Education of the People', in the *Fatherland Journal*,[80] in which his theme once again was the need to base education on the distinctive cultures of local communities, from which they could most effectively be initiated into the broader and more universal forms of knowledge associated with national and international traditions. Once again he advocated the acceleration of plans for a comprehensive provision of peasant schools in accordance with the reforms of 1864. He continued to point to the deficiencies of existing school-textbooks. On this occasion his advice was heeded when one of the texts he had attacked most vehemently— the model Reader used in the Moscow Teachers' Seminary—was withdrawn by the authorities. Various writers began to rally to his support; the poet, Nikolai Nekrasov, publicised his work in the *Fatherland Journal*, of which he was editor; another fellow-writer, the critic and essaysist, Nikolai Mikhaylovski, appealed to readers of the journal to 'peruse the fine shades of thought' in Tolstoy's article, 'On the Education of the People'.[81]

In that article Tolstoy had observed that one of the main obstacles to the promotion of elementary education amongst the peasantry was their inability to pay the salaries of teachers coming from the universities to work in their schools. In a letter to Alexandrine he described the huge wastage of talent and the great neglect of individual potential which resulted from the widespread failure of the authorities to meet the educational needs of the masses:

> I do not reason about it, but when I go into a school and see this crowd of tattered, dirty, emaciated children with their shining eyes and often angelic expressions, I am overwhelmed with a sense of agitation, terror, such as I should feel at the sight of drowning persons. Oh my, if only I can pull them out, and whom shall I save first, whom next. What is being drowned is that most precious thing, that spiritual something, which so often flashes into the eyes of children. I want education for the people only in order to save the drowning Pushkins and Lomonosovs. Every school is teeming with them.[82]

As a short-term measure to deal with the problem of inadequate educational provision for peasant children, he organised training sessions in his manor house for teachers recruited from local communities. Twelve such teachers gathered there in October 1872 to form the nucleus of what Tolstoy envisaged as a full-scale training programme for peasant teachers. He made various attempts to develop the project in the next few years and applied formally to the Ministry for Education in 1876 for permission to found a new training college that would cater specifically for the education of peasant teachers. The project was approved by the Ministry on condition that a proportion of the costs would be met by the Tula Provincial Council. In the local zemstvo, however, the whole scheme was blocked—despite Tolstoy's presence as a member—and he was forced, reluctantly, to abandon his plans. A further proposal from him to have the local zemstvo supplement the fees paid by parents to the teachers in the peasant schools was rejected also.

4 Adult Educator, 1876–1910

Following the rejection of his plans for an expansion of peasant schooling, Tolstoy ceased to engage actively in formal education, apart from continuing to promote his primer and engaging in some sporadic involvements of a related character in later years. Thenceforward his activities were concentrated in the field of adult education and specifically in the promotion of his vision of a society transformed through the simple teachings of the Christian Gospels. He sought, firstly, to disseminate his beliefs through a series of popular writings in which he explained his radically pacifist, non-materialist and non-rationalist interpretations of the message of the Gospels. Secondly, he actively supported a movement of small voluntary communities, organised in accordance with radical Christian principles and seeking to implement those principles in the circumstances of their daily lives. (Though he was reluctant to give this support initially, he gave the communities his full approval and provided some crucial advice and guidance when he became more fully aware of their work.) There are valuable lessons to be learned from each of these ventures on the ways in which moral and social ideals can be promoted through adult and community education, a matter which is increasingly attracting attention amongst twentieth century educators.

The year 1876 was a significant one in Tolstoy's life. It was the year in which he formally renewed his contacts with the Orthodox Church (though not with its hierarchy or with its major institutions), and the one in which the first instalments of *Anna Karenina* were published. This was the novel in which Levin—generally seen as a self-portrayal of Tolstoy himself, like Pierre, Prince Andrew and Nekhlyudov—proclaimed his belief in an irrationalist Christianity, based not on the dogmas of the Churches nor on the principles of an abstract theology, but on the simplicity of individual conscience and faith. That belief had already been foreshadowed in *War and Peace*, both by the dying Prince Andrew who realises that love, not reason, is the basis of faith, and by Pierre Bezukhov who echoes the simple faith of the peasant, Platon Karataev, that God is found through the love of all existent being.[83]

In July 1878 Tolstoy visited the Optina Pustyn Monastery—best known as the setting for Dostoevsky's *The Brothers Karamazov*—to seek spiritual comfort from the starets. Declaring himself deeply impressed by the wisdom of the elder, he left the monastery vowing to seek a new direction for his life. In the depths of his melancholy he concluded that faith alone would bring peace to his life. 'I lived only at those times when I believed in God', he wrote in his Diary. 'I needed only to be aware of God to live; I need only forget Him or disbelieve him and I died.'[84] He began to emulate the simple piety of the peasants, fasting, praying and attending church services, but as he read the Gospels closely, he began to question what he saw as the misrepresentation of Christ's message by the Churches through the centuries. He particularly questioned the way the Russian Orthodox Church had supported violence, in direct contravention of the teachings of Christ. A Diary entry for 22 May 1878 read: 'Went to mass on Sunday. I can find an explanation which satisfies me for everything in the church service. But prayers for a long life and the subjugation of one's enemies is blasphemy. A Christian should pray for his enemies, not against them.'[85] Thenceforward he resolved to follow the letter and spirit of Christ's teaching, which he saw disclosed in its essentials in the Sermon on the Mount. That text remained the basis of his religious, ethical, and social beliefs for the rest of his life.

In a letter to her sister early in 1879 Sofia Tolstoy complained that her husband was 'writing some kind of religious dissertation to prove that the Church disagrees with the teaching of the Gospels'.[86] Having isolated himself from society for some months, Tolstoy became totally engrossed in his scriptural studies and engaged himself in a full-scale review of his life which resulted in a major work of religious autobiography, *A Confession*. A work of powerful emotional force, full of sincere and intense self-questioning, *A Confession* has been described by one scholar as 'the finest of all Tolstoy's non-fictional works' and by another as 'one of the noblest and most courageous utterances of man'.[87] In this work he explored the nature of belief and unbelief, asserted the worthlessness of rationalist philosophy, proclaimed his admiration for the simple faith of the peasantry, denounced the hypocrisies and contradictions of Orthodoxy, and resolved to live his life in accordance with the simple precepts of the Sermon on the Mount. He emerged from the experience, greatly renewed in his energies, freed from melancholia and despair, and ready to assume the role of teacher of his people in the simple, undiluted truths of the Christian faith.

A Confession was followed by his *Critique of Dogmatic Theology*, a work in which he dismissed some of the major dogmas of Orthodoxy—such as the Incarnation, Resurrection and Ascension of Christ—and virtually the whole of its theological tradition. A year later (1882) he published a personal statement of faith, *My Religion* or *What I Believe*, in which he defined what he saw as the essential truths of Christianity—drawing his authority entirely from the scriptures—and offered a lengthy disquisition on the subject of Christian pacifism. On the latter question—in many ways the kernel of his faith—he presented a scholarly analysis of the meaning of Christ's injunction, 'Do not resist evil', in this instance drawing further support for his interpretations from the writings of the Early Fathers. In a companion work, issued at about the same time, *A Union and Translation of the Four*

Gospels, he sought to synthesise the main events of the Four Gospels in a single narrative. Reflecting on this prolific output of religious writings in the space of only three years, he was convinced that what he proclaimed was the original Christian message which the Churches had misrepresented through the centuries. 'After eighteen hundred years', he wrote, 'it so singularly happened that I discovered the meaning of the doctrine of Jesus as some new thing.'[88]

Tolstoy's meeting with Vladimir Chertkov in October 1883 was a decisive event in the propagation of this renewed vision of Christianity. Because of the suspicion with which he was regarded by government authorities—he was accused of spreading 'false and dangerous notions about the equality of man'[89]—Tolstoy had been virtually confined to his home at Yasnaya Polyana and was under constant police surveillance. In these circumstances he welcomed the arrival of a fellow Christian believer who fully shared his views on the Churches. Chertkov was to be a loyal supporter and companion for the remaining three decades of his life. A wealthy St Petersburg aristocrat who had resigned his commission in the armed forces to devote himself to the service of the poor, he was captivated by Tolstoy's writings, particularly by his insistence that violence was incompatible with Christianity. On meeting Tolstoy he declared: 'The realisation that my period of moral isolation was over gave me much joy'.[90] Both men recognised the importance of publishing as a mode of popular education; shortly after Chertkov's arrival in Yasnaya Polyana, they set up a publishing company, The Mediator, to produce inexpensive books for distribution amongst the common people.

Under Chertkov's management, the Mediator publishing house was to issue cheaply priced pamphlets (at about 5 kopecks per copy) during the next thirty years. The pamphlets were sold in their thousands all over Russia. Observing that the peasants read a good deal of popular material of the 'bast book' variety—which was sold by door-to-door pedlars all over the country—Tolstoy vowed to raise the general level of their reading. 'These millions of Russians', he wrote, 'stand before us like so many young daws with open mouths and they say to us: "Gentlemen, writers of our own land, throw us some mental food worthy of yourselves and us: write for us who crave, living, literary works, rescue us from the cheap Eruslan Lazareviches, stories about lords and other market-place wares".'[91] Tolstoy wrote a number of new stories expressly for this purpose; they included religious parables such as 'What Men Live By', 'Where Love Is God Is' and several similar stories eventually included in the *Master and Man* anthology. Ivan Sytin, a self-educated man of peasant origin, was appointed editor of these publications and charged with the task of ensuring their distribution throughout the country. As a mark of his determination to associate himself as closely as possible with the common people, Tolstoy himself went regularly to work with a cobbler in Yasnaya Polyana, and had a workshop created beside his study in the manor house, where he practised the craft of shoe- making.

By now he had come to believe that the practice of Christian love and brotherhood required an active, personal commitment to improving the material conditions of the poor. He worked tirelessly to relieve famine distress in the Caucasus; reports indicate that in a six month period he opened 147 canteens, fed 10,000 persons, and spent over 140,000 rubles on clothing, firewood and potato seeds for the starving masses.[92] In *What Then Must We Do* he gave a graphic description of the poverty of the Moscow slums, on the basis of first hand observation of the conditions in which the people were living. He had been deeply influenced by the theories of wealth distribution through taxation that were put forward in the writings of Henry George, an American economist, and expressed his approval of them in several of his writings. Echoing the theories of George, and those of Pierre Proudhon—whose ideas on social reform also appealed to him for their emphasis on individual freedom and their rejection of materialist determinism—he denounced the exploitation of the poor by the propertied classes and indicted the religious authorities for supporting them in their exploitative activities. For all this he was angrily denounced by the establishment press. 'The Count's propaganda', declared the *Moscow News*, 'is the propaganda of the most unbridled socialism.'[93] Though a keen and committed social reformer, Tolstoy, however, was deeply distrustful of doctrinaire socialism and, as might be expected from someone holding such radical Christian beliefs, was especially suspicious of the atheistic materialism of marxist socialists.

By this time large numbers of admirers were flocking to Yasnaya Polyana to meet Tolstoy and to get a deeper understanding of his teachings. They included students, writers, aristocrats, peasants, priests and teachers, many of whom stayed in the manor house—or in one of its outhouses—for several days at a time. Amongst his closest followers were the writer, Pavel Biryukov, the painter, Nicholas Gay, the literary critic and philosopher, Fyodor Strakhov, a surgeon, Ivan Rayevsky, a political activist, Wilhelm Frey, and an aristocrat, Prince Khilkov who distributed all his lands to his peasants after reading Tolstoy's writings. Abroad he also attracted widespread attention. Romain Rolland wrote to him for spiritual advice. Tomas Masaryk, the first President of Czechoslavakia , Paul Deroulede, author of *Chants du Soldat*, Raphael Lowenfeld, the writer and theatre director, and the physiologist, Charles Richet—all came to Yasnaya Polyana to discuss pacifism. A distinguished admirer—though he never, in fact, met Tolstoy—was the philosopher, Ludwig Wittgenstein. He not only espoused Tolstoy's Christianity, but followed his example further by abandoning celebrity and fame for several years to take up the simple life of a country school-master. A recently published biography describes the impact of Tolstoy's Biblical writings on Wittgenstein:

> During his first month in Galicia, he entered a bookshop, where he could find only one book: Tolstoy's *Gospel in Brief*. The book captivated him. It became for him a kind of talisman: he carried it everywhere he went, and read it so often that he came to know whole passages of it by heart. He became known to his comrades as the 'man with the Gospels'. For a time he—who before the war had struck Russell as being 'more terrible with Christians' than Russell himself—became not only a believer, but an evangelist, recommending Tolstoy's Gospel to anyone in distress. 'If you are not acquainted with it', he later told Ficker, 'then you cannot imagine what an effect it can have on a person.'[94]

Tolstoy's daughter, Sasha, who became one of his closest disciples, described the fervour of some of the people who were drawn to her father's teachings. In her *Life* she recounts the story of the preceptors of the Nicholas Institute for well-Born Young Ladies, an arch-Orthodox and monarchial establishment in Moscow.[95] On reading Tolstoy's writings the preceptors, Olga Barshteva and Maria Schmidt, decided to give up all their possessions and to live and work amongst the peasants in Yasnaya Polyana. They lived for the rest of their lives in a cottage two miles from Tolstoy's house, growing their own food, and following a simple peasant lifestyle. E.N. Drozhnin, a country teacher, refused to do military service, as a result of Tolstoy's influence, and died subsequently in a prison at Voronezh. Another conscientious objector was a man called Zalyubovski who was also sentenced to imprisonment. 'What he has done and is doing', Tolstoy wrote to his brother, 'is the greatest thing a man can accomplish in his life. I do not know whether I could have stood up to it, but I could wish nothing better for myself or my childen.'[96] Prince Khilkov and his wife were exiled to the Caucasus for attempting to found an agricultural commune in accordance with radical Christian principles. When they forbad their children to attend Orthodox services, the children were taken from them by force and entrusted to the care of their grandmother.

Another follower, Kenjiro Tokutomi, a Japanese writer and journalist, gave up his profession, went to live in a cottage in the Japanese countryside, grew his own vegetables, and dedicated himself to living in accordance with the Tolstoyan Christian philosophy. Ernest Crosby, an American, who also visited Yasnaya Polyana, devoted himself to spreading Tolstoy's teachings in the U.S.A. One of Tolstoy's most ardent supporters, Anna Dietrich, married Chertkov and together they founded a Centre for Christian education on their estate at Lizinovka, near Yasnaya Polyana. Perhaps the most self-sacrificing of Tolstoy's followers was his daughter, Masha, who refused to accept the property that he bequeathed to her, took up a simple and austere lifestyle—sleeping on bare floor-boards, living entirely on a vegetarian diet, serving the poor, the sick and unfortunate, and doing everything she could to propagate his beliefs and ideals. They were all deeply imbued with the simple Christian message that Tolstoy had communicated in his writings, their example providing powerful confirmation of the educational impact of those writings.

In these years Tolstoy gave up his own property, in accordance with his belief that the possession of material wealth was incompatible with the teachings of Christ. In 1890 he transferred all his estates to his wife and children, and the following year announced in the Russian press that he no longer claimed copyright on all the writings he had published since 1881, so that anyone was free to publish them without the obligation to pay royalties. (It was legally impossible for him to free earlier works from copyright restrictions.) In the same year he published a new prose work, *On Life* (originally called *On Life and Death*) in which he put forward his belief that death does not exist: that every human being is reborn into a higher existence through love of his/her neighbour, and that death opens up the prospect of entering into that existence eternally. That same belief is reiterated in his story, 'The Death of Ivan Ilyich', where Ivan, on his death-bed, realises that death is conquered by love. 'Where is death?', he asks. 'What is death? He was not afraid', the narrator says, 'because there was no death anymore. Instead of death there was light.'[97]

The links between these two works indicate the close convergence that existed between Tolstoy's religious and aesthetic purposes—a convergence which we shall see presently is crucial to an understanding of the nature of his role as an educator. His Christianity was based on two main principles: the all-embracing principle of love which he saw as the primary message of the Gospels, and the principle of non-resistance to evil, which he saw as its most direct, and most challenging, imperative. Rejecting most of the dogmas of the institutional Churches—e.g. the Incarnation and Divinity of Christ, the Resurrection and Ascension—he saw Christ as pre-eminently a Teacher whose message he felt obliged, as a believing Christian, to transmit through his writings. In modelling himself on Christ as a teacher he himself adopted the methods used by Christ for that purpose—the method of Gospel narrative, parable and allegorical tale i.e. a method which is distinctively literary rather than philosophical/theological.

By comparison with the complex modes of discourse used by philosophers and theologians, the literary method had the supreme merit of providing a means by which the profoundest religious truths could be communicated to the masses. That this was the purpose which underlay Tolstoy's conception of his role both as artist and religious teacher is clear from *What Is Art?*, his lengthy exposition of the complementary nature of his aesthetic and ethico-religious purposes. These two purposes converge both in his insistence throughout the work that 'the aesthetic is merely an expression of the ethical', and in his conception of the roles of artist and religious writer as ultimately educational, as is made clear in the work's concluding statements. (This issue will be examined in detail in later chapters.)

Tolstoy's teachings brought him repeatedly into conflict with the government and the ecclesiastical establishment in the last years of his life. In 1895 a particularly bitter conflict followed his championing of the cause of the Dukhobors, an old religious sect which had been banished to the Caucasus by Tsar Alexander I. They had been influenced by Tolstoy's writings in claiming their rights to pursue their beliefs without interference from state authorities. Like Tolstoy and his followers, they believed in a simple interpretation of the Gospels; they abstained from meat and alcohol, held all their possessions in communal ownership, and were totally opposed to violence. Because of their refusal to serve in the armed forces, they were constantly harrassed by the authorities. Following a large meeting on 28 June 1895, at which they proclaimed their pacifism publicly, they were brutally beaten by Cossack soldiers; many of their leaders were imprisoned, their lands were confiscated, and thousands were exiled to remote mountain villages.

Recognising that they had been influenced by his writings in deciding to take a stand publicly for their beliefs, Tolstoy took up their cause and published an article, 'The Persecution of Christians in Russia', in which he made a virulent attack on the authorities for their brutal treatment of the Dukhobors. Together with Chertkov he issued a manifesto, 'Give Help', in which he called for international support for the Dukhobors. The authorities retaliated swiftly and ruthlessly. The homes of Tolstoy and his followers were searched, their papers were confiscated, and some of the leading figures in the movement, including Chertkov and Biryukov, were forced to leave the country. Undeterred by all this, Tolstoy continued to campaign for justice for the Dukhobors. Hearing that he was being considered for the recently inaugurated Nobel Prize, he requested the Swedish Academy to make the prize-money (estimated at 100,000 rubles) available for their support, if he were chosen. In the event, the prize did not go to Tolstoy. (When his nomination was unsuccessful again in 1902 he wrote: 'I was very pleased to learn that the Nobel Prize was not given to me. First, because it spared me the great problem of disposing of the money, which like all money, can lead only to evil, in my view; and second, because it has given me the honour and great pleasure of receiving such expressions of sympathy from so many highly esteemed although unknown persons'.)[98]

Eventually, he succeeded in raising money from various other sources for the Dukhobors and the government finally authorised their exile from Russia. Over 7000 emigrated to Canada, where they settled as farmers in a newly cleared region of the country, the cost of their passage having been raised almost entirely by Tolstoy. Much of the money had come from royalties from his latest novel, *Resurrection*, a powerful exploration of Christian faith and penitence. As well as providing a vivid and compelling restatement of his Christian beliefs, the novel exposed the vices of the Tsarist regime, its authoritarianism, brutality and inhumanity. 'All Russia is living and feeding on this book', one correspondent told Tolstoy. 'You cannot imagine the conversation and debates it is provoking. I think there are only a few imbecilic and decadent degenerates against you in all of Russia.'[99]

Meanwhile Chertkov and Biryukov continued from their locations in London and Geneva to spread the Tolstoyan teaching internationally. They founded a new journal, *Free Thought*, to make his writings available to a wider public. Tolstoy himself continued to issue pamphlets, especially on the evils of war. In two of these he condemned both the suppression of the Philippine uprising by the Americans and the war then being waged by the British against the Boers in the Transvaal. He condemned exploitative work practices in *The Slavery of Our Times*, and offered a new exposition of his ethical teachings in *The Kingdom of God is Within You*. He stressed the crucial principle that the struggle to be good, rather than the victory, is what matters for a Christian believer. In a letter on the question of sexual morality to one of his followers, E.I. Popov, he reiterated this point: 'In our struggle with temptation we are weakened by setting victory as our goal; we set ourselves a task beyond our powers, a task which it does not lie within our power to fulfil or not to fulfil. There can be only one aim: to achieve the greatest degree of continence, given my character, temperament, the cir-cumstances of my past and present—continence not in the eyes of people who do not know what I have to contend with, but in my own eyes and those of God.'[100]

Some years earlier, in 1886, he had been condemned as a heretic by the Orthodox Church—a very serious charge since heresy was a criminal offence in Russia at the time. He was now further denounced as an 'impious infidel' and declared an outcast from the Church.[101] His excommunication was announced formally on 24 February 1901. Yet he was still revered by the people, thousands of whom continued to flock to Yasnaya Polyana to pledge their support. Of the essential nature of his mission he had no doubt. In July 1900 he had entered this note in his Diary:

> I must remember that I am not an ordinary individual, but an emissary, and my vocation is as follows:
> 1) never to prostitute the dignity of Him whom I represent;
> 2) always to act according to his prescriptions (love)
> 3) always to work to accomplish the mission I have been given (Kingdom of God);
> 4) whenever its interests conflict with mine, to sacrifice mine.[102]

He was shocked at the outbreak of the Russo-Japanese war in February 1904. Evidence of the war was apparent all over Russia as large numbers of soldiers were drafted into the forces from every town and village in the country. In a pacifist pamphlet, *Bethink Yourselves!* Tolstoy vehemently condemned the propaganda of the war-makers: 'I cannot read these articles that glorify the grandeur and beauty of acts of bloodshed in order to excite the people's patriotism', he declared.[103] He reasserted the need for religious renewal to combat the evil of war: 'I have thought deeply about the war that is beginning. I would like to write that at the beginning of something as dreadful as war, everybody offers hundreds of suppositions as to the meaning or consequences of the conflict, but not one person thinks about himself . . . this is the best and clearest evidence that nothing can provide a remedy for evil, except religion'.[104] Following the defeat of the Russians at Port Arthur and Mukden, he wrote of the conflict he felt between his pacifist faith and his sympathy for his Russian compatriots: 'It has become plain to me that things could not and cannot happen any other way. No matter how poor Christians we are, we cannot avoid the fact that war is contrary to the Christian doctrine. . . . That is why in any conflict with a non-Christian people for whom the highest ideal is military heroism, a Christian people must be defeated. . . . I am not saying this to console myself for the fact that we have been beaten by the Japanese. The shame and humiliation are as sharp as ever'.[105]

He was further distressed when the workers of St. Petersburg, demonstrating before the Winter Palace in January 1905, were massacred by Tsarist troops and police. While sympathising with the workers, and recognising the need for social reform, he was appalled at the violence that followed from their actions. He bitterly condemned the authorities but, significantly, warned of the dangers of a revolution based on the principles of marxist socialism. In his pamphlet, *The Government, the Revolutionaries and the People*, he asserted the primacy of individual conscience and its transcendence of all political ideologies. 'The more savage this revolution becomes', he told Chertkov, 'the more I want to withdraw into myself and have no more part, whether by act, word, or even opinion, in the whole dirty business'. 'They are killing on both sides', he wrote. 'The contradiction, as always, lies in wanting to stop violence by violence.'[106]

Tolstoy's interest in pedagogy was re-awakened in 1907 when he undertook a new project aimed at promoting reading amongst school-children. He prepared a new anthology, *The Circle of Reading for Children*, as well as a simple version of the scriptures, *The Teachings of Jesus Explained to Children*, for general circulation by The Mediator. The need for both works was prompted by his experience of teaching the nine-year old stepson of his daughter, Tanya. Again he started classes for local children in his library, basing his teaching on the two textbooks. 'Lately', he wrote in his Diary for 17 March 1907, 'I have been completely occupied giving lessons to the children. The farther I go the more clearly I see the difficulties of the task, and at the same time the greater the success I look forward to.'[107] His last formal involvement in education was a meeting he held with a group of Moscow teachers who expressed a wish to hear his views on education.[108] On this occasion he attended a film in a Moscow theatre and remarked on the great potential of the cinema for education—a far-seeing comment in 1908, though not altogether surprising from someone who had already anticipated some of the most significant principles of twentieth century pedagogic theory in his educational writings.

In the last two years of his life Tolstoy continued to issue pamphlets, letters and manifestoes on the themes that had occupied him since he completed *War and Peace* three decades previously. Sensing that a major social upheaval would shortly erupt amongst the downtrodden masses of Russia, he warned the authorities repeatedly of the injustices inherent in their society. Writing to the prime minister, Stolypin, in July 1907, he urged him to 'strive to abolish the oldest and greatest injustice of all, which is common to all peoples: the individual ownership of land'.[109] In his pamphlet, *I Cannot be Silent*, he traced the roots of violence to the unjust distribution of the country's wealth. His condemnation of capital punishment in the same document attracted widespread attention internationally. This work was followed by *The Law of Violence and The Law of Love*, Tolstoy's most mature statement of the principles of Christian pacifism. Both works were condemned by the Church and Government censors, and the Bishop of Saratov, echoing the general attitude to Tolstoy's writings amongst the Orthodox hierarchy, denounced him as an 'infidel and anarchist', a 'corrupter of the young' and 'a Russian Judas, reviled, accursed' and 'morally rotten to the core'.[110]

Chertkov, who had returned to Yasnaya Polyana in 1907 from exile in England, now set about preparing a definitive collection of all of Tolstoy's writings, which was to be edited by the critic and philosopher, Fÿodor Strakhov. Still harrassed by the police, Chertkov again had to flee from Yasnaya Polyana, this time to Moscow where he was joined by Tolstoy in September 1909 to make further plans for their publishing activities. Mobbed by great numbers of admirers at the railway station in Moscow, Tolstoy, then eight-one years old, suffered a stroke, the first in a series of illnesses that culminated in his death at Astapovo on 7 November 1910. Shortly after his return from Moscow he had received a message from a 'humble follower of your doctrine'—Mahatma Gandhi, then a young lawyer in Johannesburg'. I, as well as some of my friends, have for some time firmly believed in the teaching of non-resistance to evil by force, and we still believe it', Gandhi wrote. 'Besides it has fallen to my good luck to study your writings which have profoundly affected my outlook on life.'[111] Coming from the greatest of all practitioners of the doctrine of non-violence, this tribute appropriately testifies to the huge impact that Tolstoy had made on all those who came under the influence both of his writings and his personal exemplification of the beliefs which they sought to convey.

IV

Principles of a Liberating Pedagogy

1   Fostering the Spirit of Freedom

> ... the success of the school depends on love. But love is not accidental. Love can exist only with freedom. In all the schools founded with the convictions of the school at Yasnaya Polyana the same phenomenon has been repeated: the teacher fell in love with his school; and I am sure that the same teacher, with all the idealisation possible, could not fall in love with a school where the children sit on benches, walk by the ringing of bells, and are whipped on Saturdays.[1]

> We are endeavouring to find that common mental law which has guided man's activity in education, and which therefore, could be a criterion for the correct human activity in education, whereas the historical view to all our questions answers only by saying that Rousseau and Luther were the products of their time. We are searching for the eternal principle which found its expression in them. ... The common eternal law is written in the soul of each man. The law of progress, or perfectibility, is written in the soul of each man and is transferred to history only through error. As long as it remains personal, this law is fruitful and accessible to all; when it is transferred to history, it becomes an idle, empty prattle, leading to the justification of every insipidity and to fatalism.[2]

Both these statements, the one proclaiming the aim of education as the fostering of individual freedom, the other proclaiming its purpose as the communication of eternal truths, encapsulate the paradox at the heart of Tolstoy's educational philosophy. That paradox is the simultaneous celebration of the permanent and the changing, the finite and the infinite, the sacred and the secular, the earthly and the spiritual which is the basis of his whole vision of the educational process and of the values he believed it must seek to transmit. As was indicated in the opening chapter of this book, it has been the practice of educational theorists and historians to place Tolstoy in the company of progressive educators from Rousseau to Dewey, firstly on the basis of his assertion that 'the sole method of education is experience and its sole criterion freedom',[3] and on the further basis of his application of those principles in the conditions of the schools he founded at Yasnaya Polyana. Tolstoy shared much with Rousseau and progressive educators; he shared their dislike for coercion and authoritarianism and, with them, he affirmed the essential freedom of the learning process and the need to foster the free spirit of enquiry through the various activities of schooling. But, unlike most of them, he also asserted the permanence of spiritual truths and proclaimed a vision of the ultimate meaning and purposefulness of human existence that was radically, if unconventionally, located in the traditions of scriptural Christianity. He would almost certainly have abhorred the excesses of moral and epistemic relativism which eventually came to dominate the progressive movement, especially in its later pragmatist forms in the U.S. and Western Europe. Yet he insistently committed himself to the principles of a learner-focused view of education and would be generally regarded as offering radical and highly innovative perspectives on all the main issues affecting the central educational processes of learning and teaching.

The key to this synthesis of apparently conflicting positions lies in Tolstoy's conception of the idea of freedom i.e. in his conviction that freedom originates in, is sustained by, and must ultimately be focussed on the primary and all-embracing experience of love in all its complex and varied forms. Reference was made in an earlier chapter to the unity of all his interests—the religious, the literary, the socio-political and the educational—and to the extent to which this has been stressed in critical assessments of his work. In all the major novels, from *War and Peace* to *Resurrection*, in his autobiographical and confessional prose, in his socio-political and pedagogic writings, the conviction that is consistently pro-claimed is that the meaning of life, and the basis of all faith, is the wisdom and truth which are disclosed through love. On his death-bed Prince Andrew declares that 'love is the essence of the soul'. 'Love hinders death. Love is life', he reflects. 'All, everything that I understand, I understand only because I love. Everything is, everything exists', he says, 'only because I love. Everything is united by it alone.'[4] That vision is re-echoed by Pierre Bezukhov when he declares that faith is founded not on rationally estab-lished principles, but on the simplicity and spontaneity of human brother-hood, a lesson he has learned from the peasant, Platon Karatev. The same lesson that 'to love life is to love God'[5] is learned by Levin, Nekhlyudov, Natasha, Maslova, Ivan Ilyich and Father Sergius—all of them, in one way or another, fictional projections of Tolstoy himself. It is reiterated in the direct statements of his confessional writings. 'I believe', he declared in one of his autobiographical essays, 'that the meaning of every man's life lies only in increasing the store of love within him'—and in another he declared: 'It is becoming more and more evident in our age that the true significance of the Christian doctrine is that the essence of human life is the evergrowing manifestation of the source of everything indicated in us through love, and therefore that the essence of human life and the highest law governing it is love.'[6] Love, he repeatedly asserted, is the originating source and the only truly secure foundation for human freedom. 'Begin to live', he tells the reader in *The Law of Violence and the Law of Love*, 'by seeing the purpose and well-being of your life in the daily progress of your soul's liberation . . . in the increasing perfection of love . . . and you will experience a new and joyous sensation of the awareness of complete freedom and well-being flowing ever increasingly into your soul.'[7]

In his *Diary*[8] Tolstoy recorded his determination to promote this Christian message of a faith founded on love and freedom several years before he proclaimed it explicitly in *War and Peace*, and before he began his first major experiment in education at Yasnaya Polyana. His early educational writings are imbued with the spirit of this message just as pervasively as the fictional and confessional writings he produced in later years. It finds expression specifically in his conception of the relationship of teacher and learner as one of loving reciprocation—a truth vividly conveyed in his employment of the mother-child relationship as its paradigmatic metaphor—and correspondingly in his conception of the processes of learning and knowing as being similarly rooted in the principle of loving encounter. The ways in which these complementary truths are disclosed in Tolstoy's educational writings will be the principal concern of this chapter. Firstly, certain general principles will be identified as a background against which the specific issues relating to learning and teaching can be explored. These will be considered in this first section of the chapter; a further section will focus particularly on the nature of learning, a third on the process of teaching, and a fourth will undertake some comparisons between Tolstoy's educational theories and those of three other educators—Rousseau for whom he had a deep and enduring, but profoundly critical, admiration; and his two close contemporaries, Pestallozzi with whom he shared a lifelong concern for the educational needs of the poor, and Ushinsky, his fellow countryman, whose ideas, like his own, were prompted by their shared contempt for the policies of the educational establishment of Tsarist Russia.

'Love can exist only with freedom', Tolstoy declared in the words from 'Progress and Education' which were cited at the beginning of this chapter. Throughout his educational writings he campaigned relentlessly against all the forces that might inhibit the growth of individual freedom: authoritarianism, compulsion, dogmatism, the fostering of social conformity, didacticism, regimentation and indoctrination were the main objects of his condemnation, as he passionately asserted both the right of every child to pursue the truth in a spirit of free enquiry and the corresponding obligation of educators to provide the conditions in which this could most favourably take place. 'By the word "school"', he wrote, 'I understand not the house in which the instruction is given, not the teachers, not the pupils, not a certain tendency of instruction, but, in the general sense, the conscious activity of him who gives culture upon those who receive it.'[9] The transmission of culture would have to occur, he argued, in a spirit of 'non-interference', one in which the learner could discover meaning and truth independently of all external, i.e. non-personal, influences. This spirit of non-interference would be created, he writes, 'by granting the person under culture the full freedom to avail himself of the teaching which answers his need, which he wants, and to avail himself of it to the extent to which he needs and wants it, and to avoid the teaching which he does not need and does not want'.[10]

But, side by side with this insistence on education as a process of freely oriented discovery, Tolstoy emphasised the formative role of the educator and stressed his responsibility, as one consciously engaged in the transmission of culture, to guide and direct the pupil in his search for the truth in a spirit of individual freedom. The potential conflict between these two aspirations is transcended, he suggests, by the quality of loving reciprocation in which the activities of teaching and learning are conducted. The formative element in teaching does not impinge on the freedom of the learner when it is conducted in the unifying mutuality of loving reciprocation. It is essential, he argues, if teaching is to be truly influential, that it be charged with a love for learning: 'The educational element, let us say, in mathematics or in history, is only imparted to the students when the teacher is passionately fond of his subject and when he knows it well; only then his love is communicated to the students and has an educational influence on them.'[11] In 'Education and Culture' he gives this advice to his teachers:

> It is said that science has in itself an educational element; that it is true and not true, and in this very statement lies the fundamental error of the existing paradoxical view of education. Science is science and has nothing in itself. The educational element lies in the teaching of the sciences, in the teacher's love for his science, and in the love with which it is imparted—in the teacher's relation to his students. If you wish to educate the students by science, love your science and know it, and the students will love both you and the science, and you will educate them; but if you yourself do not love it, the science will have no educational influence, no matter how much you may compel them to learn it. Here again there is the one measure, the one salvation, the same freedom for the students to listen, or not to listen to the teacher, to imbibe or not to imbibe his educational influence, that is, for them to decide whether he knows and loves his science.
>
> Well, what then, will the school be with the non-interference in education?

> An all-sided and most various conscious activity directed by one man on another, for the purpose of transmitting knowledge, without compelling the student by direct force or diplomatically to avail himself of that which we want him to avail himself of.[12]

It is on this fundamental conception of education as a free, loving, intersubjective relationship that Tolstoy has been most widely misunderstood and misrepresented by his interpreters. Citing his words from the Introduction to his journal, *Yasnaya Polyana*, that 'the sole method of education is experience and its sole criterion freedom',[13] Michael Armstrong writes: 'Tolstoy's ambition is nothing less than a reconstruction, almost a reinvention, of the science of education.' 'This reconstruction', he argues, 'is effected by means of a systematic study of the free child, of his intellectual environment, his social relationships, his developing thought and action.' 'It is a study', he says, 'which will embrace the organisation, methods and curricula of schools in their social context, the interelationships of adults and children, learners and teachers, the nature of knowledge and the means of intellectual growth.'[14] It is indeed all of these, but the central and unifying principle is omitted in Armstrong's commentary: the spirit of interhuman mutuality and love in which all these objectives were to be realised.

The whole position is even more misleadingly stated by Archambault in his Introduction to another edition of Tolstoy's educational writings. Tolstoy, he writes, 'insists upon characterising education as essentially a process of freeing the individual for creative improvisation through understanding'. 'A graduate', he says, 'is not to be trained rigidly to conform to a present society, but rather . . . to enable him to reshape that society to meet new needs and new challenges.' And, then, he adds the extraordinary comment that Tolstoy's 'entire approach is characterised not only by a lack of ultimacy but a lack of definiteness.'[15] The excerpts just cited on the whole issue of the aims of education from Tolstoy's educational writings, the support and further elucidation for them which has been cited from his fictional prose, together with the evidence of his passionate, lifelong quest for ultimate truths which has been described in the previous chapter, should provide sufficient refutation of this absurd and untenable claim.

Much of the confusion in both these commentaries derives from a failure to grasp the meaning of the central concept of 'experience' in Tolstoy's educational writings. It is essential, in view of its importance for his entire view of the educational process, that the meaning of the term be carefully and accurately defined. To understand the precise sense in which he used it, it is necessary to look further into his conception of the tensions of the eternal and the contingent, the permanent and the circumstantial, and of the ways in which he applied them to education. Repeatedly, as has been already suggested, he stressed the constancy of certain truths, though he conceived of them as being disclosed in the inwardness of individual conscience and faith, and in the intersubjective mutuality of love, rather than in any conceptualised or objectified form. This is the point of his assertion in 'Progress and Education' that 'the common eternal law is written in the soul of each man',[16]—a position which is reiterated in Prince Andrew's, Pierre's and Nekhlyudov's declarations that faith and the meaning of existence spring ultimately from the depth of human and divine love. But Tolstoy also affirmed the contingency of the historical conditions of our existence, he stressed the relativity of all social reality, and the volatile character of the circumstances in which everyday life is conducted. Because of the necessary tension and interdependence that exists between the eternal and the changing, he acknowledged the need for continuously validating the former in terms of the latter, and insisted that the entire heritage of culture and received wisdom—in which eternal or permanent truths are historically embodied—needs to be reinterpreted constantly in the light of contemporary and experiential standpoints. Experience, by this conception, becomes a highly complex phenomenon, simultaneously disclosing both the permanent and the changing, the temporal and the intemporal, the finite and the infinite.

This is a prominent theme in *War and Peace* where the dialectic of necessity and freedom, of the historical and experiential modes of awareness, are explored against the background of major political and social occurrences. The problematic of history is seen in the novel as a dilemma embracing both a necessary relation to the past, and one which is rooted in the contingency of individual freedom. It is through the latter, he suggests, that the meaning and relevance of history is constantly validated. Pointing in his essay, 'Education and Culture', to the absence of cultural certainties in the modern age—as contrasted with the cultural stability of earlier periods in history, such as those of classical Greece and medieval Christianity[17]—he speaks of the urgent necessity, in present conditions, of seeking a renewal of culture through a critical reassimilation of its received or historical forms. Paradoxically, he says, that process has been manifested throughout history as a persistent assertion by successive societies of their freedom from the legacy of the past, from which, paradoxically, they emerge with a stronger and more renewed sense of its relevance to the conditions of their own time.

Applied to the practical conditions of schooling, this whole issue finds expression in Tolstoy's insistence that the work of the school must be firmly rooted in the conditions of the society from which it springs: that a close conjunction must be maintained, by way of its curricular and pedagogic agencies, between the historical traditions of culture and the popular forms of it that are manifested in everyday life. This is the main theme of his essay, 'Education and Culture', where he differentiates between the concepts of 'education' and 'instruction'—terms he claims are confused frequently by educators. He sees the first as implying a free assimilation of all the varied manifestations of culture, and the second as a selective extrapolation of certain modes of culture, such as its more sophisticated aesthetic forms, from the whole complex of elements constituting its total reality. The second he condemns as a divorcing of education from the wholeness of the culture which it is its function to transmit:

> The so-called science of pedagogy is interested only in education, and looks upon a man receiving his culture as upon a being entirely subject to the educator. Only through him does the man in the formative period of culture receive cultural or educational impressions, whether these impressions be books, stories, memorising, artistic or bodily exercises. The whole external world is allowed to act upon the pupil only to the extent to which the educator finds it convenient. The educator tries to surround his pupil with an impenetrable wall against the influences of the world, and allows only so much to pass through his scholastico-educational funnel as he deems to be useful. I am not speaking of what has been done by so-called unprogressive men—I am not fighting windmills. I am speaking of the comprehension and application of education by so-called excellent, progressive educators. Everywhere the influence of life is removed from the cares of the pedagogues; everywhere the school is surrounded with a Chinese wall of book-knowledge, through which only so much of the vital cultural influence is admitted as may please the educators. The influence of life is not recognised. Thus the science called pedagogy looks upon the matter, for it assumes the right to know what is necessary for the formation of the best man, and it considers it possible to remove every extra-educational influence from its charge; even thus they proceed in the practice of education.[18]

Tolstoy saw this selective process of acculturation as leading inevitably to a conception of education as induction—one by which the learner is systematically oriented towards socially sanctioned values and norms. Such a process can only be maintained, he says, through some form of compulsory enforcement. 'Of late', he writes, 'the best pedagogues have come to the conclusion that instruction is the best means of education, but that the instruction is to be compulsory, obligatory, and thus have begun to confuse all three concepts of education, culture and instruction.'[19] The compulsion consists, he suggests, in the selection of those aspects of culture considered to be educationally valuable, and in the consequent denial of the free assimilation of influences which he saw as the essential prerequisite of a genuinely liberating education. He insists that to be truly meaningful education must freely embrace all the intellectual, cultural, social and other influences impinging on the mind and consciousness of the learner. 'Education as a premeditated formation of men according to certain patterns is sterile, unlawful and impossible',[20] he declares. He argues that an education related to the immediate experience of the learner, and linked with the conditions of life as a whole, is more fruitful, simply because it mirrors the spontaneity of learning in its ordinary, everyday forms. So he calls on schools to create conditions conducive to fostering the free assimilation of knowledge in accordance with the informal, non-compulsory and intrinsically self-motivating modes of learning which occur in society as a whole. This is the basis of his pedagogic model for all education, from the lowest level of the elementary school to the higher echelons of the university:

> If I am told that such non-interference, which is possible for the higher institutions and for grown-up people, is not possible for the lower schools and for minors, because we have no example for it in the shape of public lectures for childen, and so forth, I will answer that if we are not going to understand the word 'school' in the narrowest sense, but will accept it with the above-mentioned definition, we shall find for the lower stages of knowledge and for the lower ages many influences of liberal culture without interference in education, corresponding to the higher institutions and to the public lectures. Such is the acquisition of the art of reading from a friend or a brother; such are popular games of children, of the cultural value of which we intend writing a special article; such are public spectacles, panoramas, and so forth; such are pictures and books; such are fairy-tales and songs; such are work and, last, the experiments of the school at Yasnaya Polyana.[21]

Tolstoy's thinking on these issues was to some extent prompted by the draconian statutes on education that were introduced by Nicholas I in 1828 as a basis for the creation of a stringently regulated state system of education.[22] Tolstoy commented in detail on the statutes in his paper, 'A Project of a General Plan for the Establishment of Popular Schools'. Apart from denouncing the blatant inequities which the statutes were intentionally designed to create, Tolstoy complained that a state-controlled system of education would lead inevitably to the kind of compulsion just described. 'Leaving out of consideration the impossibility of subjecting the whole population of Russia to the same treatment as regards popular education, it seems to me, in addition, to be exceedingly inconvenient and dangerous in this manner forcibly to bring education to one common level',[23] he wrote. Arguing strongly for local control of education—a position, in fact, which was eventually recognised in the reforms of the 1860s—he particularly

insisted that schools should be free to make their own decisions on matters
of curriculum policy, not because schools should not be required to teach
certain forms of subject-matter but, significantly, because he insisted no
limits should be set to what they should teach:

> We have expressed our conviction that the definition of a course of instruction
> for the popular schools is quite impossible, especially in the sense in which
> the Project is trying to make it—in the sense of setting limits to the subjects
> of instruction. . . . I do not mention that this is unjust; that it is injurious to
> the development of education; that it excludes the possibility of all lively
> interest of the teacher in his work; that it gives rise to endless abuses (the
> writer of a programme or of a textbook need only make one mistake, and that
> mistake becomes obligatory for the whole of Russia). I say only that every
> programme for the popular school is absolutely impossible, and every such
> programme is only words, words, words. I can comprehend a programme
> which defines the obligation which teachers, or the power establishing the
> school, tàke upon themselves; I can understand how one may say to the
> Commune and to the parents: I am the teacher; I open the school; and I
> undertake to teach your children this or that, and you have no right to ask of
> me that which I have not promised you; but to open a school and to promise
> that one *will not teach* this or that is both imprudent and absolutely
> impossible. And it is precisely such a negative programme that the Project
> proposes for all of Russia and for the popular primary schools.[24]

His admiration for the American system of education was based quite
simply on its freedom from state controls, unlike most European systems,
such as the Prussian, where every facet of educational policy was strictly
monitored by the state.[25] The prescriptive, compulsory, authoritarian approach to education—which, he argued, must follow inevitably from state
control—is the root cause, he says, for popular resistance to education. 'The
people want education', he declares; 'the need for education lies in every
man; the people love and seek education as they love and seek the air for
breathing.'[26] Equally, he writes, governments strive to satisfy this popular
thirst for knowledge—'the government and society burn with desire to
educate the masses'—yet this coincidence of popular demand and government response fails miserably to achieve its basic objective: 'The masses
continually counteract the efforts made for their education by society or by
the government . . . and these efforts are frequently frustrated', he writes.
'Notwithstanding all the force and cunning and the persistency of governments and societies, the masses constantly manifest their disaffection with
the education which is offered to them, and step by step submit only to
force.'[27] Citing the evidence of the school systems of Prussia, Switzerland
and France—which he had observed closely during his long tour of

1860–1—he writes of the loathing and contempt with which the common people regarded the kind of education provided for them:

> This is what reality has shown to us: a father sends his daughter or son to school against his wish, cursing the institution which deprives him of his son's labour, and counting the days up to the time when his son will become *schulfrei* (this expression alone shows how the people look at the schools). The child goes to school with the conviction that the only power of which he knows, that of his father, does not approve of the power of the state, to which he submits upon entering school.
>
> The information which he receives from his older companions, who were in that institution before, is not calculated to enhance his desire to enter school. Schools present themselves to him as an institution for torturing children—an institution in which they are deprived of their chief pleasure and youthful needs of free motion; where *Gehorsam* (obedience) and *Ruhe* (quiet) are the chief conditions; where he needs a special permission to 'go out for a minute'; where every misdeed is punished with a ruler . . . or by the continuation of study—the more cruel condition for the child.
>
> School justly presents itself to the child's mind as an establishment where he is taught that which nobody understands; where he is generally compelled not to speak his native *patois, Mundart*, but a foreign language, where the teacher for the greater part sees in his pupils his natural enemies, who, out of their own malice and that of their parents, do not wish to learn that which he has learned; and where the pupils, on their side, look upon their teacher as their enemy, who only out of personal spite compels them to learn such difficult things. In such an institution they are obliged to pass six years and about six hours every day.[28]

Tolstoy attributed these negative attitudes to the divorcing of the activities of the school from the spontaneous and 'unconscious' conditions of learning occuring in everyday life. He speaks of the 'stupefying influence' of an education which is based on compulsion, its 'continuous contortion of the mental faculties', its suppression of the basic potentialities on which all learning is founded: the spontaneity of free enquiry, the natural spirit of curiosity which are present in every child.[29] What he had witnessed in Prussia and France were mechanistic modes of learning, divorced from the stimulus of immediate experience, focussed on abstract knowledge, promoted through rote memorisation, rigid styles of didactic teaching and highly prescriptive curricula—all of which resulted in widespread failure by the pupils to comprehend or assimilate knowledge adequately. 'I could write whole books on the ignorance I have witnessed in the schools of France, Switzerland and Germany', he declared.[30] The children could not answer the simplest questions, their knowledge being largely undigested and unrelated to meaningful experience.

Unfolding his own vision of popular education, he asserts the need to reproduce in the school the conditions of spontaneous learning observable in everyday life. All the factors conducive to this—the stimulation of natural curiosity, the respect for individual needs, the provision of resources to motivate and sustain the process of learning, above all, the fostering of a spirit of loving reciprocation between teacher and learner—would constitute the authentic ethos of the school. Its objective would be to imitate the 'unconscious', intrinsically motivated learning of the streets, the cafes, or the market-place:

> Whether this education is good or bad is another matter; but here it is, this unconscious education which is so much more powerful than the one by compulsion; here is the unconscious school which has undermined the compulsory school and has made its contents to dwindle down almost to nothing. There is left only the despotic form, with hardly any contents. I say with hardly any contents, because I exclude the mere mechanical ability of putting letters together and writing down words—the only knowledge which is carried away after five or six years of study. Here it must be remarked that even the mere mechanical art of reading and writing is frequently acquired outside of school in a much shorter period, and that frequently the pupils do not carry away from school even this ability, or it is lost, finding no application in life, and that there where the law of compulsory school attendance exists there is no need of teaching the second generation to read, write and figure, because the parents, we should think, would be able to do that at home, and that, too, much earlier than at school.
>
> What I saw in Marseilles takes place in all the other countries: everywhere the greater part of one's education is acquired, not at school, but in life. There where life is instructive, as in London, Paris and, in general, in all large cities, the masses are educated; there where life is not instructive, as in the country, the people are uneducated, in spite of the fact that the schools are the same in both. The knowledge acquired in cities seems to remain; the knowledge acquired in the country is lost. The direction and spirit of the popular education, both in the cities and in the villages, are absolutely independent from, and generally contrary to the spirit which it is intended to instil into the schools. The education goes on quite independently of the schools.[31]

'Learning through experience', therefore, was a central principle in Tolstoy's vision of the school. But it was a principle that was conceived in quite a different manner from the one that was proclaimed so stridently in progressive educational theory. It was central to his educational philosophy insofar as he believed that all learning should embrace the synthesis of the permanent and the contingent, the eternal and the temporal, the spiritual and the material, that was at the heart of his beliefs about the nature and purpose of life. His understanding of the concept must be seen in the context of his quest for an eternal reality behind and beyond the flux of phenomena enveloping the temporal conditions in which men live. It was because of his understanding of the *ultimate* significance of experience—and especially of the all-embracing experience of love—that he believed it had a fundamental place in man's quest for the eternal, the unconditioned and the infinite. It was through the world of everyday experience, he believed, that man could reach the eternal, and all truly meaningul modes of learning would need to embrace that conjunction. While fundamentally rooted in experience, his theory of learning could not, therefore, be called 'empirical' in the sense in which that term was used by Dewey and his precursors of the nineteenth century. Tolstoy, who saw all experience *sub specie aeternitatis*, could never accept the finality of the empirical conveyed in assertions such as 'the real is what we experience', 'that which guides us truly is true', 'mind exists within the flow of experience', and other such propositions associated with pragmatist educational theory.[32] This can be demonstrated more precisely as his treatment of specific issues relating to the nature of learning and teaching is examined in the forthcoming sections of this chapter, and as his application of these basic principles to the particular spheres of religious, moral and aesthetic education are examined in subsequent chapters.

2   Nurturing the Desire to Learn

> Rational knowledge, as presented by the learned and wise, negates the meaning of life, yet the vast masses—humanity as a whole—recognise that this meaning lies in irrational knowledge. And this irrational knowledge is faith, the very thing that I could not help rejecting. . . .
>
> Thus, in addition to rational knowledge, which I had hitherto thought to be the only knowledge, I was inevitably led to acknowledge that there does exist another kind of knowledge—an irrational one—possessed by humanity as a whole: faith, which affords the possibility of living. Faith remained as irrational to me as before, but I could not fail to recognise that it alone provides mankind with the answers to the question of life, and consequently with the possibility of life.[33]

It is essential, before attempting to deal with Tolstoy's conception of the nature of learning, that some consideration be given to the kind of inductive methodology on which his educational writings were based. That, in turn, requires some understanding of the distinctively non-rationalist view of knowledge and meaning that underlies all his work, both in its fictional and non-fictional modes. *A Confession*, from which the above passages are taken, records his personal disillusionment with rationalism as he concluded that the ultimate truths which he sought would be disclosed, not through the categories of abstract philosophy, but through the simple wisdom of the kind of faith he observed in the unlearned masses of the peasantry amongst whom he lived. That same distrust of rationalist abstraction dominates his approach to education, and is the basis both of his rejection of philosophically-based theory and his adoption of a radically descriptive methodology, founded on detailed empiric observation of the educational process. The inductive character of his educational writings reflects his aesthetic preference for a wholeness of meaning transcending the rational, and results in a harmonisation of theory and practice that closely parallels the poetic synthesis achieved in his fictional writings. Observing his pupils closely—their religious, moral, intellectual, imaginative, social, emotional and psychological needs, their interests, attitudes, and individual learning styles—he drew his insights from direct interpretations of the processes of learning and teaching as they were manifested in the everyday conditions of his schools. Denouncing the very concept of 'theoretical pedagogics' in his essay, 'On Popular Education', he declared that education should be fashioned, not in accordance with general norms and principles, but on the basis of an unmediated perception of individual needs in the situations and conditions directly confronting the educator:

> At the basis of our activity lies the conviction that we not only do not know, but we cannot know, wherein the education of the people is to consist; that not only does there not exist a science of education—pedagogics—but that the first foundation of it has not yet been laid; that the definition of pedagogy and of its aims in a philosophical sense is impossible, useless and injurious. We do not know what education is to be like, and we do not acknowledge the whole philosophy of pedagogy because we do not acknowledge the possibility of a man's knowing what it is he ought to know. Education and culture present themselves to us as historical facts of one set of people acting on another; therefore the problem of the science of education, in our opinion, is only the discovery of the laws of this action of one set of people on another. We not only do not acknowledge in our generation the knowledge, nor even the right of a knowledge of what is necessary for the perfecting of man, but are also convinced that if humanity were possessed of that knowledge, it would not be in its power to transmit, or not to transmit such knowledge.[34]

He argued that pedagogic method should be guided by the teacher's personal judgement of the requirements of the individual learner: it should be eclectic, flexible, and adapted to the particular conditions encountered by the teacher. 'The best teacher', he wrote, 'will be he who has at his tongue's end the explanation of what it is that is bothering his pupil. These explanations give the teacher the knowledge of the greatest possible number of methods, the ability of inventing new methods, and, above all, not a blind adherence to one method, but the conviction that all methods are one-sided, and that the best method would be the one which would answer best to all the possible difficulties incurred by a pupil, that is, not a method, but an art and talent'.[35] He stressed the need to integrate learning with the total experience of the learner. In his essay, 'On Teaching the Rudiments', he points to the common misapprehension that the basic needs of the learner can be reduced to certain specifiable skills in the spheres of literacy and numeracy. 'Maybe this skill of composing words is necessary in order to introduce man into the first step of education, and maybe there is no other road? This we do not see at all', he replies. 'We very frequently perceive the diametrically opposite, if, in speaking of education, we shall understand not alone the scholastic, but also the vital education'.[36] Stressing the self-evident truth that 'education is acquired by people quite independently of their knowledge of reading and writing',[37] and that their educability therefore involves potentialities of a more fundamental character than the mastery of such rudimentary abilities, he argues that education becomes fully meaningful only when it is integrated in the existential totality of everyday life:

> The discussion in our literature of the usefulness or injuriousness of the rudiments, which it was so easy to ridicule, is in our opinion a very serious discussion, which will elucidate many questions. Some say that it is injurious for the masses to be able to read books and periodicals, which speculation and political parties put into their hands; they say that the ability to read takes the labouring class out of their element, innoculates then with discontent with their condition, and breeds vices and a decline of morality. Others say, or infer, that education cannot be injurious, but must always be useful. The first are more or less conscientious observers, the others are theorists. As is always the case in discussions, both are entirely right. The discussion, we think, is due to the fact that the questions are not clearly put. . . .
>
> Looking more closely at the result of the rudiments in the form in which they are transmitted to the masses, I think the majority will express themselves against the rudiments, taking into consideration the protracted compulsion, the disproportionate development of memory, the false conception of the completeness of science, the loathing for a continued education, the false vanity, and the habit of meaningless reading, which are acquired in these schools. In the school at Yasnaya Polyana all the pupils who come to it from the primary schools constantly fall behind the pupils who enter from the school of life; they not only fall behind, but their backwardness is in proportion to the time they have spent in the primary school. . . . The popular school must respond to the exigencies of the masses—that is all which we can positively assert in regard to this question.[38]

Far from questioning the importance of developing literacy and numeracy—we shall see presently how vigorously he sought to promote these abilities in his own schools—Tolstoy was pointing to the complex processes involved in achieving this objective successfully, and was warning of the dangers of isolating the 'teaching of the basics' from the entire formation of the individual person. He particularly emphasised the need to develop the motivation to learn as a precondition of developing a mastery of the rudiments. And this closely parallels his thinking on the interrelationship of learning and everyday experience. The intrinsic motivation to learn is rooted, he said, in the natural curiosity of the learner: a curiosity manifested in the myriad forms of spontaneous learning and knowing that occur in the course of his daily activities. It is this informal, intrinsically motivated process of spontaneous enquiry that must be fostered through education, he argues, if the work of the school is to be conducted in the same spirit of immediate and uncontrived meaningfulness that characterises the learning that occurs in the home, the street, the cafe, or the marketplace. 'In order that a man of any age should begin to learn it is necessary that he should like learning', he declares . . .

> In order that he should like learning he must recognise the falseness and insufficiency of his view of things and he must divine the new world conception, which the instruction is to open to him. Not one man or child would be able to learn, if the nature of his learning presented itself to him only as an art of reading, writing, and counting; not one teacher would be able to teach, if he did not have in his power a higher world conception than what the pupils have. In order that the pupil may entirely surrender himself to the teacher, there must be lifted for him one side of the shroud which has been concealing from him all the charm of that world of thought, knowledge and poetry, to which instruction was to introduce him. Only by being under the spell of that brilliant world ahead of him is the pupil able to work over himself in the manner in which we want him to.[39]

Two closely related principles, the one pedagogic, the other curricular, are affirmed throughout these essays. The first is the obligation of the school to ensure continuity between formal and informal learning. 'It is time to convince ourselves', he writes, 'that these (home) conditions are the chief foundation of all education and that they are far from being inimical and hindrances to the school, but that they are its prime and chief movers. A child could never learn to distinguish the lines which form the distinctive letters, nor numbers, nor could he acquire the ability to express his thoughts, if it were not for these home conditions'.[40] The instructional process, he suggests, must be rooted in what Paulo Freire a century later described as the 'thematic universe' of the learner. 'The interest in knowing anything whatever and the questions which it is the problem of the school to answer are created only by these home conditions', he writes in his essay, 'On Popular Education'. 'Every instruction ought to be only an answer to the questions put by life'.[41] But while he insists that the learning processes fostered by the school should imitate those of the home and the conditions of life as a whole, Tolstoy makes a crucial distinction between the different kinds of knowledge that stimulate and sustain learning in each instance. The specific role of the school, he suggests, is to introduce the child to the entire heritage of knowledge and culture—a heritage not generally available outside the formal world of schooling—but he urges the teacher to ensure tht this is meaningfully related to the entire experience of the child through the resources of a learner-centred pedagogy. In modern parlance, his position would be described as both 'learner-centred' and 'curriculum centred'. The process is vividly described in this passage from 'The School at Yasnaya Polyana':

> What means have we then, to lift that edge of the curtain for the pupil? As I have said, I thought, just as many think, that being myself in that world to which I am to introduce the pupils, I could easily do so, and I taught the rudiments, I explained the phenomena of nature, I told them, as it says in the ABCs, that the fruits of learning are sweet, but the pupils did not believe me and kept aloof. I tried to read the Bible to them, and I completely took possession of them. The edge of the curtain was lifted, and they surrendered themselves to me unconditionally. They fell in love with the book, with the study, and with me. All I had now to do was to guide them on. After the Old Testament I told them the New, and they loved studying and me more and more. Then I told them universal, Russian and natural history, when we were through with the Bible; they listened to everything, believed everything, begged to go on and on, and ever new perspectives of thought, knowledge and poetry were opened up to them.[42]

In addition to its emphasis on the importance of substantive curriculum content, the further significance of this passage lies in the way that it illustrates the centrality of imagination in the pedagogic methods employed by Tolstoy. Having failed to engage the children's attention through various forms of instructional pedagogy, he discovered the power of narrative evocation to stimulate their interest in a whole range of subjects from the Russian language, its folklore and literature, to history, mathematics, nature study, geography and so on. This linking of motivation with imaginative creativity is the crucial synthesis at the heart of his pedagogy and is the key to the nurturing of educability—the 'wish to learn'—which he saw as the most pressing challenge for the educator. Believing that all thought originates in the mind as symbol, he saw the process of learning as essentially one of symbolic meaning-making, and devised a pedagogy that

would foster this effectively by basing all modes of enquiry and understanding on the unifying power of the aesthetic.

The radical principle underlying all his pedagogic practice is this
identification of intellectual with imaginative understanding. Throughout
his long essay, 'The School at Yasnaya Polyana', he offers numerous
instances of how the pupil's interest in all varieties of subject-matter can be
awakened and sustained through various forms of creative activity, but
particularly through the reading of narrative prose. The Bible, with its
powerful and inexhaustible resources as narrative, was particularly popular
in this respect. 'There is no production that I know of which unites all the
sides of human thought in such a compressed poetical form as is to be found
in the Bible', he wrote. 'The lyricism of David's psalms acts not only upon
the minds of grown pupils, but everybody for the first time learns from this
book the whole charm of the epos in its inimitable simplicity and strength.'[43]
With regard to history teaching, he suggests that what is interesting to
children is not the chronlogy of events but 'the *artistic treatment* of them
by the historian' and the evocations of their excitement and drama that are
to be found in popular tradition and folklore. 'All these persons and events
are interesting for the student not to the extent of their importance in history,
but to the extent of the artistic composition of their activities, to the extent
of the artistic treatment of them by the historian, and even more so—not by
the historian but by the popular tradition.'[44]

What particularly commends Tolstoy's pedagogy to the modern educator
is not only his emphasis on the central role of the symbolic—an emphasis
not generally found in pre-twentieth century educational theory—but the
further insistence on the need to provide *universal* access for children to the
richness of their cultural, and specifically their aesthetic heritage, to nurture
this potentiality. Anticipating Buber's affirmation that 'everyone is
elementally endowed with the basic powers of the arts',[45] he recognised the
importance of an aesthetic harmony as the foundation of all moral, religious,
cultural and intellectual development, and therefore proclaimed the right of
all children to have access to this. Considering for instance, whether the arts
should be taught to peasant children (a question he considered absurd in
itself) he declared: 'To deprive him (the peasant child) of the right of
enjoying art, to deprive the teacher of the right of introducing him into that
region of better enjoyments, toward which his being strives with all the
powers of his soul, is the greater absurdity.' 'Have the children of the masses
a right to art?' he asks. 'Asking this is like asking whether the children of
the masses have a right to eat beef, that is, have they the right to satisfy their
human needs'. 'I assume'. he writes, 'that the necessity of enjoying art and
serving art are inherent in each human personality, no matter to what race

or milieu he may belong.' 'Everybody', he declares, 'without distinction of classes and occupations, has a right to it and a right to devote himself to it, on the ground that art does not brook mediocrity.'[46] He insists that not only have the masses the right to be taught art, but the right to be given access to the full riches of the heritage:

> When the question is put whether the fine arts are necessary for the masses, the pedagogues generally become timid and confused (Plato was the only one who boldly decided the question in the negative). They say that they are necessary, but with certain limitations; that it is dangerous for the social structure to give all a chance to become artists. They say that certain arts and a certain degree of them may exist only in a certain class of society; they say that the arts must have their own especial servants who are devoted to but one matter. They say that the highly gifted natures must have the chance to get away from the mass of the people and to devote themselves exclusively to the service of art. This is the greatest concession which pedagogy makes to the right of each individual to make of himself what he pleases. All the cares of the pedagogues in respect to the arts are directed toward attaining this one aim.
>
> I regard all this as unjust. I assume that the necessity of enjoying art and serving art are inherent in each human personality, no matter to what race or milieu he may belong, and that this necessity has its rights and ought to be satisfied. Taking this assumption as an axiom, I say that if inconveniences and inconsistencies arise for each person in the enjoyment of art and its reproduction, the cause of these inconveniences lies not in the manner of the transmission, not in the dissemination or concentration of art among many or among a few, but in the character and direction of the art, upon which we must look with doubt, in order not to foist anything false upon the younger generation, and also in order to give that younger generation a chance to work out something new, both as to form and contents.[47]

Later these issues will be discussed in more detail when a full chapter will be devoted to Tolstoy's ideas on aesthetic education. For the moment, there remains an important principle, arising from the view that the masses must be given access to the heritage of culture and art, that needs to be further explained. This is the formative role of the teacher in awakening the pupil's interest in art and sustaining it through imaginatively enriching content. Tolstoy envisaged a significant, but subtle and non-directive, role for the teacher in fostering creative expression and response amongst his pupils. This is especially evident in his approach to the teaching of reading where the teacher is urged, through a process of subtle, purposeful but non-directive intervention, to guide and motivate individual creativity through sensitive and resourceful pedagogy and through the use of substantial, carefully planned and imaginatively enriching content. Tolstoy's own *ABC* textbook was a particularly good example of the kind of content that he considered was suitable for this purpose. The principle was further in evidence in his reports on the writing lessons at the school in Yasnaya Polyana where freedom of expression was consistently encouraged, but the teacher, through persistent but gentle evaluation of the pupils' work, guided them towards mastery of the formal and technical procedures necessary to refine and structure their writing to the fullest possible degree.

On the one hand, therefore, he emphasised the crucial importance of the experiential, motivational and symbolic aspects of learning, and argued for a liberal pedagogic practice, in which the value of individual potentialities, the continuity of formal and informal learning, the interrelatedness of all modes of understanding, the harmonising functions of the imaginative and the symbolic, would all be appropriately recognised. But equally, he stressed the necessity for a sensitive, formative pedagogy, actively focussed on the fostering of individual potential, and the accompanying need for the substantial and enriching curriculum content that would be necessary to achieve this. This brings us to the all-encompassing paradox of his educational writings: it consists in the fact that the full potentiality of individual freedom, and the full scope of the reciprocity between teacher and learner, are both ultimately realised in the mutually constraining influence that each exerts on the other—the one by virtue of the persistent challenge represented by the nature of his learning needs, the other by his responsibility to adopt the pedagogic measures necessary to fulfil those needs. Ultimately, that paradox was rooted in the identification of love with freedom, the ideal on which all the principles of teaching and learning are founded in Tolstoy's educational writings. While he believed that love is the true source of freedom, he believed also that it imposes certain limitations on the exercise of that freedom, particularly in the close reciprocity of a relationship founded on trust, such as that between the teacher and the learner.

Thus, the whole ethos of the school at Yasnaya Polyana was designed to accommodate the demands both of individual freedom and of the discipline and order necessary for authentic teaching and learning. Classroom organisation was generally informal; there were no set places, no marching or regimentation, no bell-ringing or rigid-timetabling. Children were never compelled to underake specific tasks or duties and—though this rarely arose—they were not even compelled to attend school if they did not wish to do so. But while compulsion was consciously excluded from all school activities, there was always the presence of the teacher— encouraging, guiding, stimulating, deepening and enriching the learning process at every level—to ensure that classroom activities were serious, purposeful, imaginatively and intellectually self-fulfilling, and that they fully accommodated the needs of every child present in the school. Additionally, there was the intrinsic discipline of the content on which the learning was focussed to ensure that all these objectives were fulfilled. Tolstoy, as we have seen, insisted that pupils should have full access to their cultural heritage and ensured in every way possible that substantial subject-matter was used in all classroom activities.

It would be wrong, therefore, to see his rejection of the principle of compulsion, and his insistence that learning be based on intrinsic motivation, as leading to an aimless process of disorganised classroom activity, as Archambault does in his Introduction to an edition of Tolstoy's educational writings. He speaks of a 'pedagogy of extreme permissiveness, not only regarding teaching techniques but curricular organisation and principles of discipline as well'. 'Children are free to come and go as they please and masters to teach what, how and at whatever length they please', he writes in a passage describing the conditions at the school. 'Noise and confusion are the natural order of things. The primary role of the teacher is to listen and modify what he hears rather than talk at children who silently listen to him. There is no thought given to coverage of material, no syllabus to be finished, no required learning to be fulfilled.'[48] That this description greatly misrepresents and oversimplifies the nature of Tolstoy's views on teaching and learning should be evident from the excerpts from his pedagogic writings that have been cited throughout this chapter. What it particularly misrepresents is the delicate tension of freedom and order that was consistently maintained in the schools at Yasnaya Polyana. Tolstoy's emphasis on non-compulsion would have to be seen, in any event, in the context of the terrifying repression, the rigid and coercive didacticism, and the tyrannical methods of maintaining discipline, that were current in Russian schools in the 1860s—especially those in the Tula Province, as was illustrated earlier from contemporary reports. But this did not lead him into the greater fallacy of denying the importance of purposeful and ordered learning, of stimulating and enriching curriculum content, and of the active and formative role of a teacher in the guidance of classroom activity. This passage from 'The School at Yasnaya Polyana' illustrates how the pupils gradually realised the importance of disciplined study as they were convinced by the teacher that they should 'submit to certain conditions in order to acquire knowledge'. It shows the extent of the teacher's influence in guiding them—through encouragement and example, and especially through enlightened pedagogy—towards a serious, ordered and purposeful approach to their studies:

The farther the pupils proceed, the more the instruction branches out and the more necessary does order become. For this reason, in the normal non-compulsory development of the school, the more the pupils become educated, the fitter they become for order, and the more strongly they themselves feel the need for order, and the greater is the teacher's influence in this respect. In the Yasnaya Polyana school this rule has always been observed, from the day of its foundation. At first it was impossible to subdivide into classes, or subjects, or recess, or lessons; everything naturally blended into one, and all the attempts at separation remained futile. Now we have pupils in the first class, who themselves demand that the programme be adhered to, who are dissatisfied when they are disturbed in their lessons, and who constantly drive out the little children who run into them. . . .

School childen, small men though they be, have the same needs as we, and they reason in the same manner; they all want to learn, coming to school for this only, and so they will naturally arrive at the conclusion that they must submit to certain conditions in order to acquire knowledge. They are more than merely men, they are a company of men, united by one idea. And where three are gathered in My name, there will I be with them! When they submit only to natural laws, such as arise from their natures, they do not feel provoked and do not murmur; but when they submit to your predetermined interference, they do not believe in the legality of your bells, programmes and regulations.[49]

The passage vividly illustrates the highly formative and complex character of the pedagogy that was adopted in the schools at Yasnaya Polyana to meet the challenge of maintaining the balance of freedom and order that Tolstoy saw as being crucial to the entire process of learning. The complexities of this can now be demonstrated in more detail as the nature of his pedagogic practices is more fully explored.

3.   *The Teacher, the Curriculum and the School*

A mother teaches her child to speak only that they may understand each other; the mother instinctively tries to come down to the child's view of things, to his language, but the law of educational progress does not permit her to descend down to him, but compels him to rise to her knowledge. The same relation exists between the author and the reader, the same between the school and the pupils, the same between the state and society—the people. The activity of him who gives the education has one and the same purpose. The problem of the science of education is only the study of the conditions under which a coincidence of these two tendencies for one common end takes place, and the indication of those conditions which retard this coincidence.[50]

In this passage from his essay, 'On Popular Education', Tolstoy takes the age-old image of maternal love as his favoured analogy for the relationship between the teacher and the learner. The image conveys the spontaneous intimacy of the relationship and points to its uniqueness as something that cannot be defined in terms of values, attitudes, beliefs, modes of intention, action or behaviour, being characterised ultimately by its own authentic reality and integrity. It was in this latter sense that he argued that 'education can have no final (i.e. external) end'. 'We are compelled', he writes, 'to study all the conditions which have aided in the coincidence of the tendencies of him who educates, and of him who is being educated; we must define what that freedom is, the absence of which impedes the coincidence of both the tendencies, and which alone serves as our criterion of the whole science of education.'[51] It is significant that another Slavic educator of later years used this same image to convey the integrity and irreducibility of the teacher-learner relationship. Echoing Tolstoy, not only in his use of the maternal analogy, but also in his conception of teaching as a conversational dialogue, the aim of which is the fullest possible degree of understanding between teacher and pupil, Buber also insisted that education could have no end beyond that embraced by the central and all-embracing relationship of teacher and learner. 'The question which is always being brought forward—to where, to what must we educate—misunderstands the situation', he wrote. 'There is not and never has been a norm and fixed maxim of education'. Its ultimate focus, he said, would be the authentic character of the relationship between teacher and pupil—a trusting reciprocation comparable to the loving dialogue between a mother and her child. His words bear a remarkable similarity to those quoted above from Tolstoy's 'On Popular Education':

> The relation in education is one of pure dialogue. I have referred to the child, lying with half-closed eyes waiting for his mother to speak to him. But many children do not need to wait, for they know that they are unceasingly addressed in a dialogue which never breaks off. In face of the lonely night which threatens to invade, they lie preserved and guarded, invulnerable, clad in the silver mail of trust.
>
> Trust, trust in the world, because this human being exists—that is the most inward achievement of the relation in education. Because this human being exists, meaninglessness, however hard pressed you are by it, cannot be the real truth. Because this human being exists, in the darkness the light lies hidden, in fear salvation, and in the callousness of one's fellowmen the great love.
>
> Because this human being exists, therefore he must be really there, really facing the child, not merely there in spirit. He may not let himself be represented by a phantom; the death of the phantom would be a catastrophe for the child's pristine soul. He need possess none of the perfections which the child may dream he possesses, but he must be really there. In order to be and to remain truly present to the child he must have gathered the child's

presence into his own store, as one of the bearers of his communion with the world, one of the focusses of his responsibilities for the world. Of course, he cannot be continually concerned with the child, either in thought or in deed, nor ought he to be. But if he has really gathered the child into his life then that subterranean dialogic, that steady potential presence of the one to the other is established and endures. Then there is reality between them, there is mutuality.[52]

Significantly, Tolstoy, like Buber, saw the relationship as embodying a strong formative influence, by virtue of the greater knowledge and experience that the mother or teacher brings to the quest for mutual understanding and dialogue. Seeing the relationship as a progress towards equality i.e. a transcending of the inequality deriving from the varying degrees of knowledge and experience existing between its participants, he describes the educational dialogue as a process of involuntary formation, conducted in the spirit of reciprocated love. In 'Progress and Education' he writes: 'A mother loves her child, wants to satisfy his wants, and consciously, without the least mystical necessity, feels the need of adapting herself to his incipient reason, to speak the simplest language to him.'[53] But crucially, he adds that this is not a conscious striving after equality, but one conducted in an unselfconsciously generous spirit of interpersonal giving and receiving: 'She does not at all strive after equality with her child, which would be in the highest degree unnnatural, but, on the contrary, intentionally tries to transmit to him the whole of her knowledge.'[54] 'In this natural transmission of the mental acquisitions of one generation to the next lies the progress of education', he writes. Addressing the question, 'why does the teacher teach?' he responds:

> Only that instruction has everywhere and in all ages been regarded as good, in which the pupil becomes completely equal to the teacher—and the more so, the better, and the less, the worse. Precisely the same phenomenon may be observed in literature, in this mediate means of education. We regard only those books as good, in which the author, or educator, transmits all his knowledge to the reader or the learner. Thus, by considering the phenomena of education as a mutual activity of educator and learner, we see that this activity in either case has for its basis one and the same thing—the tendency of man towards equalised knowledge.[55]

It was in the context of an educational process determined not by prescriptive principles, but by the interpersonal integrity of the teacher-learner relationship, that he believed a genuinely individualised pedagogy could be devised. He spoke of the 'injury' done to children by a 'scholastic pedagogy' that denied the teacher the freedom to judge the individual needs of his pupils and to fashion his methods in accordance with those needs. He particularly denounced the stifling of individual initiative which followed from this: 'For the period of several centuries each school has been based on the pattern of another, itself founded on the pattern of the one before it, and in each of these schools the peremptory condition is discipline, which forbids children to speak, ask questions, choose this or that subject of instruction—in short, all measures are taken to deprive the teacher of all possibility of making deductions in regard to the pupils' needs.'[56] Far from disavowing the traditions of effective pedagogy, however—such a position would be entirely inconsistent with the emphasis on the formative role of the teacher conveyed in the maternal analogy—Tolstoy advocated what would nowadays be defined as an eclectic methodology, embracing both exploratory and instructional approaches. 'Experience has convinced us', he writes, 'that there is not one bad and not one good method; that the failure of a method consists in the exclusive adherence to one method, and that the best method is the absence of all method, but the knowledge and use of all methods and the invention of new ones according to the difficulties met with.'[57] The skilful manner in which this ideal of an eclectic methodology was implemented by Tolstoy can be illustrated by this passage on the teaching of reading from his essay, 'On Teaching the Rudiments':

> What then is the best method for teaching the reading of Russian? Neither the newest sound method, nor the oldest of the azes, letter combination and syllabication, nor the method of the vowels, nor Zolotov's method. The best method for a given teacher is the one which is most familiar to the teacher. All other methods, which the teacher will know or invent, must be of help to the instruction which is begun by any one method. In order to discover the one method, we need only know according to what method the people have been studying longest; that method will in its fundamental features be most adapted to the masses. For us it is the method of letters, combinations, syllables—a very imperfect one, like all methods and therefore capable of improvement by means of all inventions, which the new methods offer us.
>
> Every individual must, in order to acquire the art of reading in the shortest possible time, be taught quite apart from any other, and therefore there must be a separate method for each. That which forms an insuperable difficulty for one does not in the least keep back another, and vice versa. One pupil has a good memory, and it is easier for him to memorise the syllables than to comprehend the vowelessness of the consonants; another reflects calmly and will comprehend a most rational sound method; another has a fine instinct, and he grasps the law of word combinations by reading whole words at a time.[58]

A further indication of the highly effective nature of the pedagogy adopted in the schools at Yasnaya Polyana is the manner in which informality and freedom from repressive discipline were combined with highly intensive learning activities, conducted under the close guidance of teachers, and focussed on subject-matter chosen for the intellectually and imaginatively enriching nature of its content. Tolstoy's criticisms of contemporary Russian schools had been directed not only at their tyrannical policies but also at the inefficacy of their teaching methods. He strongly criticised the 1828 Statutes on the grounds that they only required schools to provide 'up to four hours of instruction'. 'I have the boldness to consider myself a good teacher', he writes, 'but if I were given seventy pupils under such conditions I should say in advance that half of them would be unable to read in two years.'[59] He would have favoured a school day that was at least twice as long as that envisaged in the statutes: 'In a sufficiently large number of schools which I know, the children study from eight to nine hours a day, and remain overnight at school so as to be able in the evening once more to recite to the teacher, and neither the parents nor the teachers observe any evil consequences from it'.[60] Thus, his description of a typical school day at Yasnaya Polyana indicates flexibility in time-tabling and a total absence of regimentation, side by side with a carefully planned and intensive sequencing of learning activities, focussed on a traditional subject-centred curriculum:

> The two lower classes meet in one room, while the advanced class goes to the next. The teacher comes, and, in the lowest class, all surround him at the board, or on the benches, or sit or lie on the table about the teacher or one of the reading boys. If it is a writing lesson, they seat themselves in a more orderly way, but they keep getting up, in order to look at the copy-books of the others, and to show theirs to the teacher.
>
> According to the programme, there are to be four lessons before noon, but there sometimes are only three or two, and sometimes there are entirely different subjects. The teacher may begin with arithmetic and pass over to geometry, or he may start on sacred history and end up with grammar. At times the teachers and pupils are so carried away, that instead of one hour, the class lasts three hours. Sometimes the pupils themselves cry: 'More, more!' and scold those who are tired of the subject. 'If you are tired, go to the babies', they will call out contemptuously. All the pupils meet together for the class of religion, which is the only regular class we have, because the teacher lives two versts away and comes only twice a week; they also meet together for the drawing class.[61]

Though he favoured flexibility in pedagogic method and advocated a judicious balancing of expositional and heuristic teaching styles, Tolstoy's descriptions of the work in the schools suggest that the latter was the one that was most commonly employed. Questioning techniques were used constantly to stimulate interest in new subject-matter and the narrative method was similarly employed to foster learning through the process of imaginative evocation that was described in the last section. The teachers were urged to introduce subject-matter if possible in terms of its local or contemporary relevance. This was a particularly favoured method in the teaching of history. In 'The School at Yasnaya Polyana' Tolstoy recalled: 'According to my observation and experience, the first germ of the historic interest makes its appearance as the result of the knowledge of con-temporaneous history, and frequently as the result of a participation in it, through political interest, political opinions, debates, reading of newspapers, and therefore the idea of begining history with the present must naturally present itself to every teacher.'[62] Yet there is evidence of a constant tension for the teachers between the application of heuristic methods and the need to give new ideas, supply new information and provide basic instruction in new subject-content. 'The children and common sense demand of me a certain harmoniousness and regularity of instruction', Tolstoy himself writes in a report on a geography lesson. 'There is left, then, nothing else but to teach geography from Obodovski's textbook or not to teach it at all.'[63] And in this passage he recalls the difficulties that he himself experienced before he learned how to use the Socratic method successfully:

> I involuntarily fell into the habitual error of the Socratic method, which in the German Anschauungsunterricht has reached the highest degree of monstrosity. I did not give the pupils any new ideas in these lessons, thinking all the time that I was giving them, and it was only due to my moral influence that I made the children answer as I pleased. Russia, Russian, remained the same unconscious tones of something hazy and indefinite belonging to them, to us. Law remained the same unintelligible word. I made these experiments about six months ago and at first I was exceedingly well satisfied and proud of them. Those to whom I read them said that it was uncommonly good and interesting; but after three weeks, during which time I was not able to work in the school, I tried to continue what I had begun, and I convinced myself that what I had done before was nonsense and self-deception. Not one pupil was able to tell me what a boundary was, what Russia, what a law was, and what were the boundaries of Krapivensk County. Everything they had learned they had now forgotten,and yet they knew it all in their own fashion. I was convinced of my mistake; but what is not determined by me is whether the mistake consisted in the wrong method of instruction or in the very thought; maybe there is no possibility, up to a certain period of a general development and without the aid of newspapers and travel, of awakening in the child a geographical and historical interest; maybe that method will be found (I am still endeavouring to find it) by means of which it will be possible to do it.[64]

Underlying the experience described here is one of the most fundamental tensions in the activity of teaching: the tension between two distinct but interrelated responsibilities—the one requiring the teacher to respond to the needs of the learner to encounter meaning through the individually focussed processes of enquiry and discovery, the other requiring him to communicate the heritage of knowledge and culture that is necessary for the child's full development and formation. Put more simply, perhaps, it is the tension between the *process* of education and its *content*, between the ways in which the pupil learns and the challenge of the curriculum on which his learning is focussed. While clearly sensitive to the needs of the learner and concerned that his teachers should seek in every way possible to accommodate those needs through their pedagogic practice, Tolstoy was equally conscious of their responsibility to communicate knowledge effectively and to give their pupils the fullest possible access to their cultural heritage. Thus, in 'Education and Culture' he defined education as 'an all-sided and most varied conscious activity directed by one man upon another, *for the purpose of transmitting knowledge*, without compelling the student by direct force or diplomatically to avail himself of that which we want him to avail himself of'.[65] And at the end of 'Progress and Education' he concluded that 'the law of educational progress means only that inasmuch as education is the tendency of people toward an equality of knowledge, this equality cannot be obtained on a lower stage of knowledge, but may be obtained only on a higher stage, for the simple reason that a child may find out what I know, while I cannot forget what I know; and also, because I may be acquainted with the mode of thought of past generations, while past generations cannot know my mode of thought.'[66]

The dilemmas which all this represents are to be seen particularly in his views on the curriculum. On the one hand, his curricular policies were guided by the same liberating principles as those that determined his pedagogic methods. In the same way that he denounced authoritarianism and compulsion in his views on the role of the teacher and the needs of the learner, he emphatically rejected the concept of a set curriculum on the grounds that it denied the freedom of choice which he considered to be a fundamental requirement of the entire process of learning. Thus in his essay, 'On Popular Education'[67] he insisted that the prescriptive criteria by which curricula had traditionally been selected—e.g. historical, philosophical, religious or pragmatic—would not be employed in the schools at Yasnaya Polyana. Such an approach, he argued, would be quite alien to the manner in which children encounter subject-content; it would depersonalise the act of learning by divorcing knowledge from its meaning-giving roots in individual experience. In addition, it would have the further disadvantage of 'setting limits to the subjects of instruction',[68] thus diminishing the pupil's potential for learning by denying him the freedom of enquiry by which this potential is nurtured.

But side by side with all this, Tolstoy insisted on the pupil's right of access to culture in its highest and most accomplished forms. While, for example, he condemned the prescribed curriculum, he still insisted that ultimately decisions on what children were taught would be the decision of the teachers, not the children themselves. And in the primer that he prepared for the education of peasant children he himself exemplified the great wealth of subject-matter that he considered appropriate for this purpose. The *ABC Book*, as we have seen from a previous chapter, included excerpts from Russian, Ukrainian, Greek, Latin, Hebrew, Indian, Arabic, Persian, Chinese and German literature. Following the principle that 'in order that the pupil may study well he must study gladly', Tolstoy provided selections from the finest traditions of world literature and presented them in a manner that made them attractive and comprehensible to simple peasant pupils, thereby justifying his conviction that all children have a right of access to 'high culture' and that this objective can be achieved if certain pedagogic requirements are met. He did not understate the difficulties inherent in this. 'I have for years vainly endeavoured to transmit to the pupils the poetical beauties of Pushkin and of our whole literature . . . I have struggled for years without being able to obtain any results', he exclaimed in one of his essays.[69] But, through patient experiment and the use of a variety of pedagogic strategies, he did succeed to a considerable degree in bridging the huge chasm that exists between popular and sophisticated culture and in cultivating an interest in art, literature and music amongst the peasant children. (This will be discussed in detail in a later chapter.) What needs to be signified at this point is his commitment to teaching a non-prescribed, but nevertheless highly traditionalist, curriculum that would ensure that the children in his schools had access to the full range and wealth of their cultural heritage. In the opening passage from 'The School at Yasnaya Polyana' he describes the curriculum that was taught by all teachers at the school:

> We have no beginners. The lowest class reads, writes, solves problems in the first three arithmetical operations, and reads sacred history, so that the subjects are divided in the programme in the following manner: (1) mechanical and graded reading, (2) writing, (3) penmanship, (4) grammar, (5) sacred history, (6) Russian history, (7) drawing, (8) mechanical drawing, (9) singing, (10) mathematics, (11) talks on the natural sciences (12) religion.[70]

Though he believed that the different sections of the curriculum should be linked—especially in the early years of elementary schooling—Tolstoy was strongly committed nonetheless to maintaining the identity of the different disciplines constituting the curriculum, and to an orderly sequencing of school activities, as is evident from the reports that he published on the work of the schools. In one of these he observes: 'At first it was impossible to subdivide into classes, or subjects, or recess, or lessons, everything naturally blended into one, and all the attempts at separation remained futile. Now we have pupils in the first class who themselves demand that the programme be adhered to.'[71] The reports he cites from the parents of the region indicate not only that he taught an extremely broad and wide-ranging curriculum, but that high levels of attainment were consistently achieved in his schools. These are some examples of the popular impressions of the schools which are cited in 'The School at Yasnaya Polyana':

> The view of the masses as regards our school has much changed from the beginning of its existence. Of the former view we shall have to speak in the history of the Yasnaya Polyana school; but now the people say that in the Yasnaya Polyana school 'they teach everything and all the sciences, and there are some awfully smart teachers there—they say they can make thunder and lightning! And the boys comprehend well—they have begun to read and write.'
>
> Some of them—the rich innkeepers—send their children to school out of vanity 'to promote them into the full science, so that they may know division' (division is the highest conception they have of scholastic wisdom); other fathers assume that science is very profitable; but the most send their children to school unconsciously, submitting to the spirit of the time.
>
> Out of these boys, who form the majority, the most encouraging to us are those who were just sent to school and who have become so fond of study that their parents now submit to the desire of the children, and themselves feel unconsciously that something good is being done to their children and have not the heart to take the children out of school.
>
> One father told me that he once used up a whole candle, holding it over his boy's book, and praised both his son and the book. It was the Gospel.
>
> 'My father', another pupil told me 'now and then listens to a fairy-tale and laughs, and goes away; and if it is something divine, he sits and listens until midnight, holding the candle for me.'
>
> The common opinion is, I think, as follows: They teach everything there (just as to gentlemen's children), many useless things, but they also teach them to read and write in a short time—and so it is alright to send the children there.[72]

The decisive factor, he insisted repeatedly, was the teacher's love for the subject-matter which he taught and the spirit in which his knowledge was transmitted to the pupils. If, he argued, the curriculum were determined prescriptively by the state authorities, it would remain remote from the immediate experience of the individual learner. Conceived, however, within the closeness and immediacy of a trusting relationship, its personal meaningfulness would be assured. We shall see later that he objected in a similar fashion to external controls on matters of religious faith and argued for a churchless spirituality, rooted simultaneously in the traditions of Christianity and in the radical freedom of individual conscience and belief.

Tolstoy's commitment to the view that fruitful and productive learning could be promoted only through caring, encouraging, non-coercive class-room relationships was further manifested in the policies he adopted on matters relating to school discipline and pupil assessment. There were no externally imposed sanctions or punishments of any kind in the schools at Yasnaya Polyana, as might be expected in view of his repeated denunciations of the tyrannical methods generally used to enforce discipline in contemporary Russian schools. He believed that discipline could be maintained normally through the intrinsic motivation of intellectually and imaginatively absorbing classroom activities, and through the full involve-ment of the pupils in the work of the school. More fundamentally, however, he considered that discipline would emerge naturally from the trusting relationships existing between teachers and pupils, and that the ultimate guarantee of good behaviour would be the mutual respect and affection resulting from this. His policies on assessment rested on a similar justification. Basically, the heuristic method of teaching, being heavily dependent on question-response exchanges between teacher and pupil, afforded regular evidence of the progress and attainment of the pupils in Tolstoy's schools, and could probably be regarded as a rudimentary form of continuous, school-based assessment. But this was as far as Tolstoy was prepared to go in the matter of evaluating pupil progress and attainment. Believing that competitiveness was profoundly in conflict with the spirit of true learning, that it was founded on false and highly egocentric forms of motivation, that it undermined the self-confidence of the less able, and generally had a destructive impact on classroom relationships, he con-demned all forms of assessment that were likely to generate rivalry between his pupils. Thus, he recommended that the use of marks and grades be gradually phased out from the work of his schools. 'Marks are left with us from the old order and are beginning to fall into disuse', he wrote, as he advised his teachers to discontinue the practice of grading as soon as they could.[73] But if he was prepared to compromise even temporarily on the issue of grades and marks, his condemnation of examinations was clear and unambiguous, as is evident from these comments on the government's proposal to introduce annual state examinations under the Statutes of 1828:

> The bad and baneful side of the examinations in a popular school must be evident to anybody: they lead to official deceit, forgery, useless mustering of children, and the consequent interruption of the cusomary occupations. The uselessness of these examinations is totally incomprehensible to me. It is injurious by means of examinations to awaken a spirit of rivalry in children eight years old, and it is impossible by means of an examination of two hours' duration to determine the knowledge of eight-year old pupils and to judge of the merits of a teacher.[74]

On all these matters Tolstoy was entirely consistent with his own repeatedly proclaimed objective of promoting teaching and learning in his schools in the spirit of freedom and love. The complexities of this deceptively simple aspiration, and the huge challenges that it entailed for those entrusted with the responsibilities of working in his schools, should be apparent from the foregoing commentary. Exceptionally, amongst nineteenth century educators, he argued for the reconception of all aspects of educational practice and method in the context of mutually caring and enriching relationships between teacher and learner. In his reports on the schools at Yasnaya Polyana he demonstrated the immense difficulties that were involved in implementing these beliefs and the radical character of the changes which they involved in all aspects of schooling. By and large, the reports suggest that he and his teachers were remarkably successful in achieving their goals, albeit for a period of only two years. Tolstoy, though exceptional, was not alone, however, in holding such beliefs. There were other reformers of the period who were similarly concerned to release education from the stranglehold of authoritarian and excessively didactic teaching. One of these, Rousseau, had preceded Tolstoy by some years; two others, Ushinsky and Pestalozzi, were his near contemporaries. Some brief comparisons between Tolstoy's writings and those of these three educators will now be undertaken to provide a more complete picture of the nature and scope of his work and of his standing as an educational reformer.

4   *Tolstoy, Rousseau, Ushinsky & Pestalozzi*

It is inevitable perhaps that Tolstoy should be compared with Rousseau in view of his repeated acknowledgement of the latter's influence on his formation and development. Earlier a Diary entry was cited in which he recorded his youthful passion for Rousseau, especially for the *Confessions* which he read in their entirety while still in his teens. 'I have read the whole of Rousseau', he wrote. 'I was more than enthusiastic about him. I worshipped him'.[75] And in a projected sequel to *Youth* he recalled: 'I will never forget the strong, joyful impression, the contempt for human lies, and the love of truth which Rousseau's *Confessions* made on me.'[76] In later years he wrote with a similar sense of excitement of his admiration for *Emile*, the work of Rousseau's which most directly influenced his writings on education. Methodologically, the work holds much in common with his own writings. Its narrative style and its concrete evocations of the nature of the educational process greatly appealed to him and probably confirmed his dislike for theoretical pedagogics. He shared not only Rousseau's contempt for formal didactics, but his denunciations of authoritarianism and compulsion, his championing of the educational rights of the poor, his commitment to educational democracy, and his belief that in all respects education should seek to foster the spirit of individual freedom.

In general terms, the similarities between the two of them are quite striking. But this conceals considerable differences in their perceptions of both the aims and practicalities of the educational process. Like Rousseau, Tolstoy believed that education should be rooted in individual experience, but it is highly unlikely that he would have approved of the child-indulging manner in which Rousseau conceived of this. It is unlikely, for example, that he would have idolised the state of childhood so euphorically as Rousseau did in this passage from *Emile*: 'Love childhood, indulge its sports, its pleasures, its delightful instincts. Who has not sometimes regretted the age when laughter was ever on the lips, and when the heart was ever at peace? Why rob these innocents of the joys which pass so quickly, of that precious gift which they cannot abuse?'[77] While, again, he would probably have agreed with Rousseau that school learning should emulate the spontaneous modes of learning occurring in everyday life, it is unlikely that he would have gone so far as Rousseau did in seeing the natural environment as the whole focus of the young child's education. He would certainly have applauded Rousseau's assertion that 'the art of teaching consists in making the pupil wish to learn',[78] and that 'education is a matter of guidance rather than instruction'.[79] He would not, however—as should be clear from the views cited earlier on the school curriculum—have given the same emphasis as Rousseau did to 'learning by doing', and he clearly envisaged a far more prominent role for book-learning for his own pupils than Rousseau did for Emile. And though he might have agreed with Rousseau's views on the contaminating impact that social institutions could have on the life of a young child—his own condemnations of Church and state would strongly suggest this to be the case—he would certainly not have isolated the child from these institutions in the manner that Rousseau advocated in *Emile*.

Whatever the similarities in their treatment of certain aspects of teaching and learning, there are fundamental differences between Tolstoy and

Rousseau on the ultimate purposes and goals of education. For Tolstoy the primary responsibility of the educator was the fostering of the spirit of love, and this he interpreted in terms of the wholly altruistic and self-sacrificing ideals put forward in the Christian scriptures. The values informing his entire vision of education were those of New Testament Christianity, especially those conveyed in the Sermon on the Mount, and he argued that all the resources of the educational process should be used to promote them. There is no such commitment to the promotion of Christian values in Rousseau. The sentiments conveyed, for example, in this passage from *Emile* are directly in conflict with the Christian ideal of service advocated in the Sermon on the Mount: 'Love of self is always right, always beneficial. As every individual is especially charged with his own preservation, his first and greatest anxiety is and ought to be to watch over it continually, and how could he do this well if it were not his chief interest.'[80] It would be difficult to imagine Tolstoy writing a passage such as this. The self-centred values that it describes directly contravene the fundamentally other-directed character of the Christian ideals that dominated all his writings— autobiographical, fictional and educational—from the 1840s until his death in 1910.

Some commentators have seen links between Tolstoy's Christian beliefs and those advocated by the Savoyard priest in *Emile*.[81] A Diary entry for 1855 provides some support for this. 'Read *Profession de foi d'un Vicaire Savoyard* and as always when reading it, it provided an immensity of useful and noble thoughts in me',[82] the entry said. But this can be taken to indicate little more than an entirely predictable admiration on Tolstoy's part for the unconventional faith of the priest and for his courage in distancing himself from the corruptions of institutional religion. The faith of the priest, like that of Rousseau himself, owed far more to the rationalism of the Deist tradition than it did to the Christian scriptures, whereas Tolstoy's faith was based entirely on these scriptures and they provided the basic content for much of the education that was offered in his schools. By comparison, there is no suggestion whatever that the scriptures be used in the education of the young Emile.

The differences between Tolstoy and Rousseau on matters of religious faith are further manifested in their treatment of the whole sphere of moral education. Rousseau's doctrine of natural goodness is the basis of his thinking on moral issues, and the kind of education he proposed for Emile consisted essentially in awakening all the propensities towards goodness he believed to be inherent in his nature. Tolstoy, to judge from the evidence of his writings, would not have endorsed this assumption of the intrinsic goodness of nature, nor would he have supported the view that this could be fostered through contact with the 'natural' environment, in isolation from the corruptions of society. Though his sense of the potential for evil in man is not explicitly emphasised in his pedagogic writings, it is of course powerfully conveyed in his treatment of the themes of guilt and repentance in all the major novels and forms an essential element in the broader vision that permeates his entire view of education. That became especially evident in the crusades he launched in later years to re-educate the masses on the evils of materialism, violence and greed, and to foster the Christian ideals of justice, self-sacrifice and brotherhood.

These differences on the ethico-religious aims of education are paralleled by further differences on the kind of curriculum that each believed children should be taught. Rousseau argued that book learning should have no place in the years of elementary education, and Emile did not encounter books until he reached adolescence, sometime between the ages of 12 and 15. Believing that the special modes of thought that are peculiar to childhood need to be sustained exclusively through playful activities of a purely 'natural' or non-formal character, he warned of the dangers of an education based on scholastic learning. 'Give your scholar no verbal lessons', he wrote. 'He should be taught by experience alone. Reading is the curse of childhood. . . . When I thus get rid of children's lessons I get rid of the chief cause of their sorrow.'[83] Just as it would be difficult to imagine Tolstoy declaring that 'love of self is always right', it seems highly improbable that he would ever have described reading as 'the curse of childhood'. On the contrary, the greater part of the curriculum that was taught at Yasnaya Polyana was based on book learning, and most of the schools' activities were centred on reading and writing or closely related activities. Unlike Rousseau, he believed profoundly in the responsibility of the teacher to introduce the child to the full riches of the cultural heritage, and argued vigorously for the highly traditionalist curriculum that would be needed to achieve this.

In Rousseau, therefore, we witness the extremes of a learner centred view of education, while in Tolstoy we see a careful and meticulously sustained balancing of learner-centred and curriculum-centred ideals. Those differences are rooted, in turn, in two widely diverging views of the aims and purposes of the entire process of education. Though both men believed passionately in the liberating potential of education, and though both were firmly committed to promoting more humane and more caring relationships than existed in the conventional institutions of schooling in their time, they differed greatly on the fundamental objectives of the whole process. Rousseau's belief in education as simply the 'cultivation of natural tendencies' contrasts sharply with Tolstoy's vision of a formative development of religious, moral, aesthetic, cognitive and physical potentialities under the firm but caring guidance of a teacher, committed to transmitting a substantial body of knowledge and a heritage of traditional values and beliefs.

Comparisons between Tolstoy and his fellow-countryman, Konstantin Ushinsky, are more fruitful in some respects. A democrat, appalled at the socially discriminatory policies of Nicholas I, Ushinsky fully shared Tolstoy's abhorrence of the inequities and injustices of the Tsarist education system. Before the Emacipation Act he too had written extensively on the moral, social and economic evils of serfdom, and had bitterly denounced the exclusion of the serf and peasant classes from the schools. Like Tolstoy, he further condemned the excessive bureaucratisation of education in the state regulated system, which he had witnessed first-hand in his work as an inspector of schools. 'Having taken this road it must even be explained how one must write, whether with a slate-pencil or with a pen, with a quill or with a steel pen-nib, with or without lines, from copybooks or without models', he wrote satirically in one of his journal articles.[84] He shared much of Tolstoy's suspicion of foreign influences on Russian education and condemned Russian educators for their uncritical adoption of West European models for school curricula, with their preponderant emphasis on the teaching of classical languages. In an article praising the policies of N.I. Pirogov, the Minister of Public Instruction, he wrote: 'When we take the trouble to extract the basic idea on which the public education of one or another country of Western Europe rests, we would find that more than anything else the educational ideas of every people are permeated with the national spirit, permeated to such an extent that to even consider transferring them to an alien soil would be out of the question, and then we would not wonder why in transferring these ideas to us we bring only their dead form, their lifeless corpse, and not their living and vivifying content.'[85] Judging from the sentiments expressed in several of the articles from his pedagogic journal, this was a view which Tolstoy would have unreservedly endorsed.

Interestingly, Ushinsky took a median position on the progressive/traditionalist controversy that resembles the one taken by Tolstoy quite closely. He too condemned the excesses of authoritarian didactics. 'There is no doubt', he wrote, 'that the old scholastic method of teaching had a disastrous effect on the mind; the reason for that, however, lay not in the seriousness of the lesson but in its inanity.'[86] But he also condemned the naivete and spurious liberalism of the 'child centred' movement. 'If grinding away over prayerbook and psaltery were really harmful to mental development', he declared, 'the facetious pedagogics, by amusing children destroys a person's character in the very bud.'[87] Though he placed less emphasis than Tolstoy did on the freedom of individual enquiry, his concept of learning as 'work full of meaning' corresponded with much of what the latter described in the reports of school activities at Yasnaya Polyana. 'Learning', Ushinsky declared, 'is work, and should remain work, but work full of meaning, so that the interest itself of learning depends on serious thought and not on embellishments of some sort that have nothing to do with the matter.'[88] Significantly, both Tolstoy and Ushinsky sought to advance this ideal of guided or teacher-stimulated learning by producing textbooks that attracted an extremely wide readership throughout the Russian Empire. Ushinsky's *Children's World* was published the same year as Tolstoy embarked on his major schooling initiatives at Yasnaya Polyana, and it remained a popular text with elementary schools for many years. A companion text, *Native Language*, went into 137 editions and remained in circulation until 1908, surpassing even the huge sales of Tolstoy's *ABC Book*. (The fact that both texts were banned by the authorities—*Children's World* in 1867 and *Native Language* in 1885—did little to diminish their popularity.)[89]

There are definite parallels between Tolstoy's and Ushinsky's ideas on matters such as motivation, interest and attention, the importance of individual experience, the role of the environment, and the centrality of imagination in all modes of learning. Ushinsky's distinction, for example, between the active and the passive imagination finds strong echoes in Tolstoy, as does his linking of attention with interest in *Man as the Subject of Education*, where one of the factors identified as being necessary to sustain attention is 'the interestingness of the teaching'.[90]

Again his distinction between extrinsic and intrinsic interest corresponds with much of Tolstoy's thinking on this issue. The use of narrative, which he advocates as an extrinsic method of awakening interest, and the fostering of intrinsic interest through direct questioning, for example, were precisely the methods used in the schools at Yasnaya Polyana. Both men recognised the crucial importance of vernacular literacy and both attached great importance to the fostering of literacy through access to the indigenous cultural heritage. 'A nation's language is the flower of all its spiritual life and the means of penetrating the character of its people',[91] Ushinsky declared in an article where he argued that mastery of the mother-tongue was the key to the realisation of the democratic ideal of universal educability. His description in the same article of the ways in which the teaching of reading and writing could be linked with nature study has much in common with Tolstoy's ideas on the subject.

For all the similarity between Tolstoy and Ushinsky on each of these issues, there are fundamental differences between them, both in the methodology of their educational writings and in their conception of the ultimate goals of education. Tolstoy's method was based, as has been said, on direct and immediate observation of the ways in which children learn, and of the ways in which the teacher can guide and fashion the learning process. There is a good deal of this kind of basic empiric observation in Ushinsky also, but his major works unquestioningly belong in the realm of theoretical pedagogics and employ the kind of methodology which Tolstoy had condemned so vociferously in his essay, 'On Popular Education'. This applies especially to his mammoth study, *Pedagogic Anthropology*, where he drew heavily on the 'anthropological sciences'—anatomy, physiology, pathology, psychology, logic, philosophy, geography, statistics, political economy—to construct a body of educational theory which Tolstoy would have rejected not only for its 'faculty' view of the mind, but for the generalised and abstract character of most of its content. It is on the ultimate purpose they envisage for education, however, that Tolstoy and Ushinsky diverge most fundamentally. A profoundly moralistic thinker in certain respects, Ushinsky spoke of the necessity for self-discipline to achieve the ultimate goals of life. 'Every free and conscious human activity presupposes a goal', he wrote. 'In itself the goal is even more necessary to man than its attainment.' 'If you want to make a man thoroughly and profoundly un-happy, deprive him of an end in life and instantly satisfy his every desire', he warned.[92] The goal he envisaged, however, was one that was inherently humanist and rational. 'It is his mental state, which does not depend on pleasure and is not subordinated to a striving after it, which is man's normal state and his greatest happiness', he wrote. This happiness, he argued, lies not in the attainment—which may be beyond man's reach—but in the constant striving for the fulfilment of this goal. 'Why', he asks, 'is an end so important in man's life?' 'Precisely because it rouses the mind to activity, to conscious free activity, i.e, stimulates the mind to work. In that way and from that point of view we conclude', he says, 'that conscious free labour alone is capable of constituting the happiness of man, and that pleasure is only a side effect accompanying it.'[93] It should not be necessary, at this stage, to dwell on the vast and unbridgeable gulf that exists between this severely rationalist, but also vague and unspecified, conception of the goals of human existence and the vision of fulfilment through the limitless potentiality of love that is proclaimed throughout Tolstoy's fictional and educational writings.

Turning to the Swiss educator, Jean Heinrich Pestalozzi, one finds a good deal of common ground with Tolstoy once again on the need both to provide for the education of the poor and the destitute and to develop more humani-tarian approaches to education than those generally existing in the early years of the nineteenth century. Acutely aware of the serf-like conditions in which the majority of the Swiss peasant classes were living, Pestalozzi sought to develop a system of popular schools to make some basic provision for their needs. Education, he declared, 'must embrace all mankind, it must be applicable to all without distinction of zones or nations in which they may be born. It must acknowledge the rights of man in the fullest sense of the word . . . and embrace the rightful claims of all classes to a general diffusion of useful knowledge, a careful development of the intellect, and judicious attention to all the faculties of man—physical, intellectual and moral.'[94] The various ventures on which he embarked—the Stanz reform school for the destitute, the experiments at Burgdorf and Yverdun, the projects at Clindy and Neuhof which he initiated when he was over seventy years old to cater for the poor children of those regions—were all motivated by the kind of ideals that are described in this letter. Seeing the denial of elementary education to the great masses of the poor as an intolerable outrage, he dedicated himself not only to rectifying this in every way that he could, but to ensuring that the kind of education provided was inspired by a humane pedagogy that contrasted sharply with the kind which was generally practised in the conventional schools of the time—all of which indicates strong parallels with Tolstoy's educational activities and the ideas and policies underlying them.

The closeness of Pestalozzi's ideals to those of Tolstoy is particularly exemplified by their common use of the maternal image to intimate the trust and loving mutuality of a genuine teacher-learner relationship. Reference was made earlier to Tolstoy's use of this image in the essays from his pedagogic journal, and to the ways in which it inspired the work of the schools at Yasnaya Polyana. Much of what he wrote had been anticipated by Pestalozzi in *Leonard and Gertrude* and *How Gertrude Teaches Her Children*. In both works a fictional mother—generally thought to have been inspired by Pestalozzi's real-life mother, whom he idolised from infancy— is his exemplar for the caring, unsentimental, efficient and resourceful teacher whose influence and moral authority derives from her firm but affectionate exercise of her responsibilities. 'She never adopted the tone of instructor toward her children', he wrote, but sought to develop their moral and intellectual abilities through 'example and guidance given in the spirit of maternal love.'[95] He urged educators to emulate her methods in their schools: 'Here you must not trust nature; you must do all in your power', he said, 'to supply the place of her guidance by the wisdom of experience.'[96] Moral education, he suggested, should be conducted through example, not through homilies and sermons. 'Words alone cannot give a real knowledge of things', he wrote. 'The school ought to stand in closest connection with the life of the home. . . . Home is the great school of character and of citizenship.'[97] The teacher, he declared, should emulate the mother who inspires love of neighbour and virtuous action through the direct witness of her own life. Pestalozzi attested directly to this belief when he organised his first school for waifs and orphans in his own home—as Tolstoy did in *his* own home at Yasnaya Polyana—and there pioneered the methods of elementary teaching which eventually attracted the attention of educators from all over Europe.

Pestalozzi and Tolstoy both believed that all education—not only its moral and character-forming aspects—should be modelled on the informal learning of the home, and both emphasised the need to relate the formal modes of learning occurring in the school to the informal modes occurring in everyday life. That commitment to the unitary character of the act of learning was greatly strengthened by their common belief in the harmonising power of religious faith, and in its potential as a focus for the integration of all facets of school learning. Though he would almost certainly have disapproved of the denominational character of Pestalozzi's Christianity—and would probably have seen some sinister links between his Protestantism and the rationalism of the Enlightenment—Tolstoy would probably have endorsed sentiments such as the following, which reflect the all-embracing character of Pestalozzi's faith: 'The aim of all instruction is, and can be, nothing but the development of human nature by the harmonious cultivation of its powers and talents. . . . These powers must be so cultivated that no one shall predominate at the expense of another, but each be excited to the true standard of activity; and this standard is the spiritual nature of man.'[98] He would also have endorsed the emphasis given to vernacular literacy by Pestalozzi and his sense of its importance as the key to meaningful learning. The balance of whole word and phonic instruction that the latter advocated in his schools closely parallels the methods advocated by Tolstoy for his own pupils. Indeed the curriculum taught by Pestalozzi—its basic constituents were reading, writing, arithmetic, music, drawing, history, science and nature study—coincides quite closely with the one that was taught at the Yasnaya Polyana schools. The freedom that Pestalozzi allowed in his schools, the flexibility he permitted in time-tabling, his conduct of lessons from early morning until late in the evening, the organised recreational activities that he encouraged on Sundays—all suggest strong similarities with the Tolstoyan schools.

Yet a deep divergence becomes evident in their conception of one of the most basic principles of learning: the need to relate it directly to the individual experience of the pupil. Tolstoy developed his views on this whole matter on the basis of direct observations of children, both in the schools he visited in his travels throughout Europe and in his own schools at Yasnaya Polyana. The claims he made for his pedagogic methods were based mainly on the fact that they were drawn from direct experience rather than the abstractions of theoretical pedagogics or philosophy. Pestalozzi's ideas on the nature of learning were drawn mainly, however, from Kantian philosophic theory and were to provide the basis for greater philosophic elaboration subsequently by Herbart and Fichte. In *How Gertrude Teaches her Children* he explicitly related the crucial concept of *Anschauung* to Kant's classification of the categories of space and time. 'The relation and proportion of number and form constitute the natural measure of all these impressions which the mind receives from without', he wrote. 'They are the measures and comprehend the qualities of the material world, form being the measure of space and number the measure of time.'[99] On this conception of objective reality as consisting of three main properties—form, number and name—he based the rudimentary principle of naming the objects of reality on which his ideal of 'learning through experience' is founded. The child would be trained to observe the types of objects identified by his senses, to observe their form, their number and their names. All instruction was to proceed from these three elementary activities. 'We should cultivate them with the strictest psychological technique of instruction, endeavour to strengthen and make them strong and to bring them, as a means of development and culture, to the highest pitch of simplicity, consistency and harmony', he declared.[100]

This highly systematic, philosophically determined pedagogy was far removed from the simple and flexible methodology that Tolstoy reported from the schools at Yasnaya Polyana. Yet it was concerned with the same objectives as Tolstoy proclaimed in his own writings, its main function being the ordering and enrichment of immediate experience and its direct realisation in the form of concrete, individually meaningful, empirically rooted knowledge. It seems probable, however, that apart from its abstract philosophical character, that Tolstoy would also have rejected its all-embracing status as the foundation on which all the learning was planned in Pestalozzi's schools. Additionally, the highly systematic manner in which Pestalozzi urged his teachers to plan the content of their lessons around the central principle of object-naming would have been far too contrived and prescriptive an approach for Tolstoy.

Each of these four educators, therefore, while united in some of their foremost objectives, presented quite distinctive ideas on how these should be achieved. They are distinguished, in a fundamental way, by the methodology of their educational writings, the formal, analytic style of Ushinsky and the philosophically-inspired methods of Pestalozzi contrasting radically with the narrative-evocative, almost intuitional, modes of Rousseau and Tolstoy. They are further distinguished by the ultimate goals they defined for the whole process of education, the religious and spiritual ideals that inspired the writings of Tolstoy and Pestalozzi differing even more radically from the rational-humanist ideals proclaimed by Rousseau and Ushinsky. Yet they are united by their common assertion of the right of all children to be given access to education as a basic entitlement. Seeing the deep injustices of contemporary educational policies, and the impoverishment of the masses resulting from the denial of their right to the fulfilment of their most basic potentialities, they sought to engender more enlightened attitudes on these issues amongst all those responsible for providing their education. Secondly, all four of them vehemently denounced the coercive practices that were current in school classrooms at the time and exposed the inhumanity and cruelty that resulted from these. The gradual liberation of education from the tyranny of authoritarian teaching was greatly assisted by their writings, though this process was not generally to reach fulfilment until well into the present century. Thirdly, all four of them refocussed pedagogic method and practice to take account of the individuality of the learner. In some instances this was to lead to a profound enrichment of the whole process of education; in others it was to lead to a sentimentalised misconception of individual freedom that proved to be ultimately detrimental to the needs of those it purported to serve.

Aesthetic Education: Fostering Imaginative Potential

1 Basic Principles of Tolstoy's Aesthetics

'The whole business of my life', Tolstoy wrote in a Diary entry for April, 1885, 'is the awareness of and expression of truth'. 'Unfortunately for me', he added, 'it's a slippery and deceptive path.'[1] Some time later in a further Diary entry we find him again proclaiming his belief that the primary responsibility of the artist is the revelation of truth, but this time insisting that the quest for truth is to be equated with the quest for faith. 'Art', he wrote, 'is only true art when the inner striving coincides with the awareness of fulfilling the work of God.' 'It is possible', he said, 'to strive to express what interests one but is not needed by God, and it is possible to strive by a work of art to assist the work of God, but without the inner striving towards it, it will not be art'.[2] Critical reception of Tolstoy's work indicates how closely he was guided by these convictions, and how fully he achieved the conjuncture of art and experience which they demanded. John Bayley, for example, in *Tolstoy and the Novel*, spoke of the remarkable degree of 'self-sufficiency' that is evident in his work. 'This sense of Tolstoy *being* the great world he writes about, must have struck every reader of his novels',[3] he says. Contrasting him with Dostoevsky, he sees the latter's fictional world as being characterised by dualism and self-confict, mirroring the ambiguities and contradictions in the mind of its creator, while Tolstoy's characters, he says, directly and unambiguously project the religious vision that informed all his works—at least from the time he wrote *War and Peace* until he completed, *Resurrection*, his last great work of fiction, nearly forty years later. For Tolstoy, he declares, the creation of a character was not a 'controlled shaping of abstract material' but a 'process of recognition', a recognition of his own self in the world of image and symbol, in the wholeness and harmony of artistic form.[4] The consciousness and inwardness of his faith finds complete consistency with the form of the art through which it finds expression.

This position is confirmed in several other studies of Tolstoy's work. 'In few writers', T.G. Cain said, 'is the greatness of the art so closely related to what may reasonably be called the greatness of the life, the intense spiritual struggles, the doubts, desires and vicissitudes of the man himself'.[5] What Tolstoy communicates, he says, is his belief in the existence of eternal values, the unity of his life and work being informed primarily by his continuing awareness of those values.Technically speaking, that unity is manifested most visibly, he claims, in the total integration of the themes of his novels with the lives of their major personae, most of whom were direct projections of Tolstoy himself. 'The generalised theme, whether it is family happiness, the sources of spiritual regeneration, even the nature of war, finds its convincing realisation only through the experience of his fictional protagonists',[6] he writes. All the major personae become projections of Tolstoy's own inner vision, all embody the search for spiritual fulfilment in which he was engaged throughout the greater part of his life. 'Such was the many-sided quality of Tolstoy's character', he concludes, 'such was the honesty and thoroughness of his search for the answers to those fundamental problems which continued to trouble him, that the ideal form for him was an expansive one in which as omniscient narrator he could project not one but many facets of his protean character, without having to commit himself finally to any one of them.'[7]

All the major characters, therefore—Pierre, Prince Andrew, Natasha, Levin, Maslova and Nekhlyudov—embody not only the major themes of the novels they inhabit, but closely reflect the personal quest for truth and spiritual self-fulfilment in which Tolstoy himself was engaged. The themes of the great novels, in turn, closely foreshadow the themes of his social and religious writings, particularly the more explicitly autobiographical works such as *A Confession, What I Believe, The Kingdom of God Is Within You* and *The Law of Violence and the Law of Love*. All their themes are closely intertwined and all proceed towards a decisive affirmation of the ultimate potency of faith and its transcendence of the conflicts of the finite, the conditioned and the temporal. It is this inner certainty that all the conflicts and insecurities of the finite and the temporal are finally resolved through faith that ultimately explains the close integration that Tolstoy effected between all the modes in which he sought to reveal himself—between his fictional, autobiographical, social and educational writings. In all of them he sought to fulfil the purpose he had defined for himself in the Diary entries cited earlier—all were designed to reveal the 'inner strivings which coincide with an awareness of fulfilling the works of God'.

That this was the conviction particularly informing his artistic activities is made evident in several works which define the principles of his aesthetic philosophy. In a preface entitled 'On Truth in Art', which he wrote as an introduction to a collection of children's stories, he began his exposition of the concept of art as a revelation of truth with the words of St. Matthew's Gospel: 'Out of the abundance of the heart the mouth speaketh. . . for by thy words thou shalt be justified and by thy words thou shalt be condemned.'[8] Emphasising the ultimately religious character of all truth, he declared: 'In order that there may be truth in what one describes it is necessary not to write about what is, but about what should be, to write not the truth of what is, but about the Kingom of God which is drawing nigh unto us but is not as yet.'[9] (It is significant in the context of the present study that these comments were made by way of an introduction to a work intended for use as an educational text.) The preface continues:

> Truth will be known not by him who knows only what has been, and really happens, but by him who recognises what should be according to the will of God. He does not write the truth who describes only what has happened and what this or that man has done, but he who shows what people do that is right—that is, in accord with God's will; and what people do wrong—that is contrary to God's will.
>
> Truth is a path. Christ said, 'I am the way, the truth and the life.'
>
> And he who looks down at his feet will not know the truth, but he who discerns by the sun which way to go.
>
> Verbal compositions are good and necessary, not when they describe what has happened, but when they show what ought to be; not when they tell what people have done, but when they set a value on good and evil—when they show men the narrow path of God's will, which leads to life.[10]

Taken too literally, these words might suggest an almost evangelical function for art, though even a cursory reading of Tolstoy's fiction would immediately make nonsense of such an assumption. What he seems to suggest is that an awareness of the presence of God in the universe is necessary for a complete sense of its existential reality. The stories he was introducing would be fully true, he said, if 'there was in them the truth of the kingdom of God'.[11] A complete image of reality, in other words, would have to include a sense of the religious truths which make it wholly meaningful. By this conception, art is seen as necessarily involved in the revelation of truths which belong ultimately in the realm of the religious and the spiritual.

Looking more specifically at the nature of art in his long essay, 'What Is Art?' he first addresses the question: what differentiates art from non-art. He considers three possible responses to this question: firstly, that art is distinguished from other modes of expression by the quality of its content; secondly, that its essence lies in the beauty of its formal and technical aspects; and thirdly, that its distictiveness consists in the exactness and precision of its representations of reality. These three viewpoints are developed further in this passage from the essay:

> One theory—which its opponents call 'tendencious'—says that the essence
> of true art lies in the importance of the subject treated of; that for art to be
> art, it is necessary that its content should be something important, necessary
> to man, good, moral and instructive.
>
> According to that theory the artist—that is to say the man who possesses
> a certain skill—by taking the most important theme which interests society
> at the time, can, by clothing it in what looks like artistic form, produce a work
> of true art. . . .
>
> Another theory, which calls itself 'aesthetic' or 'art for art's sake', holds
> that the essence of true art lies in the beauty of its form; that for art to be true,
> it is necessary that what it presents should be beautiful. . . .
>
> A third theory—which calls itself 'realistic'—says that the essence of art
> consists in the truthful, exact, presentation of reality; that for art to be true it
> is necessary that it should depict life as it really is.[12]

All three, however, are rejected as not adequately defining the boundary
between art and non-art. Art, he argues, is not defined by the importance or
seriousness of its content, since this may still be represented insincerely,
obscurely or inartistically. Neither is it defined by beauty of form, since this
might be used to express content which is 'insignificant or harmful'; nor is
it a matter of the realism which which it reflects reality, as this might be
inartistic or imaginatively unstimulating. The special gift of the artist, he
says, is to bring what was formerly unperceived to such a degree of clearness
that it becomes comprehensible to all. 'Artistic creation', he writes, 'is such
mental activity as brings dimly perceived feelings (or thoughts) to such a
degree of clearness that these thoughts are transmitted to other people.'[13]
And stressing the universality of the aesthetic—an emphasis which we shall
see has some crucial implications for education—he insists it is 'common
to all men and therefore known to each of us by inner experience'. He
continues:

> It is in this that the activity of an artist consists; and to this activity is related
> the feeling of the recipient. This feeling has its source in imitativeness, or
> rather in a capacity to be infected, and in a certain hypnotism—that is to say,
> in the fact that the artist's stress of spirit elucidating to himself the subject
> that had been doubtful to him, communicates itself, through the artistic
> production, to the recipients. A work of art is then finished when it has been
> brought to such clearness that it communicates itself to others and evokes in
> them the same feeling that the artist experienced while creating it.
>
> What was formerly unperceived, unfelt and uncomprehended by them, is
> by intensity of feeling brought to such a degree of clearness that it becomes
> acceptable to all, and the production is a work of art. The satisfaction of the

intense feeling of the artist who has achieved his aim gives pleasure to him. Participation in this same stress of feeling and in its satisfaction, a yielding to this feeling, the imitation of it and infection by it (as by a yawn), the experiencing in brief moments what the artist has lived through while creating his work, is the enjoyment those who assimilate a work of art can obtain.

Such in my opinion is the peculiarity that distinguishes art from any other activity.[14]

The assertion in this passage that art is primarily an act of communicating newness of meaning is subject, however, to three further qualifications. What the work of art reveals must, firstly, he says, be of 'importance to mankind'; secondly, it must be expressed so clearly and intelligibly that its meaning becomes accessible to all, and thirdly, it must be inspired by an 'inner need' in the mind of its author. A work in which these criteria are satisfied 'even to a slight degree' will be a work of art, he declares; a production from which even one of them is absent cannot be described as art.[15]

The requirement that what art reveals must be of 'importance to mankind' is interpreted by Tolstoy in terms of the moral significance of its content. 'The highest limit of content is such as is always necessary to all', he writes. And he adds: 'That which is always necessary to all men is what is good or moral.' The criterion of accessibiliy is further explained in the following terms: 'The highest limit of expression will be such as is always intelligible to all men. . . . What is intelligible is that which has nothing in it that is obscure, superfluous or indefinite, but only what is clear, concise and definite—what is called beautiful.' And thirdly, the work of art will be sincere, he writes, insofar as it 'evokes in all men an impression of reality, not so much of what exists, as of what goes on in the soul of the artist'. Its truth will consist in the author's fidelity to his subject, not in its supposed objectivity or representational accuracy. By this conception, therefore, the work of art combines the three classic elements of the scholastic tradition— the good (*bonum*), the beautiful (*pulchrum*) and the true (*verum*):

> A perfect work of art will be one in which the content is important and significant to all men, and therefore it will be *moral*. The expression will be quite clear, intelligible to all, and therefore *beautiful*; the author's relation to his work will be altogether sincere and heartfelt, and therefore *true*. Imperfect works, but still works of art, will be such productions as satisfy all three conditions though it be but in unequal degree. That alone wll be no work of art, in which either the content is quite insignificant and unnecessary to man, or the expression quite unintelligible, or the relation of the author to the work quite insincere. In the degree of perfection attained in each of these respects

lies the difference in quality betwen all true works of art. Sometimes the first predominates, sometimes the second, sometimes the third.[16]

Since he believed that the ultimate meaning of life is disclosed through faith and through the infinite potency of love, it was entirely consistent that Tolstoy should argue that a sincere vision of reality must also comprehend its religious significance. 'The purpose of human life is the brotherly union of man', he writes in the opening sentence of the eighteenth chapter of *What is Art?* When he adds the injunction that 'art must also be guided by this perception',[17] he points not only to the artist's responsibility to reaffirm the ideals of fellowship and brotherhood—ideals that are inherent in the very nature of humanity itself—but to define the significance of the traditions by which those ideals have been conveyed. What he envisages here is a crucial function of critical and independent witnessing by the artist to the traditions of religious truth. Reiterating his claim that the message of the Gospels has been corrupted and distorted by the Churches through the centuries, he argues that the function of the artist is to proclaim this message in its original, uncorrupted and undiluted form. Amongst his contemporaries he singles out Dickens, Hugo and Dostoevsky in literature, and Millet, Bastien Lepage, Breton and Lhermitte in painting, as authentically fulfilling this role:

> During the present century works of the higher kind of religious art, per-
> meated by a truly Christian spirit, have appeared more and more frequently
> both in literature and in painting, as also works of the universal art of common
> life accessible to all. So that even art knows the true ideal of our times and
> tends towards it. On the one hand the best works of art of our time transmit
> religious feelings urging towards the union and brotherhood of man (such are
> the works of Dickens, Hugo, Dostoevsky; and in painting, Millet, Bastien
> Lepage, Jules Breton, Lhermitte, and others); on the other hand they strive
> towards the transmission, not of feelings which are natural to people of the
> upper classes only, but of feelings that may unite everyone without exception.
> There are as yet few such works, but the need of them is already
> acknowledged. In recent times we also meet more and more frequently with
> attempts at publications, pictures, concerts, and theatres, for the people. All
> of this is still very far from accomplishing what should be done, but the
> direction in which good art instinctively presses forward to regain the path
> natural to it, can already be discerned.
>
>   The religious perception of our time—which consists in acknowledging
> that the aim of life (both collective and individual) is the union of man-
> kind—is already so sufficiently distinct that people have now only to reject
> the false theory of beauty—according to which enjoyment is considered to
> be the purpose of art—and religious perception will naturally take its place
> as the guide of the art of our time.[18]

Another of Tolstoy's contemporaries, who is not listed in this passage, proclaimed a similar vision in the following words: 'When religious forms become artificial then it is up to art to rescue the quintessence of religion'.[19] That quintessential meaning Tolstoy—like Wagner—conceived as the inner striving towards brotherhood and fellowship that lies inherent in the nature of humankind. To the extent that artists in every period of time give expression to this striving, they can be said to reflect the deepest religious aspirations of their age. In this eloquent passage from *What Is Art?* he explains how the artist creates new and endlessly meaningful images for this striving towards love and brotherhood—a striving which has its proto-typical models in the images of the Christian scriptures:

> To people of our circle who do not know, and cannot or will not understand, the feelings which will form the subject-matter of the art of the future, such subject-matter appears very poor in comparison with those subtleties of exclusive art with which they are now occupied. 'What is there fresh to be said about the Christian feeling of love to one's fellow-man?' 'The feelings common to everyone are so insignificant and monotonous', they think. And yet in our time the really fresh feelings can only be religious, Christian feelings, and such as are open and accessible to all. The feelings flowing from the religious perceptions of our times, Christian feelings, are infinitely new and varied, only not in the way some people imagine—not because they can be evoked by depicting Christ and Gospel episodes, or by repeating in new forms the Christian truths of unity, brotherhod, equality and love—but because all the oldest, commonest, and most hackneyed phenomena of life evoke the newest, most unexpected and poignant emotions as soon as a man regards them from the Christian point of view.[20]

Art, he further explains, is a 'vehicle wherewith to transmit religious, Christian perception from the realm of reason and intellect into that of feeling'.[21] It aims to 'draw people in actual life nearer to the perfection indicated to them by their religious perception'. And here a vital conjuncture is established—one which is full of implications for education, especially in the sphere of cultural literacy, as will shown in the next section. An art which proclaims the union and brotherhood of all men must, by definition, be intelligible and meaningful to *all* men. 'As soon as the religious per-ception, which already unconsciously directs the life of man, is consciously acknowledged, then', he writes, 'immediately and naturally the division of art into art for the lower and art for the upper classes will disappear.' 'There will', he declares, 'be one common, brotherly universal art.' He foresees the maturity of art as lying, therefore, in its potential to reveal the universally held beliefs and religious aspirations of the masses:

> Art of the future, that is to say, such part of art as will be chosen from among

all the art diffused among mankind, will consist not in transmitting feelings accessible only to members of the rich classes, as is the case to-day, but in transmitting feelings embodying the highest religious perceptions of our time. Only those productions will be esteemed art which transmit feelings drawing men together in brotherly union, or such universal feelings as can unite all men. Only such art will be chosen, tolerated, approved and diffused. But art transmitting feelings flowing from antiquated, outworn religious teaching; ecclesiastical art, patriotic art, voluptuous art; transmitting feelings of superstitious fear, of pride, of vanity, of ecstatic admiration of national heroes; art exciting exclusive love of one's own people, or sensuality, will be considered bad, harmful art, and will be censured and despised by public opinion. All the rest of art, transmitting feelings accessible only to a section of the people, will be considered unimportant, and will be neither blamed nor praised. And the appraisement of art in general will devolve not as is now the case on a separate class of rich people, but on the whole people; so that for a work to be thought good and to be approved and diffused, it will have to satisfy not the demands of a few people living under similar and often unnatural conditions, but of all those great masses of people who undergo the natural conditions of laborious life.[22]

His vision of an art that will be fully intelligible to the masses has further implications for the formal and technical aspects of artistic creation. 'The demand will be for clearness, simplicity and brevity', he writes. Art will have to lose its technical complexity: 'It will deteriorate if by technique we understand those complexities of art which are not considered an excellence. . . . But if by technique is understood clearness, beauty, simplicity and compression. . . not only will the technique not deteriorate but, as shown by all peasant art, it will be a hundred times better.'[23] What he foresees is a community-based art in which all can participate, regardless of cultural background or endowment: 'The art of the future. . . will not be produced by professional artists receiving payment for their work and engaged on nothing else besides their art. It will be produced by all the members of the community who feel need of such activity.' It will be a fully democratised art, enriched by the universality of its subject-content:

> And in the same way, that realm of subject-matter for the art of the future which relates to the simplest feelings of common life open to all will not be narrowed but widened. In our former art only the expression of feelings natural to people of a certain exceptional position was considered worthy of being tranmsmitted by art, and even then only on condition that those inner feelings were transmitted in a most refined manner, incomprehensible to the majority of men; all the immense realm of folk-art and of children's art— jests, proverbs, riddles, songs, dances, children's games, and mimicry—was not esteemed a domain worthy of art.

> The artist of the future will understand that to compose a fairy-tale, a touching little song, a lullaby, an entertaining riddle, an amusing jest, or to draw a sketch which will delight dozens of generations or millions of childen and adults, is incomparably more important and more fruitful than to compose a novel or a symphony, or paint a picture, which will divert some members of the wealthy classes for a short time and then forever be forgotten. The region of this art of the simple feelings accessible to all is enormous and it is as yet almost untouched.[24]

By democratisating art and ensuring its integration with the needs and aspirations of the masses, he foresees a linking of aesthetic excellence with popular accessiblity. 'The ideal of excellence in the future will not be exclusiveness of feeling, accessible only to some, but, on the contrary, its universality; and not bulkiness, obscurity and complexity of form, which are now valued, but on the contrary, brevity, clearness and simplicity of expression'. He points to the contradiction inherent in the view that art can attain excellence and yet remain impenetrable to the masses. 'The assertion that art may be good art and at the same time incomprehensible to a great number of people is extremely unjust and ruinous to art itself', he writes. Predictably, his chosen examples of an art that unites excellence with universal accessibility includes the Bible and the heritage of folk literature. 'The majority', he declares, 'always have understood and still understand what we recognise as being the very best art: the epic of Genesis, the Gospel parables, folk-legends, fairy-tales, and folk-songs are understood by all.' The idea of an art which is meaningless to the common people is an absurdity:

> Nothing is more common than to hear it said of reputed works of art that they are very good but very difficult to understand. We are quite used to such assertions, and yet to say that a work of art is good but incomprehensible to the majority of men, is the same as saying of some kind of food that it is very good but most people can't eat it. . . . It is said that the very best works of art are such that they cannot be understood by the masses, but are accessible only to the elect who are prepared to understand these great works. But if the majority of men do not understand, the knowledge necessary to enable them to understand should be taught and explained to them. But it turns out that there is no such knowledge, that the works cannot be explained, and that those who say that the majority do not understand good works of art, still do not explain those works, but only tell us that in order to understand them one must read, and hear, and see, these same works over and over again. But this is not to explain, it is only to habituate. And people may habituate themselves to anything, even to the very worst things. As people may habituate themselves to bad food, to spirits, tobacco, and opium, just in the same way they

may habituate themselves to bad art—and that is exactly what is being done.[25]

Rejecting the conventional prejudice that the masses cannot understand great art, he goes on to suggest that the spurious i.e. rationalist, learning of elite groups may, in fact, prevent *them* from grasping the essential simplicity of art. 'A good and lofty work of art may be incomprehensible', he writes, 'but not to simple unperverted peasant labourers—it may be, and often is, unintelligible to erudite perverted people, destitute of religion.'[26] Aylmer Maude recalled a conversation in which Tolstoy maintained that 'the test of any great philosophy is that it generalises a wide range of important ideas' in such a way that it can be explained to 'an intelligent boy of twelve in a quarter of an hour.'[27] That same principle was applied by Tolstoy to the whole process of artistic creation and was the basis of his belief in the responsiblity of the artist to disclose universally meaningful truths with the simplicity and intelligibility of their scriptural prototypes. As Bayley said: 'For him the Good was constant and unchanging and the art that revealed it should be timeless, parabolic, simple.'[28]

Most of the critical assessments of Tolstoy's novels and stories confirm the success with which he himself achieved this objective. Full of admiration for the formal clarity of his stories, James Joyce described one of them, the religious parable, 'How Much Land Does A Man Need', as 'the greatest story that the literature of the world has known'.[29] The universal appeal of stories such as 'The Kreutzer Sonata', 'The Death of Ivan Ilyich' and 'Father Sergius', another writer said, 'lies most of all in their author's power to clarify without being reductive, to simplify without dishonesty'.[30] Whether Tolstoy's extension of the criterion of popular accessibility to all great literature represented a naive and unsupportable expectation is beyond the scope of this study to decide—though it might perhaps be said that in the present age television has gone some way towards popularising the great classics of world literature in a manner that demonstrates their essential accessibility to the mass audiences that it attracts. What his beliefs particularly signify for the present study is the obligation on educators to ensure that the universal potentiality for the aesthetic be developed to the degree where his ideal of a fully democratised culture can become a realisable objective. The methods by which he suggested this might be achieved are the concern of the remaining sections of this chapter.

2   *Promoting Cultural Literacy*

Long before it became a central principle of radical educational theory, therefore, Tolstoy had proclaimed the right of the masses to the benefits of education, and particularly their right of access to the richness of their cultural heritage. What is especially significant about his perspectives on this issue, and what particularly distinguishes him from the socialist theorists of later years, in his insistence that this right derives primarily from the universal need for faith, and for the deepening and enriching impact of the cultural traditions of religion on its development and growth. Arguing in *What Is Art?* that aesthetic creation in its highest forms embodies the universal truths of faith, he further asserted the right of all people to have access to this, and emphasised the responsibility of educators to take the practical measures necessary to make it a reality. Like several educational reformers before him—one thinks particularly of Luther in this context— Tolstoy saw the attainment of literacy as the principal means by which this objective would be achieved. Much of his work at the school in Yasnaya Polyana was devoted to the development of reading and writing abilities, as has already been indicated. For this he developed an enlightened, imaginative and highly effective pedagogy that holds up well when examined against the most advanced developments in contemporary language teaching methodology.

There were two basic principles underlying his approach to language pedagogy. He insisted, firstly, that it be closely integrated with the concerns of everyday experience; and secondly, he argued that literacy should be regarded as fundamentally an aesthetic potentiality and that pedagogic method should be focussed specifically on developing this. His beliefs on the integration of school and life, of formal and informal modes of education, were explored in an earlier chapter. It will be recalled that he complained of the abstract character of the kind of knowledge that was taught in the conventional schools of the period; he spoke of the mechanical nature of the texts on which school learning was based and the monotony of the pedagogic methods generally in use. He argued that the development of literacy should be founded on the immediacy and wholeness of experience, that its focus should be the living speech of everyday life. 'Culture, in its widest meaning, forms the sum total of all those influences which develop a man, give him a wider world conception, and furnish him with new information', he wrote in his essay, 'On Popular Education'. 'Children's games, suffering, punishments of parents, books, work, compulsory and free instruction, the arts, the sciences, life—everything gives culture', he said.[31] It was on this broadly conceived definition of culture that he based his concept of literacy. His ideas on the issue closely foreshadow the methods advocated by Paulo Freire a century later—they point particularly to the Freirean principle of rooting literacy in the 'thematic universe' of the learner—and they bear a remarkable resemblance to the language growth', 'whole language', and 'language through experience' approaches adopted in contemporary linguistic pedagogy.[32]

The major pedagogic principles of this life-related literacy are set out by Tolstoy in his essay, 'On Teaching the Rudiments'. Initially, he stresses the central connection between language and meaning. Pointing to the fact that large numbers of people acquire the knowledge necessary for their daily lives without developing the skills of reading and writing, and correspondingly that many who acquire basic literacy comprehend little of what they encounter in books, he points to the need to relate school literacy to the existential conditions in which it becomes truly meaningful. In many contemporary schools, he says, a knowledge of the rudiments has provided the masses with a 'separate innoculated ability to read and write', which has inevitably alienated them from school and bred resistance to the whole process of education. The popular school, he insists, must 'respond to the exigencies of the masses'; its fostering of literacy should be rooted in the cultural realities of their daily lives:

> Looking more closely at the result of the rudiments in the form in which they are transmitted to the masses, I think the majority will express themselves against the rudiments, taking into consideration the protracted compulsion, the disproportionate development of memory, the false conception of the completeness of science, the loathing for a continued education, the false vanity, and the habit of meaningless reading, which are acquired in these schools. In the school at Yasnaya Polyana all the pupils who come to it from the ordinary schools constantly fall behind the pupils who enter from the school of life; they not only fall behind but their backwardness is in proportion to the time they have spent in the primary school.
>
> What the problem, and therefore the programme of the popular school consists in, we cannot explain here, and do not even regard such an explanation as possible. The popular school must respond to the exigencies of the masses—that is all which we can positively assert in regard to this question. What these exigencies are only a careful study of them and free experiment can teach. The rudiments constitute only one small, insignificant part of these exigencies, in consequence of which the primary schools are probably very agreeable to their founders, but almost useless and frequently hurtful to the masses, and in no way even resemble the schools of primary education.[33]

The passages in which Tolstoy describes his methods of fostering this ideal of a culturally integrated literacy are amongst the most remarkable in all his pedagogic writings. As a first step towards the cultivation of literacy, he sought to create a stimulating reading environment in the school. Books were available in sufficient variety to provide a free choice of reading matter and to encourage the practice of independent reading. In this passage from one of his essays he describes how the children gather excitedly around the teacher as they make their selections of books for a reading session. Having made their choice of reading material, they gradually became engrossed in the books, and those who were reluctant at the outset to get involved were eventually encouraged to join as a result of the infectious spirit of enthusiasm that was generated by the entire activity:

> The teacher takes the books and gives them to those who have gone with him up to the bookcase; those who are lying on top of the heap, without getting up, also ask for books. The heap becomes smaller by degrees. The moment the majority have books, the rest run to the bookcase and cry: 'Me too, me too. Give me yesterday's book, and me the *Koltsovian* book', and so forth. If there are two left who, excited from the struggle, still keep rolling on the floor, those who have the books cry out to them:
>
> 'Don't bother us! We can't hear a word! Stop now!'
>
> The excited boys submit and, out of breath, take hold of their books, and only at first, while sitting at their books, keep swinging their legs from unallayed excitement. The martial spirit takes fight, and the reading spirit reigns in the room.
>
> With the same enthusiasm with which he was pulling Mitka's hair, he is now reading the *Koltsovian* book (so they call Koltsov's works with us), almost clenching his teeth, his eyes aflame, and seeing nothing about him but his book. It will take as much effort to tear him away from fighting.[34]

Tolstoy laid great emphasis on the value of this kind of reading environment as a means of ensuring that his pupils were favourably disposed towards the activity of reading from the outset. This was the basic principle of his reading pedagogy; once the pupils were motivated to read, he could then implement the more specific features of his methodology and, as his pupils' mastery of reading competence increased, their motivation was correspondingly strengthened as well. Once an atmosphere conducive to reading had been created, he combined two main approaches to the development of reading competence. Firstly, all his pupils were given systematic instruction in the basic skills of reading; and secondly, he sought to develop individual reading interests through guided encounters with a wide variety of texts. The first method included a mixture of whole word and phonic instruction, the nature of the combination depending on the teacher's judgement of the needs of individual pupils. The flexibility he advocated, and the synthesis he sought to bring about between traditional and innovative approaches in developing these basic skills, is conveyed in this passage from 'On Teaching the Rudiments':

> Everybody who has taught another to read has made use for the purpose, though he may not know it, of all the existing methods and of all those that

may never exist. The invention of a new method is only the consciousness of that new side from which the pupil may be approached for his comprehension, and therefore the new method does not exclude the old, and is not only no better than the old, but even becomes worse, because in the majority of cases the essential method is divined in the beginning. In most cases the invention of the new method has been regarded as the annihilation of the old, although in reality the old method has remained the essential one, and the inventors, by consciously refuting the old methods, have only complicated matters, and have fallen behind those who consciously had used the old and unconsciously the new and the future methods.[35]

The method he was advocating here involved an eclectic synthesis of techniques, designed to provide instruction in matters such as letter and syllable formation, encoding and decoding skills, together with the basic skills of word recognition, and the comprehension and interpretation of text. Stressing the need for flexiblity, he insisted that the choice and balance of methods be determined entirely by the needs of individual learners. 'Every individual', he writes, 'must, in order to acquire the art of reading in the shortest possible time, be taught quite apart from any other and therefore there must be a separate method for each. That which forms an insuperable difficulty for one does not in the least keep another back and vice versa'.[36]

A highly individualised approach became the pedagogic norm, therefore, for the reading lessons in the school. He advocated a balanced combination of what he loosely termed 'mechanical' and 'graded' reading. (In reality neither term accurately describes what took place). Stressing the complementary nature of these two activities, he insisted that due attention be given to both in the work of the classroom: 'Although mechanical and graded readings in reality blended into one, these two subjects are still subdivided for us according to their aims', he wrote. 'It seems to us that the aim of the first is the art of fluently forming words out of certain signs while the aim of the second is the knowledge of the literary language.'[37] The teaching of mechanical reading included the kind of instruction in basic skills that has just been described, but this generally took place in conjunction with the guided comprehension of selected texts: this latter activity was intended, in turn, to serve as a preparation for voluntary reading by the children themselves, under the general direction of the teacher. The following passage describes a typical lesson in reading comprehension at the school; its key principle is the progression from close instruction in the reading of wall charts to the reading of individually chosen texts, usually in the sphere of narrative fiction. (In modern parlance it would be called a combination of basal reader and 'real books' approaches.) A crucial feature of the whole activity was the association of reading with pleasure and enjoyment:

Reading forms part of language instruction. The problem of language instruction consists, in our opinion, in guiding people to understand the contents of books written in the literary language. The knowledge of the literary language is necessary because the good books are all in that language.

At first, soon after the foundation of the school, there was no subdivision of reading into mechanical and graded, for the pupils read only that which they could understand—their own compositions, words and sentences written on the blackboard with chalk, and then Khudyakov's and Afanasev's fairy-tales. I then supposed that for the children to learn to read, they had to like reading, and in order to like reading it was necessary that the reading matter be intelligible and interesting. That seemed so rational and clear, and yet the idea was false.

In the first place, in order to pass from the reading on the walls to the reading in books, it became necessary to devote special attention to mechanical reading with each pupil according to any book whatsoever. As long as the number of pupils was inconsiderable and subjects were not subdivided, that was possible, and could, without much labour, transfer the children from reading on the wall to reading in a book; but with the arrival of new pupils that became impossible. The younger pupils were not able to read a fairy-tale and understand it: the labour of putting together the words and at the same time of understanding their meaning was too much for them.[38]

Reviewing the methods he used for these reading lessons in his pedagogic journal, Tolstoy spoke of five main approaches that he found especially successful, following lengthy periods of trial and error and extensive pedagogic experimentation. The first he describes—in language reminiscent of Pestalozzi's *How Gertrude Teaches her Children*—as 'not a scholastic but a domestic method . . . the one in use by the mothers of the whole world'. It consisted, he wrote, 'in the pupil's coming and asking to read with the teacher, whereupon the teacher reads, guiding his every syllable and the combination of syllables'. 'This method', he declares, 'will always remain the best and the only one for teaching people to read, and to read fluently.'[39] The second method consisted in encouraging pupils to take some preliminary steps in independent reading, even before they had acquired mastery of basic comprehension:

> The second method of teaching to read, also a favourite one, through which every one has passed who has learned to read fluently, consists in giving the pupil a book and leaving it entirely to him to spell and understand as well as he can. The pupil who has learned to read by syllables so fluently that he does not feel the need of asking the sexton to read with him, but depends upon himself, always acquires that passion for the process of reading which is so

ridiculed in Gogol's 'Petrushka' and on account of that passion advances. God knows in what manner that kind of reading assumes any definite shape in his mind, but he thus gets used to the forms of the letters, to the process of syllable combinations, to the pronunciation of words, and even to understanding what he reads, and I have had occasion to convince myself by actual experience that our insistence that the pupil should understand what he reads only retards the result. There are many autodidacts who have learned to read well in this way, although the defects of this system must be apparent to everybody.[40]

The third method was intended to promote a close and highly concentrated reading of texts. Pupils were first encouraged to learn certain hymns, poems and stories by heart, and were then asked to recite them while simultaneously re-reading the words they had memorised. The fourth method involved paired reading sessions in which pupils read collaboratively in small groups. 'The advantage of such reading in common lay', he said, 'in greater freedom of comprehension' and in 'greater precision of pronunciation' amongst those whose reading competence was limited, but who gained encouragement from seeing how other pupils comprehended texts.[41] Though he used this method frequently—to some degree it was forced on him by the scarcity of books in the school—Tolstoy felt that it had a limited usefulness and should not be extended to all the pupils in the school.

The fifth method was the culminating stage in the whole process—the stage where the pupils were 'reading books with ever growing interest and comprehension'.[42] What is especially striking about his approach to 'graded reading'—and what indicates his closeness to modern developments in reading pedagogy—is the emphasis he placed on the role of imagination and aesthetic potentialities in the growth of reading competence. Recognising that the roots of literacy lie in the domain of the imaginative and the symbolic, he sought to enrich and deepen this potentiality by providing his pupils with the greatest possible contact with literary texts. Narrative fiction of various forms, legends, parables, fables, poems, the great short stories of world literature—all of these provided the basic reading curriculum for the pupils in his school.

A difficulty arose, however, as he tried to effect a transition from popular literature to the more challenging texts to which he believed they should proceed as they developed the competence necessary to cope with them. While recognising the immediate and spontaneous appeal of fairy tale, folklore and popular reading matter for peasant children, he soon became aware of the difficulty of advancing from this to the works of writers such as Pushkin, Gogol, Homer, or Defoe. He describes the challenge that this represented in one of the most vivid sequences in 'The School at Yasnaya Polyana':

> For the study of the literary language we, naturally, thought of a means which seemed exceedingly simple, but which, in reality, was most difficult. It seemed to us that after the pupils had learned to read sentences written on the board by pupils themselves, we ought to give them Khudyakov's and Afanasyev's fairy tales, then something more difficult and more complicated as regards language, then something more difficult still, and so on, up to the language of Karamzin, Pushkin and the Code of Laws; but this supposition, like the majority of our, and in general, of any, suppositions, was not realised.
>
> From the language which they themselves employed in their writing on the boards, I succeeded in transferring them to the language of the fairy-tales, but in order to take them from the language of the fairy-tales to a higher level, we did not find that transitional 'something' in our literature. We tried Robinson Crusoe —the thing did not work: some of the boys wept from vexation, because they could not understand and tell it; I began to tell it to them in my own words, and they began to believe in the possibility of grasping that wisdom, made out the meaning of it, and in a month finished Robinson Crusoe, but with tedium and, in the end, almost with disgust.
>
> The labour was too great for them. They got at things mostly through memory, and they remembered parts of it, if they told them each evening soon after the reading; but not one of them could make the whole his own. They remembered, unfortunately, only certain incomprehensible words, and began to use them without rhyme or reason, as is generally the case with half-educated people.[43]

As a possible answer to the difficulties he describes, Tolstoy very nearly succumbed to a temptation that always exists for the teacher of disadvantaged pupils: he considered whether he should simply pander to their tastes and provide them with the kind of pastiche literature they might be expected to understand more readily than the classics of Russian literature. 'I began', he recalls, 'to give them to read all kinds of popular imitations, such as "Uncle Naum" and "Aunt Natalya", though I knew in advance that they would not like them—and my supposition came true'. The pupils rejected these works, he felt, because they instinctively recognised that they were culturally inauthentic. 'The only books that are comprehensible to the people and according to their taste are not such as are written for the people, but such as have their origin in the people, namely fairy tales, proverbs, collections of songs, legends of verses etc.'[44] When he returned to teaching Pushkin, Gogol and Homer, he identified the difficulties their works represented more specifically in terms of the remoteness of the themes in these works from the circumstances of the everyday lives of the pupils:

After *Robinson Crusoe* I tried Pushkin, namely his 'The Gravedigger'; but without my aid they were still less able to tell it than Robinson Crusoe, and 'The Gravedigger' seemed much duller to them. The author's apostrophes to the reader, his frivolous relation to his persons, his jocular characterisations, his incompleteness of detail—all that is so incompatible with their needs, that I definitely gave up Pushkin, whose stories I had assumed to be most regularly constructed, simple, and therefore, intelligible to the masses.

I then tried Gogol's 'The Night Before Christmas'. With my reading it at first pleased them, especially the grown pupils, but the moment I left them alone, they could not comprehend anything and felt ennui. Even with my reading they did not ask to have it repeated. The wealth of colours, the fantasicalness and capriciousness of the structures are contrary to their needs.

Then again I tried to read Gnyedich's translation of the *Iliad* to them, and the reading produced only a strange complexity in them; they supposed that it was written in French, and did not understand a thing so long as I did not tell the contents to them in my own words, but even then the plot of the poem made no impression on their minds. Sceptic Semka, a sound, logical nature, was struck by the picture of Phoebus, with the clacking arrows at his back, flying down from Olympus, but he apparently did not know where to lodge the image.[45]

Elaborating further on the 'culture gap' between the world of peasant life and the world of the classics of great literature, he points to the difficulty of initiating peasant children into the language of these works before they have developed an understanding of the ideas and concepts which that language conveys. 'Nearly always', he writes, 'it is not the word which is unintelligible but the pupil lacks the key conception expressed by the word.'[46] He suggests that skilfully handled comprehension lessons provide the answer to this but, as the following passage makes abundantly clear, foresees huge difficulties for the teacher in conducting these lessons successfully:

It is easy enough to say that the pupil must understand, but cannot everybody see what a number of different things may be understood while reading one and the same book? Though missing two or three words in the sentence, the pupil may grasp a fine shade of thought, or its relation to what precedes. You, the teacher, insist on one side of the comprehension, but the pupil does not at all need that which you want to explain to him. At times he may understand you, without being able to prove to you that he has comprehended, all the while dimly guessing and imbibing something quite different, and something very useful and important to him. You exact an explanation from him, and as he is to explain to you in words what impression the words have made upon him, he is silent, or begins to speak nonsense, or lies and deceives; he tries to discover that which you want of him and to adapt himself to your wishes, and so he invents an unexisting difficulty and labours over it; but the general impression produced by the book, the poetical feeling, which has helped him to divine the meaning, is intimidated, and beats a retreat.[47]

Tolstoy's thinking on this issue is consistently characterised by realism and he never underestimated the difficulties involved in overcoming the problems it presented. He warned of the naivete of assuming that the transition from one plane of understanding to the other (from the popular to the 'educated') could be accelerated. 'The relation of the word to the idea and the formation of new ideas are such a complicated mysterious and tender process of the soul', he writes, 'that every interference appears as a rude clumsy force which retards the process of development.'[48] He describes the counterproductive consequences likely to follow from any attempt to impose an alien culture on the masses:

> There is one proposition which we cannot admit, and that is, that having convinced ourselves in our mind that the knowledge of the literary language is useful, we should allow ourselves by forced explanations, memorising, and repetitions to teach the masses the literary language against their will, as one teaches French. We must confess that we have more than once tried to do so within the last two months, when we invariably ran up against an insuperable loathing in the pupils, proving the falseness of the measures accepted by us. During these experiments I convinced myself that explanations of the meanings of words and of speech in general are quite impossible even for a talented teacher, not to mention even such favourite explanations, employed by incapable teachers, as that 'assembly is a certain small synedrion', and so forth. When explaining any one word, for example, the word 'impression', you either substitute another unintelligible word in place of the one in question, or you give a whole series of words, the connection of which is as unintelligible as the word itself.[49]

There are no instant solutions in Tolstoy's pedagogic writings to this universal problem of bridging the gulf between 'highbrow' and popular culture. It is evident from his recollections that he believed—to use the terminology of contemporary pedagogy—that a 'carryover' effect exists between one and the other, but crucially, he argued that the transition will not occur spontaneously, but needs to be 'cultivated' through effective and imaginative teaching.[50] There is abundant evidence that he and his teachers dedicated themselves to stimulating an interest in high quality literature amongst their pupils, and that a wide variety of texts was used for this purpose. Tolstoy's own anthology, the *ABC Reader*, with its rich selections from the whole range of world literature, exemplifies his personal commitment to teaching the finest works in the literary heritage.

Despite his identification of the difficulties of crossing the barriers between popular and educated tastes—and this represents a valuable contribution in itself to the practicalities of reading pedagogy—it is clear from his reports that reading was a greatly enjoyed activity in the Yasnaya Polyana schools, and that the methods employed in them were rewarded with considerable success. His best advice seems to be that the teacher must strive in every way possible to awaken an interest in literature in his or her pupils, and live in hope that the transition from popular to high culture will eventually occur. How precisely this will happen is a matter, he suggests, that lies beyond pedagogic explanation or control. 'It is very likely', he concludes, 'that the graded reading, the subject of our dreams, will appear of itself, and that the knowledge of the literary language will of its own accord come to each pupil, just as we constantly see in the case of people who, without understanding, read indiscriminately the psalter, novels, judicial documents, and in that way acquire the knowledge of the literary language.'[51]

Essentially, therefore, Tolstoy's methods of teaching reading involved a judicious combination of directive and non-directive approaches, the precise degree of guided or independent learning depending on the teacher's judgement of the needs of individual pupils. A similar flexibility is evident in his approach to the teaching of writing. Here again his first requirement was that an environment conducive to the enjoyment of writing be created. The basic method he advocated was one which enabled teacher and pupils to experience the act of writing as partners engaged in a collaborative activity. 'It was', he recalls, 'a new and exciting sensation for them to be present at the process of creation and to take part in it.' In one of the most vivid sequences from his essay, 'How Peasant Children Write', he describes how he himself engaged with the pupils in constructing a piece of narrative fiction, allowing every member of the group to contribute to the progress of the work:

> I began the story, printed in the fourth number of *Yasnaya Polyana*, and wrote down the first page. Every unbiased man, who has the artistic sense and feels with the people will, upon reading this first page, written by me, and the following pages of the story, written by the pupils themselves, separate this page from the rest, as he will take a fly out of the milk: it is so false, so artificial, and written in such a bad language. I must remark that in the original form it was even more monstrous, since much has been corrected, thanks to the indications of the pupils.
>
> Fedka kept looking up from his copy-book to me, and, upon meeting my eyes, smiled, winked, and repeated:
>
> 'Write, write, or I'll give it to you!' He was evidently amused to see a grown person write a theme.
>
> Having finished his theme worse and faster than usual, he climbed on the

back of my chair and began to read over my shoulders. I could not proceed; others came up to us,and I read to them what I had written.

They did not like it, and nobody praised it. I felt ashamed, and, to soothe my literary ambition, began to tell them the plan of what was to follow. In the proportion as I advanced in my story, I became enthusiastic, corrected myself, and they kept helping me out. One would say that the old man should be a magician; another would remark: 'No, that won't do—he will be just a soldier; the best thing will be if he steals from him; no, that won't go with the proverb', and so forth.

All were exceedingly interested. It was evidently a new and exciting sensation for them to be present at the process of creation, and to take part in it. Their judgements were all, for the most part, of the same kind, and they were just, both as to the very structure of the story and as to the details and characterisations of the persons. Nearly all of them took part in the composition; but from the start, there distinguished themselves positive Semka, by his clearly defined artistic quality of description, and Fedka, by the correctness of his poetical conceptions, and especially by the glow and rapidity of his imagination.

Their demands had so little of the accidental in them and were so definite, that more than once I debated with them, only to give way to them. I was strongly possessed by the demands of a regular structure, and of an exact correspondence of the idea of the proverb to the story; while they, on the contrary, were only concerned about the demands of artistic truth.[52]

This whole project exemplifies the balance of freedom and discipline that characterises all his work in the sphere of writing pedagogy. His report indicates the intensity with which the pupils participated in the entire activity—'we worked from seven to eleven o-clock; they felt neither hunger nor fatigue and even got angry with me when I stopped writing', he recalls.[53] He describes his own sense of fulfilment as he witnessed the flowering of creativity in the most talented of the pupils, Vasilly Morozov (Fedka): 'I cannot express that feeling of agitation, joy, fear and almost regret which I experienced during that evening', he writes:

I felt both dread and joy, like the seeker after the treasure who suddenly sees the flower of the fern—I felt joy, because suddenly and quite unexpectedly there was revealed to me that stone of the philosophers, which I had vainly been trying to find for two years—the art of teaching the expression of thoughts; and dread, because this art called for new demands, a whole world of desires, which stood in no relation to the surroundings of the pupils, as I thought in the first moment. There was no mistaking. It was not an accident, but a conscious creation.[54]

Initially only two of his pupils, Fedka and Semka, joined with him in the writing project, but gradually the others, sensing the enthusiasm of their class-mates, began to participate as well. Much of the success of the project was due to the spirit of equality that existed between teacher and pupils. The non-dogmatic character of his approach is evident from the sub-title of the essay in which he describes this work—'Are the Peasant Children to Learn to Write from Us or are We to Learn to Write from Them'.

The fostering of creative potential that he describes was much more, however, than a merely spontaneous collaboration between teacher and pupil; it was also a highly formative process in which encouragement was combined with painstaking guidance in the mastery of the craft and disciplines of writing. Though conducted in the spirit of an apprenticeship between pupil and master, meticulous attention was given to revising, pruning, refining, restructuring and reshaping the writing, until it met their agreed standards of clear, exciting and lucid narrative. Observing Fedka's progress, for example, Tolstoy remarks: 'The chief quality in every art, the feeling of measure, was developed in him to an extraordinary degree. He writhed at the suggestion of any superfluous feature, made by some one of the boys.'[55] He placed great emphasis on the power of suggestion and association to stimulate creativity: 'Every artistic word, whether it belongs to Goethe or to Fedka, differs from the inartistic in that it evokes an endless mass of thoughts, images and explanations.'[56]

His comments continually stress the combination of authenticity, freedom, sincerity and discipline that he sought to encourage amongst the children. These are three examples chosen at random from 'How Peasant Children Write': 'We went to work and again the children displayed the same feeling of artistic truth, measure and enthusiasm. . . . They continued to write without me and finished two pages just as well done, just as well felt, and just as correctly, as the first. . . . I read over what they had written . . . again there was the same feeling of truth, beauty and measure.'[57] On the other hand, he warned against excessive intervention by the teacher in the highly individualised and complex processes that are involved in the experience of writing. In this comment on Fedka's work, for example, he reproaches himself for interfering in a manner that proved detrimental to the quality of the writing:

> The fault is all my own, for I could not keep, during the writing of this chapter, from suggesting to him and telling him how I should have written. If there is a certain triteness in the introduction, when describing persons and dwellings, I am exclusively to blame for it. If I had left him alone, I am sure he would have described the same in action, imperceptibly, much more artistically, without the really accepted and impossible manner of logically distributed descriptions, which consists in first describing the *dramatis personae*, even

their biographies, then the locality and the surroundings, and then only the action itself.[58]

Reflecting on the delicate balance that lies between non-interference and positive pedagogic guidance, he ended his report on this particular writing session with the following conclusion: 'It is my conviction that we cannot teach children in general and peasant children in particular to write and compose. All that we can do is to teach them how to go about writing.'[59] Within the terms of this latter objective, however, he offers a great deal of valuable advice on the pedagogic steps the teacher can take. On two issues—the selection of themes or occasions for writing, and the mastery of its grammatical and technical aspects—he offers specific guidelines on how the teacher can assist the development of writing competence. What he has to say on these issues is a more specific elaboration of the methods already outlined in the report on the writing project with Fedka, Semka and the others, but in this instance his comments are much more precise and more detailed.

With regard to the selection of themes or occasions for writing, he placed his main emphasis on the freedom of individual choice that the pupils were allowed. 'The chief art of the teacher, in the study of language, and the chief exercise with the aim in view of guiding children to write composition consist', he says, 'in giving them themes, and not so much in furnishing them as in presenting a large choice, in pointing out the extent of the composition, and in indicating the essential steps.' Sometimes he found Russian proverbs—such as the one that proved to be so successful with Fedka and Semka, 'He feeds with the spoon and pricks with the eye of the handle'—particularly suitable for this purpose. At other times he used stories from the Old Testament to stimulate writing; the children retold the stories in their own words after the teacher had narrated them from the Bible text. Sometimes the children were simply asked to describe some familar objects, though, as the following passage indicates, this apparently un- demanding exercise could present major difficulties for many of them:

> In the first and second class the choice of compositions is left to the students themselves. A favourite subject for compositions for the first and the second class is the history of the Old Testament, which they write two months after the teacher has told it to them. The first class lately began to write the New Testament, but not approximately as well as the Old; they even made more orthographical mistakes—they did not understand it so well.
>
> In the first class we tried compositions on given themes. The first themes that most naturally occurred to us were the description of simple objects, such as grain, the house, the wood and so forth; but, to our great surprise, these demands on our pupils almost made them weep, and, in spite of the aid

afforded them by the teacher, who divided the description of the grain into a description of its growth, its change into bread, its use—they emphatically refused to write upon such themes, or, if they did write, they made the most incomprehensible and senseless mistakes in orthography, in the language and in the meaning.

We tried to give them the description of certain events, and all were as happy as if a present had been given to them. That which forms the favourite description of the schools—the so-called simple objects,—pigs, pots, a table—turned out to be incomparably more difficult than whole stories taken from their memories. The same mistake was repeated here as in all the other subjects of instruction—to the teacher the simplest and most general appears as the easiest, whereas for a pupil only the complicated and living appears easy.[60]

The writing of compositions, like the narrative readings described earlier, was one of the most popular of the school's activities. Here again Tolstoy's method was founded on a recognition of the crucial importance of the imaginative and the symbolic in bringing to life the seeds of linguistic growth. The writing of fictional narrative was the activity that was most frequently chosen for this purpose. 'The moment the oldest pupils get hold of a pencil and paper outside of school they do not write "Dear Sir" but some fairy-tale of their own composition', he recalled. Of the younger pupils he wrote: 'Every pupil who has learned to make the letters, is possessed by the passion of writing and at first the doors, the outer walls of the schoolhouse and of the huts where the pupils live are covered with letters and words.'[61] He recognised the crucial importance of freedom and spontaneity in the fostering of the writing, and his pedagogic methods were primarily designed to encourage this. But equally, he was concerned to provide assistance in the revision, correction, reshaping and restructuring of the writing, and sought in various ways to achieve this objective as well. Seeing that didactic instruction in the technical aspects of writing would militate against the first of these objectives, the work of revision was done through a process of critical collaboration in which all the pupils were engaged collectively in the evaluation and redrafting of the writing. Tolstoy describes this in the following passage from 'The School at Yasnaya Polyana':

> At first I was vexed by the clumsiness and disproportionateness of the structure of the compositions; I thought I had properly inspired them with what was necessary, but they misunderstood me and everything went badly: they did not seem to recognise any other necessity than that of writing without mistakes. But now the time has come in the natural course of events, and frequently we hear an expression of dissatisfaction when the composition is unnecessarily drawn out, or when there are frequent repetitions or jumps from one subject to another. It is hard to define wherein their demands consist, but

these demands are lawful. 'It is clumsy', some of them cry, listening to the composition of a companion; some of them will not read their own after they have found that the composition of a comrade, as read to them, is good; some tear their copy-books out of the hands of the teacher, dissatisfied to hear it sound differently from what they wanted, and read it themselves. The individual characters are beginning to express themselves so definitely that we have experimented on making the pupils guess whose composition we have been reading, and the first class they guess without a mistake.[62]

Apart from his opposition, in principle, to didactic instruction in matters of grammar and syntax, he felt in any event that this was best conducted in the specific context of each individual pupil's work. 'With such writing,' he says, 'we obtain in a natural manner the most difficult thing for the initial study of language—the faith in the stability and form of the word.' He describes how they revelled in the collective activities of revision and correction. 'It affords them great pleasure to write correctly and to correct the mistakes of others', he writes. 'The older ones get hold of any letter they can find, exercise themselves in the correction of mistakes, and use their utmost endeavour to write well.'[63] On the other hand, he describes his frustration as he attempted to give formal instruction in the rules of grammar and syntax:

We have made all kinds of experiments in the instruction of grammar, and we must confess that not one of them has attained its end—to make this instruction interesting. In the second and the first classes the new teacher made this summer an attempt at explaining the parts of the sentence, and a few of the children at first took an interest in them as in charades and riddles. After lessons they frequently hit upon the idea of proposing riddles to each other, and they amused themselves in propounding each other such questions as 'Where is the predicate?' on a par with 'What sits on the bed hanging down its feet?' Of applications to correct writing there were none, and if there were, they were more faulty than correct. . . .

Having convinced ourselves of the inconvenience of syntactical analysis, we tried the etymological analysis—parts of speech, declensions, and conjugations, and we also propounded to each other riddles about the dative, about the infinite, and about adverbs, and that resulted in the same tedium, the same abuse of the influence gained by us, and the same inapplicability. In the upper class they always write correctly *ye* in the dative and prepositional cases, but when they correct that mistake in the younger pupils, they are never able to give any reason why they do so, and they must be reminded of the cases, in order to remember the rule: '*Ye* in the dative'. The youngest, who have not yet heard anything about the parts of speech, frequently call out *sebye ye*, not knowing themselves why they do so, and apparently happy to have guessed right.[64]

In these comments he anticipates the main objection of modern educators to the formal teaching of grammar: that is, that an abstract knowledge of the rules of grammar does little to promote proficiency in its use.[65] Contemporary pedagogic practice overwhelmingly favours an applied knowledge of grammar, with mastery of its rules and usages being gained in the context of the individual pupil's writing. This is essentially what Tolstoy believed also, as he indicates very clearly in these passages from 'The School at Yasnaya Polyana':

> Neither man nor child likes, without a struggle, to give up the living word to be mechanically dismembered, and disfigured. There is a certain feeling of self-preservation in the living word. If it is to develop, it tends to develop independently, and only in conformity with all vital conditions. The moment you want to catch that word, to tighten it in the vise, to plane it off, and to give it such adornments as this word ought to get, according to your ideas, this word and the live thought and meaning connected with it, becomes compressed and conceals itself, and in your hands is left nothing but the shell, on which you may expend all your cunning without harming or helping that word which you wanted to form. . . .
>
> The only explanation for the necessity of grammar, outside of the demand made at examinations, may be found in its application to the regular exposition of ideas. In my own experience I have not found this application, and I do not find it in the example of the lives of the people who do not know grammar and yet write correctly, and of candidates in philology who write incorrectly, and I hardly find a hint of the fact that the knowledge of grammar is applied to anything whatever by the pupils at Yasnaya Polyana school. It seems to me that grammar goes by itself as a useless mental gymnastic exercise, and that the language—the ability to write, read and understand, goes by itself. Geometry and mathematics in general also appear at first as nothing more than mental gymnastics, but with this difference, that every proposition in geometry, every mathematical definition, brings with it further endless deductions and applications; while in grammar, even if we should agree with those who see in it an application of logic to language, there is a very narrow limit to these deductions and applications. The moment a pupil in one way or another masters a language, all applications from grammar tear away and drop off as something dead and lifeless.[66]

Yet he recognised the importance of grammatical knowledge, and sought to provide it in the context of its usage in living speech. Frequently, for example, he gave his pupils exercises in sentence construction, using particular parts of speech (nouns, adjectives, verbs, adverbs etc.) for each of the exercises, and enabling the pupils to acquire a basic knowledge of grammatical nomenclature in the process. These exercises, he says, were designed 'to convince the pupils that the word is one having its own immutable laws, changes, endings and correlations between endings'.[67] Further instruction of this nature was incorporated into the teaching of reading comprehension. The most consistently used method for the teaching of grammar and syntax, however, was still the informal correction and revision of each pupil's work, in the course of which they learned to master the structures of the language in the natural contexts of their own writing.

Tolstoy reported high levels of success for his methods of teaching writing, and the children clearly enjoyed the activities which he organised for them. As in the case of reading, his methods were remarkably advanced for a nineteenth century educator, and they can be compared very favourably with the most widely advocated methods of the present time. On matters such as the centrality of imagination in the furtherance of writing competence, the need for freedom of choice in the selection of writing themes, the balancing of linguistic fluency with the mastery of grammatical and orthographic conventions, the integration of the latter with the spontaneous growth of writing competence, the collaborative methods of evaluation and assessment—on all of these his methods find countless echoes in modern pedagogic theory, as will be shown in some detail in a later chapter. It is a matter of considerable significance that all these principles should have had the authority of someone so distinguished in the sphere of writing creativity as Tolstoy, and that his methods should have been tested out in the challenging conditions of schools catering for deprived and underprivileged children in nineteenth century Russia.

3   Art and Music Education

> If I did not start with the opinion that I do not know what is to be taught, and why this or that is to be taught, I should have to ask myself: will it be useful for peasant children, who are placed under the necessity of passing all their lives in care about their daily bread, to study art, and what good is it to them? Ninety-nine out of every hundred will answer in the negative. Nor can one answer otherwise. The moment such a question is put, common-sense demands the following answer: he is not to be an artist—he will have to plough the ground. If he is to have any artistic needs, it will be above his strength to carry that persistent, untiring work which he must carry, and without carrying which the existence of the state would be unthinkable. When I say 'he' I mean the child of the masses. Of course, it is insipid, but I rejoice at this insipidity, do not stop before it, but try to discover its causes. There is another great insipidity. This same child of the masses, every child of the masses, has just such a right, —what do I say ?—a greater right to enjoy art than we have, the children of a happy class, who are not placed under the necessity of that untiring work, who are surrounded by all the comforts of life.[68]

Thus Tolstoy begins the section from 'The School at Yasnaya Polyana' where he deals with the teaching of drawing and music. As was pointed out in the last chapter, his belief in the need for all children to have a good education in the arts was rooted in the deeper conviction that all understanding is aesthetic in origin, and that the nurturing of learning potential depends ultimately on the enrichment of the imaginative resources of the learner. That conviction was further reinforced by his linking of aesthetic and religious sensibility in the works that were discussed in the opening section of this chapter. Insisting that *all* children be given access to the riches of their aesthetic heritage, he further argued that due attention be given to developing their mastery of the symbolic languages of art in the spheres of the visual and the musical, as well as in the sphere of the linguistic and the literary.

He foresaw the same problems, however, in applying this principle in the spheres of the visual arts and music as he did in the spheres of reading and writing. Once again he saw the gulf between popular taste and the sophisticated world of high art as the primary obstacle in the way of the realisation of his aims. On the one hand, he wondered why such a gulf should exist, and why it should be necessary to 'prepare' peasant children for the appreciation of art. 'Why', he asks, 'are the beauty of the sun, the beauty of the human face, the beauty of the sounds of a popular song, the beauty of an act of love and self-renunciation accessible to all, and why do they demand no preparation?' Why, he wonders, when the evidence of beauty is so readily observable, are the finest examples of Russian art beyond the comprehension of the masses:

> Ivanov's painting will rouse in the people nothing but admiration for his technical mastery, but will not evoke any poetical, nor religious sensation, while this very poetical sentiment is evoked by a chap-book picture of John of Novgorod and the devil in the pitchers. The Venus de Milo will rouse only a legitimate loathing for the nakedness and shamelessness of the woman. Beethoven's quartette of the latest epoch will appear only as a disagreeable sound, interesting perhaps because one plays on a bog fiddle and the other on a small fiddle. The best production of our poetry, a lyrical composition by Pushkin, will seem only a collection of words, and its meaning the veriest nonsense.
>
> Introduce a child from the people into this world; you can do that and are doing that all the time by means of the hierarchy of the educational institutions, academies, and art classes: he will feel, and will sincerely feel, the beauty of Ivanov's painting, and of the Venus de Milo, and of the quartette by Beethoven, and of Pushkin's lyrical poem. But upon entering into this world, he will no longer be breathing with full lungs—the fresh air, whenever he has to go into it, will affect him painfully and inimically.[69]

Despite the difficulties arising from the fact that art is not popular with the masses of the people, he nonetheless asserts the right of every child, regardless of his class or cultural background, to have his aesthetic potentialities fully developed. 'I assume', he writes, 'that the necessity of enjoying art and serving art are inherent in each human personality, no matter to what race or milieu he may belong, and that this necessity has its rights and ought to be satisfied.' Scorning the view that art education for peasant children should be restricted to rudimentary exercises in technical drawing, he insists that they be given the same opportunities as more privileged children to develop their creative abilities fully through the medium of the visual:

> I shall be told, and I have been, if drawing is needed in a popular school, it can be admitted only as drawing from Nature, technical drawing, to be applied to life: the drawing of a plough, a machine, a building; free-hand drawing as a mere auxiliary for mechanical drawing. This common view of drawing is also held by the teacher of the Yasnaya Polyana school, whose report we offer. But it was the very experiment with teaching drawing in this manner which convinced us of the falseness and injustice of this technical programme. The majority of the pupils, after four months of careful, exclusively technical drawing, from which was excluded all drawing of men, animals, and landscapes, ended by cooling off considerably in respect to the drawing of technical objects and by developing to such an extent the feeling and need of drawing as an art that they provided themselves with their secret copy-books, in which they drew men, and horses with all four legs coming out of one spot.[70]

Basically, what Tolstoy was urging was mastery of the language of art through various expressive activities, and especially through the kind of spontaneous ventures in artistic creativity that he describes in this passage. Regrettably, however, apart from indicating his commitment to encouraging the children to indulge their creative fantasies through the medium of drawing and painting, he provides no further information on the ways in which these activities were taught, and the extent to which they were practised during the daily life of the school. One would assume that in the art lessons he maintained the same kind of balance between expressive and formal activities as he did in the reading and writing lessons, but most of the information he provides is in fact concerned with the latter. In the penultimate section of 'The School at Yasnaya Polyana' he describes the systematic training he gave the children in the art of object drawing. Working with only the most basic resources—a painted board, a few slates and sticks of chalk—and with only the very limited pedagogic knowledge that he could glean from some illustrated albums, he nevertheless provided daily lessons in the disciplines and techniques of line drawing. He describes a typical lesson in this passage from the report:

> The drawing of figures from the board took place in the following manner: I first drew a horizontal or vertical line, divided it by points into different parts, and the pupils copied that line. Then I drew another, or several other lines, perpendicular or slanting to the first, standing in a certain relation to the first, and divided into units of the same size. Then we connected the points of division of these lines by straight lines or arcs, and this formed a certain symmetrical figure, which, step by step as it grew up, was copied by the boys. I thought that that would be advantageous, in the first place, because the boy learned objectively the whole process of the formation of the figure, and, in the second, because through this drawing in the board there was developed in him the conception of the correlation of lines much better than through the copying of drawings and originals. With such a process there was destroyed the possibility of copying directly, but the figure itself, as an object from Nature, had to be copied on a diminished scale.
>
> It is nearly always useless to hang out before the pupils a large complete picture or figure, because the beginners will be positively confused before it, just as though they were before an object from Nature. But the very evolution of the figure before their eyes has a great significance. The pupils, in this case, see the skeleton of the drawing, upon which the whole body is later formed. The pupils were constantly called upon to criticise the lines and their relations, as I had drawn them. I frequently drew the lines wrong on purpose, in order to get an idea how much judgement they had formed about the correlation and regularity of the lines. Then again I asked the children, when I drew some figure, where some line ought to be added in their opinion, and I even made now one boy, now another, suggest some figure.
>
> In this manner I not only roused a greater interest in the boys, but also a free participation in the formation and development of the figure; in this way the children's question 'Why?' which every child naturally asks himself in copying from an original, was obviated.[71]

Generally, his comments suggest that significant progress was made in these lessons, despite his heavy concentration on the 'grammar' of the art-form. 'In this manner', he writes—referring to the training methods that he employed—'I soon got more than thirty boys in a few months to learn quite thoroughly the correlation of lines in various figures and objects and to render these figures in even, sharp lines. The mechanical art of line-drawing was soon evolved as if of its own accord.'[72] There is no mention at all of craft-work, painting or art appreciation in his report on how they conducted their art lessons. Lack of resources may have been a limiting factor, though a similar difficulty did not prevent him from conducting his reading lessons in accordance with his belief that the greatest possible variety of material should be used to cater for individual tastes. But even the limited activities that Tolstoy describes in his reports on the drawing lessons were still far more wide-ranging than what was provided in most Russian elementary schools in those years. The official school curriculum made no provision at all for education in the visual arts, and only a narrow course of instruction in technical drawing was offered in the minority of private schools that saw fit to provide it.

In 'The School at Yasnaya Polyana' Tolstoy spoke of music and poetry as 'the two branches of our arts with which I am the more intimately acquainted and which formerly I loved very passionately'.[73] His childhood love of music—largely attributable to his mother's influence and to her fondness for Beethoven and Bach—was described in Chapter 3. His interests, it will be recalled, were quite varied, consisting at least of classical, folk and gypsy music, and they retained this eclectic character throughout the rest of his life.[74] That feeling for variety in music was reflected in his views on how music should be taught in the schools. Initially however, he insisted—as he had already done in the case of literature and art—that *all* children should have the right of access to the artistic heritage of music. Urging teachers to introduce children to the pleasures of music by having them play simple instruments—such as balalaikas and accordions—he insists that they must have access to the best of the heritage, on the grounds that 'art does not brook mediocrity':

> The customary programme of the popular schools does not admit singing beyond the singing of church choirs. The same thing takes place here: either it is a very dull and painful memorising for the children where certain sounds are produced by them, as though they were regarded merely as so many throats taking the place of the organ pipes, or there will be developed in them the feeling for the artistic, which finds its satisfaction in the balalaika and the accordion and frequently in a homely song, which the pedagogue does not recognise, and in which he does not think it necessary to guide his pupils. Either one or the other: either art in general is injurious and unnecessary, which is not at all so, strange as it may appear at a first glance, or everybody without distinction of classes and occupations, has a right to it and a right to devote himself to it, on the ground that art does not brook mediocrity.[75]

Tolstoy attributed his ideas on music pedagogy to two main sources: Chevet's *Repousee a l'unanimite* and Rousseau's *Dictionnaire de Musique*. Having seen some of their methods used for choral singing during a visit to Paris, he was greatly impressed by their potential, patricularly for choric harmonisation: 'An audience of from five to six hundred men and women', he recalls, 'were singing in absolute harmony and *a livre ouvert*, whatever the teacher gave them to sing'.[76] He was especially impressed by three features of the Chevet/Rousseau approach. The first was their expression of musical signs through the use of familiar numeric symbols: the figures were used as a simple strategy for introducing the children to musical notation before they were able to master the staff method. The second principle involved the teaching of sounds independently of time or *vice versa*—the pupils would first sing a tune without counting time, and then without singing the tune would count out the notes by tapping the measures of time with a stick. Sometimes one group would be asked to sing while another was counting time, until they were eventually harmonised. In all this work Tolstoy drew extensively on the children's repertoire of popular songs, a principle again for which he found strong support in *Repoussee a l'unanimite*:

> Finally, Chevet's third great idea consists in making music and its study popular. His method of instruction fully realises this aim. And that is not only Chevet's wish and my assumption, but an actual fact. I saw in Paris hundreds of labourers with horny hands, sitting on benches, underneath which lay the tools with which they were returning from their shops, singing from music, comprehending and enjoying the laws of music. As I looked at these labourers, I could easily imagine Russian peasants in their place, if Chevet but spoke Russian: they would sing in just the same fashion, would just as easily understand everything he was saying about the common rules and laws of music.[77]

Yet, in this instance again, he continued to dwell on the gulf between popular taste and the sophisticated traditions of art music. He points, however, to the continuity that exists from the one to the other, and writes regretfully of their failure in the school at Yasnaya Polyana, at least initially, to recognise the importance of this principle in their teaching. 'I came to the conclusion', he says, 'that everything we had been doing had been done along a false, exceptional path, which had no meaning and no future and which was insignificant in comparison with those demands and even with those productions of the same arts, samples of which we find amongst the people.' He pointed even to the possibility that a purer quality exists in the music of the people than in its more sophisticated classical forms: 'I convinced myself that a lyrical poem, for example, "I remember the charming moment", the musical productions such as Beethoven's last symphony, were not as unconditionally and universally fine as the song of "Steward Vanka", the tune of "Down the Mother Volga"—that Pushkin and Beethoven please us, not because there is any absolute beauty in them, but because we are as much spoilt as Pushkin and Beethoven were, because Pushkin and Beethoven alike flatter our freaky irritability and our weakness.'[78]

Whatever the difficulties that lay in the way, it becomes evident from his reports that Tolstoy very effectively utilised the natural progression from folk to art music in the lessons he conducted at the school. (This process appears to have been far less problematic in music than it was in literature and art). Starting with the spontaneous singing of the children, he led them gradually to different varieties of music and even into the arcane world of musical literacy. 'Now after eight months', he recalled, 'we sing "The Angel Lamented" and two cherubical songs, numbers four and seven, the whole common Mass and small chorus songs. The best pupils take down in writing the tunes of the songs which they know, and almost read music.' But for all the spontaneity and uninhibited enjoyment of these music lessons, it is clear, as the following passage indicates, that Tolstoy's methods involved a good deal of intensive and highly directive teaching, as he sought to develop the children's mastery of the formal/technical aspects of music:

> On the following day we tried the gamut, and the more talented went through it all, while the poorer ones could hardly get as far as the third. I wrote the notes on a staff in the alto-clef, the most symmetrical of clefs, and gave them the French names. The next five or six lessons proceeded just as merrily; we also succeeded in getting new minor keys and the passes to the majors— 'Kyrie Eleison', 'Glory Be to the Father and Son', and a song for three voices with piano accompaniment. One-half of the lesson was occupied with that, the other half with the singing of the gamut and the exercises, which the pupils themselves invented, 'do-mi-re-fa-mi-sol' or 'do-re-re-mi-mi-fa', or do-mi-re-fa-mi-sol', and so forth.
>
> I soon noticed that the notes on the staff were not clear to them, and I found it necessary to use figures instead. Besides, for the explanation of intervals and the variation of the tonic scale, the figures present greater conveniences. After six lessons some of them took the intervals by order, such as I asked them for, getting up to them by some imaginary gamut. They were particularly fond of exercises in fourths 'do-fa-re-sol', and so forth, up and down. Fa (the lower dominant) struck them more especially, by its force.
>
> 'What a whopper of a fa!' said Semka. 'It just cuts clean.'
>
> The unmusical boys soon fell away, while with the musical boys the class lasted as much as three or four hours. I tried to give them an idea of time by the accepted method, but the matter proved so difficult that I was compelled to separate time from tune and, writing down the sounds without the measure, to analyse them, and then, having written down the time, that is, the measure without the sounds, to analyse one beat by tapping the finger, and only then to continue the two processes together.[79]

On the specific issue of the teaching of intervals, his methods were especially painstaking and intensive. Though he indicates that many of his pupils could not follow him in all of this work, he nevertheless persisted for the sake of those eager to proceed beyond the singing of popular songs. (Providing fully for differences in ability was one of the foremost policies of the school, and was especially exemplified in the teaching of music.) Time and again he admits that some of the 'unmusical' pupils opted out of this—as was their fully acknowledged right under the policies of the school. 'After six lessons', he writes in a report on a particularly intensive period of instruction, 'the goslings were separated from the sheep; there were left only the musical natures, the amateurs, and we passed over to the minor scales and to the explanation of intervals'. The high standards that were reached in this work may be illustrated by the following passage from 'The School at Yasnaya Polyana'. It indicates the high level of musical attainment that could be expected, even from a group of disadvantaged pupils, and fully justifies Tolstoy's consistently asserted commitment to giving all children the fullest possible access to the riches of the arts:

> We easily found that the major scale consisted of a sequence of two large, one small, three large, and one small seconds. Then we sang 'Glory Be To God' in the minor scale, and by ear got up to the scale which turned out to be minor; then we found in that scale one large, one small, two large, one small, one very large, and one small second. Then I showed them that it was possible to sing and write a scale beginning with any sound, that when it does not come to large or small second, when necessary, we may place a sharp or flat. For convenience sake I wrote out for them a chromatic scale of the following kind:

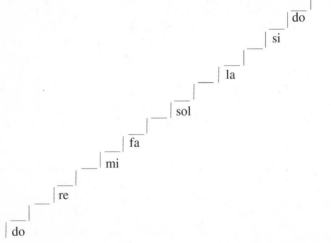

> Along this staircase I made them write all kinds of major and minor scales, beginning with any note whatever. These exercises amused them very much, and the progress was so striking that two of them frequently passed the time

between classes in writing out the tunes of the songs which they knew. These pupils are continually humming the motives of some songs which they cannot name, and they hum them sweetly and tenderly, and, above all, they now second much better and cannot bear to hear all the children sing inharmoniously together.[80]

Yet, for all the intensity of the instruction that he provided in the basic skills of music, Tolstoy's overriding objective was to ensure that at all times the children found their music lessons entertaining and enjoyable. Significantly, he argued that this would be ensured so long as the *skills* of music-playing were always subordinated to its primary status as an art. 'In order', he said, 'that musical instruction should leave traces and should be cheerfully received, it is necessary from the very start to teach the art and not the skill of singing and playing.' 'Young ladies', he adds, 'may be made to play Burgmuner's exercises but the children of the people it is better not to teach at all than to teach them mechanically.'[81] Though a tension was present at all times between the disciplines that he considered essential for a proper education in music and his determination that it should afford pleasure in the greatest possible degree, he appears to have maintained a successful, if sensitive, balance between these two objectives. His description of one of the major musical occasions in the life of the school—the singing of the Mass for the villagers of Yasnaya Polyana—uniquely captures the encouraging and non-coercive spirit in which the school's musical activities were conducted:

> We had hardly more than twelve lessons during the winter. Our instruction was spoiled by ambition. The parents, we, the teachers, and the pupils themselves, wanted to surprise the whole village—to sing in the church; we began to prepare the mass and the cherubical songs of Bortnyanski. It seemed to be more amusing for the children, but it turned out quite differently. Although the desire to be in the choir sustained them, and they loved music, and we, the teachers, put forth our special effort in this subject and made it more compulsory than the rest, I often felt sorry, looking at some tiny Kiryushka, in torn leg-rags, as he rolled off his part, 'Secretly fo-o-o-o-orming', and was requested to repeat it ten times, which finally vexed him so much that he beat the music with his fingers, insisting that he was singing right.
>   We once travelled down to the church and had a success; the enthusiasm was enormous, but the singing suffered from it: the lessons were growing tedious to them, and they fell out by degrees, and it was only at Easter that it was possible by great effort to get together a choir. Our singers began to resemble archiepiscopal singers, who frequently sing well, but with whom, on account of that skill, all desire for singing is killed, and who absolutely know nothing about notes, though they think they do know. I have frequently

seen those who come out of such a school undertake to study themselves without knowing anything about notes, but they are quite helpless the moment they try to sing that which has not been shouted into their ears.[82]

Tolstoy's policies on music education, like his policies on reading and writing, compare quite favourably with those generally advocated for primary school pupils at the present time. His pupils were given a good basic training in the disciplines of music, in aural and vocal skills, in the mastery of musical scales, in choral singing, in the playing of popular instruments, and in the basics of musical literacy. A varied repertoire, with a good blending of folk and religious music, was taught, and every effort was made to ensure that the primary aim of fostering a love for music was pursued consistently. What he offered was immeasurably superior to the 'music' programme officially prescribed for Russian primary schools. It merely required teachers to 'familarise the pupils with the chants and hymns most frequently used in the Church', and urged them 'where possible to make national and patriotic songs part of the instruction'.[83] In many instances even these crude and rudimentary requirements were ignored by the teachers in the state and parochial primary schools. Believing that all children had a right to be introduced to the finest traditions of music, literature and art, Tolstoy made remarkable strides towards making that seemingly idealistic vision a fully realisable goal. At a time when most Russian children were denied even one year of primary education, the peasant children that were taught in his schools could be described as amongst the most privileged in the Empire, their lives being immeasurably enriched by the broad and varied programme of aesthetic studies that he provided for them.

VI

Religious and Moral Education

1   A Faith Given Freely
Tolstoy's disagreements with the Russian Orthodox Church and his repeated condemnations of institutional religion have been well documented both by himself and his biographers. His Diary, his novels, his auto-biographical and socio-political writings, all attest strongly to his passion-ately held belief that the Churches through the ages had corrupted and distorted some of the most fundamental teachings of the Christian scriptures. Side by side with all this, there is evidence in the same writings of a fervent commitment to proclaiming the message of Christianity in the simple, undiluted and unambiguous form in which it had been originally disclosed. It is essential that both of these positions be explored if the nature of Tolstoy's religious beliefs is to be properly defined. That will be the main objective of the first part of this chapter. It will be necesary, in the first instance, to examine the evidence of his own writings, and some relevant biographical and critical commentaries on them, to ascertain the precise nature of his beliefs. Secondly, these beliefs can be more fully illuminated, if comparisons are made with some contemporary (or near contemporary) figures in literature and philosophy who shared both his disaffection with institutional religion and his wish to reassert the pure and and radical faith of scriptural Christianity. These include his fellow writers, Dostoevsky and Pasternak, and a number of modern philosophers, the most significant of whom are Kierkagaard, Unamuno, Buber and Levinas. Comparisons with all these are instructive not only on the nature of Tolstoy's beliefs, but on the degree to which they represented a more widely held view of the relevance of the Christian Gospels to the needs of the present time.

   Tolstoy's basic quarrel with the Churches was their rationalisation of the teachings of the Gospels and their intellectualised distortion of some of their most fundamental precepts. Throughout his writings he emphasised the ultimately irrational character of faith and its irreducibility to the categories of abstract thought. At an early point in *War and Peace* the Freemason tells Pierre that 'the infinite God in His omnipotence is not to be apprehended by reason but by life.' 'The highest wisdom is not founded on reason alone', he says. 'The highest wisdom is one attained through the light of conscience that God has implanted in our souls.'[1] Natasha, repenting of her wrong-doings, similarly asserts that 'the wish to understand everything is pride' and she sees that the conquest of intellectual pride is a pre-condition of the rediscovery of her faith.[2] Pierre, contemplating the uncomplicated character of the faith of the peasant, Platon Karataev, concludes that 'there is no greatness there where simplicity, goodness and truth are absent'.[3] Levin's torment and self-conflict, as he seeks to unravel the causes of his disbelief by immersing himself in rationalist philosophy, leads him to conclude that the attempt to explain all through intellectual speculation can lead only to the nihilism of total subjectivity. 'In infinite time, in infinite matter, in infinite space is formed a bubble organism and that bubble lasts awhile and bursts, and that bubble is Me', he muses. 'What I know', he declares, 'I know not by reason, but it has been given to me, revealed to me, and I know it with my heart by my faith in the chief thing taught by the church.' The simplicity of the faith he finally attains is underlined vividly in this passage from the end of the novel:

> Under every article of faith of the church could be put the faith in the service of truth instead of one's desires. And each doctrine did not simply leave that faith unshaken, each doctrine seemed essential to complete that great miracle, continually manifest upon earth, that made it possible for each man and millions of different sorts and kinds of men, wise men and imbeciles, old men and children—all men, peasants, Lvov, Kitty, beggars and kings to understand perfectly the same one thing, and to build up thereby that life of the soul which alone is worth living, and which alone is precious to us.
>
> Lying on his back, he gazed up now into the high cloudless sky. 'Do I not know that that is infinite space, and that it is not a round arch?' But, however, I screw up my eyes and strain my sight, I cannot see it not round and not bounded, and in spite of my knowing about infinite space, I am incontestably right when I see a solid blue dome, and more right than when I strain my eyes to see beyond it'.
>
> Levin ceased thinking, and only, as it were, listened to mysterious voices that seemed talking joyfully and earnestly within him.
>
> 'Can this be faith?' he thought, afraid to believe in his happiness. 'My God, I thank Thee!' he said, gulping down his sobs, and with both hands brushing away the tears that filled his eyes.[4]

Levin's conclusion that the force that gives meaning to life is the faith of simple men, unacquainted with the complexities of philosophic or theological rationalism, is paralleled in Tolstoy's words from *A Confession* which were cited earlier: 'Rational knowledge, as presented by the learned and the wise negates the meaning of life, yet the vast masses—humanity as a whole—recognise that this meaning lies in irrational knowledge.'[5] Of his own search for faith he says: 'In addition to rational knowledge which I had hitherto thought to be the only real knowledge I was inevitably led to acknowledge that there does exist another kind of knowledge—an irrational one possessed by humanity as a whole: faith which affords the possibility of living.' 'Where there is life there is faith', he declares. 'Since the day of creation faith has made it possible for mankind to live, and the essential aspects of that faith are everywhere the same.'[6] The aspects to which he referred were its radical simplicity, its irreducibility to the categories of rational thought, and its accessibility to the whole of humankind. He contrasts the existentially meaningful, life-related faith of the unlearned masses with the self-indulgent, spurious faith of learned elites:

> And I began to grow close to the believers among the poor, simple uneducated folk: pilgrims, monks, sectarians, and peasants. The belief held by these people was the same Christianity as that of the pseudo-believers of my circle. They too had mixed a great deal of superstition alongside Christian truths, but the difference was that while superstition was quite unnecessary to the believers of my circle, had nothing to do with their lives and simply provided some kind of epicurean distraction, the superstitions of the believers belonging to the labouring section of the population were so interconnected with their lives that they could not have conceived of life without them; they were a necessary condition of their lives. The whole way of life of the believers of my own circle stood in contradiction to their faith, whereas the whole way of life of the believers from the working population reaffirmed the meaning their faith gave to life. And I started to look more closely at the life and faith of these people, and the further I looked the more convinced I became that theirs was the true faith, that their faith was essential to them, and that it alone provides a sense of the meaning and possibility of life. In contrast to what I saw among the people of my class where it is possible to live without faith and where among the thousands there is barely one who can admit to being a believer, among them there is hardly one in a thousand who does not believe. . . . All our activities, our discussions, our science and our art struck me as sheer indulgence. I realised that there was no meaning to be found there. It was the activities of the labouring people, those who produce life, that presented itself to me as the only true way. I realised that the meaning provided by this life was truth and I accepted it.[7]

Like Kierkegaard, therefore, Tolstoy saw faith as ultimately 'absurd', as unintelligible—focussed on modes of reality and meaning such as 'thought cannot think'—yet also 'paradoxical', insofar as it is endlessly enlivened by the same powers of reason which it finally transcends.[8] In a Diary entry for September 1895 he wrote: 'There is not one believer who does not suffer moments of doubt in the existence of God. These doubts are not harmful;

on the contrary they lead to a higher understanding of God.'[9] He would probably have endorsed Kierkegaard's view that 'the loss of faith is the dialectical factor in everything Christian', and would probably also have approved of a distinction made by Unamuno between the negative 'Cartesian doubt'—which merely reinforces analytic thought—and the 'impassioned doubt' which springs from 'the eternal conflict between reason and feeling, science and life, logic and biotic'.[10] This latter form of doubt Unamuno described as 'the very foundation of the spiritual and emotional life.' The torment of self-questioning and doubt which Tolstoy chronicles in *A Confession* and *What I Believe* would strongly suggest that, while scorning the claims of rationalist philosophers to explain the nature of ultimate truths, he also saw faith as being enlivened and renewed by the persistent challenge of critical and sceptical thought.

Like his fellow-countryman, Dostoevsky, he saw the challenge of scepticism and doubt as intimating the fundamental freedom of the act of belief. And again, like Dostoevsky, he saw that freedom as being threatened by the dogmatism and authoritarianism of the institutional Churches. Echoing the words of the Grand Inquisitor, he spoke of the dogmatism of the Churches as an assault on the most fundamental principle of Christ's teaching: the radical freedom of individual conscience and faith. 'From the moment when the first members of the Church Council said "We believe in the Holy Spirit", that is to say, placed external authority above internal and considered the pitiful deliberations of Councils to be more important and holier than that which is truly sacred to man—his reason and conscience— from that moment,' he writes, 'commenced the lie which lulls man's body and soul and which has murdered millions of human beings and continues its dreadful deeds to this day.'[11]

The only authority to which he believed a Christian should subscribe was that of the scriptures, and this, as will be shown presently, held profound implications for the manner in which he believed religious and moral education should be conducted. It was the existence of the scriptures, he wrote in *The Law of Violence and the Law of Love*, which ensured that the misrepresentation of Christian teaching by the Churches was constantly resisted and corrected through the ages. The renewal of Christianity through its history is to be attributed, he writes, to individuals and groups prepared to act on the basis of individual conscience and faith and to reassert the essential message of the Biblical text:

> While the majority of people, deceived by the doctrines of the Church, had only a vague understanding of the true meaning of Christ's teaching, and instead of worshipping their former idols worshipped Christ-God, His

Mother, the Saints, bowed to relics and icons, believed in miracles, the sacraments, the Redemption, and the infallibilty of the Church hierarchy, the pagan structure of the world could be maintained and could satisfy people. All men alike believed in the explanation of the meaning of life which the Church gave them, and in the guidance for conduct that followed from it, and this faith drew people together. This is how it was until people noticed what was hiding behind the Church faith that had been given to them as the truth. But the misfortune of the Church faith was the existence of the Scriptures, which even the Church recognised as sacred. Despite the efforts made by the Church to conceal from people the essence of the teaching revealed in the Gospels, neither the prohibition of their translation into languages more accessible to the people, nor the false interpretation of them, could extinguish the light filtering through the deceit of the Church and illuminating men's souls as they grasped the enormous truths of the teaching with ever-increasing clarity. With the spread of literacy and the printing press people began to discover the Scriptures and to understand what was written in them, and could no longer, despite all the manoeuvres of the Church, avoid seeing the contradiction staring them in the eye between the political structures supported by the Church and the Gospel teachings.[12]

Amongst those he singles out as exemplifying this willingness to take a stand against dogmatism are the Early Fathers—he particularly mentions Tatian, Clement of Alexandria, Origen, Tertullian, Cyprian and Lactancius —and even some of the socialists and anarchists of later years in whom he saw 'partial manifestations of Christian consciousness', despite his rejection of the humanist and materialist principles on which their beliefs were based.[13] What they all exemplified was something he considered crucial to Christian morality: the assumption of responsibility in the light of the dictates of individual conscience and faith. In this key passage from *The Law of Violence and the Law of Love* he speaks of the weight of the responsibility that lies on the Christian to take a stand against the forces of evil and corruption:

A dreadful weight of evil hangs over the people of the world and oppresses them. The people standing beneath this weight are becoming more and more crushed by it, and are searching for a means of freeing themselves from it.

They know they can lift the weight and throw it off through joint effort; but they cannot agree to do it all together. Everyone is sinking lower and lower, leaving the weight to rest on someone else's shoulders; the weight is pressing more and more heavily and would have crushed them long ago if it were not for people who are guided in their actions not so much by considerations of external behaviour, as by the inner compatibility between their behaviour and their conscience. These kind of people are, and always have been, Christians because instead of setting themselves an external goal which needs the cooperation of others to be achieved, they set themselves an inner goal, which requires cooperation from no one else and which is the essence of Christianity in its true meaning.[14]

That same theme was developed some years later by Pasternak in *Dr Zhivago*, where a minor character, Nikolai Vedniapin, proclaims the central message of the novel: that Christanity stands above all else for the ideal of individual conscience and freedom. Though initially enthused by the ideals of socialism—especially when confronted with the appalling miseries to which the masses of the Russian people were subjected, with the full blessings of 'Christian' Orthodoxy—Nikolai nonetheless condemned the collectivist tendencies he saw in the new ideology. 'It is always', he says, 'a sign of mediocrity in people when they herd together, whether this group loyalty is to Soloviev or to Kant or to Marx. The truth is sought only by individuals and they break with those who do not love it enough.' He sees the latter tendency as one specifically linked with Christianity; the coming of Christ, he says, marked the inauguration of a new age of freedom in which the destiny of individual man superseded that of the collective. Like Tolstoy, Pasternak saw this celebration of the free personality as the essence of the Christian vision:

> And then into this tasteless heap of gold and marble, He came, light-footed and clothed in light, with his marked humanity, his deliberate Galilean provincialism, and from that moment there were neither gods nor peoples, there was only man—man the carpenter, man the ploughman, man the shepherd, with his flock of sheep at sunset, man whose name does not sound in the least proud but who is sung in lullabies and portrayed in picture galleries the world over.[15]

The freedom which is the defining characteristic of man's nature is most potently manifested, Nikolai says, in the universal capacity for love. 'The love of one's neighbour is the supreme form of living energy', he declares; 'once it fills the heart of man it has to overflow and expend itself.'[16] In his autobiography, *Safe Conduct*, Pasternak himself had written: 'We have all become people only to the measure in which we have loved people and had the opportunity to love. To love selflessly and unreservedly, with a strength equal to the square of the distance'—this, he says, 'is the task of our hearts while we are children'.[17] His words echo those of Tolstoy's Prince Andrew who finds faith also in the power of love and sees it as affording the ultimate freedom: the triumph over suffering and death. Lying wounded on the battlefield he concludes:

> Love hinders death. Love is life. All, all that I understand, I understand only because I love. All is, all exists, only because I love. All is bound up in love

alone. Love is God and dying means for me, a particle of love, to go back to the eternal and universal source of love.[18]

Pierre Bezhukov similarly learns from the peasant, Platon Karataev, that faith is not to be found in 'any kind of rule, or words, or ideas', but in the loving witness to an 'everliving God' whose presence is 'everywhere manifest'.[19] And Levin, confronted by the spectacle of his dying brother, also finds hope in the power of fraternal love: 'He felt that love saved him from despair and that this love, under the menace of despair, had become still stronger and purer. The one mystery of death had scarcely passed before his eyes when another mystery had arisen, as insoluble, urging him to love and to life.'[20] Later as he ponders on the nature of this mystery, he concludes that life's meaning is disclosed through an irrational force inexplicable to reason—the unfathomable but universally experienced power of fellowship and brotherhood. This is the moment when he attains faith:

> And he briefly went through, mentally, the whole course of his ideas during the last two years, the beginning of which was the clear confronting of death, at the first sight of his dear brother hopelessly ill.
>
> Then, for the first time, grasping that for every man, and himself too, there was nothing in store but suffering, death and forgetfulness, he had made up his mind that life was impossible like that, and that he must either interpret life so that it would not present itself to him as the evil jest of some devil, or shoot himself.
>
> But he had not done either, but had gone on living, thinking, and feeling, and had even at that very time married, and had had many joys, and had been happy, when he was not thinking of the meaning of his life.
>
> What did this mean? It meant that he had been living rightly, but thinking wrongly. . . .
>
> 'I looked for an answer to my question. And thought could not give me an answer to my question. It is incommensurable with my question. The answer has been given me by life itself, in my knowledge of what is right and what is wrong. And that knowledge I did not arrive at in any way, it was given to me as to all men, given, because I could not have got it from anywhere.
>
> 'Where must I have got it? By reason could I have arrived at knowing that I must love my neighbour and not oppress him? I was told that in my childhood, and I believed it gladly, for they told me what was already in my soul. But who discovered it? Not reason. Reason discovered the struggle for existence, and the law that requires us to oppress all who hinder the satisfaction of our desires. That is the deduction of reason. But loving one's neighbour reason could never discover because it's irrational'.[21]

The theme of loving faith dominates *Resurrection*, Tolstoy's most explicitly Christian novel, though its complexity is made fully apparent as the novel explores the conflict of sense and spirit, of the self-directed eros and the other-directed agape, which lies at the heart of all human relationships, and which is particularly exemplified in the intimacy of heterosexual feeling, as is demonstrated in the lives of the novel's protagonists, Nekhlyudov and Maslova. Deeply estranged at first by the consequences of an unloving sexual encounter, they are gradually reconciled as they recognise the truth of Christ's teaching that altruistic love alone saves man from brutality and corruption. This is the 'eternal, immutable law' of which Nekhlyudov speaks at the end of the novel:

> If a psychological problem were set to find means of making men of our time—Christian, humane, kind people—perform the most horrible crimes without feeling guilty, only one solution could be devised: simply to go on doing what is being done now. It is only necessary that these people should be governors, inspectors, policemen; that they should be fully convinced that there is a kind of business, called government service, which allows me to treat other men as things without having human brotherly relations with them; and that they should be so linked together by this government service that the responsibility for the results of their deeds should not fall on any one of them individually. Without these conditions the terrible acts I witnessed today would be imposssible in our times. It all lies in the fact that men think there are circumstances when one may deal with human beings without love. But there are no such circumstances. We may deal with things without love—we cut down trees, make bricks, hammer iron without love—but we cannot deal with men without it.[22]

Examples such as these could be multiplied from Tolstoy's writings, all of them reiterating his fundamental theme that love is the basis of faith, the ultimate source of life's meaning, and the essence of the teaching of Christ as disclosed in the scriptures. In an Address which he delivered shortly after he was excommunicated by the Orthodox Church, he declared: 'I believe that the meaning of every man's life lies only in increasing the store of love within him; that this increase of love leads a man to greater and greater blessings.'[23] In *The Law of Violence and the Law of Love* where he set out the basis of his pacifist beliefs—the logical outcome of his belief in Christian fellowship and brotherhood—he wrote: 'It is becoming more and more evident in our age that the significance of the Christian doctrine is that the essence of human life and the highest law governing it is love.'[24] One is reminded, inevitably, of the episode in *The Brothers Karamazov* where Madame Hohlakov visits Father Zosima to ask how she can recover her lost faith. 'If one has faith where does it come from?' she asks. 'How can I prove that God exists?' 'There is no proving it', the elder replies, 'though you can be convinced of it.' 'You can be convinced of it', he says, 'by the experience of active love. Strive to love your neighbour actively and indefatigably. In so far as you advance in love you will grow surer of the reality of God and of the immortality of your soul. If you attain to perfect self-forgetfulness in the love of your neighbour, then you will believe without doubt and no doubt can possibly enter your soul.'[25]

This identification of faith with 'active love' by Tolstoy, Dostoevsky and Pasternak finds many parallels in modern philosophic literature. In a key passage from the *Postscript*, for example, Kierkegaard wrote: 'The object of faith is the reality of another and the relationship is one of infinite interest. The object of faith is not a doctrine for then the relationship would be intellectual.'[26] And in the Journals he wrote: 'Faith expresses a relation from personality to personality. Personality is not a sum of doctrines . . . it is that which is within . . . that which is within to which a man, himself in turn a personality, may be related in faith.'[27] Strongly reflecting this conception of faith as lying in the realm of the intersubjective, Unamuno spoke of it as a cointentional consciousness, its definitive character lying in the depth of its cointentionality. 'Faith in God is born of love', he wrote. 'Love person- alises all that it loves. . . . And when love is so great, so vital, so strong and so overflowing that it loves everything, then it personalises everything and discovers that the total All, that the universe is also a Person, possessing a consciousness . . . a consciousness which in turn suffers, pities and loves. . . . And this consciousness of the universe which love, personalising all that it loves, discovers, is what we call God.'[28] The religious being is the one who loves deeply and actively, his faith being the product of his limitless potentiality for altruism, fellowship and brotherhood:

> God who is Love, the Father of Love, is the Son of Love in us. There are men of an external and facile habit of mind, slaves of reason, that reason which externalises us, who think it a shrewd comment to say that so far from God having made man in his image and likeness, it is rather man who has made his gods or his God in his own image and likeness, and so superficial are they that they do not pause to consider that if the second of these propositions be true, as in fact it is, it is owing to the fact that the first is not less true. God and man, in effect, mutually create one another; God creates or reveals Himself in man and man creates himself in God. God is His own maker, Deus ipse se facit, said Lactantius and we may say that He is making himself continually both in man and by man. And if each of us, impelled by his love, by his hunger for divinity, creates for himself an image of God according to his own desire, and if according to His desire God creates Himself for each of us, then there is a collective, social, human God, the resultant of all the human imaginations that imagine Him. For God is and reveals Himself in collectivity. And God is the richest and most personal of human con- ceptions.[29]

Further examples could be cited from the works of more recent philosophers—amongst them Buber, Marcel, Jaspers and Levinas—in support of this conception of faith as being founded on love. Buber's God is the 'Eternal Thou' to whom faith is directed in the form of a dialogue of love—a dialogue addressed to the existential presence of Thouness in the created universe.[30] Marcel spoke of faith as a 'presentness', a fidelity to otherness. 'Fidelity', he wrote, 'is not a mere act of will, it is faith in the presence of an other than me to which I respond.'[31] I am present to the other when my actions are motivated by selfless love. 'Love is the absolute consciousness in its plenitude', Jasper wrote . . . 'always possible, always desired, endlessly frustrating in the unattainability of its absoluteness'. Paradoxically, the unrelenting quest for the absoluteness of the intersubjective is itself empowered by the experience of intersubjectivity. And this means that love and faith are inextricably related: 'The harmony of belonging together, unrealisable in the world, makes perceptible an absolute . . . and makes possible in it the loving struggle of unrelenting truthfulness.'[32]

That potentiality for self-fulfilment through the harmony of the intersubjective is, Levinas says, inherent in the nature of our being. 'The conceptual category of individuality is fulfilled only in the movement of love', he writes. 'In love the individual is grasped as an infinity which can never become the object of thought or knowledge.' The particular significance of his conception of this whole issue lies in the emphasis placed on active love as a responsibility, a moral imperative emerging from nature itself. 'My responsibility for the other lies deeper', he writes, 'than social obligation, it comes from what is prior to my freedom, from the givenness of the intersubjective. . . . Before the neighbour I am summoned and do not just appear; from the first I am answering to an assignation. . . . The proximity of a neighbour is my responsibility for him.' This givenness of the intersubjective is the basis of faith and the reality towards which it is inevitably directed:

> We have here come upon an imbroglio that has to be taken seriously: a relationship to . . . that is not represented, without intentionality, not repressed; it is the latent birth of religion in the other, prior to emotions or voices, prior to 'religious experience', which speaks of revelation in terms of the disclosure of being, when it is a question of an unwonted access, in the heart of my responsibility, to an unwonted disturbance of being.[33]

It will be shown presently that Tolstoy, like Buber, Jaspers, Marcel and Levinas, saw faith and individual responsibility as inextricably related, and the ethical imperatives deriving from this became the basis of his ideas on moral and religious education. But first some elaboration is necessary on a further aspect of the Tolstoyan concept of faith which has not yet been mentioned: that is, its simultaneous disclosure of both the immanent and transcendent presence of God in existence. The theme that religious living involves a communion with, rather than a retreat from, the world runs through all his fiction from *War and Peace* to the stories of his final years, such as 'The Death of Ivan Ilyich' and 'Father Sergius'. 'The erroneous belief that it is better for a man to retire from the world than to expose himself to temptations . . . is entirely foreign not only to Christianity but to the Jewish religion also', he declared in *What I Believe*.[34] Man, he says, attests to God's immanent presence in creation by his love for all existent being. 'The principal commandments of Jesus', he writes, 'are that his followers shall love others and spread his doctrine. Both exact constant communion with the world.'[35]

Thus Father Sergius, in the story of that name, discovers that he can find God, not by retreating from the world to his hermitage, but by returning to serve humankind directly through the practice of active love. He envies the simple faith of his cousin, Pashenka: 'She is precisely what I ought to have been and what I have not been. I lived for man, pretending I lived for God, but she lives for God imagining that she lives for man. Yes, one good deed, a cup of water offered without thought of reward is dearer than all those I have helped for the sake of man's approval.'[36] The same theme finds further expression in various passages from the novels celebrating the beauty of nature as a physical intimation of the immanent presence of the divine. Thus Pierre, at the end of *War and Peace* , concludes that the visible confirmation of his faith in the existential presence of God lies in the beauty of the universe that God created:

> He could see no object in life now, because now he had faith—not faith in any sort of principles, or words, or ideas, but faith in a living, ever palpable God. In old days he had sought Him in the aims he set before himself. That search for an object in life had been only a seeking after God; and all at once in his captivity he had come to know, not through words or arguments, but by his own immediate feeling, what his old nurse had told him long before; that God is here and everywhere. In his captivity he had come to see that the God in Karataev was grander, more infinite, and more unfathomable than the Architect of the Universe recognised by the Masons. He felt like a man who finds what he has sought at his feet, when he has been straining his eyes to seek it in the distance. All his life he had been looking far away over the heads of all around him, while he need not have strained his eyes, but had only to look in front of him. . . .
>
> Now he had learned to see the great, the eternal, and the infinite in everything; and naturally therefore, in order to see it, to revel in its con-

templation, he flung aside the telescope through which he had hitherto been gazing over men's heads, and looked joyfully at the ever changing, ever grand, unfathomable and infinite life around him. And the closer he looked at it the calmer and happier he was. The terrible question that had shattered his edifices in old days, the question: What for? had no existence for him now. To that question, What for? he had now always ready in his soul the simple answer: Because there is a God, that God without whom not one hair of a man's head falls.[37]

There are echoes here of Father Zosima's last words to the monks as he lies on his deathbed: 'If you love everything you will perceive the divine mystery in things. Once you perceive it you will begin to comprehend it better every day.' 'Love a man even in his sin', he tells them, 'for that is the semblance of divine love and is the highest love on earth. Love all of God's creation, the whole and every grain of sand in it. Love every leaf, every ray of God's light.'[38]

Pointing to the paradox that the transcendent reality of God is perceived by man through his immanent presence in existence, Karl Jaspers wrote: 'A proved God is no God. Accordingly, only he who starts from God can seek him ... the *deus absconditus* recedes into the distance when I seek to fathom him, he is infinitely near in the absolute historicity of the unique situation—and the situation is always unique.'[39] Tolstoy, like Jaspers, suggests that love, being directed towards the finite, the temporal, the earthly, discloses the immanent possibility of the infinite, the intemporal, the transcendent, and thereby sustains faith in its everpresent possibility. Thus Prince Andrew declares that love conquers death and discloses the possibility of the eternal. 'Love hinders death', he reflects. 'Love is life. . . . Love is God and to die means that I, a particle of love, shall return to the general and eternal source.'[40]

One of Tolstoy's favourite passages from scripture was this one from the Gospel of St John: 'We know that we have passed from death into life because we love the brethren. He that loveth not his brother abideth in death'. When he quoted these words in *The Law of Violence and the Law of Love* he added this comment: 'The teaching of Christ (on love) amounts to saying that what we call our "self" or our life is really the divine principle, limited in us by our body and manifesting itself as love, and that therefore the true life in each man, divine and free, expresses itself as love.'[41] The term 'divine' here signifies the infinite and intemporal, the transcendent principle in existence, which is disclosed through love. While Tolstoy's use of the term clearly indicates his belief in the immortality of the spirit, this must be taken in conjunction with his rejection of the widely propagated teaching of the Churches on a personal resurrection. In *What I Believe* he argued that this doctrine was not only never taught by Christ himself, but that he explicitly rejected it on a number of occasions:

> According to all the Gospels the object of Jesus' teaching was the life eternal. And, strange as it may seem, Jesus, who is supposed to have been raised in person, and to have promised a general resurrection—Jesus not only said nothing in affirmation of individual resurrection and individual immortality beyond the grave, but on the contrary, every time that he met with this superstition (introduced at this period into the Talmud, and of which there is not a trace in the record of the Hebrew prophets), he did not fail to deny its truth. The Pharisees and the Sadducees were constantly discussing the subject of the resurrection of the dead. The Pharisees believed in the resurrection of the dead, in angels, and in spirits (Acts xxiii, 8), but the Sadducees did not believe in resurrection, or angel, or spirit. We do not know the source of the difference in belief, but it is certain that it was one of the polemical subjects among the secondary questions of the Hebraic doctrine that were constantly under discussion in the synagogues. And Jesus not only did not recognise the resurrection, but denied it every time he met with the idea. When the Sadducees demanded of Jesus, supposing that he believed with the Pharisees in the resurrection, to which of the seven brethern the woman should belong, he refuted with clearness and precision the idea of individual resurrection, saying that on this subject they erred, knowing neither the Scriptures nor the power of God.[42]

Later in the same work Tolstoy wrote that 'the basis of faith is not the prospect of resurrection but the meaning we derive from life, the meaning that determines whether we look on life as important and good, or trivial and corrupt'.[43] That meaning, he repeatedly asserted, lies in the infinite potency of love, and the prospect of immortality lies in man's hoped for participation in the infinity of love's existence—the hope that he, 'a particle of love, will return to the general and eternal source'.[44]

It is interesting to compare his conception of this issue with that of Pasternak in *Doctor Zhivago*. In one of the most moving sequences from Pasternak's novel, its hero, Yury Zhivago, comforts the dying Anna Gromeko, with an assurance of her immortality: 'You in others are yourself, your soul. That is what you are. This is what your consciousness has breathed and lived on and enjoyed throughout life, your soul, your immortality, your life in others. . . . You have always been in others and you will remain in others.'[45] His conviction that life is transformed through love—through 'life in others'—underlies his confident prediction on the certainty of immortality, in support of which *he also* cites the words of the Gospel of St John: 'There will be no death says Saint John, and just look at the simplicity of his argument. There will be no death because the past is over; that's almost like saying there will be no death because death is already done with, it's old and we are tired of it. What we need is something new and that new thing is life eternal'.[46] The essential message of the novel is that love conquers death: the same message conveyed by Father Zosima in his words to Madame Hohlakov—'in so far as you advance in love you will grow surer of the reality of God and the immortality of your soul'—and by the dying Prince Andrew in his declaration that 'love hinders death' and marks the soul's return to 'its general and eternal source'.[47]

The same concept of self-transcendence through love has been developed by Levinas in his essay, 'God and Philosophy'. Transcendence of self occurs, he says, in the depth of the intersubjective. 'The infinite in me', he writes, 'is the desire for the Infinite. This endless desire for what is beyond self, being, for alterity, is the desire for the infinite.' This is a desire,' he says, 'which cannot be filled, which nourishes itself with its own augmentation. . . . It is a desire that is beyond satisfaction and unlike a need does not identify a term or an end.' The selflessness of love is the guarantee of its infinity: 'Affected by the infinite, desire cannot proceed to an end which it were equal to . . . it is desire for what is not I, for the infinite which is God—the other with an alterity prior to the alterity of the other.'[48] The passion for the infinite—for the absoluteness of alterity—is the 'passion for the Good', he writes, and manifests itself primarily therefore as morality.[49] Love is the *will to love*, just as faith, as Unamuno wrote in *The Tragic Sense of Life*, is essentially the will to faith:

> . . . faith is in its essence simply a matter of will, not of reason . . . to believe is to wish to believe, and to believe in God is, before all and above all, to wish that there may be a God. In the same way, to believe in the immortality of the soul is to wish that the soul may be immortal, but to wish it with such force that this volition shall trample reason under foot and pass beyond it.[50]

In *The Law of Violence and the Law of Love* Tolstoy similarly asserted the essentially ethical character of the act of love. 'In all the pre-Christian doctrines', he wrote, 'love was regarded as one of the virtues, but not as that which the Christian teaching acknowledges it to be: metaphysically the origin of everything, practically the highest law of human life . . . and the guidance for conduct that must follow from it.'[51] The implications of this will be addressed in detail presently. There remains one issue, however, which still needs to be clarified, and which can now be more fully explained in the light of the emphasis given to Tolstoy's conception of faith as active love. Earlier some reference was made to his condemnation of the institutional Churches, and a number of reasons were suggested for this. The most fundamental of his objections, as should now be apparent, sprang from the conviction that denominational religion—especially in the intolerant form in which it was historically practised—was basically incompatible with the precepts implicit in the law of love. The kind of loving faith that he espoused was directly in conflict with the dogmatism and exclusivity of the institutional Churches, and much of the negative comment he directed at formal religion was prompted by this. A radical ecumenist—long before that term was used by the Churches themselves to designate the spirit of religious tolerance—he denounced religious exclusivity on the grounds that its basic *raison d'etre* was sectarian dominance and prejudice. Its incipient violence he saw as being directly in conflict with the message of love that it purported to preach. 'The conviction that the knowledge of truth can be found only in one way led me to doubt the rightness of my life', he writes in the passage from *A Confession* where he describes his conversion to non-sectarian Christianity:

> At the time, as a result of my interest in religion, I had come into contact with believers of various denominations: Catholics, Protestants, Old Believers, Molokans and others. Among them I met many deeply moral men with sincere beliefs. I wished to be a brother to these people. And what happened? The teaching which had promised me unity of all through one faith and through love, that very teaching, speaking through its highest representatives, told me that all these people were living a lie, that the thing that gave them strength of life was a temptation of the devil, and that it is we alone who are in possession of the only possible truth. And I saw that the Orthodox Church regarded as heretics all those who did not profess an identical faith to theirs, just as the Catholics and the others consider the Orthodox followers to be heretics. And I saw that the Orthodox, although they may try to hide it, regard with hostility all those who do not practise their faith by using the same external symbols and words as themselves. And this could not be otherwise, first of all because the assertion that you live in falsehood and I in truth is the most cruel thing that one man can say to another, and secondly, because a man who loves his children and his brothers cannot help feeling hostile towards those who want to convert his children and his brothers to a false belief. And this hostility increases in proportion to one's knowledge of theology. And assuming that truth lies in union by love, I was struck by the fact that theology was destroying the thing it should be advancing.[52]

The perversion of the original Christian injunction to 'love thy neighbour', resulting from the intolerance and dogmatic exclusivity of the Churches, together with their misrepresentations of the teachings of the scriptures, had been largely responsible, he suggests, for the widespread decline of religion in the modern age. The whole institutional fabric of the Churches was based, he says, on principles explicitly rejected by Christ—

the law of property, the 'just war' theology, the defence of social inequity—
all were given rational justification through the distortions of theological
casuistry, despite the unambiguous teachings of Christ on non-resistance to
evil, the sharing of material goods, and the pursuit of justice and righteousness. Perceiving the inherently contradictory character of the teachings of
the Churches, the masses had largely abandoned religious practice, he
writes: 'Men of the Christian world, having accepted under the guise of
Christian teaching a perversion of it, compiled by the Church . . . have ceased
with time to believe in this perverted Church Christianity and have finally
reached the point where they are left without any kind of religious understanding of life or guidance or conduct resulting from it.'[53]

Yet he proclaimed his own unequivocal acceptance of the truths of
Christianity, and pledged his unswerving devotion to the faith of the
scriptures. In his Reply to the Edict of the Orthodox Church, which proclaimed his excommunication, he declared: 'I began by loving my Orthodox
faith more than my own peace, then I loved Christianity more than my own
Church, and now I love truth more than anything else in the world. And to
this day truth corresponds for me to Christianity as I understand it. And I
hold to this Christianity and in so far as I hold to it I live calmly and joyfully,
and calmly and joyfully approach my death.'[54] It was this non-sectarian,
non-dogmatic Christianity that he sought to promote through education; its
focus was to be the unadulterated message of love that was revealed through
the scriptures, and we shall see that the methods that were used to promote
it were wholly consistent with the spirit of individual freedom in which it
was conceived.

2   Religion and Morality

It is essential, however, before an attempt is made to examine Tolstoy's ideas
on religious education, that his sense of the interdependence of religion and
morality be appropriately emphasised. In his identification of faith with
active love we find the key to his understanding of the whole relationship
between the spheres of the religious and the ethical. He spoke of the
distinctive character of Christianity—when compared, for example, with the
teachings of the Egyptian sages, the Brahmins, the Stoics, the Buddhists and
Taoists—as consisting in the fact that it made the principle of active love
the 'supreme *law* that should be not only the chief but the only guiding
principle in people's *conduct*'[55] (my italics). The moral emphasis conveyed
by the terms 'conduct' and 'law' points to the ethico-religious character of
his entire understanding of the Christian faith, indicating that he saw faith
ultimately as a responsibilty manifested in the practical expression of love
for the whole of humankind. 'The love which defines these laws is only love

when it admits no exceptions, when it is applied equally to foreigners, to all sectarians and likewise to the enemies who hate us and wrong us', he writes. In support of this all-embracing concept of love as universal resposibility, he cites the words of Christ as revealed in the scriptures, especially in the Sermon on the Mount:

> The guidance for conduct that follows from this understanding of the law of love that admits no exceptions is expressed in many parts of the Gospels, and with particular clarity and precision in the fourth commandment of the Sermon on the Mount: 'You have heard that it hath been said: An eye for an eye, a tooth for a tooth (Ex., xxi, 24). But I say unto you, That ye resist not evil' is said in verse 38 of the fifth chapter of St Matthew's Gospel. In verses 39 and 40, as if foreseeing those exceptions which might appear necessary, when the law of love is applied to life, it is clearly and definitively stated that there are, and can be, no circumstances when it is permissible to deviate from the very simple and vital requirement of love: not to do to others that which you would not have them do to you . . . 'but whosoever shall smite thee on thy right cheek, turn to him the other also. And if any man will sue thee at the law, and take away thy coat, let him have thy cloak also'.[56]

Again in *The Kingdom of God Is Within You* he stresses the ethical character of Christian love: 'However people may try', he writes, 'it cannot be denied that one of the first principles of a Christian life is love, *not in words but in deed*'[57] (my italics). Like Father Zosima, his consistent affirmation is that 'each is responsible for all',[58] and, like the elder, he recognises that love 'is possible only through effort and will', that it is 'won slowly by long labour',[59] and, above all, that it requires the conquest of selfishness and pride. In *What I Believe* he responded to the objection that the teaching of Christianity is 'excellent but impracticable', both by recognising the enormity of the challenge that it represents, and by insisting that such a commitment is nonetheless required of a believing Christian, willing to respond to the inner dictates of his conscience:

> The dogma of the fall and the redemption has debarred man from the most important and legitimate field for the exercise of his powers, and has entirely deprived him of the idea that he can of himself do anything to make his life happier or better. Science and philosophy, proudly believing themselves hostile to pseudo-Christianity, only carry out its decrees. Science and philosophy concern themselves with everything except the theory that man can do anything to make himself better or happier. Ethical and moral instruction have disappeared from our pseudo-Christian society without leaving a trace. . . .
> 　　The reasonable activity of man has always been—it could not be otherwise —to light by the torch of reason his progress towards beatitude. Philosophy

tells us that free will is an illusion, and then boasts of the boldness of such a declaration. Free will is not only an illusion; it is an empty word invented by theologians and experts in criminal law; to refute it would be to undertake a battle with a wind-mill. But reason, which illuminates our life, and impels us to modify our actions, is not an illusion, and its authority can never be denied. To obey reason in the pursuit of good is the substance of the teachings of all the masters of humanity, and it is the substance of the doctrine of Jesus; it is reason itself, and we cannot deny reason by the use of reason.[60]

By emphasising action and deed as the practical modes by which love is manifested, Tolstoy characterises it clearly as an obligation: an obligation to discharge the responsibility enjoined in the Christian imperative, 'Thou shalt love thy neighbour as thyself.' It is interesting to compare him with Buber on this issue, since both were clearly aware of the emotional and even sentimental connotations of the idea of love, and both sought earnestly to emphasise the moral responsibility which it entails. In *I and Thou* Buber explains that, while intersubjective dialogue is normally accompanied by emotion or feeling, it is not 'constituted' by it; nor, he argues, is love manifested primarily through affectivity, but rather through the exercise of personal responsibility:

> Feelings accompany the metaphysical and metapsychical fact of love, but they do not constitute it; and the feelings that accompany it can be very different. Jesus' feeling for the possessed man is different from his feeling for the beloved disciple; but the love is one. Feelings one 'has'; love occurs. Feelings dwell in man, but man dwells in his love. This is not metaphor but actuality: love does not cling to an I, as if the 'You' were merely its content or object; it is between I and You. Whoever does not know this, know this with his being, does not know love, even if he should ascribe to it the feelings that he lives through, experiences, enjoys, and expresses. Love is a cosmic force. For those who stand in it and behold in it, men emerge from their entanglement in busy-ness; and the good and the evil, the clever and the foolish, the beautiful and the ugly, one after another become actual and a You for them; that is, liberated, emerging from a unique confrontation. Exclusiveness comes into being miraculously again and again—and now one can act, help, heal, educate, raise redeem. *Love is responsibility of an I for a You*: in this consists what cannot consist in any feeling—the equality of all lovers, from the smallest to the greatest, and from the blissfully secure whose life is circumscribed by the life of one beloved human being to him that is nailed his life long to the cross of the world, capable of what is immense and bold enough to risk it: to love man[61] (my italics).

The same distinction is maintained by Tolstoy, especially in 'Religion and Morality', the work in which he most explicitly sets out his understanding of the interelationship of the religious and the ethical. In this work he once again stresses the universality of the religious experience. 'It is impossible', he writes, 'for there to be a person with no religion (i.e, without any kind of relationship to the world) as it is for there to be a person without a heart. He may not know that he has a religion, just as a person may not know that he has a heart, but it is no more possible for a person to exist without religion than without a heart.'[62] Again, he insists that faith is rooted neither in 'philosophic nor scientific knowledge'—he even suggests an 'abundance of knowledge encumbering consciousness is liable to be an impediment to faith'—and equates it with the childlike simplicity of the beliefs of the uneducated masses. 'It is very often the simple, unlearned and uneducated people who can quite lucidly, consciously and easily grasp the highest Christian concepts of life', he writes, 'while educated and cultured people continue to stagnate in extremely crude paganism.'[63] It would appear from the context in which these words were written, however, that the object of his criticism was not education *per se*, but the kind of objectified, abstract knowledge that is conventionally thought to constitute the basic content of education, and which, he suggests, leads to a diminished sense of the value of the 'unphilosophic method of comprehension', on which faith is largely dependent:

> In my opinion the chief error, and the one that more than any other impedes the true progress of our Christian people, lies precisely in the fact that the scientists of our time, now seated on the throne of Moses, are guided by the pagan view of life that was reinstated at the time of the Renaissance. They have accepted as the essence of Christianity something that is a very coarse perversion of it, and have decided that Christianity is a condition that people have outlived, while at the same time, adhering to the ancient pagan social-State understanding of life, which mankind has truly outlived, as the very highest understanding of life and the one that mankind must unwaveringly hold on to. Thus they not only fail to understand the truth of Christianity, which comprises the highest understanding of life towards which man is moving, but they do not even attempt to understand it. The chief source of this understanding lies in the fact that the scientists, recognising the incongruity between their science and Christianity, have divorced themselves from Christianity and decided that it is to blame and not their science. In other words they imagine something other than the truth: that is, they believe that Christianity is 1800 years behind science, whereas the truth is that science is 1800 years behind Christianity, which already influences a large part of contemporary society.[64]

The basis of religion, he states, is 'the relationship man establishes between himself and the infinite never-ending universe, or its origin and first cause'.[65] What he rejects in the scientific mode of thinking is its limited i.e. finite and objectified interpretation of man's relation to the universe. By focussing the relationship on the sphere of finite, phenomenal, rationally explicable realities, science, he suggests, comes directly into conflict with the reaching towards the infinite which manifests itself in the experience of love and faith. From this emerges a distinction which is crucial to his linking of the religious and the ethical. 'If religion is the establishing of a relationship between man and the universe, defining the meaning of life, then morality', he writes, 'is an indication and explanation of those activities which automatically result when a person maintains one or other relationship to the world.'[66] From the scientific, finite view of the universe there emerges a relativist, secular and humanist morality, while from the relation of faith emerges an ethic which is focussed on the absolute, the unconditioned and the infinite.

Differentiating further between secular and religious values, he speaks of the first as being manifested in two main forms: firstly, as a striving towards individual well-being (as in hedonism or epicureanism)—a morality he describes as 'primitive, savage and personal'; and secondly, as a striving towards social well-being, towards the welfare of the group, the community or the state. The latter he sees as the dominant ethic in modern society and, by implication, the conventional value system generally promoted by educators. He distinguishes both from the religious ethic, which he defines as the subordination of individual will to the absoluteness of love, service and alterity, i.e. the subordination of the self to the infinity and transcendence of the selfless:

> From the third, Christian relationship to the world, which consists in man's recognising himself as an instrument for fulfilling the aims of a higher will, follow the moral teachings that correspond to this understanding of life, and clarify the dependence of man on the higher will, defining its demands. All the highest moral teachings known to man stem from this relationship: the highest manifestations of the Pythagorean, Stoic, Buddhist, Brahmin and Taoist religions, and Christianity in its true sense. They all demand the abdication of the individual will, and of the well-being, not just of the individual, but of family, society and state, in the name of fulfilling the will revealed to us by our awareness of Him who has given us life.[67]

Like Buber, who discussed this issue at length in his *Eclipse of God*, Tolstoy attributes the decline of the religious ethic to the attempts to derive moral principles from the rationalist abstractions of philosophy and theology, instead of from the dictates of loving faith. In *Eclipse of God* Buber described the modern prevalence of atheos as a temporary darkening or 'eclipse' of God's presence, resulting from rationalist reductionism i.e. the reduction of the reality of God to the level of an Idea, with a resultant weakening of the relational character of faith.[68] Tolstoy similarly traces the decline of religious faith, and of the religious ethic, to the distortions of abstract reason:

> The Christian ethic—that which we acknowledge as a consequence of our worldly outlook—demands not just the sacrifice of the individual to the individuality of the group, but demands the renunciation of both personal and group individuality for service to God. Pagan philosophy only explores the means of acquiring the greatest well-being for the individual, or for a group of individuals, and the contradiction is inevitable. The only method of concealing this contradiction is to accumulate abstract conditional concepts, one on top of the other, and to avoid departing from the nebulous sphere of metaphysics. This is what the majority of philosophers have done since the time of the Renaissance, and it is to this circumstance—the impossibility of reconciling the previously accepted demands of Christian philosophy with a moral philosophy based on paganism—that one must attribute the peculiar abstraction, lack of clarity, unintelligibility, and irrelevance to life, of modern philosophy. With the exception of Spinoza, whose philosophy, despite the fact that he did not consider himself a Christian, is derived from religious foundations that are sincerely Christian, and of Kant, who presented his ethics as being quite independent of his metaphysics, all other philosophers, even the brilliant Schopenhauer, evidently invented artificial links between their ethics and their metaphysics.[69]

Buber blamed the decline of faith amongst the peoples of the West on the 'Hellenisation' of Christianity: a process, he said, which was initiated by St Paul—whom he charged with introducing the rationalist traditions of Greece into Christian teaching. This process, he says, was maintained by philosophers from St Augustine to the German idealists, all of whom further contaminated the mythic simplicities of Hebraic Christianity with the abstractions of Hellenism.[70] Tolstoy condemned the rationalisation of faith on the same basic grounds that an intellectualised faith would lead inevitably to the relativism of a humanist ethic. 'All such clauses (i.e. philosophic) appear', he said, 'to justify the Christian ethic, but only so long as they are being examined in the abstract.' 'The moment they are applied to problems concerning practical life not only does disagreement arise but a blatant contradiction between what we regard as the philosophic premises and what we regard as morality emerges in full force.' The ethics, he said, which derive their justification from abstract thought, inevitably culminate in the self-oriented humanism of a pseudo-morality, of which an extreme example was the Nietzschean doctrine of the Superman:

> The unfortunate Nietzsche who has lately become so famous, made a valuable exposition of this contradiction. He cannot be refuted when he says

that from the point of view of existing non-Christian philosophies all laws and morality are mere lies and hypocrisy, and that it is far more pleasant and reasonable for a man to create his own fellowship of supermen and to be one of them, than to be one of the crowd that serves as the stage for these supermen. None of the philosophical arguments stemming from a religious view of life that is pagan can prove to a person that it is more dangerous and reasonable not to live for his own well-being, which he desires, understands, finds possible, or for the well-being of his family, or society, but for the well-being that is unknown, undesired, incomprehensible, and unattainable by human means. A philosophy founded on an understanding of human life and confined to the welfare of man will never be in a position to prove to a rational person, who knows that he might die at any moment, that it is good for him and that he must deny himself his own desired, appreciated, and undoubted well-being, and do so not for the good of others (because he will never know the results of his sacrifices) but simply because it is necessary and worthy, and a categorical imperative.[71]

Implied in this passage is one of the foremost conditions identified by Tolstoy for the fostering of the ethic based on active love: the conquest of egotism, selfishness and intellectual pride. Two further conditions which he specified were the pursuit of self-illumination and the active reparation of guilt. The conquest of pride is exemplified in the progress made by all his fictional protagonists towards the attainment of religious faith. 'By reason could I have arrived at knowing that I must love my neighbour and not oppress him?' Levin asks. 'I was told that in my childhood and I believed it gladly for they told me what was already in my soul.'[72] He rediscovers the faith of his childhood, having conquered the illusory belief in the powers of reason which were the main obstacles to its re-emergence. In the same vein, Princess Mary feels envious of the 'holy fools', the despised and impoverished pilgrims who come to her door seeking alms. They 'leave family, home and all the cares of worldly welfare in order, without clinging to anything, to wander in hempen rags from place to place, doing no one any harm, but praying for all'[73]—in the committed pursuance of their Christian faith. In their spirit of total selflessness they epitomise the humility which is necessary for the subordination of individual will to the service of God.

A more insidious pride than the one which Levin describes—the pride of the spirit—is described in the story, 'Father Sergius', where the hero resolves on a life of self-abnegation for the purpose of avenging a wrong done to him by the Tsar. In the words of his sister, he wished to be a monk 'in order to stand above those who wanted to show him that they stood above him. . . . By becoming a monk he showed that he despised all that seemed important to others . . . and he now ascended a height from which he could look down from above on those people he had formerly envied'.[74] The story suggests that the quest for saintliness holds particularly sinister temptations: that spiritual pride, not holiness, is nourished by a life devoted to the service of an abstract, and ultimately solipsistic, concept of God. Repenting of his actions, he prays to be cleansed from 'the sin of worldly vanity'. Paradoxically, he is saved through the humiliation of sexual seduction, abandons his cell, and rediscovers faith in the humble service of others. His new model of holiness is his cousin, Pashenka, through whose example of unselfconscious goodness he finds a more Christ-like fulfilment than that which he had sought in the isolation of his hermitage. Like the *yurodivyy*—the 'holy fools'—like Dostevsky's Prince Myshkin, Pashenka symbolises the triumphant power of the humble and the meek, the power possessed by those in complete harmony with the essential nature of their own being:

> 'Pashenka is precisely what I ought to have been, and what I have not been. I lived for man, pretending to live for God; but she lives for God, imagining that she lives for man. Yes, one good deed, a cup of water offered without thought of reward, is dearer than all those I have helped for the sake of man's approval.' 'But', he asked himself, 'was there not some particle of the true wish to serve God?' And he had to answer, 'Yes, but all that was defiled, overgrown by the wish for glory among men. No, there is no God for one who has lived, like me, for glory among men. But I shall go, then, and search for Him'.
>
> And he went, as he had come to Pashenka, wandering from village to village, now joining, now parting with other pilgrims, men and women; asking food and shelter in Christ's name. At times some ill-tempered housewife might scold at him, or some peasant in his cups abuse him: but far more often he would be given food and drink, and even provision for his way. His appearance, betraying his aristocratic origin, inclined some people in his favour. Others, on the contrary, seemed well pleased to see one of the gentry reduced to beggary. But his gentle ways conquered all with whom he came in contact.
>
> Often, finding the Gospel in some home, he would read aloud from it; and always, everywhere, people would listen, touched and amazed, as to something ever new, though long familar.
>
> If he had an opportunity to help people, by advice, or by writing letters or documents for the illiterate, or by conciliating wranglers, he never heard their gratitude, for he would leave before it could be tendered. And, by little and little, he began to find his God.[75]

The illumination of conscience is the second of the conditions identified by Tolstoy for the fostering of the ethic of active love. 'Conscience is our best and surest guide', he wrote in his Diary for June 1852, shortly after he abandoned the practice of Orthodoxy. 'But where are the signs that distinguish this voice from other voices?' he asked. 'The voice of vanity speaks with equal force. I believe in goodness and love but I don't know what can show me the way to it. Conscience reproaches me', he mused, 'for actions with good intentions which have bad consequences'. However conflicting the promptings of conscience, he nonetheless asserted its primacy as the sole authority that would guide him in the pursuit of the ultimate Good:

> The aim of life is goodness. This feeling is inherent in our souls. The means to a good life is the knowledge of good and evil. But is one's whole life enough for this? And if we dedicate our whole life to it, may we not err and involuntarily do evil? We shall be good when all our strength is constantly directed towards this aim. One can do good without a full knowledge of what is good and evil. But what is our immediate aim: study or action? And is the absence of evil good? Inclinations and fate indicate the path we must choose, but we must always work hard with goodness as our aim.[76]

Insisting that morality must be derived from an internal rather than externally sanctioned authority, he declared emphatically that consistency between the promptings of the 'inner voice' of conscience and the practicalities of everyday action and behaviour is the basis of moral progress, and the key to spiritual advancement. 'Human life in its totality advances and cannot help moving forward towards the ideal of perfection, only if each individual person advances towards his own personal and unrestricted perfection', he wrote in *The Law of Violence and the Law of Love*. 'Man', he said, 'need only divert his attention from searching for the solution to external questions and pose the one true inner question of how he should lead his life, and all the external questions will be resolved in the best possible way.'[77] He quoted the words of the radical activist, Alexander Hertzen (in retrospect a very significant source), on the primacy of personal over social morality: 'If only instead of wishing to save the world people wished to save themselves, to liberate themselves rather than humanity, they would be doing much more for the salvation of the world and the freedom of humanity.'[78] The general welfare can only be served, he says, through 'fulfilling the law of goodness that has been revealed in the scriptures.'[79] The distinction, we shall see presently, proved crucial for his teaching on social morality, and for his evaluation of the newly emerging radicalism of socialists and marxists. His position on the whole issue can be stated quite succinctly: since love originates in the interpersonal, since, of its nature, it personalises all that it addresses, the pursuit of the Good must necessarily begin in the realm of the interpersonal and expand therefrom into the realm of the social and the political. Thus, in the most explicit statement of his faith that he recorded—his reply to the edict on his excommunication—he stressed the radically personal character of Christian morality and declared that the moral progress of society would aways depend on the growth of brotherly love. The key to progress in love is prayer, he declared—not the public prayer of the pharisees, but the private prayer of self-illumination, in which the individual communes with the voice of conscience and responds authentically to its promptings:

> What I believe is this: I believe in God, who I understand as spirit, and in Love as the beginning of everything. I believe that the will of God is most clearly and understandably expressed in the teachings of the man called Christ, but I consider it the greatest of blasphemies to look on this man as God and to pray to Him. I believe that man's true good lies in following the will of God, and that God's will is for men to love one another and so do unto others as they wish others to do unto them; according to the gospels, this is the whole of the law and the prophets. I believe that the meaning of every man's life lies only in increasing the store of love within him; that this increase of love leads a man to greater and greater blessings in this life, and to blessings after his death that are in proportion to the amount of love within him; and I believe that it contributes more than anything else towards the establishment of the kingdom of God on earth, that is, towards the establishment of an order under which the discord, deception and violence that now hold sway will be replaced by free agreement, truthfulness, and brotherly love between all people. I believe that there is only one way to progress in love and that that is prayer: not the public prayer in churches that Christ expressly forbade (Matthew 6:5-13), but the solitary prayer of which Christ gave us an example and whose essence lies in the renewal and affirmation in our own consciousness of the meaning of our life and of our dependence on God alone.[80]

Part of the task of conscience illumination consists, he further suggests, in active resistance to the tendency, common to all of us, to surrender ethical responsibility to a source outside ourselves, thus evading the dictates of the inner voice for the security of an external authority. 'What people need most', he wrote in a Diary entry, 'is to develop their own conscience, to clarify it to themselves, and then live in accord with it; what they do instead is to choose some foreign, inaccessible conscience, and then live quite without conscience, lying and lying in order to make it seem as though they are living in accord with this foreign conscience.'[81] Characteristically, he sees the impersonal, systematised ethic of rationalist philosophy as particularly facilitating this kind of evasion: 'Really', he writes, 'I prefer some jovial, hard-drinking fellow, someone who keeps all reasoning at arm's length, to the philosopher who lives in accord with someone else's conscience i.e. without any conscience at all. The former may develop a conscience, while the latter will never do so until he returns to the condition of the former.'[82]

There are strong reminders here of Dostoevsky's words in the Legend of the Grand Inquisitor—'Nothing is more seductive for man than his freedom of conscience, for nothing is a greater cause of suffering. . . . I tell Thee that man is tormented by no greater anxiety than to find someone quickly to whom he can hand over that freedom with which the ill-fated creature is born.'[83] There are strong parallels also with Buber's treatment of the problem of conscience evasion in his essay, 'The Education of Character', where he stresses the need to *discover* the voice of conscience by penetrating the wall of evasion which stands between the individual and the process of true self-illumination that will lead to the assumption of personal responsiblity. 'We find the ethical in its purity', he writes, 'only where the human person confronts himself with his own potentiality and distinguishes and decides in this confrontation without asking anything other than what is right or wrong in this his own situation.' In this passage from the essay he particularly echoes Tolstoy in his characterisation of the act of conscience evasion as ultimately a denial of faith:

> The attitude which has just been described means for the man of faith, when he encounters it, his fall from faith—without his being inclined to confess it to himself or to admit it. It means his fall, in very fact, from faith, however loudly and emphatically he continues to confess it not merely with his lips but even with his very soul as it shouts down inmost reality. The relation of faith to the One Present Being is perverted into semblance and self-deceit if it is not an all-embracing relation. 'Religion' may agree to be one department of life beside others which like it are independent and autonomous—it has thereby already perverted the relation of faith. To remove any realm basically from this relation, from its defining power, is to try to remove it from God's defining power which rules over the relation of faith. To prescribe to the relation of faith that 'so far and no further you may define what I have to do; here your power ends and that of the group to which I belong begins' is to address God in precisely the same way. He who does not let his relation of faith be fulfilled in the uncurtailed measure of the life he lives, however much he is capable of at different times, is trying to curtail the fulfilment of God's rule of the world.[84]

There are some striking evocations of the whole process of conscience illumination at various points in Tolstoy's fiction. In *Anna Karenina* the pain and self-conflict arising from two kinds of love—Anna's love for her child and the consuming force of her passion for Vronsky—presents her with a terrible and ultimately unresolvable dilemma. Seeking outside marriage the love she was denied within it, she is tormented by the prospect of losing the love of her son and, being unable to face the consequences of her choice, takes refuge in vain and illusory hopes: 'When she thought of her son, and his future attitude to his mother, who had abandoned his father, she felt such terror at what she had done, that she could not face it; but, like a woman, could only try to comfort herself with lying assurances that everything would remain as it always had been, and that it was possible to forget the fearful question of how it would be with her son.'[85] Trapped by her fate and tortured by the voice of her conscience, she proceeds inexorably towards her own destruction. Significantly, her last words as she leaps to her death are a plea to God for forgiveness: 'She tried to get up, to drop backwards, but something huge and merciless struck her on the head and rolled her on her back: "Lord forgive me all", she said, feeling it impossible to struggle.'[86]

While death marks the culmination of Anna's tragedy, its imminence initiates the process of self-illumination for the protagonist of a later story, 'The Death of Ivan Ilyich'. Looking back on a lifetime lived in accordance with trivial values, Ivan discovers its true meaning at last in the loneliness of impending death: 'He cried because of his helplessness, because of his dreadful loneliness, because of the heartlessness of people and of God, because of the absence of God'.[87] Illumination comes as he listens to 'the voice of his soul' and he recognises the self-fulfilment that lies in fellowship, compassion and familial love:

> 'I am torturing them'. he thought. 'They feel sorry for me, but things will be better for them when I am gone . . .' He wanted to tell them this, but lacked the strength. 'But what is the use of speaking? I must do something', he thought. He turned to his wife and indicated his son with his eyes.
>
> 'Take him away'. he said. 'Poor boy . . . and you . . .' He wanted to add, 'Forgive', and it came out, 'Forget', but he had not the strength to correct himself; he merely gave a little wave of his hand, knowing that the one who was to understand would understand.
>
> And presently it became clear to him that all he had been tortured by and been unable to throw off, was now falling away of itself, falling away on two sides, ten sides, all sides at once. He felt sorry for them, he must do something to ease their pain. He must relieve them and himself of this suffering. 'How good and how simple', he thought. 'And the pain?' he asked himself. 'How am I to dispose of it? Here, where are you, pain ?'
>
> He felt for the pain.
>
> 'Ah, here it is. What of it? Let it be.'
>
> 'And death. Where is death?'
>
> He searched for his accustomed terror of death and could not find it. Where was death? What was death? There was no fear, because there was no death.
>
> 'So that is it!' he suddenly said out loud. 'What happiness!'[88]

Resurrection also enacts the process of conscience illumination through its two leading characters, Nekhlyudov and Maslova. Nekhlydov recognises that his failure to heed the voice of conscience is the main cause of his downfall: 'He had ceased to believe himself and had taken to believing others. This he had done because it was too difficult to live believing oneself: believing oneself one had to decide every question not in favour of one's animal I, which is always seeking for easy gratification, but in almost every case against it. Believing others there was nothing to decide; everything had been decided already, and always in favour of the animal I and against the spiritual.'[89] Confronted with the visible consequences of his actions, as he sees Maslova in the courtroom, his conscience is moved, though he still resists its promptings:

> Still he would not give in to the feelings of repentance which began to arise within him. He tried to consider it all as a chance incident, which would pass without affecting his manner of life. He felt himself in the position of a puppy, when its master, taking it by the scruff of its neck, rubs its nose in the mess it has made. The puppy whines, draws back, and wants to get away as far as possible from the effects of its misdeed, but the pitiless master does not let go.
>
> And so Nekhlyudov, feeling all the repulsiveness of what he had done, felt also the powerful hand of the master, but he did not yet understand the whole significance of his action, and would not recognise the master's hand. He did not wish to believe that it was the effect of his deed that lay before him, but the pitiless hand of the master held him, and he had a foreboding that he should not escape. He was still keeping up his courage and sat on his chair in the first row in his usual self-possessed pose, one leg carelessly thrown over the other, and playing with his pince-nez. Yet all the while, in the depths of his soul, he felt the cruelty, cowardice and baseness, not only of this particular action of his but of his whole self-willed, depraved, cruel, idle life; and that dreadful veil which had in some unaccountable manner hidden from him this sin of his, and the whole of his subsequent life for ten years, was begining to shake, and he caught glimpses of what was covered by that veil.[90]

The novel points to a danger similar to that which was described in 'Father Sergius'—that repentance will degenerate into a spiritual solipsism even more corrupting that the original sources of guilt. Thus, in the episode of the dinner party at the governor's mansion, Nekhlyudov appears to lapse temporarily into a state of self complacency that turns out to be a more insidious barrier to the process of reform that his resistance to the urgings of his conscience. He falls 'into a spiritual state of complete satisfaction with himself such as he had not known for a long time as if he had only now found out what a good man he was'.[91] As he overcomes the temptations of spiritual pride, he proceeds to assert the final paradox of the process of self-reform: that while spiritual growth begins in the loneliness of individual conscience, it is fulfilled in the practice of brotherly love, in the love of neighbour and in active communion with humankind.

The third of the conditions identified by Tolstoy for the practice of the ethic of love is the active reparation of guilt. If moral responsibility requires the recognition of the causes of guilt it must, by implication, further require the reparation of the offence which gave rise to this guilt. Again, the theme of forgiveness and reconciliation runs through all the main novels, and is presented as the condition of the progress towards loving faith in which all the major characters are engaged. It is epitomised in the reconciliation scene between the dying Prince Andrew and Natasha. With forgiveness comes understanding and a love purified of guilt and remorse: 'Yet how many people have I hated in my life', he reflects. 'And of them all I loved and hated none as I did her. And he vividly pictured to himself Natasha, not as he had done in the past with nothing but charms which gave him delight, but for the first time picturing to himself her soul. And he understood her feelings, her suffering, shame and remorse. He now understood for the first time all the cruelty of his rejection of her, the cruelty of his rupture with her.'[92] There follows one of the tenderest love scenes in all of Tolstoy's fiction, as both forgive the offences they have suffered and are reconciled in a union profoundly enriched by the purifying power of repentance.

That the act of forgiveness is problematic and complex, requiring immense self-sacrifice and self-humiliation, is made evident in the portrait of Karenin. Feeling deeply wronged and betrayed, he cannot bring himself to forgive his wife: 'Forgive I cannnot and do not wish to. I regard it as wrong', he says. 'I have done everything for this woman and she has trodden it all in the mud to which she is akin. I am not a spiteful man. I have never hated anyone, but I hate her with my whole soul and I cannot ever forgive her because I hate her too much for all the wrong she has done me.'[93] Yet he too finds the strength to forgive as he kneels by the bedside of his ailing wife:

> The nervous agitation of Alexey Alexandrovich kept increasing, and had by now reached such a point that he ceased to struggle with it. He suddenly felt that what he had regarded as nervous agitation was on the contrary a blissful spiritual condition that gave him all at once a new happiness he had never known. He did not think that the Christian law he had been all his life trying to follow, enjoined on him to forgive and love his enemies; but a glad feeling of love and forgiveness for his enemies filled his heart. He knelt down, and laying his head on the curve of her arm, which burned him as with fire through the sleeve, he sobbed like a little child. She put her arm around his head, moved towards him, and with defiant pride lifted up her eyes.[94]

The reconciliation is temporary and does not survive Anna's recovery from her illness. But it is interpreted by the narrator, nonetheless, as the action of divine grace on Karenin, even though he himself did not consciously think of it in this way. 'He knew that when, without the slightest idea that his forgiveness was the action of a higher power, he had surrendered directly to the feeling of forgiveness, he had felt more happiness than now when he was thinking every instant that Christ was in his heart, and that in signing official papers he was doing His will'.[95]

'Repentance', Nadezhda Mandelstam wrote, 'commands unique and powerful words . . . it may be the language of a specific moment in time, but it lasts forever'. 'What', she exclaimed, 'is catharsis but a cleansing or illumination of the spirit. . . . The European world was based', she said, 'on the supreme catharsis accessible only to the religious mind, the conquest of death by atonement.'[96] That catharsis is evoked splendidly in *Resurrection* where the regeneration of the fallen is described by Tolstoy in the specific language and imagery of the Gospels. In the novel Nekhlyudov appears both vacillating and resolute in his efforts to unburden himself of his guilt. In his weakness he listens to the voice of the tempter who exploits his waning confidence—'Have you not turned before to perfect yourself and become better, and nothing has come of it'—but he resolves nonetheless to purge himself of his sin: 'At any cost I will break the lie that binds me; will tell everybody the truth and act the truth.' A beautiful sequence of lyrical imagery conveys the triumphant joy of his unburdening:

> He prayed, asking God to help him, to enter into him and cleanse him; and what he was praying for had happened already; the God within him had awakened in his consciousness. He felt himself one with Him, and therefore felt not only the freedom, fullness and joy of life, but all the power of righteousness. All, all the best that a man can do, he felt capable of doing.
>
> His eyes filled with tears as he was saying all this to himself; good and bad tears: good because they were tears of joy at the awakening of the spiritual being within him, the being that had been asleep all these years, and bad tears because they were also tears of tenderness to himself at his own goodness.
>
> He felt hot, and went to the window and opened it. The window faced the garden. It was a moonlit, quiet, fresh night; something rattled past, and then all was still. The shadow of a tall poplar fell on the ground just opposite the window, and all the intricate pattern of its bare branches was clearly defined on the clean-swept gravel. To the left the roof of a coach-house shone white in the moonlight—in front the black shadow of the garden wall was visible through the tangled branches of the trees. Nekhlyudov gazed at the roof, the moonlit garden, and the shadows of the poplar, and drank in the fresh invigorating air.

'How delightful, how delightful; oh God, how delightful', he said, meaning that which was going on in his soul.[97]

Significantly, the act of repentance radically changes his attitudes towards others, fostering in him the faith that manifests itself as love and brotherhood: 'From the moment he recognised that it was he who was so bad and disgusting, others were no longer disgusting to him.'[98] Yet, having come to terms with his guilt, he still has to face the huge obstacles that lie in the way of its reparation. As he pleads with Maslova to forgive him, he finds that great emotional barriers lie in the way of their reconciliation: 'He felt that there was in her soul one who was hostile to him, and who was supporting her, as she now was, preventing him from getting at her heart.' 'Strange to say', the narrator says, 'this did not repel him but drew him nearer to her by some fresh peculiar power.'[99] As they are finally united, he concludes that the answer to the problem of evil lies in the ever present willingness to forgive—'not until seven times, but until seventy times seven.' The cycle of evil is reinforced, he says, by those who pass judgement on the corruptions of others, while being unaware of the corruption in their own hearts. The cycle is broken only by those who, being humbly aware of their own guilt, are prepared endlessly to forgive the evil in those around them. That, he reflects, is the central message of the Sermon on the Mount:

And it happened to Nekhlyudov as it often happens to men who are living a spiritual life. The thought that at first seemed strange, paradoxical, or even only a jest, being confirmed more and more often by life's experience, suddenly appeared as the simplest, truest certainty. In this way the idea that the only certain means of salvation from the terrible evil from which men are suffering is, that they should always acknowledge themselves to be guilty before God, and therefore unable to punish or reform others, became clear to him. It became clear to him that all the dreadful evil he had been witnessing in prisons and jails, and the quiet self-assurance of the perpetrators of this evil, resulted from men attempting what was impossible: to correct evil while themselves evil. Vicious men were trying to reform other vicious men, and thought they could do it by using mechanical means. And the result of all this was that needy and covetous men, having made a profession of this pretended punishment, and reformation of others, themselves became utterly corrupt, and unceasingly corrupt also those whom they torment. Now he saw clearly whence came all the horrors he had seen, and what ought to be done to put an end to them. The answer he had been unable to find was the same that Christ gave to Peter. It was to forgive always, everyone, to forgive an infinite number of times, because there are none who are not themselves guilty, and therefore none who can punish or reform. .... Hoping to find a confirmation of this thought in the Gospel Nekhlyudov began reading it from the beginning. When he had read the Sermon on the Mount, which had always touched him, he saw in it to-day for the first time not beautiful abstract thought, setting forth for the most part exaggerated and impossible demands, but simple, clear practical laws which if carried out in practice (and this is quite possible) would establish perfectly new and surprising conditions of social life.[100]

3   The Process of Ethico-Religious Education

Tolstoy's approach to religious and moral education was largely determined by the foregoing considerations on the nature of religious faith and the imperatives for ethical conduct that arise from it. As we have seen, he conceived of faith as primarily a manifestation of love, as the product of a supra-rational consciousness, as radically free and undogmatic, and, while being focussed on the immanent and existential, as simultaneously dis-closing the possibility of the transcendent, the intemporal and the infinite. He saw it as essentially ethical in character, manifesting itself in the exercise of individual responsibility, and requiring three main conditions for its nurturing: the illumination of conscience, the conquest of selfishness and pride, and the reparation of guilt through active love.

The central question, for the purposes of the present study, is to determine how he saw the educator's role in the fostering of the spirit of faith and the promotion of its ethical imperatives. Essentially, there were two main ways in which he believed this could be achieved. Firstly, as was intimated in an earlier chapter, he saw the whole teacher-learner relationship as embodying the spirit of active love, and therefore as a practical realisation of the religious and ethical principles that have just been described. To that degree, it could be said that his entire philosophy of education was permeated by the ethico-religious spirit, and that he sought through every facet of the school-ing process to realise his religious and moral ideals. Secondly, conceiving of faith as essentially a manifestation of consciousness, there were specific ways in which he suggested this could be nurtured. The most important of these, as becomes evident from his reports on the schools at Yasnaya Polyana, was the awakening in his pupils of a love for the scriptures, and the development of their ability both to encounter and comprehend the meaning of the revealed word, and to determine its relevance in the con-ditions of their daily lives.

As has been shown in Chapter IV, the nurturing of a trusting, morally authentic, loving relationship between teacher and pupil was the cornerstone of his entire pedagogic philosophy. In this was exemplified the full character of the intersubjective reciprocity on which all his beliefs about religion and morality were based. Using the time-sanctioned metaphor of motherhood to convey the spontaneous nature of this reciprocity, he conceived of the whole educational process as a practical realisation of the spirit of altruism he believed to be the essence of the religious spirit. Exemplifying the spirit and practice of active love, the whole ethos of the school was designed to promote the development of the religious and moral potentialities of its pupils. It aimed to foster the relationships between them that Tolstoy believed were essential for the religious and moral formation of society as a whole.

'Only in his whole being, in all his spontaneity, can the educator truly affect the whole being of his pupil',[101] Martin Buber wrote. The reports on the schools at Yasnaya Polyana suggest that this was the ideal that Tolstoy and his colleagues constantly sought to achieve, as has been indicated in an earlier chapter. The particular concern of the present chapter is the *specific* curricular and pedagogic methods that were employed to achieve that objective. Basically, Tolstoy saw this as a matter of promoting the ethical-religious conjuncture that he considered to be central to the whole process. Much of the criticism that he directed at the institutional churches, as we have seen, was focussed on the abstract character of their teachings, their remoteness from the conditions of everyday life. 'Religious doctrine', he complained, 'is professed in some other realm, at a distance from life, and independent of it. If we encounter it, it is only as an external phenomenon, disconnected from life.'[102] Accordingly, he spoke of the need to foster a faith that embraced the wholeness of life, that was grasped in the depth of subjective consciousness, and manifested in the closest possible conjuncture between thought and action. Nurturing the spirit of faith would require a fundamental 'modification of consciousness', such as he describes in this passage from *The Law of Violence and the Law of Love*. Though referring to a particular principle of Christian teaching—the doctrine of non-resistance to evil—the passage clearly identifies both the fundamental character of the attitudinal change, and the linking of thought and action, which the idea of 'modified consciousness' implies:

> All external changes of life's forms that are not founded on shifts of con-sciousness not only fail to improve people's situation but, by and large, worsen it. It was not government decrees that abolished child-beating, torture and slavery, but a change in people's consciousness that called for the necessity of these decrees. And life is only improved as far as it is based on modified consciousness: that is, to the extent that in people's consciousness the law of violence is exchanged for the law of love. People think that if a shift in consciousness influences the forms of life, it must also work the other way, and since it is more pleasant, easy, and the effect more apparent, to direct energy at external changes, they always prefer to direct their energy not at changing consciousness but at changing forms. Therefore for the most part

they are preoccupied not with the essential matter, but with some semblance of it. The external, vain and useless activity based on establishing and adapting the external forms of life shields people from the essential inner activity, which alone can improve their lives. And this superstition, more than anything else, hinders the general improvement of people's lives. A better life can only come when the consciousness of men is altered for the better; and therefore, those who wish to improve life must direct all their efforts towards changing both their own and other people's consciousness.[103]

A key passage for an understanding of Tolstoy's thinking on ethico-religious education, it underlines the need to integrate faith with the whole-ness of consciousness and the wholeness of life, and to translate it directly into the exercise of active responsibility. Nurturing this integrated consciousness had been his own avowed objective as a writer, not only in the explicitly propagandist writings on religious and social reform that he produced so prolifically in the last thirty years of his life, but also in his fictional writings, where the proclamation of his moral and religious beliefs was always a dynamic purpose underlying the workings of his artistic imagination. As Renato Poggioli wrote: 'Tolstoy had always been, even before his conversion, a writer with a message; and even after his conversion he magnificently performed his artist's task, as he had himself defined it at the time when he was writing his two greatest novels.'[104]

Whether seeking directly to influence the lives and beliefs of the masses through his propagandist writings, or seeking to influence them indirectly through his fiction, Tolstoy's objective was fundamentally the same: to convey as forcefully as he could the radical meaning and content of scriptural Christianity as he understood it. The scriptures constituted the basic curriculum for all his activities in the sphere of ethico-religious education, whether these were aimed at the adult readers whom he addressed in his writings, or the children whom he taught in his schools. Repeatedly he had asserted his belief that the scriptures were the only authoritative source of Christian truth. Through the centuries they had ensured the survival of Christianity, despite the ways in which it had been distorted and corrupted. 'Despite the efforts made to conceal from people the essence of the teaching revealed in the Gospels', nothing, he said, could extinguish 'the light filtering through and illuminating men's souls as they grasped the enormous truth of the teaching with ever-increasing clarity.'[105] In *What I Believe* he attributed his own reconversion to Christianity entirely to the reading of the Gospels. 'For thirty years of my life', he wrote, 'I was, in the proper acceptance of the word, a nihilist, a man who believed in nothing. Five years ago my faith came to me; I believed in the doctrine of Jesus and my whole life underwent a sudden transformation.'[106] What he rediscovered, like his fictional protegees, Levin and Pierre, was the simplicity of his childhood understanding of the scriptures. 'From my childhood', he continues, 'from the time I first began to read the New Testament, I was touched most of all by that portion of the doctrine of Jesus which inculcates love, humility, self-denial and the duty of returning good for evil. This to me has always been the substance of Christianity; my heart recognised its truths in spite of scepticism and despair.'[107] In a particularly self-revealing passage from *What I Believe* he describes how he decided to set aside all external sources for an understanding of the words of Christ, in favour of a personal response to the pure, undiluted and unambiguous message conveyed in the Gospel text. The essence of this message, he concluded, was conveyed in a single injunction, 'Resist not evil':

> Of all the other portions of the Gospels, the Sermon on the Mount always has had for me an exceptional importance. I now read it more frequently than ever. Nowhere does Jesus speak with greater solemnity, nowhere does he propound moral rules more definitely and practically, nor do these rules in any other form awaken more readily an echo in the human heart; nowhere else does he address himself to a large multitude of the common people. If there are any clear and precise Christian principles, one ought to find them here. . . . These chapters I read very often, each time with the same exceptional ardour, as I came to the verses which exhort the hearer to turn the other cheek, to give up his cloak, to be at peace with all the world, to love his enemies—but each time with the same disappointment. The divine words were not clear. They exhorted to a renunciation so absolute as to entirely stifle life as I understood it; to renounce everything, therefore, could not, it seemed to me, be essential to salvation. And the moment this ceased to be an absolute condition, clearness and precision were at an end. . . .
>
> It was only after I had rejected the interpretations of the wise critics and theologians . . . that I suddenly understood what had been so meaningless before. I understood, not through exegetical fantasies or profound and ingenious textual combinations; I understood everything, because I put all commentaries out of my mind. This was the passage which gave me the key to the whole: 'Ye have heard that it hath been said, An eye for an eye and a tooth for a tooth: But I say unto you, that ye resist not evil'. One day the exact and simple meaning of those words came to me; I understood that Jesus meant neither more nor less than what he said. What I saw was nothing new; only the veil that had hidden the truth from me fell away, and the truth was revealed in all its grandeur.[108]

It was this kind of response that he sought to encourage through his lessons in religious education in the schools at Yasnaya Polyana. The curriculum for religious and moral education that was taught in all these schools consisted entirely of the scriptures, both the Old and New

Testament. Bible study was one of their most popular activities. 'I discovered', he recalls, 'that of all oral information which I had tried in the
period of three years nothing so fitted the comprehension of the boys' minds
as the Bible.'[109] The stories from the Old Testament seemed to have an
especially powerful appeal for them. 'The Old Testament left such an
impression on the children', he wrote, 'that two months after it had been
told to them, they wrote down sacred history from memory in their note-
books, with but few omissions.' In this passage from 'The School at
Yasnaya Polyana' he attributes the popularity of scripture both to its
narrative excitement and to its accessibility even for the simplest of the
peasant children attending his schools:

> It seems to me that the book of the childhood of the race will always be the
> best book of the childhod of each man. It seems to me impossible to put
> another book in its place.... When I read it to peasant children I did not leave
> out a single word. And nobody giggled behind somebody's back, and all
> listened with trepidation and natural awe. The story of Lot and his daughters,
> the story of Judas, provoke horror, not laughter. How comprehensible and
> clear, particularly for a child, everything is, and at the same time, how stern
> and serious! I can't understand what kind of an education would be possible
> if it were not for that book.[110]

The methods he used in these lessons were designed to foster the greatest
possible degree of individual thinking on the part of his pupils. Seeing the
dangers of didactic methods in such a crucial matter as the study of the
scriptures—not to mention the more extreme forms of indoctrination generally practised in Russian schools at the time—he advocated an enquiry-
based approach that would ensure that the lessons were conducted in the
spirit of critical thought and interpretation he considered essential for a
genuinely personal encounter with the Biblical texts. Much of his comment
in the reports on these lessons is directed at the unsuitability of the 'single
questioning' method that was widely used at the time; this required children
to regurgitate large amounts of memorised material in response to questions
directed at them by the teacher. 'I have convinced myself in practice', he
writes, 'that there is nothing more injurious to the development of the child
than that kind of single questioning and the authoritarian relation of teacher
to pupil arising from it, and for me there is nothing more provoking than
such a spectacle.'[111]

Rejecting the argument generally advanced in support of this method—
that it was necessary to ascertain how much a pupil had learnt before the
teacher could enable him to progress further in his comprehension of the
text—Tolstoy insisted that a truly capable teacher 'always feels the measure

of this knowledge without the pupils' answer', and can proceed with his teaching on the basis of this, without recourse to coercive questioning. In this passage from his review of the scripture lessons he gives a penetrating profile of the harmful effects of coercive questioning on one of the most diffident, sensitive and nervous of his pupils. Savin's inability to articulate his thoughts was due mainly to his acute shyness and low self-esteem, problems that had been greatly exacerbated by the kind of agresssive questioning to which he had been subjected by a teacher in the school he attended before coming to Yasnaya Polyana:

> Savin is a ruddy, chubby boy, with gleaming eyes and long lashes, the son of an innkeeper or a merchant, in a tanned fur coat, in small boots that fit him well, as they are not his father's, and in a red cotton shirt and trousers. The sympathetic and handsome personality of that boy struck me more especially because in the class on arithmetic he was the first, on account of the force of his imagination and merry animation. He also reads and writes not at all badly. But the moment he is asked a question he presses his pretty curly head sidewise, tears appear on his long lashes, and he looks as though he wanted to hide somewhere from everybody, and it is evident that he is suffering beyond endurance. If he is made to learn by heart, he will recite a piece, but he is not able, or has not the courage, to express anything in his own words. It is either some fear inspired by his former teacher (he had studied before with a teacher of the clerical profession), or lack of confidence in himself, or his awkward position among boys who, in his opinion, stand below him, or aristocratism or annoyance that in this alone he is behind the rest and because he once showed himself in a bad light, or his little soul was offended as some careless word escaped from the teacher, or all these causes acting together— God knows which—but his bashfulness, though not a good feature in itself, is certainly inseparably connected with everything that is best in his childish soul. It is possible to knock all that out with a physical or moral stick, but the danger is that all the precious qualities, without which the teacher would find it hard to lead him on, might be knocked out at the same time.[112]

On Tolstoy's advice, the teacher at Yasnaya Polyana directed no questions at all at Savin, and simply allowed him to mix gradually with the other pupils until he eventually developed the confidence to express himself. (When this finally happened the teacher considered it sufficiently noteworthy to record the event in his Diary. His entry read: 'Stubborn Savin said a few words!') Spontaneity of response, therefore, was the objective of the methods used in the scripture lessons: the pupils were simply encouraged to read the psalter, either individually or in groups—though generally under the active guidance of the teacher—and subsequently to recount their impressions of the narrative in their own words:

From the foundation of the school even up to the present time the instruction in sacred and Russian history has been carried out in this manner: the children gather about the teacher, and the teacher, being only guided by the Bible, and for Rusian history by Pogodin's *Norman Period* and Vodovozov's collection, tells the story, and then asks questions, and all begin to speak at the same time. When there are too many voices speaking at the same time, the teacher stops them, making them speak one at a time; the moment one hesitates, he asks others. When the teacher notices that some have not understood anything, he makes one of the best pupils repeat it for the benefit of those who have not understood. This was not premeditated, but grew up naturally, and it has been found equally successful with five and with thirty pupils if the teacher follows all, does not allow them to cry and repeat what has once been said, and does not permit the shouts to become maddening, but regulates that stream of merry animation and rivalry to the extent to which he needs it.[113]

The particular appeal of scripture, as has been noted, lay in the richness of its aesthetic content and this, to a considerable degree, determined the pedagogic methods that were used in Tolstoy's schools. It will be recalled from an earlier chapter that he insisted that all learning is aesthetic in origin—originating in the comprehension of images and symbols—and is therefore most effectively nurtured through the development of aesthetic potentialities. This principle was applied with particular effect to the study of the scriptures. 'There is no book like the Bible to open up a new world to the pupil and to make him without knowledge love knowledge', he declared. 'I speak even of those who do not look upon the Bible as Revelation. There is no production I know of which unites all the sides of human thought in such a compressed poetical form as in the Bible. Without it', he declares, 'the development of a child is unthinkable in our society.' He continues:

Who has not wept over the story of Joseph and his meeting with his brothers? Who has not narrated with a sinking heart the story of Samson bound and deprived of his hair, as he, taking vengeance on his enemies, himself perishes under the ruins of the fallen palace, and a hundred other impressions, on which we have been brought up as on our mother's milk?

Let those who deny the educational value of the Bible, who say that the Bible has outlived its usefulness, invent such a book, such stories, which explain the phenomena of Nature, or the phenomena from universal history, or from their imagination, which will be as readily received as the Biblical accounts, and then we shall admit that the Bible has outlived its usefulness.
. . .

I repeat my conviction, which perhaps is deduced from a one-sided experience. Without the Bible the development of a child or man is unthinkable in our society, just as it was unthinkable in Greek society without

Homer. The Bible is the only book for the first reading of children. The Bible, both as to its contents and to its form, ought to serve as a model of all manuals and readers for children.[114]

The spontaneity of response that he sought to promote did not, however, preclude a highly formative role for the teacher in the lessons on scripture. Tolstoy stressed the importance of opening up new vistas of experience for his pupils, and of awakening and developing the religious consciousness which was the ultimate aim of this work. He emphasised the need for the teacher to communicate his 'higher world conception' to the child, to enlarge the scope of childhood sensitivity and awareness, to 'lift the shroud' which had been 'concealing from the child the world of thought, knowledge and poetry' that the scriptures could disclose. In all these respects their efforts seem to have been met with spectacular success:

> A child or man entering school (I make no distinction between one of ten, thirty, or seventy years of age), brings with him his familar and favourite view of things, as taken away by him from life. In order that a man of any age should begin to learn, it is necessary that he should like learning. In order that he should like learning he must recognise the falseness and insufficiency of his view of things and he must divine the new world conception, which the instruction is to open to him. Not one man or child would be able to learn, if the future of his learning presented itself to him only as an art of reading, writing, and counting; not one teacher would be able to teach, if he did not have in his power a higher world conception than what the pupils have. In order that the pupil may surrender himself to the teacher, there must be lifted for him one side of the shroud which has been concealing from him all the charm of that world of thought, knowledge and poetry, to which instruction was to introduce him. Only by being under the spell of that brilliant world ahead of him is the pupil able to work over himself in the manner in which we want him to.
>
> What means have we then to lift that edge of the curtain for the pupil? As I have said, I thought, just as many think, that being myself in that world to which I am to introduce the pupils, I could easily do so, and I taught the rudiments, I explained the phenomena of Nature, I told them, as it says in the ABCs, that the fruits of learning are sweet, but the pupils did not believe me and kept aloof. I tried to read the Bible to them, and I completely took possession of them. The edge of the curtain was lifted, and they surrendered themselves to me unconditionally. They fell in love with the book, with the study and with me. All I had to do now was to guide them on.[115]

It is significant that Tolstoy insisted that all these lessons should be based on the authentic version of the Biblical text. He warned vehemently against the use of 'abridged versions' of scripture, seeing them as a corruption 'both of its holiness and its poetry', and he condemned the various popular renderings of scripture then in general circulation for their 'triteness' and banality. He further condemned the use of didactic teaching in any form, insisting that it would destroy the sense of wonder essential for an appreciation of the richness and variety of the text:

> All the short sacred histories in the Russian language I consider a double crime: against its holiness and against poetry. All these rifacimentos, having in view the facility of the study of sacred history, only make it more difficult. The Bible is read as a pleasure, at home, leaning the head on the arm; the abbreviated stories are learnt by heart with the aid of a pointer. Not only are these short stories dull and incomprehensible, they also spoil the ability to understand the poetry of the Bible. I have observed more than once that bad, unintelligible language impairs the receptiveness of the inner meaning of the Bible. Unintelligible words, however, such as occur in the Bible, are remembered together with the incidents; they arrest the attention of the pupils by their novelty, and, as it were, serve as guide-posts to the stories. . . .
>
> Very frequently, a pupil speaks only in order to make use of a pretty phrase for which he has taken a liking, and then the simplicity of imbibing the contents only is gone. I have also observed that pupils from other schools always feel much less or not at all the charm of the Biblical stories, which is destroyed by the necessity of memorising and by the rude methods of the teacher connected with it. These pupils have even spoiled the younger pupils and their brothers in the manner of whose narration there was reflected certain trite methods of the abbreviated sacred histories. Such trite stories have, by means of these injurious books, found their way among the masses, and frequently the pupils bring with them from home peculiar legends of the creation of the world, of Adam and of Joseph the Beautiful. These pupils do not experience that which the fresh pupils feel when they listen to the Bible and with trepidation catch each word and think that now, at last, all the wisdom of the world will be revealed to them.[116]

In addition to the oral activities that have just been described, Tolstoy generally favoured teaching methods which encouraged the children to narrate their impressions of the Biblical text through the medium of their own writing. The examples of this work that he cites are amongst the most striking of his pedagogic anecdotes, and fully confirm his claim that his pupils 'fell in love with the book, with the study, and with me'.[117] This extract comes from a ten-year old pupil's account of the story of Abraham and Isaac:

> God commanded Abraham to bring his son Isaac as an offering. Abraham took two servants with him. Isaac carried the wood and the fire, and Abraham carried the knife. When they came to Mount Hor, Abraham left his two servants there and himself went with Isaac up the mountain. Says Isaac: 'Father, we have everything, where then is the victim?'

Says Abraham: 'God has commanded me to sacrifice thee.'

So Abraham made a fire and put his son down.

Says Isaac: 'Father bind me or else I will jump up and kill thee.'

Abraham took and tied him. He just swung his arm, and an angel flew down from the heavens and held back his arm and said: 'Abraham, do not place thine hand on thy young son, God sees thy faith.'

Then the angel said to him: 'Go into the bush, a wether is caught there, bring him in place of thy son', and Abraham brought a sacrifice to God.

Then came the time for Abraham to marry off his son. They had a servant Eliezer. Abraham called up the servant and says he: 'Swear to me that thou wilt not take a bride from our town, but that thou wilt go where I send thee.'

Abraham sent him to Nahor in the land of Mesopotamia. Eliezer took the camels and went away. When he came to a well he began to speak: 'Lord give me such a bride, as will come first, and will give to drink to me and also to my camels—she shall be the bride of my master Isaac.'[118]

Similar reports are cited on the stories of Jacob and Esau, Jacob and his wife Rebecca, and Jacob and his twelve sons. The following extract is taken from a composition by an eight year old pupil; it indicates not only a mature grasp of the narrative but an ability, unusual for a child of his age, to convey the interplay of character and the exchanges of dialogue in vivid, colourful and fluent prose:

Jacob had twelve sons. He loved Joseph best of all, and had made for him a many-coloured dress. Then Joseph saw two dreams, and he told them to his brothers: 'It was as though we were reaping rye in the field and we reaped twelve sheaves. My sheaf was standing straight, and the eleven sheaves were bowing before my sheaf.'

Say the brothers: 'Is it really so that we shall bow to thee?'

And he had another dream: 'It was as though there were eleven stars in heaven, and the sun and moon were bowing to my star.'

Say father and mother: 'Is it possible we shall bow before thee?'

His brothers went a long distance away to herd cattle, then the father sent Joseph to take some food to his brothers. His brothers saw him and say they: 'There comes our reader of dreams. Let us put him down in a bottomless well.'

Reuben was thinking to himself: 'The moment they turn away I will pull out.' And there merchants came by. Says Reuben: 'Let us sell him to the Egyptian merchants.'

They sold Joseph, and the merchants sold him to Potiphar the courtier. Potiphar loved him and his wife loved him. Potiphar was absent somewhere and his wife says to Joseph: 'Joseph let us kill my husband and I will marry thee.'

Says Joseph: 'If thou sayest that a second time I will tell thy husband.'

She took him by his garment and cried out loud. The servants heard her and came rushing in. Then Potiphar arrived. His wife told him that Joseph had intended to kill him and then to marry her. Potiphar ordered him to be put in jail.[119]

Though his own religious beliefs were drawn overwhelmingly from the New Testament —especially from the Gospel of St Matthew and its extensive account of the Sermon on the Mount—Tolstoy appears, nonetheless, to have given far greater attention to the Old Testament in the scripture lessons in his schools. This, he explains, was due to the popularity of its narrative content—'it was remembered and gladly repeated, with enthusiasm both at home and at school',[120] he writes. But having stimulated their interest in the scriptures through the excitement of the Old Testament narrative, he gradually introduced them to the New Testament as well. Here again he employed the same teaching methods, giving particular attention to oral discussion and encouraging the retelling of Gospel episodes in writing. The following is an excerpt from an account by one of his pupil's of the Last Supper and the events leading to Christ's Crucifixion:

Once upon a time Jesus Christ sent his disciples to the city of Jerusalem and said to them: 'If you come across a man with water, follow him and ask him: Master show us a room where we can prepare the passover. He will show you and you prepare it there.

They went and saw what he had told them, and they prepared it. In the evening Jesus himself went there with his disciples. During the supper Jesus Christ took off his garment and girded himself with a towel. Then he took the laver and filled it with water and went to each disciple and washed his feet. When he went up to Peter and wanted to wash his feet Peter said:

'Lord! thou wilt never wash my feet'.

And Jesus Christ said to him: 'If I am not going to wash thy feet, thou wilt not be with me in the kingdom of heaven.'

Then Peter was frightened and says he: 'Lord! Not only my feet, but even my head and my whole body.'

And Jesus said to him: 'Only the pure one has to get his feet washed.'

Then Jesus Christ dressed himself and sat down at the table, took the bread, blessed it, and broke it and began to give it to his disciples, and he said: 'Take it and eat it—this is my body.'

They took it and ate it. Then Jesus took a bowl of wine, blessed it and began to carry it around to the disciples, and he said: 'Take it and drink it—it is my blood of the New Testament.'

They took it and drank it. Then Jesus said: 'One of you will betray me.'

And the disciples began to say: 'Lord ! Is it I?'

And says Jesus Christ: 'No.'

Then Judas says: 'Lord, is it I?'

And Jesus Christ said half aloud: 'Yes.'

After that Jesus Christ said to his disciples: 'He to whom I shall give a piece of bread will betray me.'

Then Jesus Christ gave Judas a piece of bread. Then Satan took his abode in him, so that he was abashed and went out of the room.[121]

For children whose ages ranged from 8 to 12—especially the disadvantaged peasant children who attended Tolstoy's schools for a period of one or, at most, two years—these were remarkable achievements, and they indicate the extraordinary effectiveness of the methods that were employed. The reports vividly illustrate the effective manner in which informal and instructional teaching techniques were blended in the lessons; they demonstrate their highly successful appeal to imaginative and aesthetic responses, their effective integration of oral-aural, reading and writing activities, and their scrupulous concentration of classroom activity on the unabridged, authentic text of the scriptures. The scriptures were the focus of all the work that Tolstoy conducted in these religion lessons as they had been the inspiration of his personal rediscovery of the Christian faith.

Seldom in the history of pedagogy does religious and moral education seem to have evoked so much pleasure and been so eagerly pursued as it was in the Yasnaya Polyana classrooms. When Tolstoy's methods are contrasted with the rigid moralism, the crudely employed didactics, and the dogmatism that passed for religious and moral education in contemporary Russian classrooms—and indeed in European schools generally at that time—the far-seeing and enlightened nature of his methods will be realised. His work at the schools, however, represented just one facet in his plans to communicate the truths of scriptural Christianity to the masses of the Russian people. Being deeply conscious of the far-reaching social as well as moral and religious implications of the Christian message that he taught, he sought to communicate this in the most effective way that he could to the larger public beyond the limited confines of the schools he had founded at Yasnasya Polyana. The logical extension to his experiments in ethico-religious education in his schools, therefore, were the major ventures in social and community education to which he devoted the last three decades of his life. These will be considered in detail in the coming chapter.

Social and Community Education

1   The Aims of Social and Community Education

> Konstantin Levin regarded his brother as a man of immense intellect and culture, as generous in the highest sense of the word, and possessed of a special faculty for working for the public good. But in the depths of his heart, the older he became, and the more intimately he knew his brother, the more and more frequently the thought struck him that this faculty of working for the public good, of which he felt himself utterly devoid, was possibly not so much a quality as a lack of something—not a lack of good, honest, noble desires and tastes, but a lack of vital force, of what is called heart, of that impulse which drives a man to choose someone out of the innumerable paths of life, and to care only for that one. The better he knew his brother, the more he noticed that Sergei Ivanovitch, and many other people who worked for the public welfare, were not led by an impulse of the heart to care for the public good, but reasoned from intellectual considerations that it was a right thing to take interest in public affairs, and consequently took interest in them. Levin was confirmed in this generalisation by observing that his brother did not take questions affecting the public welfare or the question of the immortality of the soul a bit more to heart than he did chess problems, or the ingenious construction of a new machine.[1]

Through Levin's reflections on the ambivalent character of his brother's humanitarianism, Tolstoy pinpoints an issue that lies at the heart of his own social philosophy. He points to the essentially abstract character of a generalised love of mankind: that is, a love that reaches out towards a vague and unspecified ideal such as the 'common good' or the 'public welfare', without being rooted in the immediacy of interpersonal mutuality from which an authentic love must ultimately spring. Sergei's humanitarianism lacked a 'vital force', his brother says; it was not inspired by an 'impulse of the heart' but was 'reasoned from intellectual considerations'. In essence it was an impersonal concern, lacking the humility and selflessness of a genuinely personalised love. For Sergei it gratified a selfish pride by affording him an image of himself as a philanthropic benefactor of mankind.

That same distinction is emphasised repeatedly in the writings of Kierkegaard, Buber, Levinas and Dostoevsky, all of whom shared some of the essential principles of Tolstoy's social philosophy. 'The neighbour', Kierkegaard writes in *The Works of Love*, is 'the one who is nearer to you than all others.' 'That neighbour who is nearest to you implies all men like the Good Samaritan',[2] he writes—simultaneously affirming both the radically interpersonal nature of the act of love and its non-selective character as a responsibility embracing the whole of humankind. The same principle is affirmed by Buber in his conception of the I-Thou and the I-We—the interpersonal and intercommunal—as intersecting modes of relation, each requiring its complete authentication in its interdependence with the other.[3] It is affirmed again by Levinas in statements such as 'the *proximity* of the neighbour is my responsibility for him', and 'responsibility does not come from fraternity but fraternity denotes responsibility for another, antecedent to my freedom'.[4]

That this responsibility requires an exceptional degree of altruistic commitment is made evident in the words of Ivan Karamazov, when he declares that he cannot see how he can love his neighbour—'it is just my neighbour to my mind that one cannot love'—while asserting that he can love 'those at a distance'—that great impersonal mass of humanity beyond his immediate sphere of contact and responsibility:

> 'I must make you a confession', Ivan began. 'I could never understand how one can love one's neighbour. It's just one's neighbours, to my mind, that one can't love, though one might love those at a distance. I once read somewhere of John the Merciful, a saint, that when a hungry, frozen beggar came to him, he took him into his bed, held him in his arms and began breathing into his mouth, which was putrid and loathsome from some awful disease. I am convinced that he did that from "self-laceration", from the self-laceration of falsity, for the sake of the charity imposed by duty, as a penance laid on him. For anyone to love a man he must be hidden, for as soon as he shows his face love is gone.'[5]

What Dostoevsky emphasises is the greater degree of effort that is required to fulfil one's responsibility towards a neighbour than to the generality of mankind. Zosima speaks of a 'love won by hard labour', something 'possible only through effort and will', implying that the love of neighbour is primarily a duty and responsibility, requiring a subordination of the interests of the self to the greater good of the other.[6] Like Kierkegaard, he suggests that if love is to be stripped of its selfishness, if its inherent selflessness is to be released, a commitment is required which is dictated by moral duty rather than the expectation of reciprocation or reward. 'Only when it is a duty to love, only then is love everlastingly free in blessed independence', Kierkegaard wrote, suggesting that a purely altruistic love is always impelled by duty—a duty identified primarily in the responsibility towards those 'who are nearest', and by extension towards the universality of mankind.[7] A generalised love, unauthenticated in the immediacy of the interpersonal, is, he suggests, an evasion of responsibility, is essentially ego-directed, merely an elaborate form of self-love. That distinction is strikingly illustrated by Zosima in his anecdote about the doctor who 'loved humanity' but could not love those nearest to him. He was addressing the society lady who had come to ask his advice on how she could recover her lost faith:

> He was a man getting on in years, and undoubtedly clever. He spoke as frankly as you, though in jest, in bitter jest. 'I love humanity', he said, 'but I wonder at myself. The more I love humanity in general, the less I love man in particular. In my dreams', he said, 'I have often come to making enthusiastic schemes for the service of humanity, and perhaps I might actually have faced crucifixion if it had been suddenly necessary; and yet I am incapable of living in the same room with anyone for two days together, as I know by experience. As soon as anyone is near me, his personality disturbs my self-complacency and restricts my freedom. In twenty-four hours I begin to hate the best of men: one because he's too long over his dinner; another because he has a cold and keeps on blowing his nose. I become hostile to people the moment they come close to me. But it has always happened that the more I detest men individually the more ardent becomes my love for humanity.'[8]

Persistently, Tolstoy suggests, both through the words of his major fictional personae, and through the explicit language of his non-fictional essays, that the pursuit of social ideals is endlessly open to the corrupting force of self-interest masquerading as an altruistic devotion to mankind. 'I imagine the mainspring of all our actions is after all self-interest', Levin declares to his brother, as they debate the need for social reform amongst the poverty-stricken masses. 'No sort of activity is likely to be lasting unless it is founded on self-interest . . . that's a universal principle, a philosophical principle',[9] he says. Largely because it is a philosophical, that is, an abstract principle, he subsequently repudiates all such solutions to the problems of social inequity and injustice. We learn at the end of the novel that, when he rediscovered the faith of his childhood, he had at that stage abandoned all interest in 'Spencer and his theories'. 'I'm fully convinced', he reflects—referring to Spencer's evolutionary socialism—'that the solution of the problems that interest me I shall never find in him and his like.'[10]

For all that, Spencer reappears in *Resurrection* where Nekhlyudov, experiencing some pangs of conscience at the spectacle of so much poverty and injustice, looks for an answer in 'Spencer's *Social Studies* and Henry George's ideas on social reform'. 'He felt with his whole being', the narrator says, 'a loathing for the society in which he had lived till then: the society that so carefully hides the sufferings borne by millions to assure ease and pleasure to a small minority'.[11] However, when he meets a committed socialist, Markel Kondratyev, he sees a cold-blooded fanatic, self-disciplined and single-minded in his pursuit of theoretical objectives, but driven by a venomous and indiscriminate hatred for his comrades and for all those to whom he attributes responsibility for the ills of society. The horror of the portrait presented by Tolstoy is unalleviated by some intimations of a limited manifestation in Kondratyev of some fellow-feeling for one of his comrades and for Maslova:

> His religious views were of the same negative nature as his views of existing economic conditions. Having seen the absurdity of the religion in which he was brought up, and having freed himself from it with great effort—at first with fear but later with rapture—he, as if wishing to revenge himself for the deception that had been practised on him and on his ancestors, was never tired of venomously and angrily ridiculing priests and religious dogmas.
>
> He was ascetic by habit, contenting himself with very little, and like all who have been used to work from childhood and whose muscles have been developed, he could work much and easily and was quick at any manual labour; but what he valued most was the leisure in prisons and at the halting-stations, which enabled him to continue his studies. He was now studying the first volume of Karl Marx, and carefully hid the book in his sack, as if it were a great treasure. He behaved with reserve and indifference to all his comrades except Novodvorov, to whom he was greatly attached, and whose arguments on all subjects he accepted as irrefutable truths.
>
> He had an infinite contempt for women, whom he looked upon as a hindrance in all useful activity. But he pitied Maslova and was gentle with her, for he considered her an example of the way in which the lower are exploited by the upper classes. The same reason made him dislike Nekhlyudov, so that he talked little with him and never pressed his hand, but when greeting him only held out his own to be pressed.[12]

Nekhlyudov's grim portrait of the revolutionist, Kondratyev, is followed by a similar one of his comrade, Novodvorov. Equally dogmatic and single-minded in his pursuit of his socialist ideals—'everything seemed quite simple, clear and certain to him'—his revolutionary activity, like Kondratyev's, 'was founded on nothing but ambition and the desire for supremacy'. 'He did not love anyone and looked on all men of note as rivals', Nekhlyudov says, and he placed all his faith in his powers of rational analysis. 'The intellectual powers of man—his numerator—were great; but his opinion of himself—his denominator—were immeasurably greater, and had far outgrown his intellectual powers.' He was unloved by his comrades, but commanded their loyalty by virtue of the courage and resoluteness with which he pursued his goals:

> Being devoid of those moral and aesthetic qualities which call forth doubts and hesitation, he very soon acquired a position in the revolutionary world which satisfied him—that of a party leader. Having once chosen a direction, he never doubted or hesitated, and was therefore certain that he never made a mistake. Everything seemed quite simple, clear and certain. And the narrowness and one-sidedness of his views did make everything simple and clear; one only had to be logical, as he said. His self-assurance was so great that it either repelled people or made them submit to him. As he carried on his activity among very young people who mistook his boundless self-assurance for depth and wisdom, the majority did submit to him and he had great success in revolutionary circles. His activity was directed to the preparation of a rising in which he was to usurp power and call together an assembly. A programme composed by him was to be put before this assembly, and he felt sure that this programme of his solved every problem, and that it would be inevitably carried out. His comrades respected him for his courage and resoluteness but did not love him. He did not love anyone, and looked upon all men of note as rivals, and could he have done it would willingly have treated them as old male monkeys treat young ones. He would have torn all mental power, all capacity, from other men, so that they should not interfere with the display of his talents. He behaved well only to those who bowed before him.[13]

Ultimately, Nekhlyudov finds moral fulfilment, not in revolutionary social ideals, but in the spiritual self-renewal that comes from repentance of his sins and reconciliation with those he has wronged. The message conveyed by the novel is that the spiritual fulfilment attained through the selfless love of neighbour (the nearest implying the universal) is the only true basis for the exercise of social and communal responsibility. This is stated even more explicitly by Tolstoy in his non-fictional writings than it is in the novels. In one of the most impassioned sequences from *The Law of Violence and the Law of Love* he condemns revolutionary movements for assuming the responsibility to act on behalf of the masses to change the conditions of their lives. 'The belief that some people can arrange the lives of the majority in the name of which the greatest crimes are committed is the greatest hindrance to achieving the true well-being of humanity', he declared. 'Rivers of blood have been shed in the name of this, inestimable suffering has been caused by such movements and these', he asserts, 'form the greatest obstacle to society's successful creation of those particular improvements in life appropriate to our time.'[14]

The reason revolutionary movements fail in their attempts to transform society is to be traced, he says, to their failure to begin the process of reform with the moral perfection of their own members: 'Under the pretext of altering and improving social conditions, they put all their energy into influencing other people, thus neglecting their own inner self-perfection which alone can enhance a change in the structure of society as a whole.' 'Human life in its totality', he declares, 'advances and cannot help moving forward towards the eternal ideals of perfection only if each individual person advances towards his own personal and unrestricted perfection'. He cites the revolutionary propagandist, Alexander Hertzen, in support of the premise that the general welfare can only be served by individuals seeking to effect a moral transformation in their own lives. 'If instead of wishing to save the world', Hertzen wrote, 'people wished to save themselves, to liberate themselves rather than humanity, they would be doing much more for the salvation of the world and the freedom of humanity.' Endorsing Hertzen, Tolstoy insists that reform must be sought, not through the pursuit of 'external aims'—a process he condemns as 'vain and stupid'—but by each individual confronting the root causes of society's ills in the corruption of his own soul:

> All you suffering men of the Christian world, both rulers and rich and poor and oppressed, need only free yourselves from the deception of false Christianity and government (concealing what Christ revealed to you and what is demanded by your reason and your heart) and it will become clear to you that it is in yourselves and only in yourselves that you will find the cause of all the bodily suffering (want), and spiritual suffering (awareness of injustice, envy and annoyance) that torments you—the oppressed and poor. And that it is also in yourselves, the rich and powerful, that you will find the cause of those fears, pangs of conscience and awareness of the sinfulness of your lives, all of which disturbs you in varying degrees according to your moral sensitivity. . . .
>
> 'Come unto me, all ye that labour and are heavily laden, and I will give you rest. Take my yoke upon you and learn of me; for I am meek and lowly in heart: and ye shall find rest unto your souls. For my yoke is easy and my burden is light'. (Matt. 1, 28-31) You will be saved and delivered from the evil you endure and receive the true well-being you so clumsily strive after, not through personal desire nor envy, nor through adherence to a party programme; nor through hatred, indignation, or the pursuit of fame, nor even through a sense of justice, and above all not through troubling yourselves about the organisation of other people's lives. However strange it may seem, it is only through an activity within your own soul, involving no external aim and no consideration of what might come of it.
>
> Understand that the assumption that a man may organise the lives of others is a crude superstition that people have only accepted because of its antiquity.

And understand that those who are preoccupied with organising the lives of others, be they monarchs, presidents and ministers, or spies and executioners, or members and leaders of a party, or dictators, understand that these people manifest nothing worthy—as people seem to think—but, to the contrary, are pitiable, deeply misled people, preoccupied with a task that is not only vain and stupid, but is one of the most horrible things a man can choose to do.[15]

This insistence on the priority of individual over social renewal runs through all of Tolstoy's writings, both fictional and non-fictional, and constitutes the primary objective of his thinking on social and community education. It is especially evident in works such 'Bethink Yourselves!' where he condemned the ravages of the Russo-Japanese War of 1905 and in 'The Slavery of our Times' where he condemned the unjust and exploitative practices that were common in Russian society at the end of the ninteeenth century.[16] Describing the calamites that result from conflict in all its forms, he insists the solution must be sought internally by each individual in the tendency towards violence present in his own soul. 'Is it not evident that if there is to be a salvation from this position', he cries, 'it is only one—that one which Jesus teaches, "Seek ye first the kingdom of God and his righteousness (that which is within you) and all the rest (that is all the practical welfare towards which man is striving) will of itself be realised".'[17] And while condemning the injustices and inequities in contemporary society, he again insists that the best prospect for reform lies in the individual potential for moral self-renewal. A revolution that is not based on this will simply reproduce the corrupt and egotistical society it is seeking to replace. While conceding their basic sincerity, he therefore condemns revolutionary movements that are inspired by purely political and social objectives:

> If on the other hand, you belong to the category of sincere people desiring to serve the nation by revolutionary, socialistic activity, then (apart from the insufficiency of aim involved in that material welfare of men towards which you are striving, which never satisfied anyone) consider those means which you possess for its attainment. These means are, in the first place and above all, immoral, containing falsehood, deception, violence, murder; in the second place these means can in no case attain their end. The strength and caution of governments defending their existence are in our time so great that not only can no ruse, deception, or harsh action overthrow them, they cannot even shake them. All revolutionary attempts only furnish new justification for the violence of governments, and increase their power.
>
> But even if we admit the impossible—that a revolution in our time could be crowned with success—then, why should we expect that, contrary to all which has ever taken place, the power which has overturned another power can increase the liberty of men and become more beneficent than the one it

has overthrown? Or, if that conjecture, though contrary to common sense and experience, were possible, and one power having abolished another power could give people the freedom necessary to establish those conditions of life which they regard as most advantageous for themselves, then there would still be no reason whatever to suppose that people living an egotistical life could establish amongst themselves better conditions than the previous ones.[18]

The belief that socio-political reform can alter the 'character and life-conception' of men he sees as a reversal of the natural order of things— 'taking the result for the cause and the cause for the result of an accompanying condition'.[19] It is to be compared, he says, to moving around the wet firewood in a stove in the hope that somehow it may eventually catch fire—a futile and hopeless activity. Thus, in this eloquent passage from 'An Appeal to Social Reformers', he pleads with all revolutionaries to devote their energies to the fulfilment of Christ's injunction, 'Be you perfect as your heavenly Father is perfect', as the only fruiful means to the realisation of their social ideals:

> Think only what enormous and splendid mental powers are now spent in the service of the state and in its defence from revolution; how much youthful and enthusiastic effort is spent on attempts at revolution, on an impossible struggle with the state; how much is spent on socialistic dreamings. All this is not only delaying, but rendering impossible the realisation of the welfare towards which all men are striving. How would it be if all those who are spending their powers so fruitlessly, and often with harm to their neighbours, were to direct them to all that, which alone affords the possibility of good social life—to their inner self-perfection?
>
> How many times would one be able to build a new house out of the new solid material, if all those efforts which have been and are now being spent on propping up the old house were used resolutely and conscientiously for the preparation of the material for a new house and the building thereof, which, although obviously it could not at first be as luxurious and convenient for some chosen ones as was the old one, would undoubtedly be more stable, and would afford the complete possibility for those improvements which are necessary, not for the chosen only, but for all men!
>
> So that all I have said here amounts to the simple, generally comprehensible, and irrefutable truth, that in order that good life should exist amongst men, it is necessary that men should be good. There is only one way of influencing men towards a good life: namely, to live a good life onseself. Therefore the activity of those who desire to contribute to the establishment of good life amongst men can and should consist in efforts towards inner perfection in the fulfilment of that which is expressed in the Gospel by the words: 'Be ye perfect even as your Father in Heaven is perfect'.[20]

In one of his last pamphlets, a work simply entitled 'Love one Another', which he addressed to the peasants of Yasnaya Polyana,Tolstoy once again reiterated the conviction that he had asserted repeatedly through all his treatises on the ills of modern society—that true reform would be achieved only through the power of love. 'To desire the welfare of all is to love men', he wrote. 'And to love men is a thing no one and nothing can hinder. The more a man loves the more his life gains in freedom and joy', he declared. Again he insisted on the need to found social progress on the bedrock of individual morality: 'There is but one way in which life can become good, namely, by men themselves becoming better. And when men are better life will arrange itself in the way proper for good people'. Quoting his favourite verses from the Gospel of St John—'We know that we have passed out of death into life because we have loved the brethren'—he makes three crucial assertions: one, that love is truly genuine only when motivated by its own absolute selflessness, that is, without concern for reciprocation or reward; two, that love transforms everything to which it is directed, regardless of how it is received; three, that the process of loving is set in motion by the simple ethical imperative of 'beginning now'—by an act of direct and immediate resolve:

> Love gives blessedness to man not by its consequences: the love itself gives blessedness quite independently of how other people act, and, in general, of all that takes place in the outside world. Love gives blessedness in that man, when loving, unites with God, and not only desires nothing for himself, but wishes to give all he has, and his life itself, for others; and in surrender of himself to God, he finds his welfare. Therefore all that others do, and all that goes on in the world, can have no influence on his conduct. To love means to yield oneself to God, and to do what God wishes; and God is love, that is to say, He wishes the welfare of all, and therefore cannot wish man to perish, fulfilling his law. The loving man alone does not perish among the non-loving. Or if he perishes among men, as Christ perished on the cross, then his death is joyful to himself, and important for others; not despairing and insignificant, as is the death of worldly people.
>
> So the excuse that I do not yield myself to love because not everyone does the same, and I should be left alone, is both incorrect and bad. It is as though a man who ought to work to feed himself and his children, were not to begin because others were not working. . . .
>
> One cannot know whether anything is good or bad, unless one tastes it in life. If a farmer is told that it is good to sow rye in rows, or a bee-keeper that it is good to use frame-hives, a reasonable bee-keeper or foreman will experiment to find out whether what he has been told is true; and he will follow or not follow the advice, according to the degree to which his experiment succeeds.

So it is with the whole business of life. To know surely in how far the doctrine of love is applicable—try it![21]

The first aim of social and community education, therefore, is the nurturing of ethico-religious awareness and behaviour through the self-perfection of the individual—through a self-perfection attained in the practice of active love in the interpenetrating spheres of all the interpersonal and social relations in which individual life is conducted. Tolstoy identified two distinct but interdependent ways in which an educator could promote these objectives: firstly, through the direct fostering of an individual consciousness of personal and social responsibility; secondly, through a personal witnessing or exemplification of the ideal of active love. The term 'consciousness' is used in these writings, as in the writings on the teaching of scripture discussed in the last chapter, with the distinctly modern connotation of an awareness grasped in the depth of personal subjectivity—an awareness sufficiently intense as to be manifested directly in decision, action and deed (almost a co-intentional praxis in the Freirean sense of that term).[22] In 'Bethink Yourselves!' he addresses the question: how are social corruption and immorality to be countered? It cannot be done, he declares, merely through the dissemination of ideas, nor through the process of institutional change. It requires a fundamental transformation effected in the depth of individual consciousness. 'The only relief from evils men inflict on themselves is attainable not by any external measure but by that simple appeal to the consciousness of each separate man which one thousand nine hundred years ago was proposed by Jesus—that every man must bethink himself and ask himself why he lives and what he should and should not do.' In this passage from the essay he deliberately employs Biblical language to underline the essentially religious character of the transformation that he describes:

> Jesus said, 'Bethink yourselves', that is, 'Let every man interrupt the work he has begun and ask himself: Who am I? Whence have I come, and whence am I going? And, having answered these questions according to the answer to decide whether that which he is doing is in conformity with his destination'. And every man of our world and time who is acquainted with the essence of the Christian teaching, needs only for a minute to interrupt this activity, to forget the capacity in which he is regarded by men, be it of emperor, soldier, minister or journalist, and seriously ask himself who he is and what is his destination, in order to begin to doubt the utility, lawfulness, and reasonableness of his activity. 'Before I am emperor, soldier, minister or journalist', every man of our time and of the Christian world must say to himself, 'before any of these I am a man. I am a living being sent by the Higher Will into a universe endless in time and space, in order, after staying in it for an instant,

to die, and to disappear from it. And therefore all those personal, social, and even universal, human aims which I may place before myself and which are placed before me by men, are all insignificant owing to the shortness of my life, as well as to the boundlessness of the life of the universe, and should be subordinated to that higher aim, for the attainment of which I am sent into the world. This ultimate aim, owing to my limitations, is inaccessible to me, but it does exist (as there must be a purpose in all that exists), and my business is that of being its tool. My end is that of being a workman of God, of fulfilling His work'. And having understood this destiny, every man of our world and time, from emperor to soldier, cannot but regard differently those duties which he has taken upon himself or which other men have imposed upon him.[23]

The transformation to which he refers is to be achieved, not through intellectual persuasion, but through the nurturing of faith, the unified consciousness transcending the abstractions of the rational. The man of faith, he wrote, is 'guided in his activity, not by the presumed possible consequences of his action, but by the consciousness of the destination of his life'. It is that sense of ultimate purpose, he says, which impels a man to act in accordance with the ethical imperatives of his conscience—the final arbiter of the rightness and truthfulness of all action:

> A factory workman goes to his factory, and in it accomplishes the work which is allotted him without considering what will be the consequences of his labour. In the same way a soldier acts, carrying out the will of his commander. So acts a religious man in fulfilling the work prescribed to him by God, without arguing as to what precisely will come of that work. Therefore, for a religious man there is no question as to whether many or few men act as he does, or of what may happen to him if he does that which he should do. He knows that, besides life and death, nothing can happen, and that life and death are in the hands of God whom he obeys.
>
> A religious man acts thus and not otherwise, not because he desires to act thus, not because it is advantageous to himself or to other men, but because, believing that his life is in the hands of God, he cannot act otherwise.
>
> In this lies the distinction of the activity of religious men.[24]

Fostering the consciousness of faith, inculcating and deepening an awareness of the moral imperatives through which it is manifested, were the central preoccupations of Tolstoy's writings in the years he devoted to adult education. We have seen from the last chapter that instruction in the scriptures was his chief method of promoting religious consciousness amongst the young. With the adult population to whom he addressed his interpretations of Christian truth, the process was basically the same. For thirty years he conducted a dialogue with the adult masses through the medium of his writings, employing the same basic methods of questioning, interpreting and explicating the message of the scriptures as he did in his schools, and defining their relevance to the major social and political issues of the day.

To see this merely as an exercise in mass communication would be to misunderstand the nature of the dialogue in which he was engaged. His method of communication derived its force and authority, not only from the skill with which he delivered his message, but from his own personal exemplification of the truth of what he conveyed. All his writings were imbued with the authority of his own personal attestation to the moral validity of the message that was taught—whether this was the rejection of violence, the surrender of personal property, the practice of private prayer, the regular study of the scriptures—in all cases he gave visible and enduring witness to the truth of what he preached. And he imposed a similar responsibility on his followers. The deliverance of mankind from the 'calamities which men inflict upon themselves', will come, he says, not from initiatives in social and political reform, but from the example of those personally committed to enacting the truths of faith in the conditions of their everyday lives. That witness was provided in the past, he said, by 'simple men' like the Dukhobors in Russia, the Nazarenes in Austria, Condatier in France, Tervey in Holland—all of whom sought 'the closest fulfilment in themselves of the will of Him who has sent them into life and directed all their powers to this realisation'. 'Only such people', he said, 'realising the Kingdom of God in themselves, in their souls, will establish, without directly aiming at this purpose, that external Kingdom of God for which every human soul is longing.'[25]

Of such men, he further asserts, there are millions in the Christian, Buddhist, Mohammedan, Brahmin and Confucian faiths, all determined to give witness in their lives to the 'chief law of God and of all religions: to act towards others as one wishes others to act towards oneself.'[26] Their witness, he explains, consists both in their attestation of the truths of faith and in their willingness to give protest—even to the point of martyrdom— against all activities and practices that are in conflict with these truths. He insists on the moral responsibility of the believer not only to give direct witness to his faith, but to protest against evil in all its forms—against state violence, for example, institutionalised poverty and injustice, against exploitative work practices, inhuman methods of taxation, child labour, the subjugation of women etc. In all instances the individul has a duty in conscience, he says, to give voice to his dissent and disapproval. In a highly self-revealing passage from 'I Cannot be Silent' he explains how he himself decided on such a course as he contemplated the manner in which he was benefitting personally from the violence and injustice perpetrated by the government in his name:

> Strange as is the statement that all this is done for me, and that I am a participator in these terrible deeds, I cannot but feel that there is an indubitable interdependence between my spacious room, my dinner, my clothing, my leisure, and these terrible crimes committed to get rid of those who would like to take from me what I use. Though I know these hopeless, embittered, depraved people, who but for the government's threats would deprive me of all I am using, are products of that same government's actions, still I cannot help feeling that at present my peace is dependent on all the horrors that are now being perpetrated by the government.
>
> Being conscious of this, I can no longer endure it, but must free myself from this intolerable position.
>
> It is impossible to live so! I, at any rate, cannot and will not live so.
>
> That is why I write this and will circulate it by all means in my power, both in Russia and abroad; that one or two things may happen, either that these inhuman deeds may be stopped, or that my connection with them may be snapped, and I put in prison, where I may be clearly conscious that these horrors are not committed on my behalf; or, still better (so good that I dare not even dream of such happiness) they may put on me, as on those twenty or twelve peasants, a shroud and a cap, and may push me also off a bench, so that by my own weight I may tighten the well-soaped noose round my own throat.[27]

That protesting action was extended by Tolstoy to the non-payment of government taxes and to the refusal to support the armed forces in their bloody conflicts with Russia's enemies. In 'The Slavery of Our Times' he urged his followers to engage in civil disdobedience against the government for its evil and inhuman policies at home and abroad. 'Such a man', he wrote, in his profile of the moral dissenter, 'should not voluntarily pay taxes to governments, either directly or indirectly, nor should he accept money collected by taxes . . . nor should he make use of government institutes supported by taxes collected by violence from the people.' Civil disobedience, he argued, was always justified when the government's policies ran counter to the law of God. Referring specifically to the inequities in contemporary European society, he writes: 'One cannot be free while transgressing the higher universal law of mutual service, as it is transgressed by the life of the wealthy. . . . A man can be free only to the degree to which he fulfils the higher law. The fulfilment of this law is not only difficult but almost impossible . . . where man's success is founded upon contest with other men.'[28]

Reading Tolstoy's reflections on the importance of a personal witnessing to the truths of faith, one thinks of Buber's characterisation of the zaddik teacher as someone whose influence on his followers consisted in the manner by which his teachings were embodied in every facet of his own life. The impact of the zaddik's teaching derived, he said, from 'the fact that he lived in a certain way. . . . He did not proceed fom a teaching, but moved to a teaching in such away that his life worked as a teaching, a teaching not yet grasped in words'.[29] That Tolstoy had a similar impact on his readers and followers—they included some of the most notable figures of the age, as well as the masses of simple workers and peasants to whom he particularly addressed himself—should be evident from the details of his activities in the sphere of adult education that were provided in an earlier chapter. Of the themes on which he dwelt most frequently in his writings, two have a particular relevance to social and community education: the problem of justice and the problem of peace. Each of these will be examined in the next two sections of this chapter. Though the two are closely interrelated, the theme of non-violence is by far the more prominent in Tolstoy's writings, and it seems logical therefore that this should be examined first. Following some discussion of the issues relating to social justice and equity, brief consideration will be given also to the activities of the Tolstoyan communities—the various groups who came together all over the world to live in accordance with the principles of Tolstoy's teachings. Their activities provide the most striking testament that exists on the special impact of those teachings, an impact deriving both from their intrinsic moral validity and from the manner in which they had been taught.

2 'Resist Not Evil': Education for Peace

Tolstoy, therefore, saw the goal of community education as the fostering of the spirit of altruistic love in the realms of the social and the political with the same degree of ethical authenticity as he had advocated it in the more immediate and more intimate realm of the interpersonal. He conceived the process as involving a twofold dialogue: a dialogue, firstly, through which the educator would seek directly to penetrate the consciousness of those to whom he addressed his message; and secondly, a dialogue of witness in which he would simultaneously seek to exemplify in his own life, in his words and in his deeds, the truth of the messsage that he sought to convey. For Tolstoy this process was focussed on the two main themes that have already been mentioned—the theme of non-resistance to evil and the closely related theme of social justice and reform.

The first of these—the theme of non-violence—is central to his writings on religion and morality and to those which deal with the socio-political, moral and economic issues of his day. For more than fifty years he had persistently asserted his belief that violence in all its forms is intrinsically evil, and is directly in conflict with the teachings enunciated by Christ in the Sermon on the Mount. Assessments of his position on this issue range from the highly critical views of contemporaries such as Dostoevsky—who ridiculed it as 'insensibility side by side with sentimentalism'[30]—to the adulation of Mohandas Gandhi who confessed himself a convert to the whole philosophy of non-violence (though not without significant quali-fications), and who drew immense support from the letters he received from Tolstoy, advocating such a course, in the early years of his political activities in the Transvaal.[31] Regrettably, the more common reaction to Tolstoy's views is probably typified by a recent biography which describes his pacifism as 'being marked by a remarkable simplicity of moral outlook', there being no 'ambivalences, no circumstances where the idea of a just war might have demanded consideration'.[32]

That the position is much more complex than this is intimated by a rarely discussed preface to Tolstoy's social and political writings, which was written by his fellow countryman, the philosopher, Nikolai Berdyaev.[33] Berdyaev argues that Tolstoy's pacifist teachings have been widely mis-understood in two main respects. There has been, firstly, he suggests, a general failure, or reluctance, to appreciate the full significance of his belief in the ultimate power of the spirit. Underlying his teachings on non-violence was a 'quietistic conviction', Berdyaev says, that led him to assert that if evil were not resisted, it would finally be conquered by the infinite poten-tiality of the spirit. What the conviction reflected was a growing awareness by Tolstoy in his later years of the compatibility of certain Buddhist teachings with the teachings of Christ—a position which was greatly reinforced by his belief in religious tolerance and in the common ground to be found between all religions committed to the propagation of the 'law of love'.

He was drawn particularly to the Buddhist doctrine of *ahimsa* which he found to be fundamentally consistent with Christ's injunction not to resist evil. There are numerous instances, in his correspondence and in his diaries, of his interest in this and in other aspects of Buddhist teaching. In a letter to his fellow-writer, A.A. Fet, for example, he described how he saw the practice of non-resistance to evil as the means to spiritual perfection and the gateway to Nirvana. He confessed his own 'religious reverence for, and terror of Nirvana', adding that nothing could be more welcome than the 'extinction of will and desire', and that he found it 'much more interesting than life'.[34] There are many such instances of his affirmation of the Buddhist teaching on the ultimacy of spirit and its survival of the death of material existence—a doctrine he found to be especially compatible with Christian teaching on immortality.[35] Thus he declared that it was better to die than to inflict injury on a fellow human being. 'I run the risk', he said, 'only of death . . . and death in fulfilling the will of God is a blessing.' 'By resisting force', he added, 'I run the risk of acting quite contrary to the law of Christ—which is worse than death.'[36] A claim for which both authoritative Christian and Buddhist support could be cited could hardly be described as 'simplistic', unless that term were to be used to describe an unusually strict and un-ambiguous reassertion of some of the most fundamental principles of both traditions—a position which Tolstoy himself defended with characteristic ease, clarity and consistency.

The second issue on which his pacifist teaching has been misunderstood involves what Berdyaev describes as the 'ethical maximalism' of his inter-pretations of the Christian scriptures—a term that Berdyaev, in turn, had borrowed from the philosopher, Zenkovsky.[37] On the one hand, Tolstoy insisted on the absolute commitment demanded of Christians to the ethical teachings of Christ and, like Kierkegaard, urged an unqualified inter-pretation of the meaning of the injunction, 'Be ye therefore perfect as your heavenly Father is perfect.'[38] But equally, he said, on several occasions, that what matters for a Christian is not the victory but the intensity of his struggle to achieve it. In a letter to his disciple, Yevgeny Popov, for example, he wrote: 'In our struggle with temptation we are weakened by setting victory as our goal; we set ourselves a task beyond our powers. . . . The aim is constant struggle with temptation.'[39]

And, even more significantly, in a letter to Adin Ballou, the author of *Christian Non-Resistance*, he wrote that 'compromise, inevitable in prac-tice, cannot be admitted in theory'. 'The great sin', he said, 'is compromise in theory, is the plan to lower the ideal of Christ in order to make it attainable.'[40] In other words, while recognising the inevitability (but not the rightness) of some compromise on the doctrine of non-violence in practice, he insists that the ideal itself can never be diluted. Like several other Christian axioms it becomes, therefore, a 'counsel of perfection'. As Kierke-gaard had argued throughout his *Christian Discourses*, what matters is the process of *becoming* a Christian, and man becomes virtuous only in the degree to which he aspires towards the perfection which Christianity entails. That, broadly speaking, was Tolstoy's position also. By this conception, the law on violence must be seen as absolute and its principles can never be diluted; however imperfectly they may be implemented in practice, their absolute validity must always be upheld. On this reasoning, Berdyaev saw Tolstoy's 'ethical maximalism' as an indispensable feature of his entire moral and religious outlook—as a beacon light in his struggle against evil and, for all its limitations, a position profoundly relevant to the needs of the present age:

> Tolstoy used to say that the only thing in which he had unshakeable faith was the Good. The Good for him was God. This shews his greatness, but also his limitations. Unlike Dostoevsky he remained unaware of the mysterious, mystical aspect of Christianity: and it is not easy to acquit him on the charge of stuffy moralism, though this applies perhaps more to the 'Tolstoyans' than to Tolstoy himself. But, however much he may have put a moral strait-jacket upon himself and upon those to whom he preached, his very moralism was a sign of his clear and utterly truthful conscience and of his love for unadulterated truth. Like a true Russian he was a maximalist, and we may reiterate how important it is that the testimony of maximal moral truth should sound in our age when truth is dimmed or falsified or lost. In the great conflict between Tolstoy's artistic genius and his moral convictions, in which the former was, in the end, sacrificed for the latter, there was revealed something eternally human as well as morally significant. His ethical maximalism was itself bound up with his belief in true, undivided, integral humanity, and with his awareness that life is doomed to unrelieved isolation and atomisation unless men recover their original, uncorrupted manhood.[41]

Seen therefore in terms of its roots both in Buddhist spirituality and in the ethical maximalism of the Russian religio-philosophic tradition, Tolstoy's pacifism seems a more credible doctrine than has generally been acknowledged. Both its strengths and weaknesses become more clearly apparent when it is judged from the standpoint of the conditions in which it was conceived. It dominated his writings for many years and led him repeatedly to denounce the Churches, the government, the war-makers and revolutionaries, for their employment of violence and force to achieve their ends. His anger was directed particularly at the Churches for what he saw as their betrayal of the teachings of Christ through the specious logic of a 'just war' theology. In *A Confession* he recalls that it was the Church's teaching on war that initially shocked him into recognising the false nature of its interpretations of the Christian scriptures:

> At the time Russia was at war. And, in the name of Christian love, Russians were killing their fellow men. It was impossible not to think about this. It was impossible to avoid the fact that killing is evil and contrary to the most basic principles of any faith. And yet prayers were said in the churches for the success of our armies, and our religious teachers acknowledged this killing as an outcome of faith. And this was not only applied to murder in time of war, but, during the troubled times that followed the war, I witnessed members of the Church, her teachers, monks, and ascetics condoning the killing of helpless, lost youths. As I turned my attention to all that is done by people who profess Christianity, I was horrified.[42]

Looking for historical explanations of the misrepresentation of Christ's teaching on violence by the Churches, Tolstoy turned his attention to his old enemies, the theologians and rationalists, blaming them for providing intellectualised justifications for the distortion of the meaning of the original Christian message. Insisting that Christ's words on non-violence admit of no exception, that they encapsulate the very essence of his conception of the law of love, he argues that an interpretation of Christianity that admits the use of violence 'presents an inner contradiction resembling cold fire or hot ice'. 'It would seem evident', he continues, 'that if some people, despite recognising the virtue of love, can admit the necessity of tormenting or murdering certain people for the sake of some future good, then others, by just the same right, and also acknowledging the virtue of love, can claim the same necessity in the name of some future good.'[43] The admission of any exception to Christ's words 'diminishes the whole significance' of his teaching, he writes, as he cites an impressive array of sources from early Christian teaching in support of his interpretations of those words. (Since this is a key passage for an understanding of his treatment of the whole theme of pacifism, it is worth quoting at some length):

> The Christian community of the first to the fifth centuries A.D. categorically declared, through its leaders, that Christianity forbids any murder, including murder in war.
>
> In the second century, the philosopher Tatian, a convert to Christianity, declared that killing in war was inadmissable for Christians, as was any kind of murder, and he regarded the honoured military wreath as an obscenity for a Christian. In the same century Athinagoras of Athens stated that not only must Christians themselves not kill, but they must not be present at any scene of murder.
>
> In the third century Clement of Alexandria contrasted the warrior-like pagans with the peaceful race of Christians. But it was the renowed Origen who most clearly expressed the Christians' dislike of war. Applying to the Christians the words of Isaiah, who said that a time would come when people would beat their swords into ploughshares and their spears into pruning-hooks, Origen says firmly: 'We will not raise arms against any other nation, we will not practise the art of war, because through Jesus Christ we have become the children of peace.' Replying to the accusation made by Celsus against the Christians who refused military service (for in the opinion of Celsus the Roman Empire would collapse if it became Christian), Origen says that Christians fight more than others for the sake of the Emperor, but they do it through good deeds, prayers, and by setting a good example to others. As for armed combat, Origen quite rightly says that a Christian will not fight in the Emperor's armies, not even if the Emperor forced them to.
>
> Tertullian, a contemporary of Origen, expressed himself equally decisively

on the impossibility of Christians becoming soldiers. He said of military service: 'It is not fitting to serve the emblem of Christ and the emblem of the devil, the fortress of light and the fortress of darkness. One soul cannot serve two masters. And how can one wage war without the sword which the Lord himself has taken away? How can it be possible to practise using the sword when the Lord has said that anyone who takes up his sword will perish by the sword ? How can a son of peace participate in combat?

The celebrated Cyprian said: 'The world is going mad in mutual bloodshed. And murder, which is considered a crime when people commit it singly, is transformed into a virtue when they do it en masse. The offenders acquire impunity by increasing their ravaging'.

In the fourth century Lactancius said the same thing: 'There must not be any exception to God's commandment that it is always a sin to kill a person. It is not permitted to bear arms, for our only weapon is the truth.'[44]

From the time that Christains joined the armies of Constantine, he says, the 'simple indubitable and evident truth that the profession of Christiantity is incompatible with the readiness to commit any kind of violence' was systematically concealed by the Churches from their followers, and for fifteen centuries a corrupt and contradictory version of Christ's teaching was propagated. The most dreadful crimes were perpetrated in the name of Christianity, he says, while those small groups of believers who remained loyal to the original teaching on non-violence—the Manicheans, Montanists, Cathars, Molokans, Quakers, Jehovists, Klisti, Skoptsi, Dukhobors and Moravians—were despised for their strict adherence to the message of the scriptures.[45] He uses a term more frequently used by revolutionaries—*odureniye*[46] or 'stupefaction'—to convey the mental domination exercised by the Churches over their followers through the centuries. In *The Law of Violence and the Law of Love* he urges those believers to rediscover the simplicity of the original Christian injunction on love, and specifically to abide by the command not to inflict violence on a fellow human being. In this passage from *What I Believe* he describes his own rediscovery of this truth and his subsequent reassessment of the version of Christianity taught by the Churches:

When I understood that the words 'Resist not evil' did indeed mean 'Resist not evil', my whole understanding of Christ's teaching was suddenly changed; I was appalled at the peculiar way in which I had understood it until then. I knew—we all know—that the meaning of the Christian teaching lies in love for other people. To say 'Turn your cheek, love your enemies', is to express the very essence of Christianity. I had known all this since childhood, but why had I not understood these straightforward words in a straightforward manner? Why had I searched instead for some allegorical meaning in them? 'Do not resist him that is evil' means 'Do not ever resist him that is evil, do not commit acts of violence, acts that are contrary to the spirit of love'. And if you are insulted, then suffer the insult and still do not commit acts of violence. It is impossible to say any of this more clearly and straightforwardly than Christ did.[47]

There are clear implications for the educator in all this: it is necessary, he suggests, to penetrate the cloud of stupefaction preventing believers from appreciating the true meaning of Christ's teaching and to enable them to rediscover this for themselves through a conscientious reading of the scriptures, unimpeded by the abstractions of exegetic 'scholarship' or theology. In moral terms the imperatives are equally clear: for a Christian there are no circumstances in which the use of violence or force would be permissable. He quotes the words of the French socialist writer, Anatole France: 'War will only be annihilated when people cease to have any share in violence and are prepared to suffer all the persecutions they will bring upon themselves for doing so.'[48] Recognising, like France, that violence originates in the desire to dominate, Tolstoy argued that the only possible solution to conflict lies in the refusal to respond to force with more force, a stance which requires exceptional humility and self-sacrifice in the individual respondent.

He cites the Stoic philosopher, Epictetus, to give a more explicitly religious character to the same theme. Submission to the will of God, the latter declared, is paradoxically, the true source of freedom: 'When you can say in all truth with your whole heart: "My Lord, my God, do with me as you will", only then will you free yourself from slavery and be completely free.' Domination of others, Epictetus asserts, is itself a form of slavery: 'If you see a person wishing to control not himself, but others, you know that he is not free, he has become a slave of his desire to dominate people.'[49] That desire to dominate, which is the root cause of violent conflict, will be overcome, Tolstoy concludes, only when each individual is awakened to the voice of conscience urging him to refuse to respond to force with more force, to counter evil with more evil, in direct contravention of the words of Christ. 'The salvation of men' will only be achieved, he writes, 'by every person who is called upon to participate in violence over his fellow man and his own self recognising the true spiritual I within himself and asking in amazement, "Well why should I do that?".'[50] Such a man, he says, will refuse to engage in violent conflict, on the grounds that violence is itself intrinsically evil and cannot therefore be employed for the conquest of evil. Addressing the classic dilemma of the pacifist—what must he do in the face of violent attack—his response is a clear and emphatic reassertion of the absolute and binding character of the law of non-violence enjoined in the commandment, 'Thou shalt not kill':

> ... the question of what I should do to counteract acts of violence committed
> before my eyes is always based on the same primitive superstition that it is
> possible for man not only to know, but to organise, the future in the way he
> likes. For a man free of this superstition the question does not and cannot
> exist.
>
>   A rogue has raised his knife over his victim. I have a pistol in my hand and
> kill him. But I do not know, and cannot possibly know, whether the purpose
> of the raised knife would have been implemented. The rogue may not have
> carried out his evil intention, whereas I certainly commit my evil deed.
> Therefore the only thing that a person can and must do in this and similar
> instances is what he must always do in all possible circumstances: he must
> do what he believes he ought to do before God and before his own conscience.
> A man's conscience may demand that he sacriifice his own life but not that
> of another person. The same principle can be applied to the method of
> counteracting social evil.
>
>   Thus, to the question of what a person should do in the face of the evil
> committed by one, or a number of persons, the answer given by a man free
> of the superstition that it is possible to foresee, and to employ violence to
> organise, the conditions of the future, is always the same: do unto others as
> you would have them do unto you.[51]

Tolstoy's condemnation of the Churches for their failure to preach the
Christian doctrine of non-violence is reinforced by a vociferous condemnation of all war-makers, especially governments who hold the power to
initiate or to prevent the obscenity of mass slaughter. Ever since he served
as an officer in the Crimean War and witnessed the atrocities committed in
the name of 'patriotism' and 'freedom', he had been loud in his condemnation of the horrors of war. All this reached a climax with 'Bethink
Yourselves!' his manifesto on the immorality of warfare, which he issued
after the outbreak of the Russo-Japanese War in 1904. Denouncing those
responsible for this 'universal stupefaction and brutalisation', he declared:
'Men who are separated from each other by thousands of miles, hundreds
of thousands of such men (on the one hand, Buddhists whose law forbids
the killing, not only of men, but of animals, on the other hand, Christians
professing the law of brotherhood and love) like wild beasts, on land and on
sea, are seeking out one another in order to kill, torture and mutilate each
other in the most cruel way possible.'[52] Brought by the 'deceit of centuries'
to recognise the greatest crime on earth—the murder of one's fellow
man—as a 'virtuous act', they are the victims, he says, of a giant fraud on
the part of churchmen and statesmen who have consistently sought to
provide 'moral' justification for their actions. 'How', he asks, 'can so-called

enlightened men preach war, support it, participate in it, and worst of all, without suffering the dangers of war themselves, incite others to it, sending their unfortunate, defrauded brothers to fight.' The same men who recently proclaimed the 'futility and senselesness of war' were now, he says, 'exciting the passion of hatred in peaceful, harmless industrious men and inciting them to deeds contrary to conscience and faith'. There is an element of pathos as well as anger in his description of the deluded masses who leave families and homes, on the urging of their leaders, to risk their lives in pursuit of utterly false and misguided ideals:

> Stupefied by prayers, sermons, exhortations, by processions, pictures and newspapers, the cannon-fodder—hundreds of thousands of men, uniformly dressed, carrying divers deadly weapons, leaving their parents, wives, children, with hearts of agony but with artificial bravado—go where they, risking their own lives, will commit the most dreadful acts of killing men whom they do not know and who have done them no harm. And they are followed by doctors and nurses who somehow imagine that at home they cannot serve simple peaceful suffering people but can only serve those who are engaged in slaughtering each other. Those who remain at home are gladdened by news of the murder of men, and when they learn that many Japanese have been killed they thank someone whom they call God.
>
> All this is not only regarded as the manifestation of elevated feeling, but those who refrain from such manifestations, if they endeavour to disabuse men, are deemed traitors and betrayers, and are in danger of being abused and beaten by a brutalised crowd, which in its defence of its insanity and cruelty can possess no other weapon than brute force.[53]

As has already been indicated, Tolstoy saw the refusal to fight as the only legitimate moral option open to a Christian, and he repeatedly advised his followers that they must be prepared to adopt this course of action, regardless of the consequences to themselves. He warned they would have to expect personal vilification for their stance and would be accused of cowardice, treason against their country, betrayal of the good of their fellow-man, and so on. While tolerating certain forms of political dissent—largely because they afford a semblance of democratic normality to their actions— governments, he further warns, will not countenance the 'refusal to fight', because they know that 'such refusals expose their fraud and strike at the root of their power'.[54] Thus, in a letter to a group of Swedish citizens, who had written to him in 1899 about a forthcoming Peace Conference,[55] he warned that 'conscientious objectors' would have to endure the con- demnation of their leaders and the opprobrium of their fellow citizens, but could look forward to a time when their actions would create the conditions in which those who take up arms will themselves become an object of contempt to their fellow men:

> Armies can be reduced and abolished only in opposition to the will, but never by the will of governments. Armies will only be diminished and abolished when people cease to trust governments, and themselves seek salvation from the miseries that oppress them, and seek that safety, not by the delicate and complicated combinations of diplomats, but in the simple fulfilment of the law, binding upon every man, inscribed in all religious teachings, and present in every heart, not to do to others what you wish them not to do to you—above all, not to slay your neighbours.
>
> Armies will first diminish, and then disappear, only when public opinion brands with contempt those who, whether from fear, or for advantage, sell their liberty and enter the ranks of those murderers, called soldiers; and when the men now ignored and even blamed who, despite all the persecution and suffering they have borne, have refused to yield the control of their actions into the hands of others, and become the tools of murder, are recognised by public opinion, to be the foremost champions and benefactors of mankind.
>
> Only then will armies first diminish and then quite disappear, and a new era in the life of mankind will commence.[56]

He sees the outrage of war, however, as merely the most extreme expression of the institutionalised violence universally manifested in the functioning of the modern state. In 'I Cannot Be Silent' he condemned the criminal practices—e.g. interrogation, torture, cruel methods of punishment and execution—commonly practised by states in the guise of law enforcement.[57] Reasserting the principle that violence simply breeds more violence, he castigates government authorities for exemplifying the antithesis of the values which they purport to serve, and thereby creating a climate in which violence is legitimised. Arguing that the violence of individual criminals may be understandable in some degree as being motivated by impulse, degenerate character, or quite simply ignorance, he condemns the cold-blooded violence engaged in by governments, not only for the conscious and deliberate manner in which it is conducted, but for the implicit justification it provides for similar activities on the part of the masses:

> That is how the crimes committed by the government act on the worst, the least moral, of the people, and these terrible deeds must also have an influence on the majority of men of average morality. Continually hearing and reading about the most terrible, inhuman brutality committed by the authorities, that is, by persons whom the people are accustomed to honour as the best of men, the majority of average people, especially the young, preoccupied with their own affairs, instead of realising that those who do such horrid deeds are unworthy of honour, involuntarily come to the opposite conclusion, and

argue that if men generally honoured do things that seem to us horrible, probably these things are not as horrible as we suppose.[58]

Considering the links between violence and injustice, he points to the inequitable distribution of material wealth as a prime cause of the social discontentment that breeds violence. The existence, for example, of huge estates side by side with massive poverty amongst small landlholders leads inevitably, he says, to criminal and subversive activities. 'It is plain', he writes—addressing himself to the Russian political authorities—'that you cannot pacify the people unless you satisfy the demand of the most elementary justice advanced by Russia's whole agricultural population, namely, the demand for the abolition of private property in land.'[59] What is essential, he argues in this powerfully emotive passage from 'I Cannot Endure It', is for each individual to recognise his role in implicitly supporting injustice, by continuing to accept the benefits accruing to him from the immoral policies of the political establishment:

> Everything now being done in Russia is done in the name of the general welfare, in the name of the protection and tranquillity of the inhabitants of Russia. And if this be so, then it is also all done for me, who live in Russia. For me, therefore, exists the destruction of the people, deprived of the first, most natural right of man, the right to use the land on which he is born; for me are the half million men torn away from wholesome peasant life, and dressed in uniforms and taught to kill; for me exists that false so-called priesthood, whose chief duty is to pervert and conceal true Christianity; for me are all these transportations of men from place to place; for me these hundreds of thousands of hungry workmen wandering about Russia; for me these hundreds of thousands of unfortunates are dying of typhus and scurvy in the fortresses and prisons which do not suffice for such a multitude; for me the mothers, wives, and fathers of the exiles, the prisoners, and those who are hung, are suffering; for me are these spies and this bribery; for me the interment of these dozens and hundreds of men who have been shot; for me the horrible work goes on of these hangmen, at first enlisted with difficulty, but now no longer loathing their work; for me exist these gallows, with well-soaped cords from which hang women, children and peasants; for me exists this terrible embitterment of man against his fellow-man.[60]

Amongst the crimes which he blames both on state institutions and on the 'stupefaction of the masses' is the horrific violence perpetrated against animals to provide food for popular consumption. Realising the horror of this whole practice, Tolstoy himself abandoned the habit of eating meat for the last thirty years of his life. His feeling of revulsion on the whole issue was greatly strengthened by his discovery of the prohibitions against the slaughter of animals for food in the Buddhist scriptures. In 'The First Step', the tract on vegetarianism which he published in 1891, he seeks to instil in his readers a sense of the barbarism and cruelty of animal slaughter by providing macabre descriptions of the practices occurring in state abattoirs. The following dramatic account of the killing of an ox typifies his highly evocative method of shocking his readers into a recognition of the savagery involved in the whole process:

> While I stood there, a large red, well-fed ox was led in through the opposite door, dragged by two men. It was barely inside when I saw one of the butchers raise a knife over its neck and plunge it in. The ox immediately collapsed onto its stomach, as though all four legs had been knocked from under it, rolled onto one side and began twiching its legs and hindquarters. Another butcher immediately threw himself onto the ox from the opposite side, grabbed its horns and held its head to the ground while a third butcher cut its throat. A stream of dark red blood gushed out from beneath the head and a blood-smeared boy placed a tin basin in the ground in order to catch it. While all this was going on the ox was constantly twitching its head, as though trying to get up, and waving all four legs in the air. The basin was rapidly filling up, but the ox was still alive, its stomach heaving and its legs beating the air so that the butchers had to keep their distance. When the basin was full, the boy carried it away on his head, to the albumen factory, another boy put down a second basin, which also began to fill up. The ox's stomach was still heaving and its back legs still in convulsions. When the blood stopped flowing a butcher lifted the ox's head and began stripping off the hide. The ox continued to twitch. The naked head, red with white veins, now remained in whatever position it was placed, by the butchers, the hide hanging down from either side. The ox was still twitching. Another butcher then grabbed one of the legs, broke it and cut it off. The stomach and the other legs were still shuddering. Next the other legs were cut off and thrown onto a heap of legs from oxen belonging to the same owner. The ox was then dragged to the hoist and strung up; it was no longer moving.[61]

While denouncing social corruption and injustice, and while exposing the horrific violence practised by state institutions, Tolstoy did not, however, restrict his condemnation to members of the political establishment, but extended it to those who advocated violence as a legitimate means of redressing the injustices rampant in Russian society. In an essay written shortly after the Revolution of 1905, he stressed the futility as well as the immorality of armed insurrection. 'The Russian people', he wrote, cannot help seeing that all the effort spent during the Revolution, and all the bloodshed, has not abolished poverty and the dependence of the workers on the rich and the powerful; has not prevented the expenditure of the people's strength or the seizure of foreign lands, and on wars, and has not freed the many from the power of the few.'[62] To Gandhi, who had written to him about the terrible conditions existing in the Transvaal, he also spoke of the dangers of armed resistance: 'What are needed for the Indian, as for the Englishman, the Frenchman, the German, and the Russian, are not constitutions and Revolutions, but only one thing is needful—the law of love which brings the highest happiness to every individual as well as to mankind.'[63]

Countering violence with violence is not only immoral, but is also ineffective, he argued, since it implicitly legitimises that which its victim seeks to condemn. 'The moment a man enters into strife against violence', he says, 'he thereby deprives himself of freedom, for by admitting violence on his part towards others he thereby admits also the violence against which he has striven.'[64] For the victim of violence only one course is open: the non-violent response enjoined on mankind by Christ. Despite the misrepresentation of Christ's teaching through the centuries, the truth of this teaching, he argues, is sufficiently rooted in the consciousness of Christians to be reawakened and directed towards the ideals defined in the scriptures:

> The consciousness that the slaughter of his fellow runs counter to man's nature is already in Christendom sufficiently rooted in the great majority of men. It is only necessary to understand, admit and incorporate in life the idea that we are not called on to organise other people's lives by violence, which inevitably results in murder; and that no murder we commit, in which we participate, or by which we profit, can be truly profitable to others or to ourselves, but on the contrary can only increase the evil we wish to correct. If people would but understand *that*—and refraining from all interference with other people's lives, would cease to seek to improve their own position by external, coercive organisations necessitating murder, but would seek to improve it by each man drawing personally nearer to the ideal of perfection clearly placed before him by his own best nature and the true Christian teaching, an idea quite irreconcilable with murder. Then that organisation of life which people now vainly strive to bring about by external means, only making life worse and worse, would come about by itself.
>
> There is but one way for men to free themselves from the ever-increasing ills they bear: that is by acknowledging and introducing into life in the new era now dawning on humanity, the *true* Christian teaching: that teaching which, if its basic principle—non-resistance to evil *by evil*—be not acknowledged, becomes merely an hypocrisy, that binds no one to anything, and far from altering the brutal, animal life men now live by, merely confirms it.[65]

Various commentators have questioned the practicality and realism of Tolstoy's pacifism; they include admirers, such as his biographer, Aylmer Maude, who claimed his 'misstatement of the theory of non-resistance has served more than anything else to conceal from mankind his greatness as a thinker'.[66] A more recent scholar, William Edgerton, held that what he preached was totally unrealisable in practice, and saw Gandhi's doctrine of *non-violent resistance* to evil, as distinct from Tolstoy's doctrine of total *non-resistance*, as a more realistic objective.[67] (Edgerton may not have taken sufficient account of the implications of Tolstoy's qualifying phrase 'non-resistance to evil *by evil*' in the passage just quoted. Tolstoy did not advocate total passivity before evil, as will be shown in the next section of this chapter.) All such views, as was indicated at the outset, fail to give due recognition to the spirit of ethical maximalism in which Tolstoy articulated his moral teachings. In his pacifist writings he did no more than reassert the absolute validity of the law of love and its centrality in the spheres of social and political activity as in the more immediate and more obvious sphere of the interpersonal. Just as he would not countenance any diminishing or qualifying of the absolute character of love itself, neither could he accept a conception of relationships between men that allowed for conditions in which violence—the very antithesis of the law of love—could be accorded some form of moral validity.

And, while he clearly conceived of the ethic of non-violence as an ideal to be scrupulously pursued, he was sufficiently conscious of the weakness of mankind to realise that there would always be occasions when that ideal would not be fulfilled. Thus he declared that what mattered was the struggle to abide by the law of love, not the victory or the fulfilment which might always lie beyond the reach of human endeavour—at least in any permanent or final form—and he clearly envisaged a disparity between the ideal and its practical implementation when he differentiated between 'compromise in theory' and 'compromise in practice' in his correspondence with Adin Ballou.[68] In the final analysis, he reaffirmed the primacy of conscience as the final arbiter of all morality, and urged every individual to resolve his moral dilemmas, including those relating to violence, in the privacy of his own soul.

3 'The Slavery of Our Times': Education For Justice and Righteousness
Social reform is a major preoccupation of Tolstoy's later prose writings and is closely linked with his pacifist teachings. Seeing a strong correlation between Christ's injunction on non-resistance to evil and his injunction towards justice and righteousness, he advocated radical measures for reform as the precondition for the creation of a just, harmonious and peaceful society. Far from advocating passivity or acquiescence in the face of evil, as some of his critics suggested, he repeatedly spoke of the need for protest against social corruption and gave persistent witness to that purpose in his

writings. His social writings are focussed on four main themes: the evils of contemporary work practices, the inequities of private property and the fiscal policies adopted to ensure its perpetuation, the dangers of a purely humanist socialism, and the need for the creation of a community spirit reflecting the values inherent in the Christian scriptures.

Having identified himself so closely throughout the greater part of his life with the poor and the down-trodden, it was entirely predictable that Tolstoy should have so vehemently denounced the inhuman work practices common in Russian society at the end of the nineteenth century. In 'The Slavery of Our Times' he cites example after example of the appalling conditions to which workers were subjected—conditions he considered harsher than those enforced by the slave-owners in the days of serfdom. In one example he writes about the work of the goods porters at Kursk Railway Station in Moscow who were required to work 36-hour shifts, moving bales of up to 26 stone weight on their backs, for the paltry payment of one rouble for each consignment of 16 tons of merchandise transported. This was visible evidence of the institutionalised violence he condemned in his pacifist writings:

> Only, perhaps, in that miserable hour of vain attempt to get rest and sleep do they painfully realise all the horror of their life-destroying thirty-six hour work, and that is why they are specially agitated by such an apparently insignificant circumstance as the overcrowding of their room.
>
> Having watched several gangs at work, and having talked with some more of the men, and heard the same story from them all, I drove home, convinced that what my acquaintance had told me was true.
>
> It was true, that for a bare subsistence, people, considering themselves free men, thought it necessary to give themselves up to work such as, in the days of serfdom, not one slave-owner, however cruel, would have sent his slaves to. Let alone slave-owners, not one cab proprietor would send his horses to such work, for horses cost money, and it would be wasteful, by excessive work, to shorten the life of an animal of value.[69]

In another example he describes the conditions in a silk factory where 'three thousand women stand, for twelve hours a day, at the looms, amid a deafening roar, winding, unwinding, arranging the silk threads to make silk stuffs' for the use of the rich. When they have children, he says, they send them to the Foundlings' Hospital, where 80% of them perish, and the mothers return to work within a day of giving birth, for fear of losing their jobs.[70] He blames the middle classes, who are the main beneficiaries of all this, for their apathy and indifference to the plight of their fellow citizens: 'The fact is that we, well to-do people, liberals and humanitarians, very sensitive to the sufferings not of people only, but also of animals, unceasingly make use of such labour and try to become more and more rich, that is, to take still greater advantage of such work. And we remain perfectly tranquil'. The complacency of the privileged is one of the main reasons, he says, that such conditions continue to exist:

> Having learned that the women and girls at the silk factory, living far from their families, ruin their own lives and those of their children; and that a large half of the washer-women who iron our starched shirts, and of the type-setters who print the books and papers that while away our time, get tuberculosis, we only shrug our shoulders and say that we are very sorry things should be so, but that we can do nothing to alter it; and we continue with tranquil conscience to buy silk stuffs, to wear starched shirts, and to read our morning paper. We are much concerned about the hours of the shop assistants, and still more about the long hours of our own children at school; we strictly forbid carters to make their horses drag heavy loads, and we even organise the killing of cattle in slaughter-houses so that the animals may feel it as little as possible. But how wonderfully blind we become as soon as the question concerns those millions of workers who perish slowly, and often painfully, all around us, at labours and fruits of which we use for our convenience and pleasure.[71]

Questioning the myth of historical progress, and particularly the supposed benefits accruing to mankind from developments in technology and science, he suggests that the advances made in modern society have simply issued in new forms of slavery which do not differ in essentials from those that existed in the age of serfdom. A stranger arriving in Russia at the end of the nineteenth century would, he says, see two clearly differentiated classes of people: one 'with clean hands, well nourished, clothed and lodged . . . and doing no work'; the other 'dirty, poorly clothed, lodged and fed', toiling unceasingly from morning till night, and living in conditions of abject poverty. 'The people of our time', he declares, 'are divided into slaves and slave-owners as definitely as, in spite of the twilight, each twenty-four hours is divided into day and night.' The abolition of the 'obsolete' form of slavery associated with serfdom resulted only in its replacement by the more sophisticated forms introduced into the factories and farms of Russia from the early years of the nineteenth century:

> If the slave-owner of our time has not slave John, whom he can send to the cess-pool to clean out his excrements, he has five shillings of which hundreds of Johns are in such need that the slave-owner of our times may choose anyone out of hundreds of Johns and be a benefactor to him by giving him the preference, and allowing him, rather than another, to climb down into the cess-pool.
> The slaves of our time are not only all those factory and workshop hands,

who must sell themselves completely into the power of the factory and foundry owners in order to exist; but nearly all the agricultural labourers are slaves, working as they do unceasingly to grow another's corn on another's field, and gathering it onto another's barn; or tilling their own fields only in order to pay to bankers the interest on debts they cannot get rid of. Slaves also are all the innumerable footmen, cooks, housemaids, porters, coachmen, bathmen, waiters, and so on, who all their life long perform duties most unnatural to a human being, and which they themselves dislike.[72]

The root-cause of all this, he argues, is the law of private property which allows the expropriation by one man of the fruits of another man's labour. 'In our society', he writes, 'in consequence of the right of property in required articles, the very thing happens which that right is intended to prevent: namely, all articles which have been, and continually are being, produced by working people, are possessed by, and as they are produced are continually taken by, those who have not produced them.'[73] The entire state support system through which the law of property is upheld— compulsory regulations on work, the laws on taxation, the system of compulsory schooling etc.—has created a modern form of slavery just as vicious and inhuman as the old methods that existed under feudalism:

The laws giving a master the right to compel his slaves to do compulsory work, were replaced by laws allowing the masters to own all the land. The laws allowing all the land to become the private property of the masters may be replaced by taxation laws, the control of the taxes being in the hands of the masters. The taxation laws may be replaced by others defending the right of private property in articles of use and in the means of production. The laws maintaining property in land and in articles of use and means of production, may, as is now proposed, be replaced by the enactment of compulsory labour.

So it is evident that the abolition of one form of legislation producing the slavery of our time, whether taxes, or land-owning, or property in articles of use, or in the means of production, will not destroy slavery, but will only repeal one of its forms, which will immediately be replaced by a new one, as was the case with the abolition of chattel slavery, and of serfdom, and with the repeals of taxes. Even the abolition of all three groups of laws together, will not abolish slavery, but evoke a new and previously unknown form of it, which is now already beginning to show itself, and to shackle the freedom of labour by legislation concerning the hours of work, the age and state of health of the workers, as well as by demanding obligatory attendance at schools, by deductions for old-age insurance or accidents, by all the measures of factory inspection, etc. All this is nothing but transitional legislation, preparing a new and as yet untried form of slavery.[74]

He points to the responsibility of all those who stand to gain from these injustices to dissociate themselves from the policies which allow them to occur, and he particularly reminds Christians of their duty to refuse to support capitalistic practices. 'Money and property have nothing to do with Christianity', he declares. 'According to the Gospels there is no property and woe betide those who possess it. Whatever situation a Christian may be in, all he can do with regard to property is to refuse to participate in the violence carried out in the name of property and to explain to others that property is a myth, that there is no such thing as property, but only a certain evil and habitual violence with regard to what we refer to as property.'[75] Looking at some practical proposals for social reform, he saw some merit in the fiscal policies advocated by the American economist, Henry George, but concluded that more fundamental changes were required, involving the basic political structures of society. The concentration of power in the centralised apparatus of the state he saw as the main source of the injustices that were occurring. His basic argument was that the sheer size of the state structure requires coercive agencies, such as armies, police forces and civil bureaucracies, simply to maintain its existence and to administer its affairs efficiently. This, he insists, is an inevitable feature of the large, monolithic state structure, whatever the political ideology on which it is based:

> To bind and keep togeher a bundle of wood a strong rope is necessary and a certain degree of its tension. So also to keep together in one state a great collection of men, a certain degree of applied coercion is necessary. In the case of the wood, the difference may be only in its relative position, in such and not other pieces of wood being directly submitted to the pressure of the rope, but the power holding them together is one and the same in whatever position the pieces may be placed. It is the same with any coercive state of whatever kind, a despotism, a constitutional monarchy, an oligarchy or a republic. If the union of men is maintained by coercion, by the establishment by some people of laws forcibly applied to others, then there will always exist coercion, equal in extent, of some people over others. In one place it will manifest itself in coarse violence, in another—in the power of money. The difference will be only that in one coercive state organisation, the coercion will weigh more upon a certain section of people, whilst in another organisation on another.[76]

In a state where power is vested in coercive agencies there is, he argues, an inevitable restriction, and ultimately a corruption, of basic freedoms. 'So long as the state, and the coercion necessary for its maintenance exist, there will not', he says, 'there cannot be, true freedom.' This applies, he further explains, not only to despotic governments, such as the Tsarist autocracy, but even to constitutional monarchies or democracies, such as those existing in Sweden, Portugal and Switzerland. The coercion consists, he says, in the employment of laws and regulations which ostensibly exist to ensure that order exists in the affairs of society, but which in fact are open to manipulation and corruption, as a result of which the wealth and resources, and ultimately the exercise of power, are concentrated in the hands of small, ambitious and greedy minorities. Only the most corrupt, acquisitive and self-seeking members of society have the personal resoursefulness and motivation, he says, to grasp the privileges and the power which are available in such conditions:

> In many of my writings I have repeatedly endeavoured to show that what intimidates men—the fear that without governmental power the worst men would triumph while the best would be oppressed—is precisely what has long ago happened, and is still happening in all states, since everywhere the power is in the hands of the worst men; as indeed, cannot be otherwise, because only the worst men could do all these crafty, dastardly and cruel acts which are necessary for participation in power . . . before answering the question whether the position of men would be the worse or the better without governments, one should solve the problem as to who makes up the government. Are those who constitute it better or worse than the average level of men? If they are better than the average run, then the government will be beneficent; but if they are worse it will be pernicious. And that these men—Ivan IV, Henry VIII, Marat, Napoleon, Arakcheyef, Metternich, Tallyrand and Nicolas—are worse than the general run is proved by history.
>
> In every human society there are always ambitious, unscrupulous and cruel men who, I have already endeavoured to show, are ever ready to perpetrate any kind of violence, robbery, or murder for their own advantage; and that in a society without government these men would be robbers, restrained in their actions partly by strife with those injured by them (self-instituted justice, lynching), but partly and chiefly by the most powerful weapon of influence upon men—public opinion. Whereas in a society led by coercive authority, these same men are those who will seize authority and will make use of it, not only without the restraint of public opinion, but, on the contrary, supported, praised and extolled by a bribed and artificially maintained public opinion.[77]

It would be wrong if this were to be characterised as a case for the dismantling of all the structures necessary to maintain law and order in a civilised society. Tolstoy's anarchism was of the same variety as Proudhon's and Kropotkin's, being directed towards the transformation of existing structures into new forms of political organisation, in which order would be rooted in the small, voluntaristic units of closely knit communities. This becomes more clearly apparent when we consider the case he made against the vision of a revolutionary social order then being put forward by marxist socialists. He detected, with prophetic accuracy, the totalitarian character of the society that this would create, and condemned it as vehemently as he did the excesses of the tsarist autocracy. Denouncing the 'unrealisable teachings' of the socialists, and ridiculing their claim that, once their objectives were fulfilled, 'everyone would be free and have at their disposal everything that is now made use of by the well to-do classes', he spoke of an inherent contradiction in all their political activities. The contradiction consisted in their proposal to use violence to destroy the structures of a tyrannical state—a course, he predicts, which can lead only to the replacement of one political order with another that will be just as coercive:

> The means of realising the objects of a revolution for the freedom of men obviously must be other than that violence by which men have hitherto attempted to raise equality. The men of the great French revolution wishing to retain equality might make the mistake of thinking that equality is attainable by coercion, although it would seem evident that equality cannot be secured by coercion, as coercion is in itself the keenest manifestation of inequality. But the freedom constituting the chief aim of the present revolution cannot in any case be attained by violence. Yet at present the people who are producing the revolution in Russia think that the Russian revolution, having repeated all that has taken place in European revolutions with solemn funeral procession, destruction of prisons, brilliant speeches, *Allez dire a votre maitre*, constitutional assembles and so forth, and having overthrown the existing government, and having instituted constitutional monarchy or even a socialistic republic, they will attain the object at which the revolution aimed. But history does not repeat itself. Violent revolution has outlived its time. All it can give men, it has already given them, but at the same time it has shown what it cannot attain.[78]

It is impossible, he argues, to create a freer society through violent revolution; it simply transfers power from one group to another, without any transformation of existing social structures. Being limited to the sphere of the political and the social, marxism did not offer the prospect of such a transformation. It would, he predicted—with profound and tragic accuracy —lead to a political enslavement of the Russian people more repressive that anything they had previously experienced:

> Nothing demonstrates so clearly the increasing enslavement of nations as the growth, spread and success of socialistic theories: that is, the tendency to greater and greater slavery . . . Those who are now endeavouring to produce in Russia a political revolution according to the model of European revolutions, however, possess neither any new foundations nor any new ideals. They strive merely to substitute for one old form of coercion another new one, also to be realised by coercion, and carrying with it the same calamities as those from which the Russian people now suffer, as we see in

Europe and America, groaning under the same militarism, the same taxation, the same seizure of the land. The majority of revolutionaries put forward as their ideal a socialistic organisation which could be obtained only by the cruellest coercion, and which, if it ever were attained, would deprive men of the last remnants of liberty.[79]

The social transformation that Tolstoy envisaged was one that he believed would be realised through the spread of a community spirit, sufficiently inclusive to embrace the religious and moral, as well as the purely social and political, ideals of a society based on genuine fellowship and love. It was a vision that he conceived specifically in terms of the ideals of the Christian scriptures and one that he believed would be achieved, not through the imposition of a revolutionary political order, but through the voluntary efforts of all those inspired by these ideals. His essay, 'An Appeal to Social Reformers', opens with the words of the Acts of the Apostles—'And all that believed were together and had all things in common'[80]—to intimate both the Christian and communalist character of the transformation he envisaged. What he was proposing was in keeping with the spirit of anarchism to the extent that it entailed a fundamental restructuring of society, though he suggested this would be facilitated, in any event, by the decline of political absolutism and the gradual spread of democratic politics. He cites the 'utopian anarchists'—Godwin, Proudhon and Kropotkin—on the need to create a new consciousness of community ideals amongst the masses, and the need to develop an awareness of their capacity to create these structures through their own consensual activities. While identifying to a considerable degree with their ideals, he complains, however, of the limitations of the purely secularised vision of community reform which they proposed:

> All these teachings are perfectly correct in this—that if power is to be abolished, this can be accomplished in nowise by force, as power having abolished power will remain power; but that this abolition of power can be accomplished only by the elucidation in the consciousness of men of the truth that power is useless and harmful, and that men should neither obey it nor participate in it. This truth is incontrovertible: power can be abolished only by the rational consciousness of men. But in what should this consciousness consist? The Anarchists believe that this consciousness can be founded upon considerations about common welfare, justice, progress or the personal interests of men. But apart from the fact that all these factors are not in mutual agreement, the very definitions of what constitutes *general welfare, justice, progress or personal interest* are understood by man in infinitely various ways. . . . Moreover the supposition that considerations about general welfare, justice or the law of progress can suffice to secure that men, freed from coercion, but having no motive for sacrificing their personal welfare, should

combine in just conditions without violating their mutual liberty, is yet more unfounded. . . . So that whilst correctly recognising spiritual weapons as the only means of abolishing power, the Anarchistic teaching, holding an irreligious materialistic life conception, does not possess this spiritual weapon, and is confined to conjectures and fancies which give the advocates of coercion the possibility of denying its true foundations, owing to the inefficiency of the suggested means of realising this teaching.[81]

Insisting that the ideals of community renewal cannot be confined to matters of social and material welfare, he returns to the original theme of all his social writings: that social renewal must be rooted in the individial pursuit of self-perfection. 'Only such a religious conception, uniting all men in the same understanding of life, incompatible with subordination to power and participation in it, can truly destroy power',[82] he writes. The abuse of power, being due primarily to human corruption, can only be changed, he says, through the moral improvement of mankind—a process that must take place in each individual soul. 'There is only one means to the good life amongst men', he declares, 'the profession and realisation of a religious teaching natural and comprehensible to the majority of mankind.'[83] Social reform therefore would consist primarily in moral rather than political change; it would most emphatically not be brought about through violent revolution. 'In order that men may live a common life without oppressing each other, there is necessary', he says, 'not an organisation supported by force, but a moral state in accordance with which people act from their inner conviction and not by coercion'. This, he suggests, is the essence of the social vision revealed in the Christian Gospels:

> Thus the rational activity proper to our time for men of our Christian Society is only one: the profession and preaching by word and deed of the last and highest religious teaching known to us, of the Christian teaching; not of that Christian teaching which, whilst submitting to the existing order of life, demands of men only the fulfilment of external ritual, or is satisfied with faith in and the preaching of salvation through redemption, but of that vital Christianity, the inevitable condition of which is, not only non-participation in the action of the government, but disobedience of its demands, since these demands from taxes and custom-houses to law courts and armies are all opposed to this true Christianity. If this be so, then it is evident that it is not to the establishment of new forms that the activity of men desirous of serving their neighbour should be directed, but to the alteration and perfecting of their own characters, and those of other people.[84]

This passage, however, clearly indicates a far more radical interpretation of the social message of Christianity than what had traditionally been taught by the Churches. In words that seem, in some respects, to anticipate the liberationist theology of a century later, he speaks of a 'revolution consisting in the replacing of false Christanity. . . . by true Christianity and the recognition of that equality and true liberty which are natural to all rational beings.'[85] Yet, he warns of the dangers of an excessively politicised Christianity, through which the service of material needs would be given precedence over the individual process of self-perfection which is the central message of the Gospels. His words on this issue have acquired immense significance with the emergence of the new 'political Christianity' in Third World societies (especially those of Latin America) in the aftermath of the liberalising reforms of the Second Vatican Council:

> . . . the alteration of the character of men must begin in themselves, and demands much struggle and labour, whereas the alteration of the forms of the life of others is attained easily without inner effort over one's self, and has the appearance of a very important and far-reaching activity. It is against this error, the source of the greatest evil that I warn you, men sincerely desirous of serving your neighbour by your lives.
>
> 'But we cannot live quietly occupying ourselves with the profession and teaching of Christianity when we see around us suffering people. We wish to serve them actively. For this we are ready to surrender our labour, even our lives', says people with more or less sincere indignation (*sic*).
>
> How do you know, I would answer these people, that you are called to serve men precisely by that method which appears to you the most useful and practical? What you say only shows that you have already decided that we cannot serve mankind by a Christian life, and that true service lies only in political activity, which attracts you.
>
> All politicians think likewise, and they are all in opposition to each other, and therefore certainly cannot all be right. It would be very well if everyone could serve men as he pleased, but such is not the case, and there exists only one means of serving men and improving their condition. This sole means consists in the profession and realisation of a teaching from which flows the inner work of perfecting one's self. The self-perfecting of a true Christian, always living naturally amongst men and not avoiding them, consists in the establishment of better, more and more loving relations between himself and other men. The establishment of loving relations between men cannot but improve their general conditions, although the form of this improvement remains unknown to man.[86]

This statement, however, is essentially a definition of priorities and does not exclude political action in pursuit of Christian objectives. The refusal to serve in the armed forces, the refusal to pay taxes, the engagement in active protest against corruption and injustice—each of which Tolstoy repeatedly advocated as peaceful methods of undermining the power of an unjust government—were all political acts, but were subordinated to what he insisted was the first requirement for the realisation of Christian ideals: the practice and exemplification of personal morality. The kind of social commitment he envisaged was one that had to be wholly compatible with the primary doctrine of non-resistance to evil. In 'The End of the Age' for example we find the following statement:

> Christian humanity in its present condition has got before it the choice of two things; either the continuation on the way in which existing civilisation will give the greatest welfare to the few, keeping the many in want and servitude, or else at once, without postponement to some far future, abandoning a portion or even all those advantages which civilisation has attained for the few, if such advantages hinder the liberation of the majority from want and servitude.[87]

The surrender of privilege, like the refusal to pay taxes, belong in the same moral category as the refusal to fight but, in so far as their purpose is to bring about radical change in the existing order of society, they must all be characterised as acts of political dissent, and were clearly so regarded by the political establishment of Russia at the time they were advocated by Tolstoy. The primary ethical goal to which all others, including the political and the social were to be subjected, however, was that conveyed in Christ's injunction to 'love thy neighbour as thyself'. The validity of this message would be determined only, he declared, by the actual practice of Christian love and by the evidence of its effectiveness in transforming interpersonal and social relationships. The process could be set in motion quite simply, he suggested, by taking certain practical steps towards its implementation in the conditions of everyday life:

> Test it. Resolve for a certain period to follow the doctrine of love in all things; to live so as in all things to remember first of all, with every man, thief, drunkard, rough officer, or dependent, not to swerve from love; that is to say, in the business you have with him, to remember his need rather than your own. Having so lived for the appointed term, ask yourself: was it hard for you, and have you injured or bettered your life? Then in accord with the result of your test, decide whether it is true that the practice of love gives welfare in life, or whether that is so only in words. Test this: try, instead of returning the offender evil for evil, instead of condemning behind his back a man who lives badly, and so on, instead of all this, try to respond to evil with good, and say no evil of any man. Treat not even a cow or a dog harshly, but treat them kindly and affectionately, and live in this way for a day or two, or more, as an experiment, and compare the state of your soul with what it was before. Make the experiment, and you will see how, instead of a surly, angry, and depressed condition, you will be bright, merry and joyous. Live thus for a second and a third week, and you will see how your spiritual gladness will

ever grow and grow, and not only will your work not fall into disorder, it will but prosper more and more.[88]

It is instructive to compare Tolstoy's vision of community reform with that of his fellow writer, Dostoevsky, since there is a considerable measure of agreement between them on the need for such a reform to be founded on ethico-religious ideals, and since both of them emphatically rejected the revolutionary methods advocated by marxist socialists. On one issue they differed fundamentally: the central issue of non-resistance to evil. Having read *Anna Karenina*, Dostoevsky detected a latent pacifism in Levin which he denounced as 'insensibility side by side with sentimentalism.' The following are his comments on the novel in *The Diary of a Writer*:

> Is it for mere vengeance, for mere killing, that the Russian people have risen? And when was it that assistance to the massacred, to those who are being exterminated by entire regions, to assaulted women and children in whose defence there is no one in the whole world to intercede, was considered a callous, ridiculous and almost immoral act, a craving for vengeance and blood-thirst! And what insensibility side by side with sentimentalism! In fact, Levin himself has a child, a boy! He loves him! When this child is bathed in a bath-tub it is almost a family event! Why doesn't his heart bleed when he hears and reads about wholescale massacres, about children with crushed heads crawling around their assaulted, murdered mothers with their breasts cut off? This happened in a Bulgarian church where two hundred such corpses were found, after the town had been plundered. Levin reads all this, and there he stands and meditates:
>
> 'Kitty is cheerful to-day; she ate with an appetite; the boy was bathed in the tub, and he begins to recognise me: what do I care about things that are transpiring in another hemisphere? *No immediate settlement for the oppression of the Slavs exists or can exist*—because I feel *nothing*.
>
> Is this how Levin brings to a close his epopee? Is it he whom the author seeks to set forth as an example of a truthful, honest man? Men, such as the author of *Anna Karenina*, are teachers of society, our teachers, while we are merely their pupils. What then do they teach us?[89]

Dostoevsky's reaction to Tolstoyan pacifism was not unusual for its time, and would probably typify the kind of response that the doctrine of non-violence would evoke even at the present time, when weapons of mass destruction threaten the very survival of mankind and render the need for a radical rethinking of traditional attitudes to war-making all the more urgent. But in his broader vision of a society transformed through the resources of the community spirit, he substantially endorsed the positions taken by Tolstoy. Father Zosima's ideal of *sobornost* i.e. of a society guided by the spirit of brotherhood—whose members follow the doctrine that 'each is responsible for all'[90]—closely parallels the vision disclosed by Tolstoy in his social writings. Zosima's insistence that such a society will be brought into being, not by radical ideological doctrines, but by fundamental changes in attitude, again corresponds closely with Tolstoy's view that radical changes in popular consciousness are necessary to realise the social ideals he envisaged. 'To transform the world, to recreate it afresh, men must turn into a different path psychologically', Zosima says. 'Until you have been really active, in fact a brother to everyone, brotherhood will not come to pass', he warns. 'No sort of scientific teaching, no kind of common interest will ever teach men to share property and privileges with equal consideration for all'.[91] Dostoevsky's further condemnation of 'scientific' socialism, through his mouth-piece, Shatov, in *The Devils*, was on the same basis as Tolstoy's: that it was essentially a rationalist view of social change, radically flawed both by its inadequacies as an abstract thought system and by the limitations of its secularised humanism:

> Socialism is by its very nature bound to be atheistic because it has proclaimed from the very first that it is an atheistic institution and that it intends to organise itself exclusively on the principles of science and reason. Reason and science have always, to-day and from the very beginning of time, played a secondary and a subordinate part; and so they will to the end of time. Peoples are formed and moved by quite a different force, a force that dominates and exercises its authority over them, the origin of which, however, is unknown and inexplicable. That force is the force of an unquenchable desire to go on to the end and, at the same time, to deny the existence of an end. It is the force of an incessant and persistent affirmation of its existence and a denial of death. It is the spirit of life, as the Scripture says, 'rivers of living water', the running dry of which is threatened in Revelation.[92]

Shatov's words in *The Devils* are re-echoed by Alyosha in *The Brothers Karamazov*. 'For socialism', he says, 'is not merely the labour question, it is before all things the atheistic question, the question of the form taken by atheism to-day, the question of the tower of Babel built without God, not to mount to heaven from earth but to set up heaven on earth'.[93]

Again, like Tolstoy, Dostoevsky points to the paradox that, side by side with its rationalist/humanist orientation, socialism appeals also to a senti-mental, quasi-religious tendency in human nature which is, in essence, irrational. Thus Stepan Verkhovensky, describing the socialist group he has joined, observes: 'What fascinates them is not realism but the sentimental and idealist side of socialism, its religious aspect, as it were, its poetry—all of it second-hand of course'.[94] This is the same 'pagan' religiosity that Tolstoy satirised in 'Religion and Morality'.[95] It is basically what accounts for the fanatical zeal of characters like Kondratyev and Novodvorov, the revolutionary activists in *Resurrection,* or of Stavrogin, the militant anarchist and atheist in *The Devils.*

The prevailing conclusion in both their writings is that the prospect of a just and harmonious society is realisable only through the practice of humility, penitence and selflessness—above all, through faith in the suprarationalist truths revealed in the Christian scriptures. Tolstoy took his models for such a society from the masses of the peasantry: from simple men who lived their lives in accordance with the tenets of an uncomplicated faith in the all-embracing vision of Christian brotherhood. That, essentially, is what Zosima reaffirmed also when he declared that 'equality is to be found only in the spiritual dignity of man', again taking as his examples the simple peasant people who retained an indestructible spiritual integrity despite their tribulations and sufferings and the impoverished conditions in which they lived:

> Fathers and teachers,watch over the people's faith and this will not be a dream. I've been struck all my life in our great people by their dignity, their true and seemly dignity. I've seen it myself. I can testify to it. I've seen it and marvelled at it. I've seen it in spite of the degraded sins and povetry-stricken appearance of our peasantry. They are not servile, and even after two centuries of serfdom they are free in manner and bearing, yet without insolence, and not revengeful and not envious. 'You are rich and noble, you are clever and talented, well be so, God bless you. I respect you, but I know that I too am a man. By the very fact that I respect you without envy I prove my dignity as a man.
>
> In truth if they don't say this (for they don't know how to say this yet) that is how they act. I have seen it myself, I have known it myself, and, would you believe it, the poorer our Russian peasant is, the more noticeable is that serene goodness, for the rich among them are for the most part corrupted already, and much of that is due to our carelessness and indifference. But God will have His people, for Russia is great in her humility. I dream of seeing, and seem to see clearly already, our future. It will come to pass, that even the most corrupt of our rich will end by being ashamed of his riches before the poor, seeing his humility, will understand and give way before him, will respond joyfully and kindly to his honourable shame. Believe me that it will end in that; things are moving to that. Equality is to be found only in the spiritual dignity of man, and that will only be understood among us. If we were brothers, there would be fraternity, but before that, they will never agree about the division of wealth.[96]

4 *'Fools for Christ': The Tolstoyan Communities*

The communities of 'Tolstoyan' Christians that sprang up all over the world in the 1890s provide some of the most compelling evidence we possess on the efficacy of Tolstoy's teachings and on the extent of their impact on the lives of his followers. As it happened, Tolstoy himself expressed some doubts about the wisdom of forming such communities, arguing that his followers could exemplify the spirit of his teachings more effectively in the conditions of society at large than they would in the isolated conditions of separate communities. 'Why in a community?' he wrote to an aspiring colonist. 'One ought not to separate oneself from other people. If there is anything good in a man let that light be spread about him wherever he lives.'[97] But, despite his reservations, large numbers of people came together in various countries throughout the world to form such communities, resolving to plan their lives entirely in accordance with Tolstoyan ideals. Their very existence demonstrates how profoundly he had touched the minds and hearts of his followers. If empirical evidence were to be sought on the success with which he had achieved his stated goal of effecting the fundamental changes in consciousness necessary for a genuine religious conversion, that evidence would, in the main, be provided by these communities.

Though they rarely survived for more than a few years, their significance consists in the fact that thousands of people were sufficiently inspired by Tolstoy's teachings to leave home, family, career, property and wealth for the austerity of life in a remote and impoverished commune. Tolstoy himself had advised the colonists that what mattered was the effort they made to live in accordance with the ideals of the scriptures, not the success with which that was achieved. 'The ideal of the material life cannot be fully realised', he wrote to one of them, 'any more than the ideal of the spiritual life. The whole point is in the constant effort to approach the ideal.'[98] It is this latter criterion rather than their ultimate success or failure in achieving their goals, that must be employed in a final assessment of their work—in which case a more positive impression emerges than has generally been accorded them by historians.

Tolstoyan communities began to spring up in Russia at the end of the 1880s. Generally they attracted young landowners and intellectuals, and lasted for short periods of time until they were forced to break up because of practical difficulties, usually related either to lack of finance or insufficient knowledge of agricultural husbandry on the part of the members. In the same period groups of people inspired by Tolstoy's writings began to form communes in the United States, the most prominent of which was the Commonwealth Colony in Georgia which remained in existence from 1896 to 1900, and was enthusiastically supported by Tolstoy himself.[99] A colony was formed by Christian Anarchists at Blaricum in Holland in 1900 and this also remained in existence for about three years.[100] Another was formed in the village of San Bernardo near Santiago in Chile in 1904 by two young writers, Fernando Santivan and Augusto d'Halmar. 'Tolstoy was our constant theme', Santivan wrote subsequently. 'We kept talking about the beauty of a simple life, about non-resistance to evil, about the work we could do as apostles among the peasants, about the need to flee from the evil pleasures of city life.'[101] And in Japan, a follower of Tolstoy called Mushakoji Saneatsu, who said his life was transformed by reading *A Confession* and *What I Believe*, organised a colony called The New Village which also survived for some years, until it was eventually forced to close because of financial difficulties.[102]

Two of the most extensively documented of the Tolstoyan movements were the Purleigh Colony founded in England in the late 1890s and the Peasant Village Communities which emerged in Russia at the turn of the century and remained in existence until the late 1930s. The kind of impact made by Tolstoy's teachings can be best illustrated by considering the activities of each of these movements. The Purleigh Colony originated with the Croydon Brotherhood Church, set up by John Coleman Kenworthy at the Salvation Army Barracks in West Croydon in 1894. Having previously been interested in the ideas of Henry George and the utopian socialists, Kenworthy encountered Tolstoy's writings during a trip to the U.S. in 1890, was instantly captivated by them, and, abandoning a promising career in business, returned to England to work with the poor in Canning Town. Here he formed the Brotherhood Church for a group of idealists like himself who had grown disillusioned with the political status quo: they included socialists, anarchists, pacifists and theosophists. A magazine was published, the *Croydon Brotherhood Intelligence* (later the *New Order*) through which they aimed to propagate their ideals amongst the populace, in the same way that Tolstoy and Chertkov had been doing in Russia for several years. The Tolstoyan influence can be seen clearly in this excerpt from the first issue of the journal:

> The Brotherhood Church, as the name implies, aims at gathering together people of ALL CLASSES, to learn and to practise the fraternal principles of the SERMON ON THE MOUNT. Nothing, to an honest and good mind, can be plainer than this purpose.
>
> Our message is, and must be, especially to the working people and the poor—the fellows of those who of old, heard Jesus gladly. Whatever work may eventually become, the duty of the hour is to carry the doctrines of SOCIAL SALVATION into every heart and home that we can reach. We desire to help every social activity that makes for righteousness; and to waken the minds of men with a gospel that calls for, and shows the way to, honest and right conditions of industry and business, which are the first needs of social

life. Upon this foundation we labour to build up the spiritual and moral natures of ourselves and of others, after the Christ-ideal.[103]

The main aim of the movement, Kenworthy declared, was to promote the values of brotherhood, cooperation, self-sufficiency, non-competitiveness and religious tolerance. Not only did he find support for these values in Tolstoy's writings, but he was deeply moved by the manner in which Tolstoy exemplified them in his own life. 'He not only believes these things but he lives them, and the crown of his teaching is the precept that the world will never be reformed until men reform themselves', he wrote in one of the articles extolling Tolstoy's personal examplification of radical Christianity. 'What is the use of talking about socialism, communism, Christianity, while you are not prepared personally to live an honest and true life', he wrote, paraphrasing Tolstoy's words on the importance of giving personal witness to faith. 'You cannot', he said,—again paraphrasing Tolstoy—'reform the world, but you can reform your own life, and the world is waiting for salvation until men do just this simple, yet how difficult thing.'[104]

While closely following Tolstoy's view that social reform must begin with individual self-perfection, he complained nonetheless of the hypocrisy of those who lead supposedly virtuous lives, while simultaneously countenancing poverty, injustice and corruption all around them. At his urging, the Brotherhood Church, therefore, organised various projects to provide for the needs of the poor; these included laundries, shoe-making and dress-making centres, and shops where groceries, fruit and vegetables were sold on a non-profit-making basis. Gradually, the idea emerged that the members of the Brotherhood Church should form an agricultural commune where they would provide their own food, drink and shelter, and live simple lives in accordance with the teachings of the scriptures. Kenworthy visited Tolstoy at Yasnaya Polyana in the winter of 1895-6 to discuss the whole venture with him, and to seek his advice on the way in which it should be organised. Tolstoy suggested that the *New Order* should publish reports on the Tolstoyan colonies in the U.S., South America and various locations in Europe, so that aspiring colonists would have some advance knowledge of the kind of life they were proposing to lead and the kind of commitment that would be expected of them.[105]

On his return to England, Kenworthy negotiated the purchase of ten acres of land at Purleigh, near Maldon in Essex, which was to be the site for the proposed colony. The financial capital was provided by the members from their own resources. One of them, Arnold Eiloart, a lecturer in chemistry at the Royal College of Science in Kensington, donated £2000 from his family fortune. Aylmer Maude, Tolstoy's friend and biographer, donated £230, and other members donated sums varying between £50 and £60. Initially, a small group of pioneers was sent to begin work on the colony—preparing the land for cultivation, tending to cattle and fowl, planting an orchard, and building simple homes for the colonists. By November 1897 there were fifteen full-time colonists in the commune, and a further thirty-five were living in homes nearby. Amongst the latter were Louise and Aylmer Maude and Chertkov—the latter living in exile as a result of his expulsion from Russia, because of his support for the Dukhobors. Maude, who had initially gone to Russia to work as an industrialist, had embraced the Tolstoyan philosophy while living with Tolstoy and preparing his mammoth biography. As a result, he decided to abandon his business interests and returned to England, resolving to live in accordance with Tolstoyan ideals amongst the colonists at Purleigh. He whole-heartedly supported the work of the colony for a year before deciding to emigrate to Canada in September 1898, following some disagreements with Kenworthy (The latter's 'eccentricities' are the subject of some unfavourable comment in Maude's biography of Tolstoy.)[106]

For almost three years the activities of the colony proceeded quite successfully, the members devoting their time to the cultivation of the land and to providing as fully as possible for their material and spiritual needs. The colony was extended by a further thirteen acres in May 1898. Relations between the colonists were subject to some strain, however, because of their strict adherence to the Tolstoyan principle of 'non-coercive' order. There were no rules or regulations of any kind so that all the work of the colony depended on the voluntary cooperation of its members—a policy that demanded an exceptionally high degree of dedication and goodwill. All decisions were taken democratically at the weekly meetings of the colonists and, unless a decision had unanimous support, it had to be deferred to a subsequent meeting.

In these conditions of excessive democracy, policy differences began to develop, leading inevitably to divisions amongst the colonists. Following one such disagreement, some members left in 1898 to join alternative colonies—they included Eiloart who was reimbursed for his £2000 donation —and others left to devote their enegies to the cause of the Dukhobors and to help with the plans which were then under way to resettle them in Canada. A substantial proportion of the colony's income was allocated to the Dukhobors (records suggest a figure of over £1200, most of it accumulated from the sale of vegetables) and this resulted in financial difficulties for the colony itself. Recognising that the needs of the Dukhobors were greater than their own, they donated almost everything they posessed, seeing this as the kind of sacrifice demanded of Christians, attempting to live by the precepts of the Sermon on the Mount. It was this loss of income, more than any other factor, which seems to have led to the break-up of the colony. Strains, already developing through differences in work patterns, were greatly exacerbated by the shortage of funds. The colony continued in existence, however, until late in 1899 when further members left to join other communities, mostly of a similar character to the one at Purleigh. Eventually, Kenworthy himself left the colony and thenceforward travelled throughout the country delivering lectures on the principles of Tolstoyan Christianity. Some attempts were made subsequently to revive the Purleigh community, but these met with little success. Though forced to close, largely as a result of practical difficulties—and these were in some degree due to the fervour with which they sought to abide by the spirit of New Testament Christianity —the Purleigh Colony must be seen, nonetheless, as an extraordinarily courageous attempt by a group of simple idealists to implement the hugely demanding precepts of Tolstoyan Christianity in the conditions of their daily lives. What matters finally—if we are to adopt the criterion laid down by Tolstoy himself—is the dedication and fervour with which they sought to realise the truth of his teachings, rather than their failure to sustain their achievements over a longer period of time.

A far greater degree of success attended the efforts of some Russian followers of Tolstoy, who also sought to implement his teachings by organising communities dedicated to the practice of Christian ideals. Two recent publications have greatly increased our knowledge of the activities of these communities. In 1983 a Soviet emigre writer, Mark Popovski, published *Russian Peasants Tell Their Story*, a commentary on the diaries, letters and records of Russian Tolstoyans which he had smuggled out of the country in 1978.[107] And in 1989 the documents themselves were published in Moscow in a volume entitled *Memoirs of Peasant Tolstoyans*.[108] Both works describe how the peasants sought to follow the teachings of Tolstoy in various villages throughout the country, largely under the influence of the publications issued by Tolstoy himself and Chertkov since the 1890s. Popovski estimates the number of these peasant Tolstoyans as amounting to several thousand by the outbreak of World War I.

The origins of the movement can be traced to the activities of the Moscow Vegetarian Society which had been founded in 1909 for the purpose of promoting Tolstoy's teachings on vegetarianism and non-violence, and with a view to making his writings available to workers and peasants throughout the country. Its headquarters, which included a meeting-hall, a bookshop and a library, were frequented by large numbers of artists and intellectuals. In June 1917 several of these Tolstoyans sought to expand their activities by founding the Society of True Freedom in Memory of Leo Tolstoy, with the aim of 'facilitating contacts among all who sympathise with the philosophy of life that Tolstoy represents, but also to assist in educational tasks'.[109] Branches of the Society were founded in Kiev, Sochi, Tsaritsyn (Volgograd), Vitebsk, Vladimir and several other towns and villages.

Almost immediately they took practical measures to promote Tolstoy's teachings on non-violence. During the October Revolution they issued a pamphlet, *Stop the Fratricide*, and distributed it amongst the revolutionaries fighting in the streets. In the spring of 1918 they sent a circular to all their members recommending that they 'raise their voice aginst war, the death penalty, pogroms, mob law, the torture of animals and other deformations of society'.[110] In November 1918 a petition was addressed to the Council of People's Commissars, advocating the abolition of the death penalty. New publishing centres were established in various provincial centres—e.g. Samara, Kharkov, Ekaterinodar and Smolensk—in defiance of the laws on censorship. Three journals were published, *The Voice of Tolstoy and Unity*, *Life Renewal* and *True Freedom*, the latter reaching a circulation of 10,000 copies. When they could no longer publish openly, because of the censorsip laws, they continued to distribute their ideas in handwritten and mimeographed documents.

The conscription laws, re-introduced on the outbreak of civil war, presented the Tolstoyans with an immediate test of their commitment to the doctrine of non-violence. Initially, their refusal to serve in the armed forces was met with a conciliatory response from the authorities. Lenin himself signed a Decree, on behalf of the Council of People's Commissars, granting complete exemption from military service to anyone who could demonstrate sincere opposition to war on grounds of religious faith. The responsibility to determine the sincerity of 'objectors' was vested in the United Council of Religious Communities, which had been founded in 1918 on the initiative of Chertkov, and included amongst its members Mennonites, Baptists and Evangelicals, as well as Tolstoyans. Documents show that in 1918 between 300 and 400 exemptions from military service were granted by the Council, almost entirely on the basis of certification by Chertkov.[111] During 1919-20 approximately 10,000 applications were examined by the Council, most of which were approved, though in some instances exemptions were disregarded by local conscription centres.

Tolstoyans were still regarded with favour by the authorities in the period immediately following the Civil War, when their exemplary methods of farming attracted the attention of officials concerned at the problem of food scarcities, resulting from the upheavals of the Revolution and Civil War. Together with Old Believers and some other small Christian sects, they were urged by the government to set up agricultural communes where they could practise their beliefs freely and where their farming methods could serve as an example to others. On 5 October 1921 the RSFSR Commissariat for

Agriculture set up a special commission to facilitate this. It issued the following proclamation, in which it quoted the words of the New Testament in support of its appeal to the believers to set up model communities where they could fully practise their 'communal, communistic way of life':

> The sectarians and Old Believers of Russia, who for the most part belong to the peasant population, have behind them many centuries of experience in communal living. We know that there are many sects in Russia whose adherents have long aspired to a communal, communistic life, in conformity with their doctrines. They ordinarily take as the foundation for this aspiration the words from the 'Acts of the Apostles': 'Neither said any of them that ought of the things which he possessed was his own; but they had all things in common. . . .' All governments, all authorities, all laws in the whole world and in all ages have been against such a life. . . . And now the time has come when all sectarians . . . can peacefully come out in the open, firmly confident that no one will ever persecute anyone among them for their beliefs. The Soviet Government of workers and peasants has proclaimed real freedom of conscience and absolutely does not interfere in any matters of religious belief, granting to everyone complete freedom of belief and unbelief.[112]

Encouraged by the words of the proclamation, large numbers of peasant believers began to organise agricultural cooperatives, of which about 100 were estimated to have been established by Tolstoyans. They continued with their work for some years, with the full approval of the state authorities, and were generally considered model farmers and an example to the rural population in the regions where they lived. A change of policy came, however, with the launching of the First Five Year Plan in 1929 and the proposal to introduce land collectivisation throughout the countryside. The peasant believers, while refraining from the use of force and engaging exclusively in peaceful methods of protest, firmly resisted all attempts to force them into the new collectives. Large numbers of them were arrested, tortured and imprisoned, and eventually entire communes were liquidated by Stalin's soldiers.

Several of the Tolstoyans managed, however, to escape to Western Siberia where they set up new communities and continued to live in accordance with their Christian beliefs. Boris Mazurin, one of the seven whose reminiscences are recorded in *Russian Peasants Tell Their Story*, was a member of one of the communities who re-settled in Siberia. In 1988, under the new freedom enjoyed by the press in the conditions of *glasnost* and *perestroika*, his recollections were published in *Noviy Mir*, *Izvestia* and *Uchitel'skaya gazeta*. He spoke of the simple faith that sustained the Tolstoyans as they sought to survive as Christian communities during the horrific upheavals of the Stalin period. 'How good it is', he wrote, 'that Leo

Tolstoy founded no church, no party, no sect, and set forth no dogmas. He pointed out to people the path of life that he considered the true one. He shared his experience on this path, set a course, and left to each individual what rightfully belongs to all individuals: to think independently and to make decisions independently, guided by their reason and their conscience according to the powers and requirements of their soul.'[113]

Mazurin's words, with their emphasis on the free, undogmatic, non-institutional character of Tolstoyan Christianity, go a long way towards explaining how it could survive even the brutality of the Stalinist regime, and how communities determined to live by the dictates of their conscience, in the spirit of the teachings of the scriptures, could remain in existence, despite the systematic attempts that were made to exterminate them. Perhaps, even more significantly, they vindicate to a remarkable degree the confidence that Tolstoy himself had placed in the simple faith of the unsophisticated peasantry. William Edgerton has remarked on the irony of the fact that the Tolstoyan communities in the Soviet Union survived so much longer than those in the U.S. and Western Europe. The remarkable thing about the experiences recorded in the memoirs of the peasant Tolstoyans, he writes, 'is that the peasants appear to have been more successful than many intellectuals in distinguishing what was primary and essential in Tolstoyism from what was derivative and optional.' 'Tolstoy's peasant followers', he says, 'recognised that the essence of his spiritual discovery was very simple and very profound and was very difficult to live by: it was what Tolstoy called the Law of Love, and it had been discovered over and over again by the world's great religious leaders all through history.'[114] In his final summing up of the lessons to be drawn from the experiences of these communities, Edgerton points to a conclusion that seems inescapable from the entire saga of their survival: that their scrupulous adherence to the Christian law of love, and especially to Christ's teaching on non-violence, afforded them a strength that ultimately enabled them to withstand whatever forces were ranged against them—even the full might of the most tyrannical state the world has ever seen. These are the concluding words of his report:

> In all the accounts I have read of the peasant Tolstoyans in the Soviet Union I have not yet found a single case in which they either consciously or involuntarily betrayed any hatred, vindictiveness, or even scorn for those who persecuted them, falsely accused them, unjustly imprisoned them, and sent hundreds of them to their death. Is it possible that these unsophisticated peasants found something in Tolstoy's teachings that lifted them beyond raw courage to the point where they could look upon even those who oppressed and tormented them as fellow human beings?[115]

VIII

Conclusion: The Modernity of Tolstoy

Seen from a modern standpoint, Tolstoy's vision of education seems remarkably far-seeing, profound and comprehensive. On the aims and goals of education, on the role of the teacher, the learner and the school, he had viewpoints to offer which are remarkably relevant to the needs and concerns of the present age. As someone who insisted that education is primarily concerned with moral and religious formation, while simultaneously denouncing most of the historical conventions of the religion which he sought to promote, his ideas seem especially pertinent at a time when—to paraphrase Heidegger—the religious need persists, despite the widespread rejection of its rituals and traditions in modern life.[1] As the greatest writer of his age (possibly the greatest in the history of the novel), he could bring the full weight of his artistic authority to bear on the problems of developing literacy—verbal, visual and musical—amongst the deprived and culturally disadvantaged children who crowded to his schools. Judged against the advances that have been made in all these spheres through modern innovations in classroom pedagogy, his ideas remain extraordinarily valid and meaningful, and provide valuable pointers on the ways in which the challenge of providing high levels of cultural literacy for the ever increasing numbers of disadvantaged learners might be met. And, as someone passionately dedicated to social and political reform, and to promoting the values and attitudes necessary to make it a realisable hope, his ideas—specifically those on the promotion of justice and peace—have become more significant than ever in the light of the endemic divisions and injustices which, together with the prospect of nuclear annihilation, threaten the future and the very survival of humankind.

On the question of the general aims of education, comparisons were made in a earlier chapter between Tolstoy and three of his near contemporaries: Rousseau, Ushinsky and Pestalozzi. Significant differences emerged between them on the matter of the ultimate aims of the entire process—the religious and spiritual perspectives of Tolstoy and Pestalozzi contrasting pointedly with the rational-humanist ideals of Rousseau and Ushinsky. Agreement could be detected between them, however, on a range of issues, such as their insistence on the universal right to education, their championing of the individuality of the learner, their emphasis on learning as a process of freely oriented enquiry, and their common opposition to excessive uses of didactic pedagogy. Comparisons between Tolstoy and some twentieth century educators can similarly help to define and illuminate the relevance of his thinking to the conditions and needs of the present time. The three to whom perhaps he can be most fruifully compared are the American pragmatist, John Dewey, the socialist educator, Vasily Sukhomlinsky, and the Jewish existentialist educator, Martin Buber. Between them they represent some of the most significant movements in modern educational thought.

It is with the first of these that Tolstoy has been compared most frequently. At first sight, there seems to be some basis for suggesting close comparisons between Tolstoy and Dewey. Their common rejection of authoritarian traditions in education—their condemnation, for example, of fixed, prescriptive curricula, of the traditional reliance of teachers on didactic pedagogy and on coercive forms of classroom discipline—is undoubtedly a significant link, as is their common emphasis on individual enquiry and discovery, on self-initiated, activity-based learning, and on individual curiosity and interest as natural sources for developing the motivation to learn. Both of them advocated pedagogic methods that could be loosely termed 'heuristic' and learner centred, and both stressed the importance of rendering knowledge meaningful by relating it to the individual experience of the learner. There is much common ground between them also in their emphasis on the benefits of learning from the environment —social, physical and cultural—and Tolstoy's repeated exhortations to his teachers to relate the work of the school to the life of society as a whole finds some significant echoes in Dewey's *The Child and the Curriculum, The School and Society* and *Democracy and Education.*[2]

But there the similarities end. Dewey's conception of the role of the teacher as some kind of facilitator of child-initiated learning seems narrowly focussed by comparison with the profoundly formative view of the teaching process put forward by Tolstoy. (This may not wholly apply to the revised view of the teacher developed by Dewey in *Experience and Education*,[3] but his impact on modern education derived largely from his early writings, and his later 'revisionist' works did little to diminish the impact of the original 'child centred' studies on a generation of school-teachers in the U.S. and abroad.) The analogy suggested by R.S. Peters for the Deweyan model of the teacher—like a 'leader in a game' or a 'football captain'[4]—could never be employed to describe the highly formative view of the teacher developed by Tolstoy in his pedagogic writings. The diminished sense of the value of subject-content in Dewey's *The Child and the Curriculum* and *The School and Society*—a position which followed logically from his instrumentalist theory of knowledge—is similarly to be contrasted with the reverential attention given to traditional subject-content in Tolstoy's writings on the curriculum. This difference is most visibly illustrated in their respective attitudes to the arts: the importance accorded to initiating the child into the riches of the cultural heritage in Tolstoy's writings contrasting dramatically with the virtual sacrificing of aesthetic appreciation and receptivity in Dewey's philosophy to a spurious identification of aesthetic creativity with various rudimentary forms of expressive activity.[5]

There are deep differences again between Dewey and Tolstoy in the basic modes and methods of their educational writings and in the ultimate goals they conceived for the educational process. The formal philosophic, predominantly rationalist and quasi-scientific method of Dewey's writings, particularly his employment of methods of deductive analysis for the formulation of educational concepts and principles, seem utterly foreign to the unified aesthetico-religious perceptions of Tolstoy, and to the direct and unmediated observations of classroom practice on which he based his educational insights. Tolstoy's ethico-religious affirmations, his insistence on the absolute primacy of the law of love, and of the moral imperatives deriving from it, and his repeated emphasis on the eternal verities on which he saw the whole process of education as being finally focussed, seem even more fundamentally in conflict with the empirical pragmatism of Dewey, with its concentration on the immediate and observable realities of the here and now, the contigent, the relative and the scientifically verifiable. While, therefore, he shared with Dewey a belief that learning should be rendered meaningful in the context of individual experience, the sense in which he used the term 'experience' differs immeasurably from the way in which it was understood by Dewey. In the latter case, experience is seen as the cornerstone of all reality, and as dynamic, changing and transient as that reality. In the former, it is related in a complex and mysterious fashion to the reality of the infinite, and has the potential to disclose the eternal and transcendent truths which ultimately embrace the full meaning of that reality.

Closer comparisons are possible between Tolstoy and his twentieth century fellow-countryman, the socialist educator, Vasily Sukhomlinsky. Their common concern for the underprivileged and disadvantaged is an obvious link between them; the war orphans taught by Sukhomlinsky in his Ukrainian school in the 1950s and 1960s seem remarkably similar to the children that Tolstoy taught at Tula in the 1860s, and the whole ethos of the school at Pavlysh was strongly reminiscent of the conditions at Yasnaya Polyana. Reading *To Children I Give My Heart*[6] one is constantly reminded of the distinctive blending of learner-centred and traditionalist elements that characterise the Tolstoyan pedagogy. Both men emphasised the uniqueness of the individual child, the importance of nurturing learning in a spirit of freedom, the need to harmonise all the formative aspects of growth in a single, unified process, the need to make the pupil receptive to learning by fostering the spirit of spontaneous curiosity and enquiry, the importance, above all, of a truly formative, effective and imaginative pedagogy in promoting all of these objectives.

In the area of classroom pedagogy some especially close affinities can be seen between them in relation to the development of literacy and the teaching of literature, music and art. Both men recognised the importance of imagination as the foundation of all learning, and both sought to develop symbolic potential in their pupils, utilising the resources of literary, visual and musical art-forms to achieve this objective in the fullest possible degree. Unlike Dewey and the progressivists, they realised that the potential for symbolic meaning-making is developed not merely by expressive activities —though these play a crucial role in fostering a mastery of the language of the particular art-form—but, more fundamentally, through guided encounters with the riches of the cultural heritage in its literary, visual and musical forms. Thus, they both stressed the importance of fostering an interest in the traditions of literature, in its popular and sophisticated forms, side by side with an intensive and concentrated development of basic linguistic skills. Both wrote of the need to master the technical aspects of music—achieving remarkably high levels of musical literacy in the process —while ensuring their pupils had access also to the best of the Russian and European musical heritage. And both gave persistent attention to the formal training of visual competencies, while developing in their pupils the critical and receptive abilities necessary for a deep and enduring appreciation of the traditions of art.

Indeed, there appear to be similarities between Tolstoy and Sukhomlinsky even in their treatment of moral education, despite the obvious differences in their basic ideological beliefs. The latter's recommendations in *To Children I Give My Heart* that altruistic potential be developed in children, both through the personal example of the teacher, and through a direct experiencing of the virtues of fellowship and communal responsibility by the children themselves, closely correspond to the policies that Tolstoy followed at Yasnaya Polyana. Yet the ultimate goals that each of them envisaged for this whole process were radically different, Sukhomlinsky's being the subordination of individual freedom to the good of the collective, and, in the final analysis, to the good of the state; Tolstoy's being a fulfilment of individual freedom through the practice of selfless love, and a belief in the infinity of being that it has the potential to disclose.

The goal in the first instance is the purely humanist one of service to the welfare of mankind; in the second it is a religious ideal, inspired by faith in the infinite character of the absolute and transcendent Good towards which its author believes that man must finally aspire.

And yet the issue seems somewhat more complex than such polarised positions would suggest. By emphasising the importance of altruistic service to the degree that he did, and by seeking so assiduously to develop individual potentialities, through a subject-matter profoundly imbued with the spirit of religion in its literature, art and music, Sukhomlinsky communicated much of the same cultural heritage through which Tolstoy sought to foster a religious and spiritual and ethical consciousness in his pupils. It might well be the case that the differences between them are indicative mainly of a dialectical tension at the heart of the culture that they shared—a tension sufficiently comprehensive to embrace their supposedly divergent views and purposes. Recent events in the USSR, which indicate a massive resurgence of values systematically repressed during the years of communist domination, would suggest that long-standing cultural traditions, including the aesthetico-religious traditions celebrated by Tolstoy and the great artists of the nineteenth century, have retained their place in the minds and hearts of the people. It seems reasonable to assume that educators like Sukhomlinsky, dedicated as they were to conserving the best of the country's cultural heritage, and doing so with spectacular success through the highly traditionalist curriculum which they taught in their schools, have played a significant part in this whole process.

The similarities between Tolstoy and Sukomlinsky are to a large degree attributable to their common Slavic culture, and to the impact on their writings of the spiritual, aesthetic, social and educational traditions of the Slavic peoples. A third educator of the modern period to whom Tolstoy can be further compared is the Jewish philosopher, Martin Buber. As the child of Galician parents and one who spent his formative years in Lvov, Buber shared much of the same Slavic heritage as Tolstoy and Sukhomlinsky. What he primarily shares with Tolstoy, however, is a belief in education as fundamentally a religious process, the basis for which is the all-embracing spirit of love in which they both believed it must always be conducted. From this they developed a conception of teaching as an activity characterised by moral integrity, authenticity, pedagogic effectiveness and caring concern for the needs of the learner, and a conception of learning as a freely oriented search for truth, conducted in a spirit of loving enquiry, in pursuit of the goal of selflesss altruism, through which they saw all human potentialities as being ultimately fulfilled.

Both men insisted on the inextricable links that exist between religious and ethical concerns, seeing the law of love as the absolute imperative that must determine the value and purpose of all human activity. They saw the law of love as religious in its orientation towards the infinite, the intemporal and the absolute, and as moral, in the manner in which it urged the regulation of human conduct in accordance with its own absolute and incontrovertible dictates. Significantly, Tolstoy and Buber both stressed the non-institutional, non-formal character of religious faith, seeing the dangers inherent in a merely conventional observance of religion and the manner in which it had been corrupted by those conventions throughout history. Each of them further conceived of the process of ethical awareness as essentially an exercise in conscience illumination, recognising that this was the only authentic and enduring basis for the fostering of moral responsibility. Both, however, emphasised the importance of religious traditions and stressed the central importance of the scriptures in fostering and deepening the consciousness of religious and ethical truth.

Further links can be seen in their treatment of aesthetic education. Each saw a vital place for the traditions of art in the nurturing of aesthetic consciousness, and therefore specified in detail the pedagogic methods that should be employed for the fulfilment of this goal. Side by side with this, they advocated intensive and systematic instruction in the languages of the different art-forms, seeing both the receptive and expressive aspects of aesthetic experience as complementary agencies in a balanced development of creative potentialities. Both men, furthermore, recognised the importance of maintaining a balance between the popular and sophisticated forms of culture, and argued for a curriculum that linked the works of the great masters in painting, literature and music with the folk traditions to which they are inextricably related. Both stressed the need for closer links between school and society, seeing adult education in particular as the bridgehead that would forge stronger links between the formal processes of education occurring in the school and the informal modes that occur in society at large. In such an extension of the entire process of education they saw the possibility of a renewal and revitalisation of society through the fostering of the community values and the more radical forms of democracy that such a conjuncture could ensure. In this also they saw the best prospect for countering the dominance of state monoliths—both of the totalitarian and capitalist modes—and the best hope for the resolution of conflict at local, national and international levels. This they saw as predominantly a matter for educators and they offered significant guidelines on the ways in which it would be achieved and the values by which it should be informed.

A key difference between Tolstoy and Buber, however, lies in the fact that Tolstoy was a practising school-teacher who directly exemplified the effectiveness of his educational ideals in the context of actual classroom practice, whereas Buber's experience lay entirely in the sphere of adult and university education. As a result, one finds a greater amount of specific pedagogic guidance in Tolstoy's writings, particularly in the spheres of reading, writing, art and music education, and in the teaching of the scriptures—all of which stands up remarkably well to comparison with modern developments in each of these fields. What particularly commends him, at the present moment, however, is his view of how the school should be organised so that the aims and ideals it sets before itself can be most effectively implemented. His views on this issue have acquired immense relevance in the 1980s, with the growing emphasis on the importance of 'school ethos' and the growth of a world-wide movement devoted to promoting the virtues of the 'effective school'. Since some of the most remarkable advances claimed by the effective schooling movement have been in the sphere of educational disadvantage,[7] Tolstoy's experience seems all the more relevant, since all his pupils belonged in a category that would nowadays be described by the term 'disadvantaged'.

Effective schools are now generally designated by certain characteristics, such as inspirational leadership, clearly defined goals for learning, good pastoral and counselling care, effective pedagogic policies, close home-school liaison, and a high degree of participation by teachers in the adminis-tration of the school. The essential synthesis comprehended in the effective schooling ideal is its combination of academic and pedagogic effectiveness with a high degree of caring concern, especially for underprivileged, less able or disadvantaged pupils. It is largely because of this distinctive blending of effectiveness with pastoral care that the schools have been so successful in dealing with disadvantaged pupils. Now that an extensive literature exists on the work of these schools, what are most needed perhaps are inspirational models of the ideals they have implemented so succesfully: indeed the absence of a coherent and explicitly formulated philosophy is probably the major weakness of the whole movement, much of its work being guided by a purely ad hoc application of organisational principles, such as those that have just been mentioned. That weakness could be rectified in part by the identification of some striking examples of schooling that embody the ideals for which the movement stands.

It is the present writer's contention that the schools at Yasnaya Polyana provide exemplary models of what constitutes an effective school, and despite their remoteness from the conditions of the present time, that they admirably exemplify the kind of ethos that needs to be created in many contemporary schools. As has been indicated in an earlier chapter, it was the special blending of the ideals of freedom, loving and caring concern, and high levels of pedagogic effectiveness, together with a closely maintained relationship with the local community, that defined the special ethos of Tolstoy's schools. While emphasising the need for the most dedicated professionalism in his teachers, yet simultaneously calling for the flexible application of teaching skills in accordance with the unique needs of every individual pupil, and while balancing highly intensive and highly directive teaching methods with a generous provision for discovery-based and learner-centred activities, he managed to ensure that the work of the school was sufficiently individualised to meet the particular needs of every child, while also seeing that it was consistently purposeful, intellectually and imaginatively stimulating, and that it provided all children with the basic knowledge necessary for their development.

He sought to accommodate the paradoxical and mutually constraining ideals of freedom and order, informality and discipline, and to provide simultaneously for the needs of the individual and the needs of the group. While stressing the importance of self-initiated learning, he ensured that every child was taught a curriculum which embraced the full range of traditional disciplines and gave full recognition to the heritage of culture and thought to which he believed each had a right of access and which every teacher had a corresponding obligation to provide. While the spirit of freedom reigned at all times in the schools, the dedication of the teachers— some of whom worked from 8 to 10 hours every day—ensured that school time was devoted to carefully guided and purposeful learning, and that the children were fully immersed in its activities throughout every part of the school day. While denouncing compulsion, he still maintained the authority of the teacher as the leader and director of all school activities, and further maintained the authority of the traditions of knowledge and culture through the broadly based curriculum that was taught in his schools. Though he rejected formal methods of assessment, and particularly the traditional written examination, his pupils were evaluated nonetheless on an informal basis by their teachers and high levels of attainment were reported in the schools.

In every respect, therefore, the schools could be called 'effective' and could serve as unusually impressive models of the kinds of conditions in which underprivileged children can be taught. An important factor in the success of the schools was the religious ethos that Tolstoy created, in accordance with his own radical interpretations of the traditions of Christianity. In this again they have much to offer modern educators seeking an approach to education that will accommodate the spiritual needs of a society grown disillusioned with conventional forms of religion. The 'churchless' Christianity that Tolstoy advocated, while having the stability and authenticity of its traditionalist origins, has the great attraction of being simply an expression of the universal potentiality for love that is present in the whole of humankind. It might be said of him, as Paul Tillich said of Buber, that he 'proclaimed the freedom from religion, including the institutions of religion, in the name of that to which religion points'.[8] He identified both the nature of the universal need for faith and the manner in which it can be fostered. His crucial message to educators was that faith is fostered not primarily through knowledge—though it may be deepened, and enriched by it—but primarily through the nurturing of altruistic love, initially in the sphere of the interpersonal, and by its extension into the realms of the communal, the social and the political.

From an educational standpoint, the most significant feature of his religious writings was his view of faith as active love i.e. as a *responsibility* to abide by, and give effect to, the law of love as the ultimate criterion by which the worth of all human action is to be judged. Seeing the dangers both of moral relativism and secularised humanism, he insisted on the absolute character of the ethical injunctions deriving from the law of love, and urged on educators their duty to develop the fullest possible awareness amongst their pupils of the responsibilities following from this. Essentially, there were two main ways in which he believed this should be done. In the first instance, he stressed the importance of a direct exemplification by educators of the spirit of love in all their relations with their pupils. In the case of the school at Yasnaya Polyana, he sought in every way possible to ensure that its whole ethos was imbued with this spirit. Secondly, he advocated the direct fostering of ethico-religious consciousness through the study of the scriptures.

While rejecting the formal conventions of religion, and while particularly rejecting the dogmatic and authoritarian traditions of the Christian Churches, he nonetheless asserted the profound relevance of scriptural Christianity to the life of modern man, and argued that the surest way to developing the spirit of selfless love was through the discovery of the radical meaning of the words of the scripture text. He urged, however, that scripture study be conducted in the same spirit of open-minded, critical enquiry as he had advocated for all other modes of school learning. His reports on the lessons at the school indicate how successful he was in awakening in his pupils an interest in the reading of scripture, and how fully they integrated its meaning into the circumstances of their daily lives. His methods demonstrate the success with which he maintained the essential freedom of the act of religious faith while communicating a sense of the relevance of the traditions through which its meaning is illuminated and defined. As a free-thinking but profoundly traditionalist Christian himself, he succeeded remarkably in maintaining that same delicate balance of authority and freedom in the way in which he developed the spirit of morality amongst his pupils.

The success of Tolstoy's work in ethico-religious education was attributable to a considerable degree to the extent to which he utilised the aesthetic appeal of the scriptures. The strong concentration on the narrative itself, through the various reading and writing activities that he encouraged, evoked in his pupils a deep and enduring awareness of the meaning of the scripture text. Behind this whole process, however, lay a twofold conjuncture. Tolstoy himself believed profoundly in the unity of aesthetic and religious truth, seeing all religious truth as having a distinct aesthetic character, and all aesthetic truth as ultimately pointing to a religious transcendence. And this was bound up, in turn, with his belief in the universality of aesthetico-religious truth and its accessibility to all of mankind. This was the guiding principle of the philosophy he set out in *What Is Art* and some related writings. It was because he believed so fervently that the literary character of scripture was the key to its religious profundities—the means by which it was made universally accessible— that he employed it so successfully in his lessons at the school.

That belief was deeply reinforced by his conviction that all learning is aesthetic in origin and is most effectively fostered, therefore, through the cultivation of imaginative propensities. Believing that all thought originates in the mind as image and symbol, he saw the process of learning as essentially one of symbolic formation and devoted his pedagogic methods primarily to promoting this potentiality and to a focussing of all enquiry on the unifying power of the aesthetic. This identification of aesthetic and intellectual understanding was the most radical principle of his pedagogic philosophy. It was radical not only in the depth of the aesthetic, religious and cognitional conjuncture that it embraced, but in the pedagogic possibilities it opened up by equating the fostering of imagination with the development of the basic powers of educability. The principle was applied to all the disciplines of the curriculum with consummate skill by Tolstoy himself and his teachers. Appealing directly to the imaginative dimensions of all varieties of subject-matter, they treated the whole curriculum as an aesthetic harmony, all the elements of which could be comprehended through the unifying power of the imagination.

Because of his insistence on the inseparability of the religious and the aesthetic, Tolstoy argued passionately for the universal right of access to the heritage of culture. Almost uniquely amongst nineteenth century educators, he proclaimed the right of the masses to the benefits of an education embracing the full range of traditional disciplines: he specifically affirmed the right of the disadvantaged and the supposedly ineducable masses to this. (He did, of course, make this case from what was primarily a religious standpoint, whereas modern educators have made the same case from ideological and egalitarian positions that are basically humanist and secular). 'The necessity of enjoying art and serving art are inherent in each human personality no matter to what race or milieu he may belong', he declared. 'Everybody, without distinction of classes or occupations has a right to it', he said.[9] From this emerged the ideal of cultural literacy—an ideal embracing both the imaginative and communicative aspects of literacy, and extending it into the spheres of the visual and the musical, as well as the linguistic. This Tolstoy envisaged as a universal, democratic right, and devised a pedagogy for it that reflects the balancing of imaginative, technical and communicative principles he considered to be crucial to its proper realisation.

Thus, in the basic area of language education he argued that the development of reading and writing competence, while being rooted primarily in the comprehension of image and symbol, should be linked as closely as possible with the 'living speech' of everyday life and with the everyday experience of the learner. The principle finds echoes everywhere in contemporary first language pedagogy—in the 'language growth', 'whole language', and 'language through experience' movements of recent years, in the pedagogic writings of Bruner, Holbrook, Abbs, Dixon, Meek, and a host of others similarly concerned to stress the centrality of the symbolic in language growth and to integrate school language with the language of ordinary life.[10] Unlike some of his modern day successors, however, Tolstoy, maintained a careful balance between the formal and informal aspects of language growth, insisting that instruction in the skills and structures of language be combined with the fostering of imaginative potentialities, to ensure that their complementary, if somewhat tensed and slightly conflicting, functions were fully realised. That balance is admirably exemplified in the reports he provided on the reading lessons at Yasnaya Polyana.

It is similarly in evidence in his accounts of the writing lessons at the school. Here again he recognised the centrality of symbolic experience in generating linguistic growth, and sought therefore to encourage imaginative uses of language in every way that he could. The modern educator whom perhaps he most closely resembles in this respect is Holbrook; the reports on the work of the school at Yasnaya Polyana find strong echoes in Holbrook's *English for the Rejected*, a collection of case studies on the development of writing abilities in a group of acutely disadvantaged children taught by the author.[11] While both men were able to record spectacular success in releasing creative potential in their pupils, Tolstoy laid far more emphasis on the importance of balancing individual freedom with some degree of formal instruction, and demonstrated the need for direct guidance from the teacher in enabling the pupils to master the formal and technical aspects of language, while providing the greatest possible degree of freedom for the development of imaginative potential. The wisdom of this approach has since been confirmed in contemporary first language pedagogy, the balance that Tolstoy advocated being particularly in evidence in the work of Protherough and Abbs in the 1980s.[12]

Tolstoy's writings on literacy have the combined attraction, therefore, of defining enlightened and well-balanced pedagogic principles and providing the evidence of their effectiveness in the difficult conditions in which he worked. At a time when so much concern is being voiced at the intolerably high levels of illiteracy amongst young school leavers, the importance of his contribution to this issue deserves the fullest attention from educators. As in the sphere of verbal literacy, the pedagogy he devised in the areas of art and music was also intended to provide access to the riches of their cultural heritage for all children, regardless of their ability or cultural background. Again his methods proved to be remarkably sucessful in developing an appreciation of music and art amongst the peasant children that he taught. In music he provided a good basic training in choral and individual singing and in the rudiments of musical literacy, while simul- taneously introducing his pupils to a wide repertoire of classical, folk and sacred music. His insistence that the whole experience be one of pleasure and enjoyment, side by side with his intensive concentration on the develop- ment of aural and vocal skills and the mastery of the technical language of music, would almost certainly have the full approval of modern music educators. In art, his range of activities was more limited, being virtually confined to lessons in technical drawing, though here again he managed to combine systematic training in the skills of drawing with some provision for art-making activities. Ultimately, the importance of Tolstoy's work in each of these fields consists not merely in the formation he gave his pupils in each of the disciplines he taught, but in the wealth and diversity of symbolic experience he provided for them in pursuit both of his broadened ideal of cultural literacy and his belief that the masses should be given the fullest access to the riches of the cultural heritage. Modern educators, struggling with the huge and seemingly insurmountable problem of illi- teracy, and seeing the inadequacies both of the pragmatist and 'back to the basics' movements in providing for the needs of the culturally impoverished masses, can derive confidence from Tolstoy's experience, and will see what can be achieved through a carefully balanced programme in cultural studies which accords its due place to the imagination and to the fostering of symbolic potentialities, while utilising a range of pedagogic methods sufficiently broad and flexible to embrace the complex and varied sensitivities which such a process must comprehend.

Tolstoy, however, saw the whole process of cultural democratisation as part of a wider vision in which the pursuit of ideals such as universal literacy would be complemented by fundamental reforms in the character of society as a whole. In his fictional and non-fictional writings he fearlessly exposed the great injustices rampant in Russian and European society at the end of the nineteenth century. But he was profoundly critical of the newly emerging socialist ideology, with the purely humanist and political solutions it offered on all these issues. While being, in some degree, sympathetic to its ideals, he pointed to a basic defect at the heart of marxist socialism: its isolation of socio-political from individual morality, and its consequent subordination of individual freedom to the good of the collective, and ultimately, the state.

Almost a century later, with the collapse of totalitarian socialism in Eastern Europe, Tolstoy's critique has assumed enormous significance retrospectively. What makes it so profoundly relevant now is not just his exposure of the inadequacies of socialist humanism—in this his position differs little from that of most Christian commentators on marxism—but his insistence that the ideals that originally inspired the emergence of socialism need to be comprehended in a more balanced doctrine of Christian responsibility. Throughout his social writings one sees a recurrent emphasis on the need for an active witnessing by every individual to the ideal of justice in accordance with the dictates of his conscience. He spoke, for example, of the need for protest against state violence, institutional poverty, exploitative work practices and socially discriminatory laws, through non-violent methods such as the refusal to pay taxes, the denial of support for unjust institutions, and so on. He indicated the duty of every individual to ask himself if, by his actions, he was giving tacit support to injustice and, if so, to withdraw that support and give voice to his dissent from the policies and activities of an unjust regime.

A crucial emphasis in all this, however, is his insistence that moral opposition to injustice must always be non-violent in character, on the grounds that violence in any form is the greatest of all evils and explicitly contravenes the teaching of Christ, as enunciated in the Gospels. To understand the nature of Tolstoy's pacifism adequately it is vital to recognise its intrinsically religious character. Being essentially an extension of the ethic of forgiveness into the sphere of the social and the political, it was conceived by Tolstoy in the same spirit of absoluteness as he conceived the law of love itself. But, like all religious acts, including the primary act of faith, it was seen by him as fundamentally aspirational in character. Just as he argued that the love for the ideal and the perfect was motivated and empowered by the absolute character of that to which it aspired (i.e. its own self-transcendence), so, he argued, the will to peace is empowered by the absolute nature of the Christian ideal of non-resistance to evil, which is yet another manifestation of the same law of love on which the act of faith is focussed. He saw the act of love as an inexhaustible yearning for the infinite, and informed by the spirit of the infinity for which it yearns. He similarly saw the ideal of absolute peace as the goal which inspires the never-ending quest for its own realisation and fulfilment. That, essentially, was his meaning when he declared that there could be no compromise on the absolute nature of this ideal, even if some compromise in its practical implementation proved to be inevitable. Pacifism he saw as the persistent and unrelenting quest for peace; that quest would find expression in an active witnessing to peace, conscientious objection to war service being its commonest mode of expression.

But, as a recent study[13] has suggested, the fundamental issue in Tolstoy's pacifist writings was his view of the relationship between conflict and power. He saw the very concept of the large corporate state, with its army, its police force, its faceless bureaucracy, as a constant threat to peace, its whole rationale being the defence of its own authority, both internally and externally, through the employment of force. By its very existence, he argued, the corporate state exemplifies the antithesis of the Christian ideal of non-violence. Normally, its attestation of the legitimacy of force could be countered, he said, by an active witnessing to the Christian ideal, whether through the refusal to support violence—either directly through war-service, or indirectly through taxation—or even by a total denial of allegiance to the state. But Tolstoy also envisaged this ideal being realised through a process of political reform by which power would be devolved from the large state structure to small, radically democratic communities, with a consequent transformation of social and political relationships. The concentration of power in the large state apparatus, he argued, inevitably led to coercion, whereas smaller communities, while still existing within the framework of the larger political structure, could be based on non-coercive principles, such as social cooperation and voluntary service for the welfare of their own members and, by extension, of society as a whole.

The term 'utopian' is entirely appropriate for such a vision, provided it is used in the sense of an entirely realisable ideal—the sense in which it was used by Proudhon, whose ideas profoundly influenced Tolstoy's own thinking on these issues, and by modern 'utopians' such as Buber and Freire, who similarly envisage the renewal of society through a process of community transformation. Like Buber and Freire, Tolstoy saw this whole process as involving the promotion of attitudes appropriate to the growth of the community spirit, and therefore, as one to be brought about primarily through education. Only through such a total transformation of social relationships could peace be ensured, he said, and this required the kind of fundamental changes in consciousness which only a truly radical process of education could bring about. What he envisaged was radical in the sense that it required a basic moral and religious reorientation of values suffi- ciently comprehensive to embrace both the process of individual self- perfection and the moral renewal of society. It is rather significant that a century after Tolstoy articulated this vision, another Slavic writer and social philosopher, Vaclav Havel, the playwright-president of Czechoslovakia, has spoken in similar terms of his vision of a society reformed and reconstituted through the growth of the community spirit. His vision of a post-marxist, post-totalitarian society—neither capitalist nor socialist, but committed to the values of 'trust, openness, responsibility, solidarity, love' —has distinct echoes of what Tolstoy was advocating in pre-revolutionary Russia in the 1890s. In 'The Power of the Powerless' Havel wrote:

> A genuine, profound and lasting change for the better . . . can no longer result from the victory (were such a victory possible) of any particular traditional political conception, which can ultimately be only external, that is, a structural or systemic conception. More than ever before, such a change will have to derive from human existence, from the fundamental reconstitution of the position of people in the world, their relationships to themselves and to each other, and to the universe. If a better economic and political model is to be created, then perhaps more than ever before it must derive from profound existential and moral changes in society. This is not something that can be designed and introduced like a new car. If it is to be more than just a new variation on the old degeneration, it must above all be an expression of life in the process of transforming itself. A better system will not automatically ensure a better life. In fact the opposite is true: only by creating a better life can a better system be developed. . . .
>
> And the political consequences? Most probably they could be reflected in the constitution of structures that will derive from this 'new spirit', from human factors rather than from a particular formalisation of political relationships and guarantees. In other words, the issue is the rehabilitation of values like trust, openness, responsibility, solidarity, love. . . . There can and must be structures that are open, dynamic and small; beyond a certain point, human ties like personal trust and personal responsibility cannot work. . . . They would be structures not in the sense of organisations or institutions, but like a community.[14]

Neither Tolstoy nor Havel has indicated in specific terms the manner in which this process is to come about. Both clearly designate it as a task for educators, and this perhaps is the great challenge that must now be faced if humanity is to be saved from the plunge towards political, social and moral deterioration of which they have warned.

On this, as on all the issues that have been discussed, Tolstoy's views have a meaningfulness that lies deeper than their relevance to the concerns of the present age. As an educator, he has the supreme attraction of having embodied in his life and work the truth and authenticity of the values which he sought to promote. In this consists the ultimate validity and authority of all his writings. 'He commands our respect to a degree that no other writer does by virtue of his love of truth', a recent commentator wrote. 'As we read him', he says, 'we realise that for Tolstoy in all things truth—to get it right, exactly right— matters more than anything else—that for this one value he will not count the cost in personal suffering, isolation, or risk of ridicule.' And he adds: 'There is another respect in which Tolstoy is unique among writers—that is the degree to which he moves our inmost and deepest feelings. The reason for this lies in Tolstoy's goodness and his love of goodness which shines steadily and unwaveringly through everything which he wrote.'[15] It is because he so consistently exemplified the ideals that he preached, and because all his activities—as novelist, religious reformer, publicist, schoolmaster, crusader for the weak and the down trodden—were directed towards promoting them, that Tolstoy stands out as a totally authentic and committed educator. But, as another of his admirers has told us, the truth is rarely simple, and, while Tolstoy may have given lifelong witness to its purity and authenticity, he also demonstrated its immense and ever challenging complexity. In this he has performed an important service to educators, as Isaiah Berlin has shown in 'Tolstoy and Enlightenment'. These are the concluding reflections in his essay:

> Everyone knows that Tolstoy placed truth highest of all the virtues. Others have made such declarations and have celebrated her no less memorably. But Tolstoy is among the few who have truly earned that rare right: for he sacrificed all he had upon her altar—happiness, friendship, love, peace, moral and intellectual certainty, and, in the end, his life. And all she gave him in return was doubt, insecurity, self-contempt, intolerable contradictions. In this sense (although he would have repudiated this most violently) he is a martyr and a hero in the central tradition of the European enlightenment. This seems a paradox: but then his entire life is in this sense a great paradox, inasmuch as it bears constant witness to a proposition to the denial of which his last years were dedicated—that the truth is seldom wholly simple and clear, or as obvious as it may sometimes seem to the eye of the ordinary, sensible man.[15]

Notes

All quotations from Tolstoy's *Pedagogic Journal* are taken from Volume 4 of *The Collected Works of Count Tolstoy*, first published by J.M. Dent of London in 1904, and republished by the University of Chicago Press in 1967. All page references relate to the Chicago edition. These are the translations of Leo Wiener, generally considered the most authentic versions of Tolstoy's educational writings currently available, not only because of Wiener's knowledge of the Russian language, but even more importantly, because of his empathy with, and appreciation of, Tolstoy's educational aims and ideals. There are some occasional obscurities and infelicities in his renderings of Tolstoy: in the few instances where these constitute a potential obstacle to precise interpretation, a paraphrase of the original Russian text has been incorporated in the commentary.

Quotations from Tolstoy's diaries and letters are, in most cases, taken from the editions prepared by R.F. Christian. In the case of letters or diary entries not included in Christian's four substantial volumes, new translations have been made from the originals in *Polnoye sobraniye sochinenii*, the definitive 90 volume edition of Tolstoy's works, edited by Chertkov and others, which was published in Moscow in 1949.

Original documents on education in Tsarist Russia have been consulted wherever possible. Where these were unavailable or inaccessible, the original documentary sources are cited, together with the secondary sources in which they were located. This applies particularly to some of the documentation available from the pioneering research conducted by Hans and Eklof within the USSR, the former in the 1920s, the latter in the 1980s.

CHAPTER I

1. *Tolstoy on Education* (translated by Leo Wiener, with an Introduction by Reginald D. Archambault) (Chicago and London: Chicago University Press, 1967), pp. v-xviii.
2. Alan Pinch and Michael Armstrong, *Tolstoy on Education: Tolstoy's Educational Writings, 1861-2* (London: The Athlone Press, 1982).
3. Ibid., p. 56.
4. Isaiah Berlin, 'Tolstoy and Enlightenment', *Encounter*, February 1961, reprinted in *Tolstoy: A Collection of Critical Essays* (ed. R. Matlaw) (Englewood: Prentice-Hall, 1967), p. 28-52.
5. Renato Poggioli, 'Tolstoy As Man and Artist', *Oxford Slavonic Papers*, X, 1962 reprinted in *Tolstoy: A Collection of Critical Essays*, p. 19.
6. N.K. Mikhaylovsky, 'The Right Hand and the Left Hand of Count Tolstoy' in *Tolstoy: The Critical Heritage* (ed. A.V. Knowles) (London: Routledge and Kegan Paul, 1978), pp. 274-81.
7. Berlin, 'Tolstoy and Enlightenment', p. 28.
8. Ibid., p. 29.
9. Ilya Tolstoy, *Tolstoy, My Father* (trans. Ann Dunnigan) (London: Peter Owen, 1972);

Alexandra Tolstoy, *Tolstoy: A Life of My Father* (Belmont: Mass., Nordland Publishing Co., 1953); Pavel Biryukov, *Leo Tolstoy: His Life and Work* (New York: Scribner, 1906); Aylmer Maude, *Tolstoy*, 2 vols. (Oxford University Press, 1987).

10. Poggioli, 'Tolstoy As Man and Artist', p. 19.

CHAPTER II

1. B.P. Yesipov and N.K. Goncharov, *Padadogik* (Berlin: Volk and Wissen Verlag, 1948). The German edition was used because of the unavailability of the Russian original.

2. For a full discussion of this see Dmitrij Tschizewskij, *Russian Intellectual History* (Ann Arbor: Ardis, 1978). See especialy pp. 41ff, 54ff, 60ff, 75ff, 98ff.

3. This was the monastic school founded by Fedor Rtischev, adviser to Tsar Alexis, in 1666. Primarily a theological institute, the school taught Slavic and classical languages, philosophy and rhetoric, as well as theology.

4. See Nicholas Hans, 'The Moscow School of Mathematics and Navigation, 1701;, *Slavonic and East European Review*, June 1951, p. 532.

5. Nicholas Hans, *A History of Russian Educational Policy, 1701-1917* (London: P.S. King, 1931), pp. 10-16.

6. Daniel B. Leary, *Education and Autocracy in Russia from the Origin to the Bolsheviks* (University of Buffalo Press, 1919).

7. Hans, *A History of Russian Educational Policy*, p. 21.

8. Ibid., p. 30.

9. Michael T. Florinsky, *Russia: A History and Interpretation* (New York: Macmillan, 1953), vol. 1, p. 601.

10. Hans, *A History of Russian Educational Policy*, p. 32.

11. Ibid., pp. 28-9.

12. Ibid., p. 45. See also William H. Johnson, *Russia's Educational Heritage* (Pittsburg: Carnegie Press, 1950), pp. 109-133.

13. Hans, *A History of Russian Educational Policy*, p. 35-40.

14. Ibid., p. 43.

15. Ibid., p. 51.

16. Statistics are from Hans, pp. 51-60, 242.

17. Ibid.

18. Ibid.

19. Ibid., p. 65.

20. Ibid., pp. 66, 21.

21. Ibid.

22. Ibid., p. 68.

23. B. Eklof, *Russian Peasant Schools* (University of Califoria Press, 1986), p. 25.

24. Hans, *A History of Educational Policy*, p. 72.

25. Ibid., pp. 72-3.

26. Ibid., p. 72.

27. Ibid., p. 78.

28. Ibid., p. 91.

29. Ibid., p. 84.

30. Ibid., pp. 83-4.

31. Eklof, *Russian Peasant Schools*, p. 29.

32. N.V. Chekhov, *Narodnoe obrazovanie v Rossii s 60-kh godov xix veka* (Moscow, 1912), pp. 92-4, cited in Eklof, p. 30.

33. M.I. Demkov, *Istoriia russkoi pedagogiki* (St. Petersburg, 1897), p. 47, cited in Eklof, p. 37.
34. Thomas Darlington, *Education in Russia*, Board of Education Special Reports on Education, vol. XXIII (London: 1909), pp. 86, 103.
35. S.I. Miropol'skii, *Shkola i gosudarstvo: obiazatel'nost obucheniia v Rosii* (St. Petersburg, 1910), pp. 66-70, cited in Eklof, p. 38-9.
36. P.S. Sheremetev (ed.), *Narodnye uchitelia i uchitel'nitsy v Tul'skoi gubernii* (Tula, 1898), cited in Eklof, p. 40.
37. N.M. Druzhinin, *Gosudarstvennye krest'iane i reforma P.D. Kiseleva* (Moscow, 1958), cited in Eklof, p. 44.
38. E.A. Zviaginstev, *Polveka zemskoi deiatel'nosti po narodnomu obrazovaniiu* (Moscow, 1915), cited in Eklov, p. 45.
39. G.T. Robinson, *Rural Russia under the Old Regime: A History of the Landlord and Peasant World and a Prologue to the Revolution of 1917* (Berkeley, 1967), pp. 126-7.
40. Eklov, *Russian Peasant Schools*, p. 25.
41. Ibid., p. 50.
42. Hans, *A History of Russian Educational Policy*, p. 96.
43. N.I. Pirogov, *Izbrannye pedagogicheskie sochineniia* (Moscow, 1952).
44. Hans, *A History of Russian Educational Policy*.
45. K.D. Ushinsky, *Izbrannye pedagogicheskie sochineniia* (Moscow, 1953); *Man As the Object of Education* (Moscow: Progress Books, 1978); *Selected Works* (Moscow: Progress Books, 1975). For Ushinsky's assessment of Pirogov see *Selected Works*, pp. 264-315.
46. J. McClelland *Autocrats and Academics: Education, Culture and Society in Tsarist Russia* (Chicago University Press, 1979).
47. See 'On the National Character of Public Education' and 'On Public Schools', *Selected Works*, pp. 100-207, 243-312.
48. Hans, *A History of Russian Educational Policy*, p. 101.
49. Ibid., p. 103.
50. Eklof, *Russian Peasant Schools*, p. 54-5.
51. Hans, *A History of Russian Educational Policy*, pp. 135-6.
52. Eklof, *Russian Peasant Schools*, pp. 68-9.
53. See Hans, *A History of Russian Educational Policy*, pp. 110-131; McClelland, *Autocrats and Academics*, pp. 26-9; Allen Sinel, *The Classroom and the Chancellery* (Cambridge, Mass., 1973).
54. Hans, *A History of Russian Eduational Policy*, pp. 123-4.
55. McClelland, *Autocrats and Academics*, p. 14.
56. Hans, *A History of Russian Educational Policy*, p. 110.
57. Sinel, *The Classroom and the Chancellery*, p. 250.
58. Ibid.
59. Hans, *A History of Russian Educational Policy*, pp. 119-20.
60. Ibid., p. 155.
61. Ibid., p. 157.
62. Ibid., p. 168.
63. Ibid., Chapter 7.
64. I.B. Petrov, *Voprosy narodnogo obrazovaniia*, cited in Eklof, *Russian Peasant Schools*, pp. 175-6.
65. Eklof, *Russian Peasant Schools*, p. 217.
66. Ibid., pp. 218-9.
67. Ibid.

68. Ibid.
69. A. Nikolaev, *Sel'skii uchitel'* (St. Petersburg, 1896), cited in Eklov, pp. 225-6.
70. I. Petrov, *Voprosy narodnogo obrazovaniia*, cited in Eklof, p. 233.
71. Eklof, *Russian Peasant Schools*, p. 233.
72. Ibid.
73. Ibid., p. 228.
74. Hans, *A History of Russian Educational Policy*, p. 233.
75. Eklof, *Russian Peasant Schools*, p. 161.
76. Ibid., p. 162.
77. Ibid., p. 165.
78. Ibid., pp, 285, 287, 293, 295.
79. Hans, *A History of Russian Educational Policy*, pp. 200, 238.
80. Ibid., Chapter 8.
81. Ibid.
82. Eklof, *Russian Peasant Schools*, pp. 285, 350.

CHAPTER III

1. Alexandra Tolstoy, *Tolstoy: A Life of My Father* (Belmont, Maine: Nordland Books, 1953); Ilya Tolstoy, *Tolstoy, My Father: Reminiscences* (London: Peter Owen, 1972); Alymer Maude, *Tolstoy* (2 vols.) (Oxford University Press, 1987); Pavel Biryukov, *Leo Tolstoy: His Life and Work* (New Yord: Scribner, 1906).
2. From an unfinished autobiographical sketch, *Notes of a Madman*, cited in Henri Troyat, *Tolstoy* (Penguin Books, 1967), p. 38.
3. Leo Tolstoy, *Childhood, Adolescence, Youth* (trans. Solasko) (Moscow: Progress Books, 1981).
4. Alexandra Tolstoy, *Tolstoy: A Life of My Father*, p. 21.
5. Ibid.
6. *Childhood, Adolescence, Youth*, p. 180-1.
7. Ibid., pp. 187-8.
8. Ibid., pp. 206-7.
9. Ibid., p. 224.
10. Ibid., p. 242.
11. Troyat, *Tolstoy*, p. 70.
12. *Childhood Adolescence, Youth*, Chapter XI.
13. Ibid., p. 321.
14. Alexander Tolstoy, *Tolstoy: A Life of My Father*, pp. 40-41.
15. From an early version of 'Adolescence' cited in Maude, *Tolstoy*, vol. I, p. 35.
16. *Tolstoy's Diaries* (ed. R.F. Christian) (London: The Athlone Press, 1985), vol. I, p. 7.
17. Ibid., p. 5.
18. Maude, *Tolstoy*, vol. I, p. 39.
19. *Tolstoy's Diaries*, vol. I, p. 11.
20. *Childhood Adolescence, Youth*, pp. 194-6.
21. Leo Tolstoy, *A Confession and other Religious Writings* (ed. Jane Kentish) (Penguin Books, 1987), p. 19.
22. Maude, *Tolstoy*, vol. I, p. 49, also see *Tolstoy's Diaries*, vol. I, p. 58.
23. Maude, *Tolstoy*, vol. I, p. 49.
24. *Tolstoy's Diaries*, vol. I, p. 92.
25. Maude, *Tolstoy*, vol. I, p. 55.

26. *Tolstoy's Diaries*, vol. I, p. 101.
27. Ibid., p. 112.
28. *Polnoye sobraniye sochinenii* (ed. Chertkov) (Moscow: 1949), vol. LV, pp. 361-2.
29. Maude, *Tolstoy*, vol. I, p. 204, 250, 257.
30. *Tolstoy's Diaries*, vol. I, p. 157.
31. *Tolstoy on Education* (trans. Leo Wiener) (University of Chicago Press, 1967).
32. Alexander Tolstoy, *Tolstoy: A Life of My Father*, p. 125.
33. Maude, *Tolstoy*, vol. I, p. 209.
34. *Polnoye sobraniye sochinenii*, vol. LX, pp. 339-40.
35. *Tolstoy on Education* (trans. Wiener), pp. 22-3.
36. Ibid., p. 22.
37. *Tolstoy's Diaries*, p. 158.
38. Victor Lucas, *Tolstoy in London* (London: Evans Bros., 1979), p. 49.
39. Ibid.
40. Maude, *Tolstoy*, vol. I, p. 224.
41. *Tolstoy's Diaries*, p. 157.
42. Maude, *Tolstoy*, vol. I, p. 248.
43. Alexandra Tolstoy, *Tolstoy: A Life of My Father*, pp. 115-6.
44. *Tolstoy on Education* (trans. Wiener), pp. 228-9.
45. Maude, *Tolstoy*, vol. I, p. 258.
46. *Tolstoy's Letters* (ed. R.F. Christian), vol. I (London: The Athlone Press, 1978), p. 151.
47. *Tolstoy's Diaries*, vol. I, p. 163.
48. *Tolstoy's Letters*, vol. I, p. 161.
49. Henri Troyat, *Tolstoy*, p. 309.
50. Maude, *Tolstoy*, vol. I, p. 259.
51. Alexandra Tolstoy, *Tolstoy: A Life of My Father*, p. 112; Maude, *Tolstoy*, vol. I, p. 258.
52. *Tolstoy's Letters*, vol. I, p. 160.
53. Ibid., p. 134.
54. Maude, *Tolstoy*, vol. I, p. 252.
55. Ibid.
56. Alexandra Tolstoy, *Tolstoy: A Life of My Father*, p. 112.
57. Vasilly Morozov, 'Recollections of a Pupil of the Yasnaya Polyana School' in *Reminiscences of Lev Tolstoi by his Contemporaries* (Moscow: Foreign Languages Publishing Houses, 1961), pp. 144-51.
58. Maude, *Tolstoy*, vol. I, p. 257-9.
59. *Tolstoy's Letters*, vol. I, pp. 157-8.
60. Maude, *Tolstoy*, vol. I, p. 290.
61. Ibid.
62. Tolstoy himself told Maude the main reason for the closure of the school was his marriage. (*Tolstoy*, vol. I, p. 291).
63. Troyat, *Tolstoy*, p. 309.
64. Maude, *Tolstoy*, vol. I, pp. 313-6.
65. Alexandra Tolstoy, *Tolstoy: A Life of My Father*, p. 197.
66. Ibid., pp. 197-8.
67. *Tolstoy's Letters*, vol. I, pp. 240-1.
68. *Polnoye sobraniye sochinenii*, vol. LXI, pp. 283-4.
69. Ilya Tolstoy, *Tolstoy, My Father*, p. 17-18.
70. Alexandra Tolstoy: *Tolstoy: A Life of My Father*, pp. 200-1.
71. *Tolstoy's Letters*, vol. I, p. 242.
72. Alexandra Tolstoy, *Tolstoy: A Life of My Father*, p. 199.

73. *Polnoye sobraniye sochinenii*, vol. LXI, pp. 304-5.
74. Ibid., pp. 276-7.
75. Troyat, *Tolstoy*, p. 460.
76. *Polnoye sobraniye sochinenii*, vol. LXI, pp. 323-4.
77. Maude, *Tolstoy*, vol. I, p. 344.
78. Alan Pinch, 'The Historical Background', *Tolstoy on Education* (eds. A. Pinch and M. Armstrong) (London: The Athlone Press, 1982), p. 27.
79. David Holbrook, *English for the Rejected* (Cambridge University Press, 1962).
80. Maude, *Tolstoy*, vol. II, pp. 344-6.
81. Ibid.
82. *Tolstoy's Letters*, vol I, p. 273.
83. Leo Tolstoy, *War and Peace* (trans. Louise and Aylmer Maude) (London: Macmillan/Oxford University Press, 1977), p. 1218.
84. *Polnoye sobraniye sochinenii*, vol. XXIII, p. 16.
85. *Tolstoy's Diaries*, vol. I, p. 192.
86. A.N. Wilson, *Tolstoy* (London: Hamish Hamilton, 1988), p. 309.
87. Derek Leon, *Tolstoy: His Life and Work* (London: Routledge and Kegan Paul, 1944), p. 194; Ernest Simmons, *Leo Tolstoy* (Boston, Little Brown, 1949), vol. I, p. 365.
88. A.N. Wilson, *Tolstoy*, p. 337.
89. Troyat, *Tolstoy*, p. 602.
90. Ibid., p. 604.
91. Alexander Tolstoy, *Tolstoy: A Life of My Father*, p. 272.
92. Ibid., p. 327.
93. Ibid., p. 319.
94. Ray Monk, *Ludwig Wittgenstein* (London: Cape, 1990), pp. 115-6.
95. Alexandra Tolstoy, *Tolstoy: A Life of My Father*, pp. 261-2.
96. Ibid., p. 279.
97. Leo Tolstoy, *Stories* (trans. Wettlin/Altschuler) (Moscow: Raduga Publishers, 1983), p. 673.
98. *Tolstoy's Letters*, vol. II, pp. 613-4.
99. Troyat, *Tolstoy*, p. 673.
100. *Tolstoy's Letters*, vol. II, p. 469.
101. Troyat, *Tolstoy*, p. 777.
102. Ibid., p. 775.
103. Leo Tolstoy, *Essays from Tula* (London: Sheppard Press, 1948), pp. 19-65.
104. *Tolstoy's Diaries*, vol. II, pp. 516-7.
105. Ibid., pp. 814-5.
106. Troyat, *Tolstoy*, p. 821.
107. *Tolstoy's Diaries*, vol. II, p. 565.
108. Alexandra Tolstoy, *Tolstoy: A Life of My Father*, p. 480.
109. Troyat, *Tolstoy*, p. 845.
110. Ibid., p. 848.
111. Ibid., p. 874. See also Alexandra Tolstoy, *Tolstoy: A Life of My Father*, p. 483 and *Tolstoy's Letters*, vol. II, pp. 692, 706-8.

CHAPTER IV

1. 'Progress and Education', *Tolstoy on Education* (trans. Wiener), p. 182.
2. Ibid., p. 159.
3. 'On Popular Education', *Tolstoy on Education* (trans. Wiener), p. 31.
4. L. Tolstoy, *War and Peace*, pp. 1083-4.
5. L. Tolstoy, *War and Peace*, p. 1296; *Anna Karenina*, pp. 492, 704-8, 763-6, *Resurrection*, pp. 457-61.
6. L. Tolstoy, *A Confession and Other Religious Writings*, pp. 172-7.
7. Ibid., p. 221.
8. See Note 26, Chapter III.
9. 'Education and Culture', *Tolstoy on Education* (trans. Wiener), p. 143.
10. Ibid.
11. Ibid., pp. 149-50.
12. Ibid.
13. 'Progress and Education', p. 31.
14. Pinch and Armstrong, *Tolstoy on Education*, p. 29.
15. R. Archambault, Introduction to *Tolstoy on Education* (trans. Wiener), pp. ix-x.
16. 'Progress and Education', p. 163.
17. 'Education and Culture', pp. 105-110.
18. Ibid., pp. 107-8.
19. Ibid.
20. Ibid., p. 111.
21. Ibid., pp. 144-6.
22. See Chapter II, Section 2.
23. 'A Project for Popular Schools', *Tolstoy on Education* (trans. Wiener), p. 63.
24. Ibid., pp. 77-8.
25. Ibid., pp. 61-2.
26. 'On Popular Education', p. 3.
27. Ibid., p. 5.
28. Ibid., pp. 11-12.
29. Ibid., pp. 12-14.
30. Ibid., p. 22.
31. Ibid., pp. 24-5.
32. For a detailed analysis of Dewey's theories of experience, knowledge and truth see Theodore Brameld, *Patterns in Educational Philosophy* (New York: Holt Rinehart and Winston, 1955), pp. 91-178. See also, John Dewey, *Essays in Experimental Logic* (University of Chicago Press, 1916), *Experience and Nature* (New York: Open Books, 1925) and *The Quest for Certainty* (New York: Minton, Batch & Co., 1929).
33. L. Tolstoy, *A Confession and Other Religious Writings*, pp. 50-1, 53.
34. 'On Popular Education', pp. 29-30.
35. 'On Teaching the Rudiments', *Tolstoy on Education* (trans. Wiener), p. 58.
36. Ibid., p. 35.
37. Ibid., pp. 36-7.
38. Ibid., pp. 39-40.
39. 'The School at Yasnaya Polyana', *Tolstoy on Education* (trans. Wiener), pp. 309-10.
40. 'On Popular Education;, p. 14.
41. Ibid., p. 15.
42. 'The School at Yasnaya Polyana, p. 310.
43. Ibid., p. 311.
44. Ibid., pp. 334-5.

45. Martin Buber, *Between Man and Man* (London: Fontana, 1979), p. 110.
46. L. Tolstoy, 'The School at Yasnaya Polyana', pp. 341-2.
47. Ibid., pp. 346-7.
48. *Tolstoy on Education* (trans. Wiener), p. xiv.
49. 'The School at Yasnaya Polyana, pp. 233-5.
50. 'On Popular Education', pp. 30-31.
51. Ibid., p. 31.
52. Buber, *Between Man and Man*, p. 125-6.
53. 'Progress and Education', p. 155.
54. Ibid., pp. 155-6.
55. Ibid., pp. 189-90.
56. 'On Popular Education', p. 18.
57. 'On Teaching the Rudiments', p. 44.
58. Ibid., pp. 57-8.
59. Ibid., p. 83.
60. Ibid.
61. 'The School at Yasnaya Polyana', p. 232.
62. Ibid., pp. 321-2.
63. Ibid., p. 338.
64. Ibid., pp. 326-7.
65. 'Education and Culture', pp. 149-50.
66. 'Progress and Education', pp. 189-90.
67. 'On Popular Education', p. 8.
68. 'A Project for Popular Schools', p. 77.
69. 'The School at Yasnaya Polyana', p. 346.
70. Ibid., p. 227.
71. Ibid., p. 234.
72. Ibid., pp. 258-60.
73. Ibid., pp. 241-2.
74. 'A Project for Popular Schools', pp. 83-4.
75. Maude, *Tolstoy*, vol. I, p. 49.
76. *Polnoye sobraniye sochinenii*, vol. II, p. 345.
77. Jean Jacques Rousseau, *Emile* (London: Dent, 1961), p. 43.
78. Ibid., p. 210.
79. Ibid., p. 19.
80. Ibid., p. 181.
81. e.g. T.G.S. Cain, *Tolstoy* (London: Paul Elek, 1977), pp. 9-10.
82. *Tolstoy's Diaries*, vol. I, p. 70. See also p. 55.
83. Rousseau, *Emile*, pp. 80, 125.
84. K. Ushinsky, *Man as the Object of Education* (Moscow: Progress Books, 1987), p. 523.
85. Ibid., p. 529.
86. Ibid., p. 545.
87. Ibid.
88. Ibid., pp. 513-4.
89. Ibid., pp. 532, 540.
90. Ibid., pp. 137-8.
91. Ibid., p. 532. See also 'The Native Language' and 'The Russian Language' in K. Ushinsky, *Selected Works* (Moscow: 1985), pp. 240-263, 315-342.
92. Ushinsky, *Man as the Object of Education*, p. 520.
93. Ibid.

94. Ibid., p. 521.
95. Jean Heinrich Pestalozzi, *How Gertrude Teaches Her Children* (London: Swan Sonnerschein, 1907), pp. 56-7.
96. Ibid.
97. Ibid.
98. J.A. Green, *Pestalozzi's Educational Writings* (London: Arnold, 1912), pp. 18, 156.
99. Pestalozzi, *How Gertrude Teachers Her Children*, pp. 86-88.
100. Ibid.

CHAPTER V

1. *Tolstoy's Diaries*, p. 226.
2. Ibid., p. 330.
3. John Bayley, *Tolstoy and the Novel* (London: Chatto and Windus, 1966), p. 33.
4. Ibid., pp. 59-60.
5. Cain, *Tolstoy*, p. vii.
6. Ibid., p. 66.
7. Ibid., p. 63.
8. L. Tolstoy, *What is Art and Essays on Art* (ed. Aylmer Maude) (Oxford University Press, 1930).
9. Ibid., p. 10.
10. Ibid., pp. 9-10.
11. Ibid.
12. Ibid., pp. 48-9.
13. Ibid., p. 51.
14. Ibid., p. 53.
15. Ibid., pp. 54-5.
16. Ibid., p. 56.
17. Ibid., 263.
18. Ibid.
19. Richard Wagner, 'Religion und Kunst' in John Chancellor, *Wagner* (London: Granada, 1980), p. 275.
20. L. Tolstoy, *What is Art*, p. 272.
21. Ibid., p. 275.
22. Ibid., pp. 268-9.
23. Ibid., p. 269.
24. Ibid., p. 273.
25. Ibid., pp. 176-7.
26. Ibid., p. 148.
27. Maude, Introduction to *What is Art*, p. vii.
28. Bayley, *Tolstoy and the Novel*, p. 15.
29. *The Letters of James Joyce* (ed. Stuart Gilbert) (London: Macmillan, 1957), p. 364.
30. Cain, *Tolstoy*, p. 139.
31. 'On Popular Education, p. 109.
32. Paulo Freire, *Pedagogy of the Oppressed* (Penguin Books, 1972), pp. 90-95. See John Dixon, *Growth Through English* (London: Oxford University Press, 1967; R. Protherough, *Encouraging Writing* (London: Methuen, 1983); Margaret Meek, *Achieving Literacy* (London: Routledge, 1983).
33. 'On Teaching the Rudiments', p. 40.

34. 'The School at Yasnaya Polyana', pp. 230-1.
35. 'On Teaching the Rudiments', pp. 44-5.
36. Ibid., p. 58.
37. 'The School at Yasnaya Polyana', p. 261.
38. Ibid.
39. Ibid., p. 267.
40. Ibid., pp. 267-8.
41. Ibid., p. 268.
42. Ibid., p. 269.
43. Ibid., p. 270.
44. Ibid., p. 271.
45. Ibid.
46. Ibid., p. 273.
47. Ibid., p. 276.
48. Ibid.
49. Ibid., p. 275.
50. See, for example, Charles Suhor, 'Content and Process in the English Curriculum', Association for Supervision and Curriculum Development Yearbook, Alexandra VA, 1988, pp. 31-52.
51. 'The School at Yasnaya Polyana', p. 275.
52. 'How Peasant Children Write', *Tolstoy on Education* (trans. Wiener), pp. 193-4.
53. Ibid., p. 197.
54. Ibid., pp. 197-8.
55. Ibid., p. 197.
56. Ibid., p. 198.
57. Ibid., p. 201.
58. Ibid., p. 207.
59. Ibid., p. 223.
60. 'The School at Yasnaya Polyana', pp. 288-9.
61. Ibid., pp. 279, 289.
62. Ibid., pp. 289-90.
63. Ibid., pp. 280-2.
64. Ibid., pp. 282-4.
65. e.g. James Britton, *The Development of Writing Abilities* (London: Macmillan, 1975); Andrew Wilkinson, *Assessing Language Development* (Oxford University Press, 1980).
66. 'The School at Yasnaya Polyana', pp. 284-7.
67. Ibid., pp. 285-8.
68. Ibid., p. 340.
69. Ibid., pp. 343-4.
70. Ibid., p. 341.
71. Ibid., pp. 349-50.
72. Ibid., p. 351.
73. Ibid., p. 345.
74. See Alexander Tolstoy, *Tolstoy, A Life of My Father*, pp. 40-41.
75. 'The School at Yasnaya Polyana', pp. 341-2.
76. Ibid., p. 355.
77. Ibid., p. 357.
78. Ibid., p. 345.
79. Ibid., pp. 354-5.

80. Ibid., pp. 357-8.
81. Ibid., p. 360.
82. Ibid., pp. 358-9.
83. See Thomas Darlington, *Education in Russia*, pp. 296-99.

CHAPTER VI

 1. L. Tolstoy, *War and Peace*, pp. 380-1.
 2. Ibid., p. 725.
 3. Ibid., p. 1180.
 4. L. Tolstoy, *Anna Karenina*, pp. 767-8.
 5. L. Tolstoy, *A Confession and Other Religious Writings*, p. 50.
 6. Ibid., p. 51.
 7. Ibid., pp. 58-9.
 8. S. Kierkegaard, *Concluding Unscientific Postcript* (Princeton University Press, 1972), p. 257.
 9. *Tolstoy's Diaries*, vol. II, p. 416.
10. S. Kierkegaard, *The Sickness Unto Death* (Princeton University Press, 1970), p. 256; Miguel de Unamuno, *Tragic Sense of Life* (New York: Dover Publications, 1954), p. 106.
11. Tolstoy, *A Confession*, p. 167.
12. Ibid., pp. 167-8.
13. Ibid., p. 171.
14. Ibid., p. 199.
15. Boris Pasternak, *Doctor Zhivago* (London: Collins and Harvill, 1958), p. 49.
16. Ibid., p. 19.
17. Boris Pasternak, 'Safe Conduct' in *Collected Prose of Boris Pasternak* (ed. Livingstone) (New York: Praeger, 1977), p. 22.
18. Tolstoy, *War and Peace*, pp. 1083-4.
19. Ibid., p. 1218.
20. Tolstoy, *Anna Karenina*, p. 492.
21. Ibid., p. 765.
22. Tolstoy, *Resurrection*, pp. 460-1.
23. 'A Reply to the Synod's Edict' in A.N. Wilson, *The Lion and the Honeycomb: Tolstoy's Religious Writings* (London: Collins, 1987), p. 129.
24. Tolstoy, *A Confession*, p. 172.
25. F. Dostoevsky, *The Brothers Karamazov* (trans. Garnett) (London: Landsborough Publications, 1958), pp. 49-50.
26. Kierkegaard, *Concluding Unscientific Postscript*, p. 290.
27. R.G. Smith, *The Last Years' Journals, 1853-55* (London: Collins, 1965), pp. 99-100.
28. Unamuno, *Tragic Sense of Life*, pp. 139, 150.
29. Ibid., pp. 169-70.
30. Martin Buber, *I and Thou* (Edinburgh: Clark, 1937). See Part III.
31. Gabriel Marcel, *The Philosophy of Existentialism* (New York: Citadel Press, 1961), pp. 35-6.
32. Karl Jaspers, *Philosophie*, vol. II (Berlin: Springer Verlag, 1932), pp. 64-5.
33. E. Levinas, 'God and Philosophy' in *The Levinas Reader* (ed. Hand) (Oxford: Blackwell, 1989), pp. 180-1.
34. L. Tolstoy, *My Religion* (London: Walter Scott, 1889), p. 176.

35. Ibid., p. 178.
36. L. Tolstoy, *Stories*, p. 338.
37. L. Tolstoy, *War and Peace*, pp. 1218-9.
38. Dostoevsky, *The Brothers Karamazov*, p. 285.
39. Karl Jaspers, *The Perennial Scope of Philosophy* (London: Routledge and Kegan Paul, 1950), p. 39.
40. Tolstoy, *War and Peace*, p. 1083.
41. Tolstoy, *A Confession*, p. 173.
42. Tolstoy, *My Religion*, pp. 143-4.
43. Ibid., p. 166.
44. Tolstoy, *War and Peace*, p. 1083.
45. Pasternak, *Doctor Zhivago*, p. 70.
46. Ibid., p. 71.
47. Dostoevsky, *The Brothers Karamazov*, pp. 49-59; Tolstoy, *War and Peace*, p. 1083.
48. E. Levinas, 'God and Philosophy', p. 177.
49. Ibid.
50. Unamuno, *Tragic Sense of Life*, p. 114.
51. Tolstoy, *A Confession*, p. 172-3.
52. Ibid., pp. 73-5.
53. Ibid., p. 158.
54. 'A Reply to the Synod's Edict' in Wilson, *The Lion and the Honeycomb*, p. 130.
55. Tolstoy, *A Confession*, p. 172.
56. Ibid., pp. 173-4.
57. L. Tolstoy, *The Kingdom of God is Within You* (trans. Garnett) (London, 1894), vol. I, p. 234.
58. Dostoevsky, *The Brothers Karamazov*, p. 286.
59. Ibid.
60. Tolstoy, *My Religion*, pp. 123-4.
61. M. Buber, *I and Thou*, p. 66.
62. L. Tolstoy, 'Religion and Morality' in *A Confession and other Religious Writings*, p. 137.
63. Ibid., p. 140.
64. Ibid., p. 141.
65. Ibid., p. 142.
66. Ibid.
67. Ibid., p. 143.
68. Martin Buber, *Eclipse of God* (New York: Humanities Press, 1972), p. 46.
69. Tolstoy, 'Religion and Morality', p. 145.
70. Martin Buber, *Two Types of Faith* (New York: Harper and Row, 1961), pp. 7-15.
71. Tolstoy, 'Religion and Morality', pp. 145-6.
72. Tolstoy, *Anna Karenina*, p. 765.
73. Tolstoy, *War and Peace*, p. 527.
74. Tolstoy, *Stories*, p. 294.
75. Ibid., p. 338.
76. *Tolstoy's Diaries*, vol. I, p. 56.
77. *A Confession*, pp. 213-4.
78. Ibid.
79. Ibid.
80. 'A Reply to the Synod's Edict', p. 129.
81. *Tolstoy's Diaries*, vol. I, p. 230.

82. Ibid.
83. Dostoevsky, *The Brothers Karamazov*, p. 226.
84. Martin Buber, *Between Man and Man* (London: Fontana Books, 1979), p. 140.
85. Tolstoy, *Anna Karenina*, p. 189.
86. Ibid., p. 738.
87. Tolstoy, *Stories*, p. 183.
88. Ibid., pp. 193-4.
89. Tolstoy, *Resurrection*, p. 65.
90. Ibid., pp. 103-4.
91. Ibid., p. 565.
92. Tolstoy, *War and Peace*, p. 1016.
93. Tolstoy, *Anna Karenina*, p. 387.
94. Ibid., p. 404.
95. Ibid., p. 498.
96. Nadezhda Mandelstam, *Hope Abandoned* (Penguin Books, 1980), pp. 303, 392.
97. Tolstoy, *Resurrection*, p. 137.
98. Ibid., p. 156.
99. Ibid., p. 197.
100. Ibid., pp. 581-2.
101. Buber, *Between Man and Man*, p. 134.
102. Tolstoy, *A Confession*, pp. 19-20.
103. Ibid., pp. 200-1.
104. Poggioli, 'Tolstoy As Man and Artist', p. 19.
105. Tolstoy, *A Confession*, p. 168.
106. Tolstoy, *My Religion*, p. ix.
107. Ibid., p. 2.
108. Ibid., pp. 6-7.
109. 'The School at Yasnaya Polyana', p. 307.
110. Ibid., pp. 308-9.
111. Ibid., p. 294.
112. Ibid., pp. 297-8.
113. Ibid., pp. 293-4.
114. Ibid., pp. 31-32.
115. Ibid., pp. 309-10.
116. Ibid., pp. 312-13.
117. Ibid., p. 310.
118. Ibid., pp. 302-3.
119. Ibid., pp. 305-6.
120. Ibid., p. 307.
121. Ibid., pp. 313-14.

CHAPTER VII

1. L. Tolstoy, *Anna Karenina*, pp. 236-7.
2. S. Kierkegaard, *The Works of Love* (trans. Swenson) (New York: Kennikat Press, 1946), pp. 18-19.
3. Martin Buber, *The Knowledge of Man* (New York: Harper and Row, 1966), p. 108.
4. E. Levinas, 'God and Philosophy', p. 181.
5. Dostoevsky, *The Brothers Karamazov*, p. 210.
6. Ibid., p. 286.

7. Kierkegaard, *The Works of Love*, p. 32.
8. Dostoevsky, *The Brothers Karamazov*, p. 50.
9. Tolstoy, *Anna Karenina*, p. 243.
10. Ibid., p. 770.
11. Tolstoy, *Resurrection*, p. 325.
12. Ibid., p. 520.
13. Ibid., p. 527.
14. Tolstoy, *A Confession and Other Religious Writings*, pp. 212-13.
15. Ibid., pp. 217-18.
16. L. Tolstoy, *Essays from Tula* (with a Preface by Nikolai Berdyaev) (London: Sheppard Press, 1988), pp. 19-64, 65-136.
17. 'Bethink Yourselves', *Essays From Tula*, p. 51.
18. 'An Appeal to Social Reformers', *Essays from Tula*, p. 150.
19. Ibid., p. 152.
20. Ibid., pp. 156-7.
21. 'Love one Another', *Essays from Tula*, pp. 284-91.
22. See Paulo Freire, *Pedagogy of the Oppressed*, Chapter II and III.
23. 'Bethink Yourselves', pp. 34-5.
24. Ibid., p. 44.
25. Ibid., p. 46.
26. Ibid.
27. 'I Cannot Be Silent', *Essays from Tula*, pp. 187-8.
28. 'The End of the Age', p. 276.
29. Martin Buber, *The Origin and Meaning of Hasidism* (New York: Horizon Press, 1960), p. 25.
30. F. Dostoevsky, *The Diary of a Writer* (Haslemere, Surrey: Ianmead Limited, 1984), pp. 783-93, 812-13.
31. *Tolstoy's Letters*, vol. I, pp. 692, 706-8. See also Alexandra Tolstoy, *Tolstoy: A Life of My Father*, p. 483.
32. A.N. Wilson, *Tolstoy*, p. 101.
33. N. Berdyaev, Preface to *Essays from Tula*.
34. *Polnoye sobraniye sochinenii*, vol. LXII, p. 7.
35. See Maxim Gorky, *Reminiscences of Tolstoy, Chekhov and Andreyev* (trans. Koteliansky and Woolf) (London: Hogarth, 1968), p. 31.
36. *Polnoye sobraniye sochinenii*, vol. LXV, p. 35.
37. Nikolai Berdyaev, Preface to *Essays from Tula*; V.V. Zenkovsky, *A History of Russian Philosophy* (trans. Kline) (London: Routledge and Kegan Paul, 1953), p. 392.
38. S. Kierkegaard, *Christian Discourses* (trans. Lowrie) (Princeton University Press, 1971).
39. *Tolstoy's Letters*, vol. I, p. 469.
40. Maude, *Tolstoy*, vol II, p. 252-3.
41. Berdyaev, Preface to *Essays from Tula*, p. 15.
42. Tolstoy, *A Confession*, p. 76.
43. Ibid., pp. 176-7.
44. Ibid., pp. 188-9.
45. Ibid., pp. 188-9.
46. S.R. Hopper (ed.), *Lift Up Your Eyes: The Religious Writings of Leo Tolstoy* (New York: Julian Press, 1960), p. 312.
47. Tolstoy, *My Religion*, p. 13.
48. Tolstoy, *A Confession*, p. 181.

49. Ibid., p. 195.
50. Ibid., p. 203.
51. Ibid., pp. 214-15.
52. 'Bethink Yourselves', p. 21.
53. Ibid., pp. 23-26.
54. 'A Letter on the Peace Conference', *Essays from Tula*, p. 220.
55. The letter was Tolstoy's response to a message he had received from a group of Swedish pacifists regarding the Tsar's Peace Conference of 1899.
56. 'A Letter to the Peace Conference', p. 221.
57. 'I Cannot be Silent', p. 177.
58. Ibid., pp. 178-9.
59. Ibid., p. 179.
60. Ibid., pp. 186-7.
61. 'The First Step' in *The Lion and the Honeycomb: Tolstoy's Religious Writings* (ed. Wilson), p. 100.
62. 'Thou Shalt Kill No One', *Essays from Tula*, p. 203.
63. *Polnoye sobraniye sochinenii*, vol. LXVII, p. 245.
64. 'The End of the Age', *Essays from Tula*, p. 237.
65. 'Thou Shalt Kill No One', pp. 210-11.
66. Maude, *Tolstoy*, vol. II, pp. 223, 258-9.
67. William Edgerton, 'The Puzzle of Tolstoy's Worldwide Social Influence', Unpublished Paper, World Conference for Soviet and East European Studies, Harrogate, July 1990.
68. Maude, *Tolstoy*, vol. II, pp. 252-3.
69. 'The Slavery of Our Times', *Essays from Tula*, p. 71-2.
70. Ibid.
71. Ibid., pp. 73-4.
72. Ibid., pp. 95-6.
73. Ibid., p. 105.
74. Ibid., p. 108.
75. A full translation of Tolstoy's letter to his son, Mikhail, is given in *The Lion and the Honeycomb* (ed. Wilson), p. 145.
76. 'The End of the Age', *Essays from Tula*, pp. 272-3.
77. Ibid., pp. 250-1.
78. Ibid., pp. 232-3. See also *Essays from Tula*, pp. 90, 150, 225.
79. Ibid., pp. 258-9.
80. 'An Appeal to Social Reformers', *Essays from Tula*, p. 137.
81. Ibid., pp. 146-7.
82. Ibid.
83. Ibid., p. 148.
84. Ibid., pp. 151-2.
85. 'The End of the Age', pp. 224-5.
86. 'An Appeal to Social Reformers', p. 152-3.
87. 'The End of the Age', p. 267.
88. 'Love One Another', pp. 291-2.
89. Dostoevsky, *The Diary of a Writer*, pp. 811-13.
90. Dosteovsky, *The Brothers Karamazov*, p. 285.
91. Ibid., p. 270.
92. Dostoevsky, *The Devils* (trans. Magarshack) (Penguin, 1971), p. 256.
93. Dostoevsky, *The Brothers Karamazov*, p. 24.
94. Dosteovsky, *The Devils*, p. 89.

95. Tolstoy, *A Confession*, p. 137.
96. Dostoevsky, *The Brothers Karamazov*, pp. 282-3.
97. A.B. Goldenweizer, *Talks with Tolstoy* (New York: Horizon, 1969), p. 173.
98. Ibid., p. 174.
99. Yaacov Oved, *Two Hundred Years of American Communes* (Oxford: Transaction Books, 1988), pp. 275, 283.
100. Rudolf Jans, *Tolstoj in Nederland* (Bussum, 1952), pp. 99-108.
101. Fernano Santivan, *Memorias de un Tolstoyano* (Santiago, Chile: 1955), cited in Edgerton, 'The Puzzle of Tolstoy's Worldwide Social Influence'.
102. C. Fisher, *Lev Tolstoi in Japan* (Wiesbaden, 1969), cited in Edgerton, 'The Puzzle of Tolstoy's Worldwide Social Influence'.
103. *Croydon Brotherhood Intelligence*, January 1985, cited in M.J. de K. Holman, *The Purleigh Colony: Tolstoyan Togetherness in the Late 1890s* in M. Jones, *New Essays on Tolstoy* (Cambridge University Press, 1978), pp. 194-222.
104. *The Labour Annual*, London, 1896, cited in Holman/Jones, p. 198.
105. Jones, *New Essays on Tolstoy*, p. 201.
106. Maude, *Tolstoy*, vol. II, pp. 378-80.
107. Mark Popovsky, *Russkie muzhiki raskazivayut: posledovateli L.N. Tolstovo v sovetskom soyuze, 1918-1977* (Russian Peasants Tell Their Story: Followers of Leo Tolstoy in the Soviet Union, 1918-1977) (London: Overseas Publications Interchange Limited, 1983).
108. *Vospominaniye krest'yan tolstovtsev, 1910-1930* (Memoirs of Peasant Tolstoyans, 1910-1930) (Moscow, 1989).
109. Ibid., pp. 459-70.
110. Ibid.
111. Ibid., pp. 465-467.
112. Popovsky, *Russkie muzhiki*, pp. 83-4.
113. *Vospominaniye krest'yan tolstovtsev*, pp. 204-5.
114. Edgerton, 'The Puzzle of Tolstoy's Worldwide Social Influence', pp. 22-3.
115. Ibid., p. 25.

CHAPTER VIII

1. For a discussion of Heidegger's views on religion see Martin Buber, *Eclipse of God*, pp. 70-78.
2. John Dewey, *The Child and the Curriculum* and *The School and Society* (University of Chicago Press, 1962); *Democracy and Education* (New York: Macmillan, 1966).
3. John Dewey, *Experience and Education* (New York: Collier-Macmillan, 1963).
4. R.S. Peters, 'John Dewey's Philosophy of Education' in *John Dewey Reconsidered* (London: Routledge and Kegan Paul, 1974).
5. In his essay Peters wrote: 'He develops a very one-sided view of man that completely ignores certain features of the human condition. First, Dewey ignores the purely personal life of human beings. By that I don't just mean his failure to emphasise the importance of respect for persons in his account of democracy, nor his attack on the 'rottenness' of individual attempts at self-improvement; I mean also his neglect of interpersonal relationships and the education of the emotions. It is significant that he makes practically no mention of the role of literature in education. Literature is

singularly unamenable to the problem-solving method of learning and often concerns itself with the predicaments of man rather than his problems'. (*John Dewey Reconsidered*, pp. 118-19).

6. V. Sukhomlinsky, *To Children I Give My Heart* (Moscow: Progress Books, 1982).
7. e.g. Michael Rutter, *Fifteen Thousand Hours* (London: Open Books, 1979); M. Gold and D. Mann, *Expelled to a Friendlier Place* (Ann Arbor: University of Michigan Press, 1984); P. Mortimore, *School Matters* (London: Open Books, 1988); B. Wilson, *Successful Secondary Schools* (Lewes: The Falmer Press, 1988).
8. Tillich's tribute to Buber was delivered at a Memorial Service held at the Park Avenue Synagogue in New York City in July 1965. For the text of his tribute see Maurice Friedman, *Martin Buber's Life and Work*, vol. III (New York: Dutton: 1983), pp. 471-2.
9. Tolstoy, 'The School at Yasnaya Polyana', p. 347.
10. Jerome Bruner, *Actual Minds: Possible Worlds* (Harvard University Press, 1986); David Holbrook, *English for Meaning* (Windsor: NFER, 1978); Peter Abbs, *English within the Arts* (London: Hodder and Stoughton, 1982); John Dixon, *Growth Through English* (London: Oxford University Press, 1967); Margaret Meek, *Achieving Literacy* (London: Routledge, 1983).
11. David Holbrook, *English for the Rejected* (Cambridge University Press, 1962).
12. Peter Abbs, *English within the Arts*; Robert Protherough, *Encouraging Writing* (London: Methuen, 1983).
13. R.V. Sampson, *Tolstoy: The Discovery of Peace* (London: Heinemann, 1973).
14. Vaclav Havel, *Living in Truth* (London: Faber, 1986), p. 118.
15. Isaiah Berlin, 'Tolstoy and Enlightenment' in *Tolstoy: A Collection of Critical Essays* (ed. Matlaw) (Englewood: Prentice-Hall, 1967), p. 51.

Bibliography

Adams, R.J. 'Tolstoy and Children's Art: Sincerity and Expression', *Art and Education*, 26, March, 1973, pp. 4-5.

Baudouin, Charles, *Tolstoy: The Teacher* (New York: Dutton, 1923).

Bayley, John, *Tolstoy and the Novel* (London: Chatto and Windus, 1966).

Berlin, Isaiah, *The Hedgehog and the Fox: An Essay on Tolstoy's View of History* (New York: Simon and Schuster, 1953)

Biryukov, Pavel, *Leo Tolstoy: His Life and Work* (New York: Scribner, 1906).

Bunnell, W.S., 'Tolstoy and Freedom: An Examination of the Implications of His Educational Ideals', *Research Studies*, 11, January, 1955, pp. 32-51.

Cain, T.G.S., *Tolstoy* (London: Paul Elek, 1977).

Calam, John, 'Tolstoy on Education', *Saturday Review of Literature*, 51, March, 1963, p. 80.

Chertkov, Vladimir, *The Last Days of Tolstoy* (New York: Kraus, 1973).

Cecil, David, 'Some Reflections on the Art of Leo Tolstoy', *Oxford Slavonic Papers*, XI, pp.60-68.

R.F.Christian. *Tolstoy: A Critical Introduction* (Cambridge University Press: 1969).

_____ *Tolstoy's War and Peace: A Study* (Oxford, Clarendon Press, 1962).

Crankshaw, Edward, *Tolstoy: The Making of a Novelist* (New York: Viking, 1974).

Crosby, Ernest H., *Tolstoy and his Message* (London: Fifield, 1911).

_____ *Tolstoy as a Schoolmaster* (Chicago: Hammersmark, 1904).

Crauford, Alexander, *The Religion and Ethics of Tolstoy* (London: Unwin, 1912).

Darlington, Thomas, *Education in Russia*, Special Reports on Education, Vol. XXIII (London, 1909).

Davis, A., 'Tolstoy's Magic Rod: The Tolstoy School and Museum at Yasnaya Polyana', *Survey*, 49, March 1923, pp. 698, 740.

Duane, Michael, 'Tolstoy at School', *New Society*, 7 March, 1968, pp. 351-2.

Eklof, B., *Russian Peasant Schools* (University of California Press, 1986).

Florinsky, Michael T., *Russia: A History and Interpretation* (New York: Macmillan, 1953).

Florovsky, George, 'Three Masters: The Quest for Religion in the Nineteenth Century', *Comparative Literature Studies*, 3, 1966, pp. 119-137.

Goldenweizer, Alexander, *Talks With Tolstoy* (New York Horizon Press, 1969).

Goncharov, N., 'Pedagogical Ideas and Practice of L.N. Tolstoy', *Soviet Education*, 4, October, 1962, pp. 3-15.

Gorky, Maxim, *Reminiscences of Tolstoy, Chekhov and Andreyev* (London: Hogarth, 1968).

Greenwood, E.B., 'Tolstoy, Wittgenstein, Schopenhauer', *Encounter*, XXXVI, April, 1971, pp. 60-72.

_____ *Tolstoy : The Comprehensive Vision* (New York: St. Martin's Press, 1975).

Gustafson, Richard, *Leo Tolstoy: Resident and Stranger* (Princeton University Press, 1986).

Hans, Nicholas, *A History of Russian Educational Policy, 1701-1917*, (London: P.S. King, 1931).

Hayman, Ronald, *Tolstoy* (London: Routledge and Kegan Paul,1970).

Heier, E., 'Tolstoy and Nihilism', *Canadian Slavonic Papers*, XI, No.4, 1969, pp. 464-465.

Jepsen, Laura, *From Achilles to Christ: The Myth of the Hero in Tolstoy's War and Peace* (Tallahassee, Florida, 1978).

Johnson, William H., *Russia's Educational Heritage* (Pittsburg: Carnegie Press, 1950).

Jones, Malcolm (ed.), *New Essays on Tolstoy* (Cambridge University Press, 1978).

Kenworthy, John, *Tolstoy: His Life and Works* (New York: Haskell, 1971).

Knowles, A.V. (ed.), *Tolstoy: The Critical Heritage* (London: Routledge and Kegan Paul, 1978).

Kuzminskaya, Tatiana, *Tolstoy as I Knew Him: My Life at Home and at Yasnaya Polyana* (New York: Macmillan, 1948).

Leary, Daniel B., *Education and Autocracy in Russia from the Origin to the Bolsheviks* (University of Buffalo Press, 1919).

Leon, Derek, *Tolstoy: His Life and Work* (London: Routledge and Kegan Paul, 1944).

Lucas, Victor, *Tolstoy in London* (London: Evans Brothers, 1979).

McClelland, J., *Autocrats and Academics: Education, Culture and Society in Tsarist Russia* (Chicago University Press, 1979).

Masaryk, Thomas, *The Spirit of Russia: Studies in History, Literature and Philosophy* (New York: Macmillan, 1961).

Matlaw, R. (ed.), *Tolstoy: A Collection of Critical Essays* (Englewood: Prentice-Hall, 1967).

Maude, Aylmer. *Tolstoy*, 2 vols. (Oxford University Press, 1987).

____ *Family Views of Tolstoy* (Oxford University Press, 1929).

Morozov, Vasilly, 'Recollections of a Pupil of the Yasnaya Polyana School' in *Reminiscences of Lev Tolstoi by His Contemporaries* (Moscow: Foreign Language Publishing House, 1961), pp. 144-51.

Mueller, R.J., 'Enter and Leave Freely: A Description of Count L. Tolstoy's School at Yasnaya Polyana', *Phi Delta Kappan*, 44, June, 1963, pp. 435-437.

Noyes, G.P., *Tolstoy* (New York, Dover, 1968).

Panichas, George, *Mansions of the Spirit* (New York: Hawthorn, 1967).

Pirogov, N.I., *Izbrannye pedagogicheskie sochineniia* (Moscow, 1952).

Popovsky, Mark, *Russkie muzhiki raskazivayut: posledovateli L.N. Tolstovo v soyetskom soyuze, 1918-1977* (Russian Peasants Tell Their Story: Followers of Leo Tolstoy in the Soviet Union, 1918-1877) (London: Overseas Publications Interchange, 1983).

Radosavlevich, Paul, 'The Spirit of Tolstoy's Experimental School', *School and Society*, 29, 737, 9 February, 1929, pp. 175-183; 29, 738, 16 February, 1929, pp. 208-15.

Robinson, G.T., *Rural Russia under the Old Regime : A History of the Landlord and Peasant World and a Prologue to the Revolution of 1917* (Berkeley, 1967).

Roszack, Theodore. 'Tolstoy: The School Was All My Life', *Times Educational Supplement*, 24 March, 1972.

Sampson, R.V., *Tolstoy: The Discovery of Peace* (London: Heinemann, 1973).

Schuyler, Eugene, 'Count Leo Tolstoy Twenty Years Ago' in *Selected Essays* (New York: Scribner, 1901).

Shestov, L., *Dostoevsky, Tolstoy and Nietzsche* (Ohio University Press, 1969).

Shneidman, N.N. 'Soviet Approaches to the Teaching of Literature. A Case Study: L. Tolstoy in Soviet Education', *Canadian Slavonic Papers*, 15, 1973, pp. 325-350.

Simmons, Ernest, *Leo Tolstoy* (Boston: Little Brown, 1949).

____ *Introduction to Tolstoy's Writings* (University of Chicago Press, 1969).

____ 'Tolstoy's University Years', *Slavonic and East European Review*, 59, 22, 1944, pp.16-36.

Sinel, Allen, *The Classroom and the Chancellery* (Cambridge, Mass., 1973).

Smith, Bradford, *Men of Peace* (Philadelphia: Lippincott, 1964).

Spence, G.W., *Tolstoy the Ascetic* (Edinburgh: Oliver and Boyd, 1967).

Steiner, George, *Tolstoy or Dostoevsky: An Essay in Contrast* (New York: Random House,1959).

Sukhotin-Tolstoy, Tatiana, *The Tolstoy Home* (New York: AMS, 1961).

Tolstoy, Alexandra, *Tolstoy: A Life of My Father* (Belmont, Mass.: Nordland, 1948).

Tolstoy, Ilya, *Tolstoy, My Father: Reminscences* (London: Peter Owen, 1972).

Tolstoy, Leo, *A Confession and Other Religious Writings* (trans. Kentish) (Penguin Books, 1987).

_____ *Anna Karenina* (trans. Garnett) (London: Heinemann, 1977).

_____ *Childhood, Adolescence, Youth* (trans. Solanko) (Moscow: Progress, 1981).

_____ *Diaries*, 2 vols.(ed. Christian) (London: The Athlone Press, 1985).

_____ *Essays From Tula* (London: Sheppard Press, 1948).

_____ *The Kingdom of God is Within You*, 2 vols. (trans. Maude) (Oxford University Press, 1937).

_____ *Letters*, 2 vols. (ed. Christian) (London: The Athlone Press, 1978).

_____ *Lift Up Your Eyes: The Religious Writings of Leo Tolstoy* (ed. Hopper) (New York: Julian Press, 1960).

_____ *My Religion* (London: Walter Scott, 1889).

_____ *On Education* (trans. Wiener) (University of Chicago Press, 1967).

_____ *On Education: Tolstoy's Educational Writings, 1861-2* (ed. A. Pinch and M. Armstrong) (London: The Athlone Press, 1982).

_____ *Polnoye sobraniye sochinenii* (ed. V. Chertkov). 90 vols. (Moscow, 1949).

_____ *Resurrection* (trans. Louise Maude (Moscow: Progress, 1972).

_____ *Stories* (trans. Wettlin, Altschuler) (Moscow: Raduga, 1983).

_____ *War and Peace* (trans. Louise and Aylmer Maude) (London: Macmillan/Oxford University Press, 1977).

_____ *What Is Art and Other Essays* (trans. Maude) (Oxford University Press, 1930).

Tolstoy, Lev Lvovich, *The Truth about My Father* (London: Murray, 1924).

Tolstoy, Sergei, *Tolstoy Remembered* (New York: Atheneum, 1962).

Tolstoy, Sofya Andreyevna, *The Autobiography of Countess Sophie Tolstoy* (trans. Koteliansky and Woolf) (London: Hogarth Press,1922).

_____ *The Diary of Tolstoy's Wife*, 1860-1891 (trans. Werth) (London: Gollancz, 1928).

_____ *The Countess Tolstoy's Later Diary, 1891-1897* (trans. Werth) (New York: Books for Libraries Press, 1929).

Troyat, Henri, *Tolstoy* (Penguin Books, 1967).

Tsanoff, Radoslav, *Autobiographies of Ten Religious Leaders* (San Antonio: Trinity University Press, 1966.

Tschizewskij, Dmitrij *Russian Intellectual History* (Ann Arbor: Ardis, 1978).

Ushinsky, K.D., *Izbrannye pedagogicheskie sochineniia* (Moscow, 1953.

_____ *Man As the Object of Education* (Moscow: Progress Books, 1978).

_____ *Selected Works* (Moscow: Progress Books, 1975).

Vospominaniye khrest'yan Tolstovtsev, 1910-1930 (Memoirs of Peasant Tolstoyans, 1910-1930) (Moscow, 1989).

Wasiolek, Edward, *Tolstoy's Major Fiction* (Chicago University Press, 1978).

Wilson, A.N., *Tolstoy* (London: Hamish Hamilton, 1988).

_____ *The Lion and the Honeycomb: Tolstoy's Religious Writings* (London: Collins, 1987).

Yaacov, Oved, *Two Hundred Years of American Communes* (Oxford: Transaction Books, 1988).

Yesipov, B.P. and Goncharov, N.K., *Padagogik* (Berlin: Volk and Wissen Verlag, 1948).

Zenkovsky, V.V., *A History of Russian Philosophy* (New York: Columbia University Press, 1953).

Zweers, A.F., 'Tolstoy on Education', *Canadian Slavonic Studies*, 4, Summer, 1970, pp. 347-8.

Index